THE BOOK OF

HEMPNALL

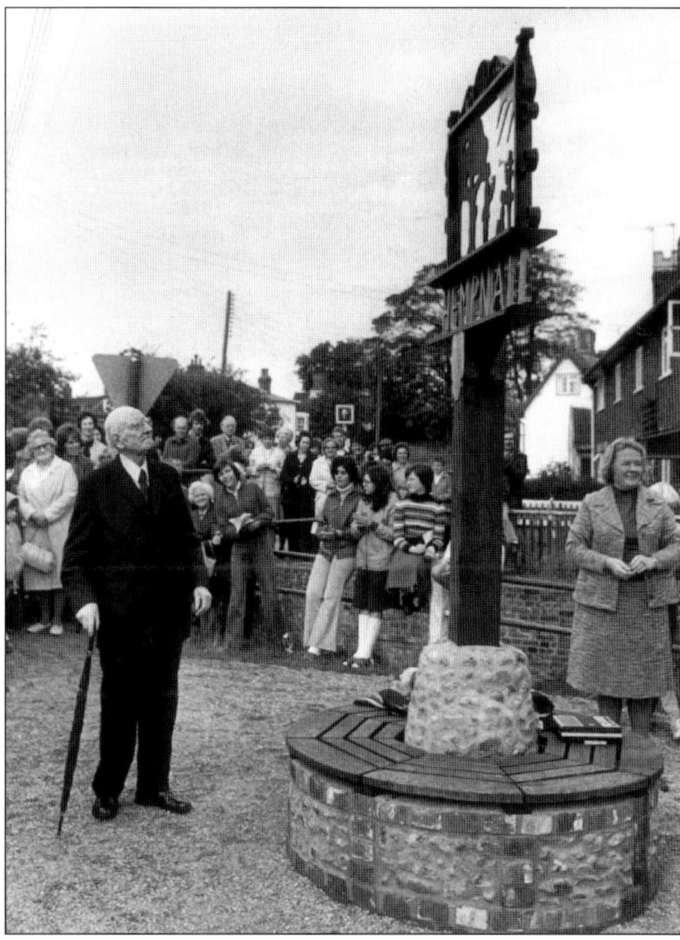

MAUREEN P. CUBITT

HALSGROVE

First published in Great Britain in 2008

British Library Cataloguing-in-Publication Data
A CIP record for this title is available from the British Library

ISBN 978 1 84114 789 5

HALSGROVE

Halsgrove House
Ryelands Industrial Estate
Bagley Road
Wellington
Somerset TA21 9PZ
T: 01823 653777
F: 01823 216796
e: sales@halsgrove.com
www.halsgrove.com

Frontispiece photograph: *George Gerald Stammers unveiling the village sign, 1977.*
(EASTERN DAILY PRESS)

Printed in Great Britain by CPI Antony Rowe, Wiltshire

CONTENTS

Acknowledgements

In the course of 30 years I have incurred many obligations. I should like to acknowledge some of them, and I hope those I have missed will forgive me. My first debt is to the residents of Hempnall, who have shared their memories, photographs and family archives and who have allowed me to photograph their timber-framed houses. In particular I should like to express my gratitude to Betty and Lawrence Chapman, Neville Day, Joan and Roy Ladbrooke, Diane Ingram, Pauline Peck, Jean Stammers and Joy Worman. I am indebted to the farmers of Hempnall who have allowed me to walk on their fields, especially Elizabeth Allen and Robert Allen, John Ellis, Michael Moore, Peter Rogers, and Stephen Wright.

The wealth of information obtained from the Hempnall records stored at Barningham Hall has been invaluable. For this I owe much to the generosity of Sir Charles and Lady Mott-Radclyffe and Mr and Mrs T. Courtauld.

I am grateful to William F. Milligan and Dr Andrew Rogerson for dating archaeological finds, and to Christopher Barringer for inspiring me with local history. I thank members of the Norfolk Record Office and Norwich Library for their expertise, help and advice. I owe thanks to Paul Cattermole and the Hylton family for information and to Geoffrey Kelly and Terence O'Rourke for translating Latin documents.

Finally, I would like to acknowledge the help and support given by my husband, David, who transcribed a greater part of the newspaper articles and who read and re-read the Hempnall document as it progressed.

Photographic Acknowledgements

Permission to reproduce a number of items in the keeping of the following institutions is gratefully acknowledged:

The *Eastern Daily Press*
Norwich Castle Museum and Art Gallery
Norfolk Record Office
The Norfolk County Library and Information Service

Abbreviations

CCR	Calendar of Close Rolls
CChR	Calendar of Charter Rolls
CFR	Calendar of Fine Rolls
CPR	Calendar of Patent Rolls
CFF	Calendar of the Feet of Fines
EDP	Eastern Daily Press
HC	Heritage Centre, Norfolk and Norwich Millennium Library
MSS	manuscripts
NA	Norfolk Archaeology
NAS	Norfolk Archaeological Society
NAC	Norfolk Archdeaconry Court
NCC	Norwich Consistory Court
NC	Norfolk Chronicle
NG	Norwich Gazette
NN	Norfolk News
NNR	*The Norfolk and Norwich Remembrancer and Vade-Mecum Norfolk & Norwich from 1701 to 1820 inclusive.* (Norwich 1822)
NM	Norwich Mercury
NA	Norwich Argus
NRO	Norfolk Record Office
NRS	Norfolk Record Society
NAU SMR	Norfolk Archaeological Unit, Sites and Monuments Records
PRO	Public Record Office (National Archives)
VCH	Victoria County Histories, *History of Norfolk* Vol.2
£.s.d.	pounds, shillings, pence

Blomefield, *Norfolk*, F. Blomefield, *An Essay Towards a Topographical History of the County of Norfolk* (Vol.2. (Norwich 1745)

Bryant, *Depwade*, T. Hugh Bryant, 'Norfolk Churches', *The Hundred of Depwade* Vol. 17 (Norwich 1906)

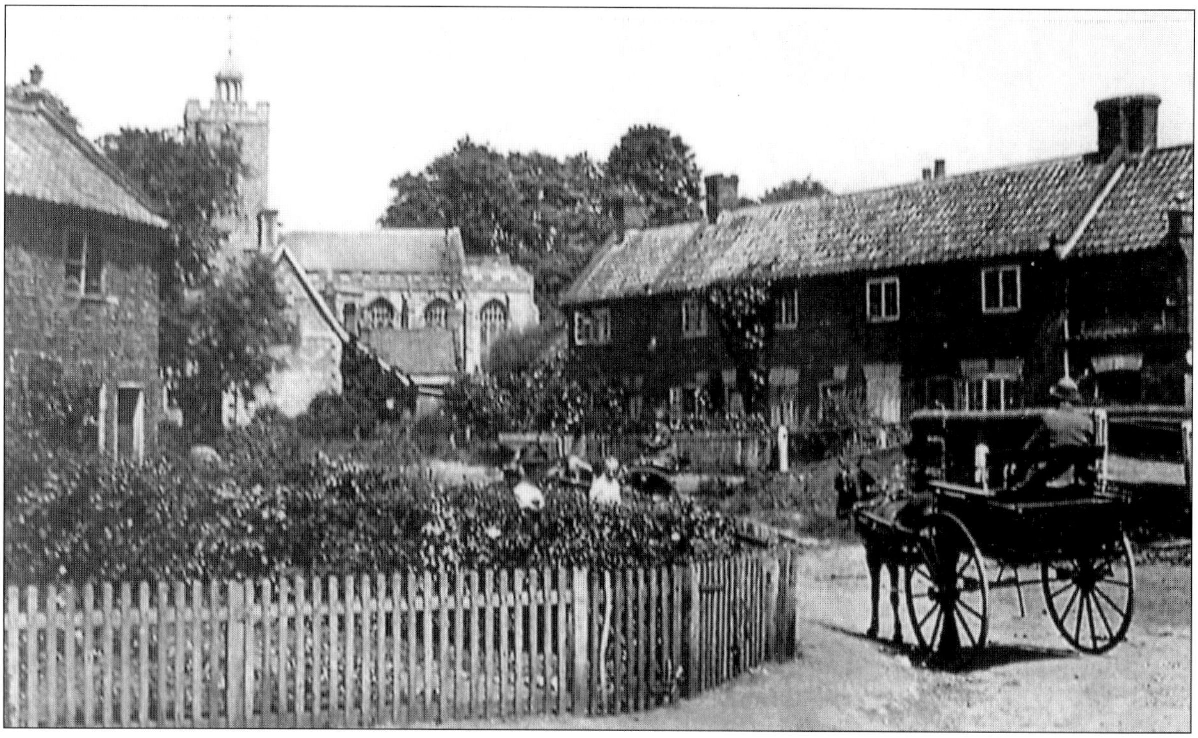

Town Bridge and the church, c.1900.

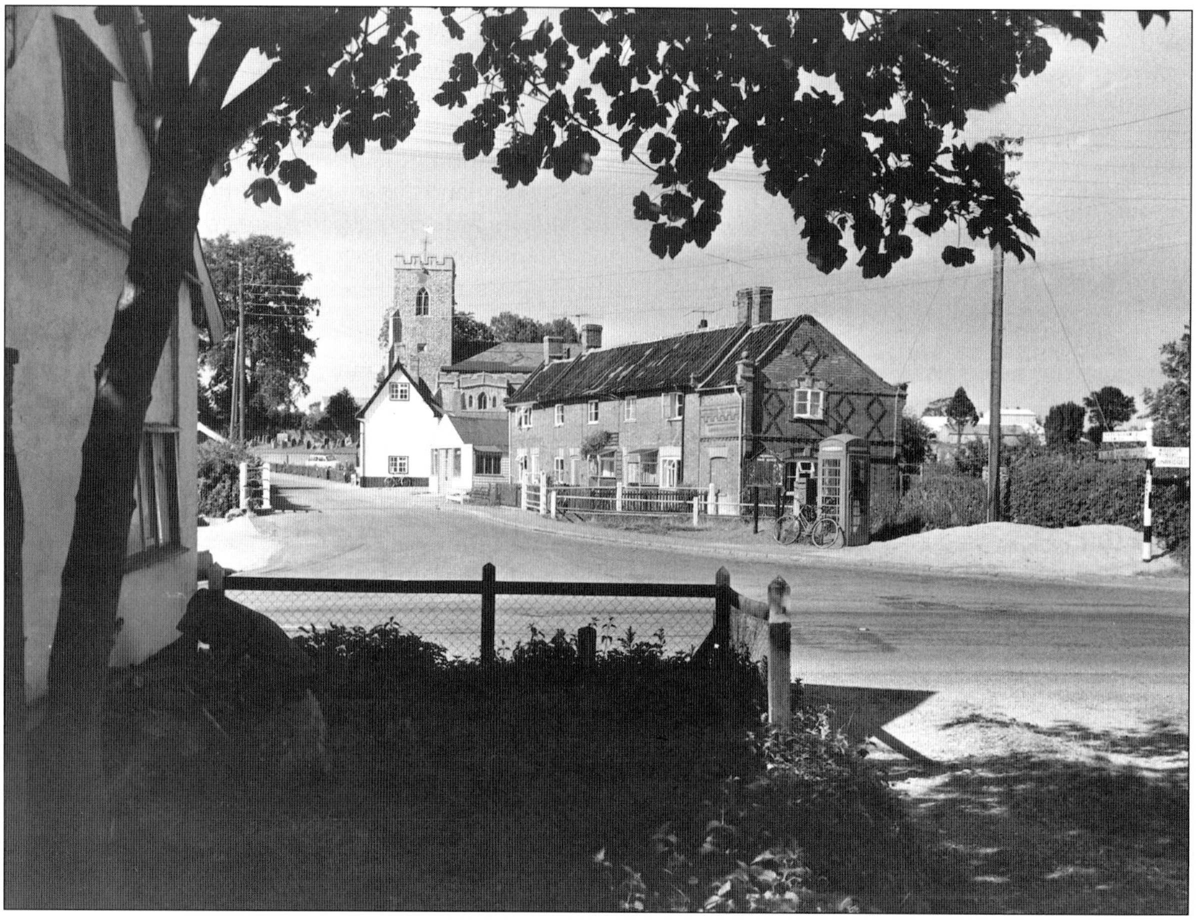

A view from the site of the old blacksmith's forge towards the church 1967. (EASTERN DAILY PRESS)

Introduction

Visualising the past is like taking a look through a keyhole, for it is impossible to learn everything about one village. Old photographs and maps allow us to imagine a walk along a familiar street in a century not long past and hazard a guess at the landscape with the help of archaeology; but the people, how can we really understand their world? Small clues appear in the multitude of documents available, but we will never understand, for instance, why Abraham Bennet stabbed Israel Dunnet and why Henry Roads hid a smuggler. Was Susanna Sporle really murdered by highwaymen, or by her own son? This is a story about one village, but the keys to discovery could apply to all.

The village of Hempnall lies in the north-east corner of the hundred of Depwade in South Norfolk, about ten miles south of Norwich, at the source of the River Tas (Fig. 1). 'Field-walking', a way of recording surface archaeology by walking across ploughed fields, provides an indication of settlement patterns and past landscapes. Dried up riverbeds become more obvious on contour maps and tracks take sensible routes along ridgeways or follow a stream. Routes taking a gentle curve appear to be following the edge of ancient woodland or a furlong within an open field (Fig. 2).

The landscape is important for its effect on the lives of its inhabitants. The heavy chalky boulder clay of South Norfolk, much of it woodland in prehistoric times, shaped the economy and also made it necessary for the inhabitants to co-operate in order to survive. As the story of each generation unfolds, the independence of the people of Hempnall becomes a common thread.

It was far enough from Norwich to make its own life, yet enjoyed a good communication system from the Roman period onwards. Rebellious, free-spirited individuals defied their masters on several occasions. Politicians and preachers visited the place, knowing that free-thinking, enterprising people would listen. There are rich documentary resources for the village. Copyhold records exist for the years 1329–99, 1533–51, 1573–90 and 1651–1920, enabling the researcher to trace the history of the sites of at least 60 houses with their holdings.[1] Wills and inventories allow the reader to imagine the interiors of ancient dwellings, some of which survive to this day. Local newspapers from 1715 provide a variety of stories, including several involving murders.

The earliest known map of part of the parish shows the Bungay Town lands in 1665.[2] A large-scale estate map, made in 1767 and covering about three-quarters of the parish, identifies demesne and copyhold land.[3] The 'Inclosure' map of 1818 was produced to show the new allotments, roads, footpaths and, unusually, the copyhold boundaries. Unfortunately, none of the three copies made can be found. However, the Award exists, and parts of the map have been reproduced on early estates maps, so the landscape of 1818 can be partially reconstructed.[4] The Tithe Redemption Map and Apportionment, made in 1842, supply field names, land use, owners and occupiers. It is possible to plot the commons, demesne, copyholds, glebe and town land by using the 1767 and 1842 maps as a base, with additional information from estate maps (Fig 3).

The landscape holds its mysteries, and ancient houses hide their own stories of extension, reduction, restoration and dilapidation. This particular village, with its remarkable variety of sources, invites and inspires exploration.

References

[1] NRO MC 1862/1/1–40, MC 1862/4862X9, MC 1817/9, 843X4, MC 1817/10, 843X5. Court books for the manors of Hempnall and Hempnall Cannons. Tin box at Barningham Hall: Court books 1651–1920

[2] NRO. Bungay Town Reeve land in Hempnall, 1665

[3] NRO MC 607/1 (MS 33540). Estate of James, Viscount Grimston, 1767

[4] NRO C/Sca 2 Inclosure Award for Hempnall, 1818

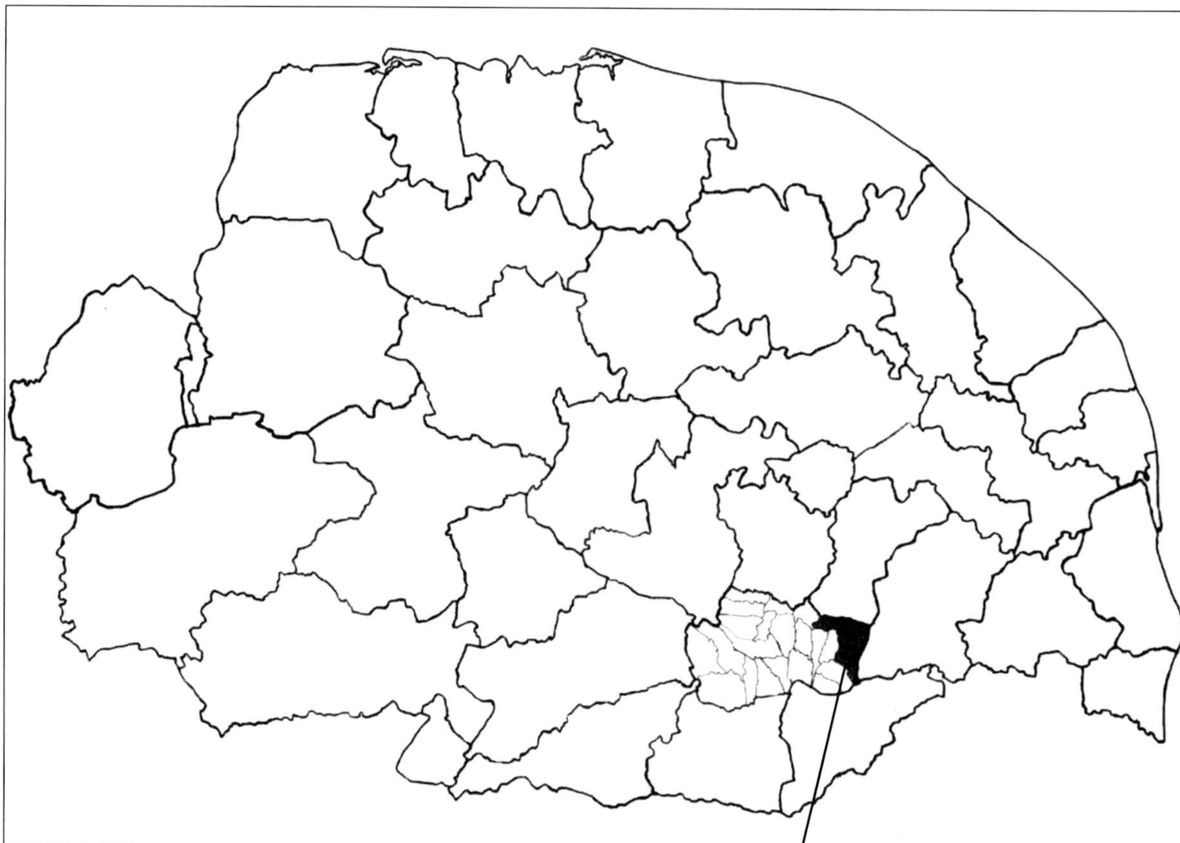

The hundred divisions of Norfolk

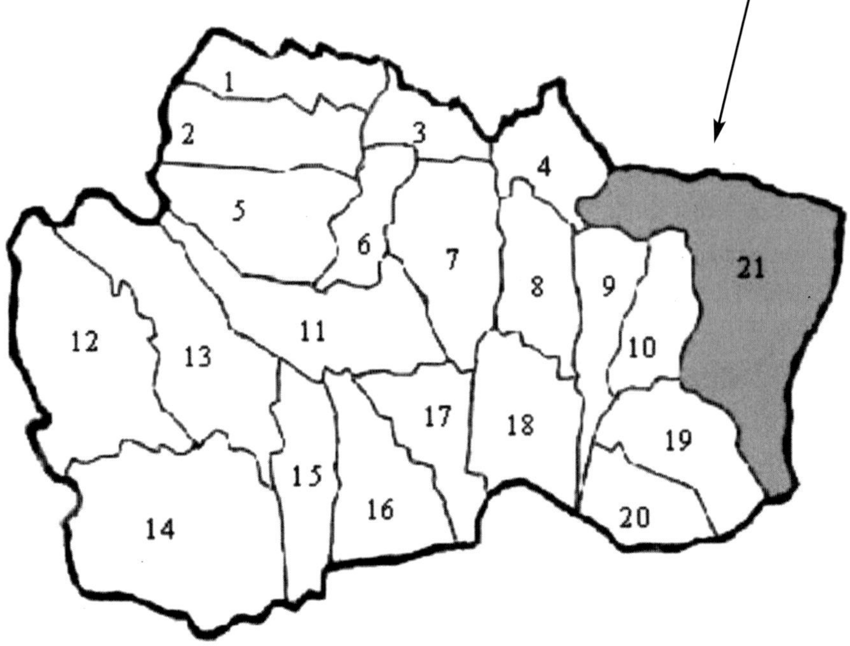

1. *Ashwellthorpe*
2. *Fundenhall*
3. *Hapton*
4. *Tasburgh*
5. *Tacolneston*
6. *Forncett St Mary*
7. *Tharston*
8. *Stratton St Michael*
9. *Morningthorpe*
10. *Fritton*
11. *Forncett St Peter*
12. *Carleton Rode*
13. *Bunwell*
14. *Tibenham*
15. *Aslacton*
16. *Moulton St Michael*
17. *Wacton*
18. *Stratton St Mary*
19. *Hardwick*
20. *Hempnall*

Fig. 1

Depwade hundred showing Hempnall.

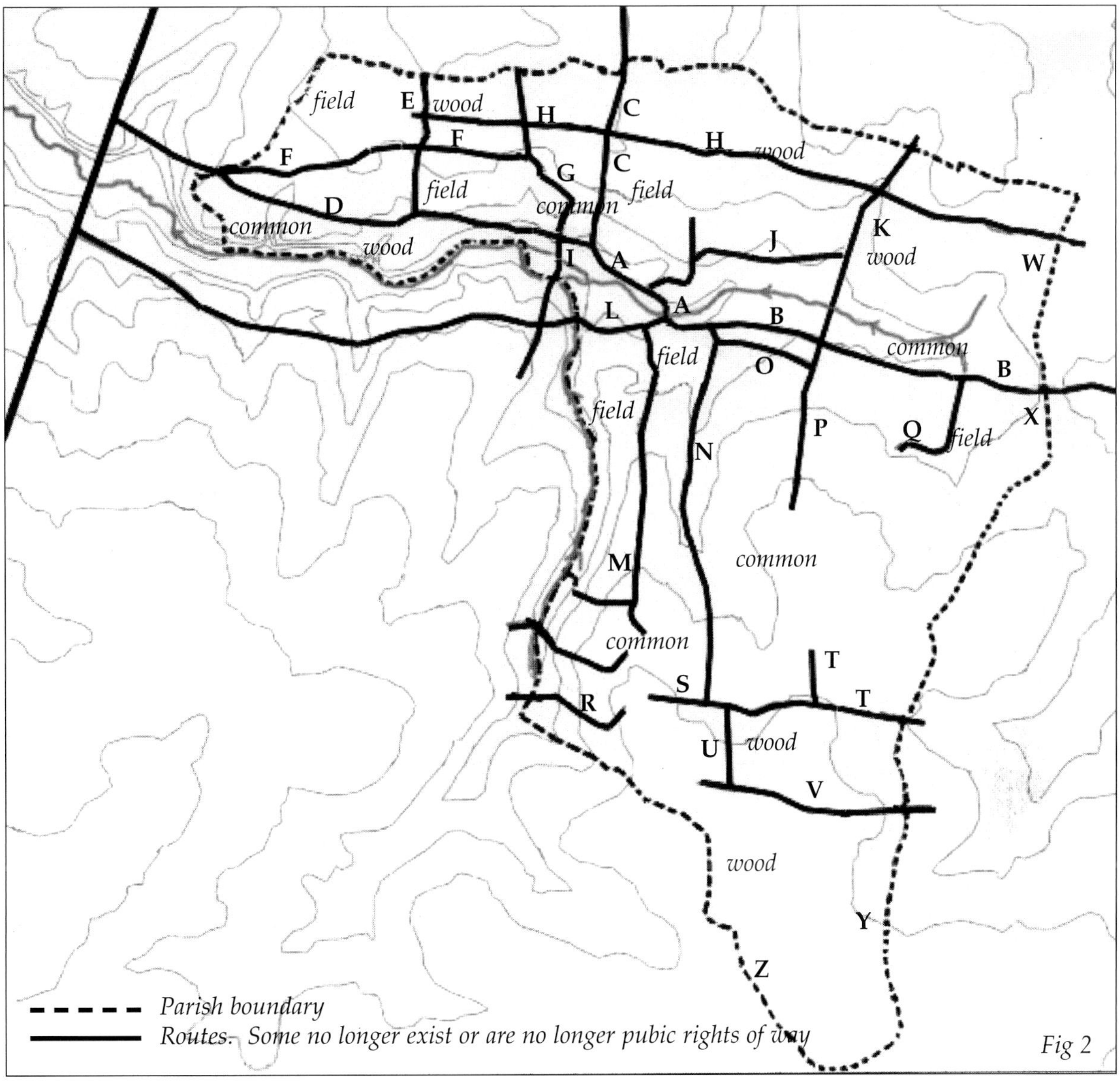

Hempnall within the Landscape – the most recent names first

NB *The names of routes without a letter are not known, or they never had a name*

A *The Street/Market Street*
B *Bungay Road/Roadway Wong/Rodeweye*
C *Broaden Lane/Broadway/common way called Cole's Green*
D *Fairstead Lane*
E *Brahamseway/Bergamswey*
F *Westgate Street/Westgatestrete (small sections exist)*
G *Pymar's Lane/Pymore Lane*
H *Marl Pit Way*
I *The Krons/Rons/Wronze/Rouans*
J *Bussey's Loke*
K *Harlesgate*
L *Mill Road/Windmill Street/Millgate*
M *Field Lane/ Upper Lane/Pea Lane*
N *Lower Lane/Pigg Lane/Chyrchwaye/ Watergate Way*
O *Back Lane/Frog's Lane*
P *Alburgh Road*
Q *Gurney Lane/Road Street*
R *Steppings Lane*
S *Workhouse Lane*
T *Spring Lane*
U *The Lawn/Launde*
V *Underwood Lane*
W *Nobb's Lane*
X *Oxnead Lane*
Y *Barondole Lane*
Z *Room Lane*

NB *W X Y Z are boundary roads, part of the processional way that would have circled the parish*

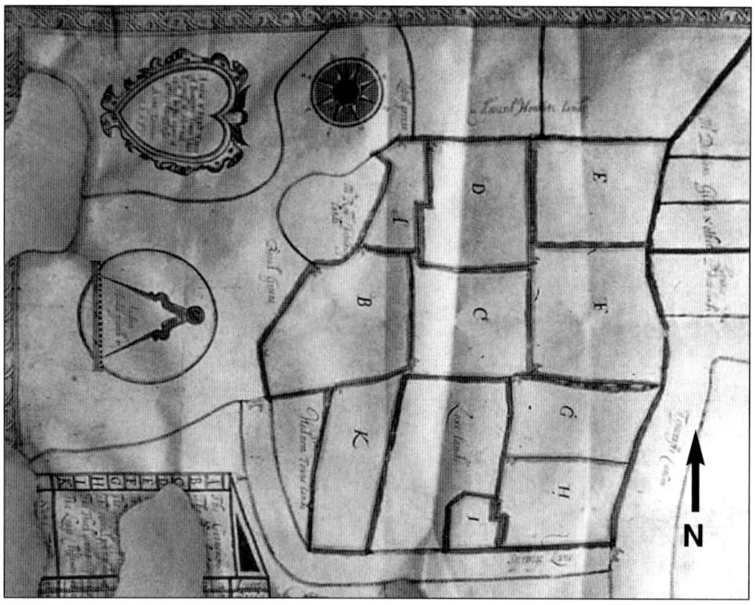

Left: *The earliest known map of a Hempnall estate, Capel Close, later Chapel Close, belonging to the Bungay Town Lands 1665. Norfolk Record Office FX 22/1.*

Below: *Demesne, copyhold and charitable lands*

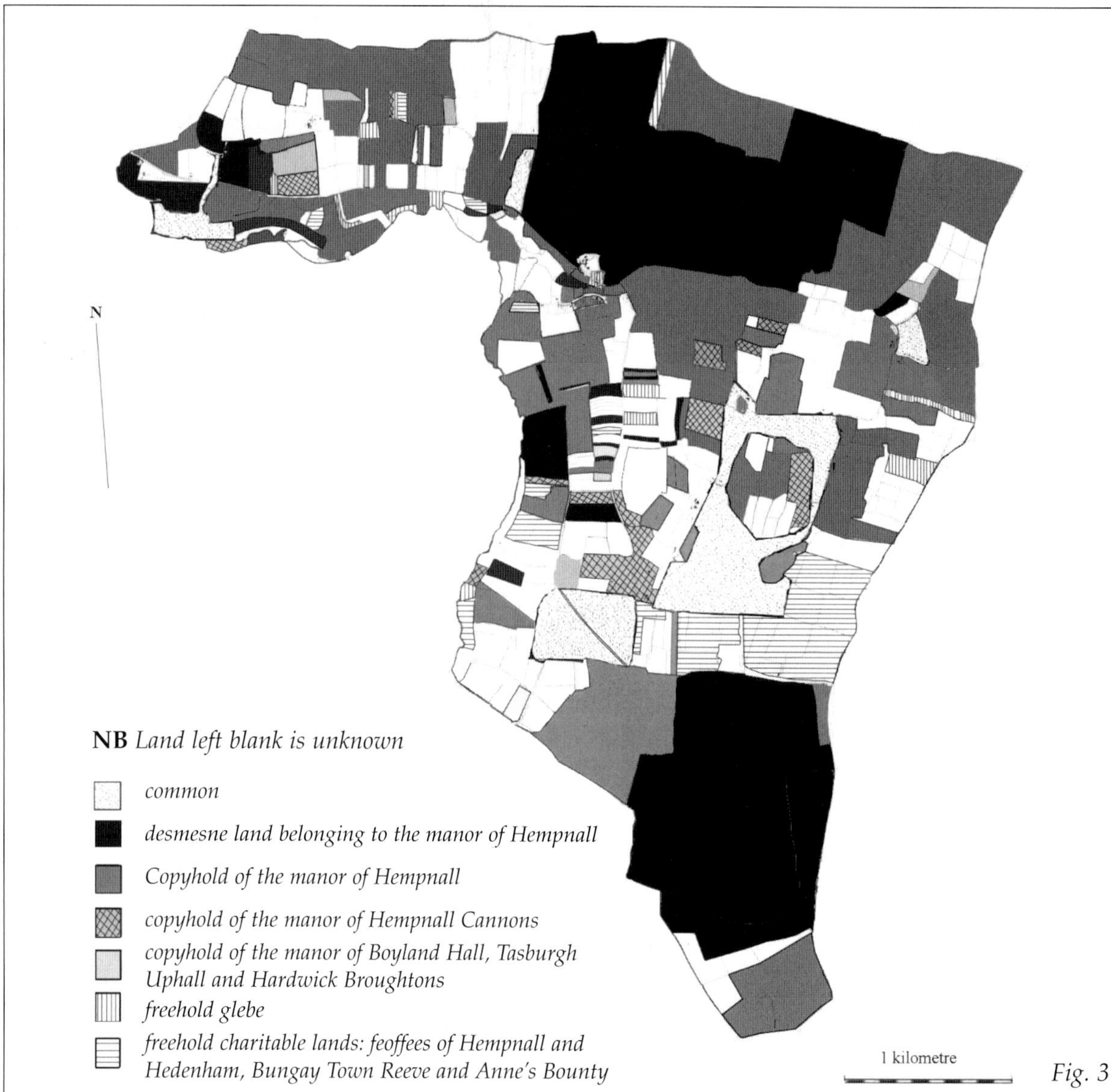

Fig. 3

CHAPTER 1

Making Tracks c.8000BC–AD410

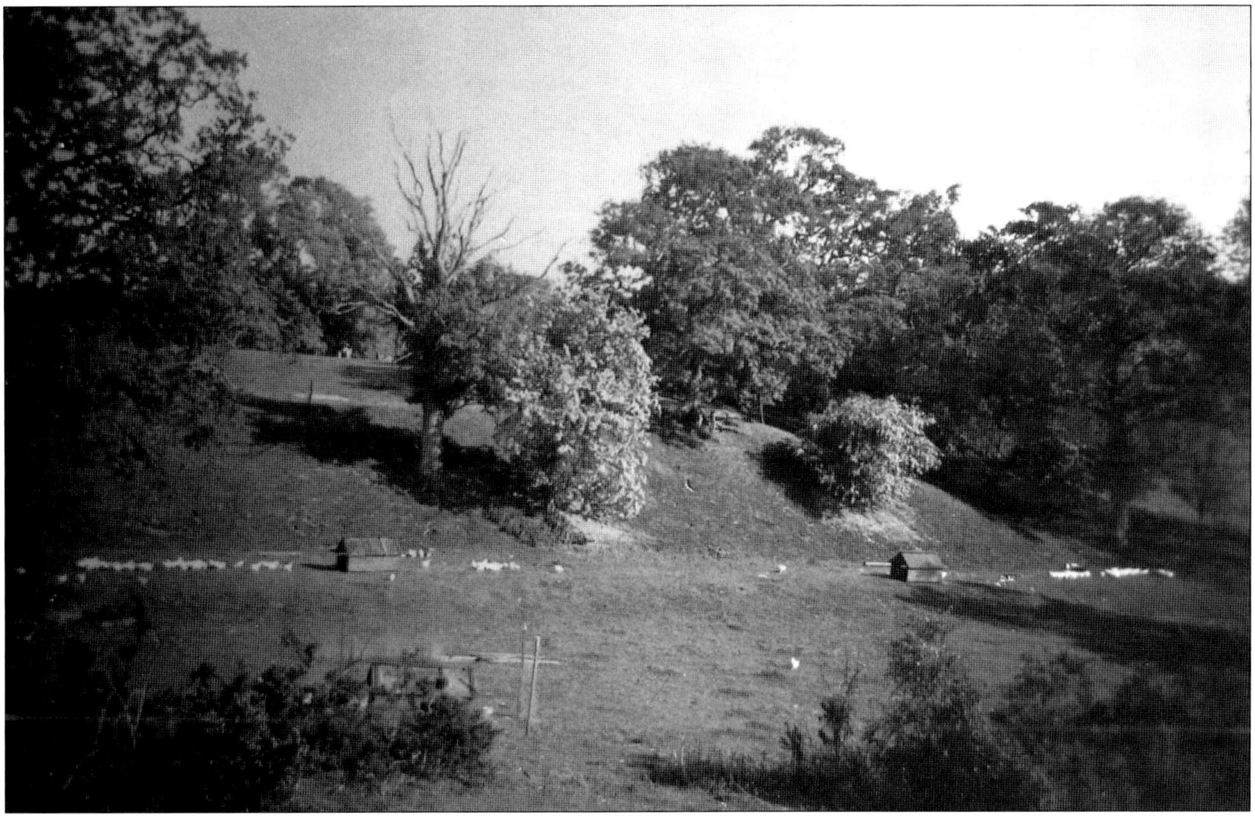

Sloping landscape between the River Tas and Fairstead Lane, c.1960.

When mixed oak forests were just beginning to colonise the heavy soils and hunting parties were making tracks through the territory, a Mesolithic hunter dropped his flint axe where Lundy Green is now.[1] During the Neolithic period Stone-Age peoples were beginning to turn their hands to farming. Fields scattered with flint scrapers, tools and prehistoric pottery may indicate that a group were beginning to clear woodland near the river to the north of Lundy Green and south of the present village.

A few traces of the Bronze Age have been found in the north of the parish. The land rises sharply from the river valley of the Tas towards Fairstead Lane, where the crop mark shows where a ring ditch perhaps once surrounded a burial mound. A copper alloy axehead from this period has been discovered on Moat Farm.

There are several areas of burnt flints in the north-east corner of the parish, indicating woodland clearance or possibly that steam was produced for ritual purposes. Crop marks show a circle on the field Stocklands and lines leading to it. Ancient field names, many traceable to the fourteenth century, suggest an interesting use of the landscape for this part of Hempnall (Fig. 4). Perhaps this solitary area, uninhabited since Roman times, hides ancient secrets of burials and pagan rituals? Field names record 70 acres of an area called Barrow (from 'beorg', Old English meaning tumulus). Nearby, Leggatts, from the Old English 'leger', also means a burial place or grave. Street Wood, formerly Asket Hall Wood and before that Askethawe Wood, and Little Wood, previously called Inhams Wood, once Easthawe Wood, both have the 'hawe' element, which is Old Norse for tumuli. In the centre of this area lies the Harsley, alias the Harrow. Harsley comes from 'haursely' or 'haer', Old English for a rock, heap of stones or tumulus, and Harrow is derived from 'hearg', a heathen temple. Connecting these fields is an ancient road, perhaps Roman, but in 1328 its name was Harsleygate, 'gate' being the Viking name for a road. Barrow sites would not have been in woodland, so these areas must have been clearings since prehistoric times. During the Iron Age, one group lived in this part of Hempnall. They were probably members

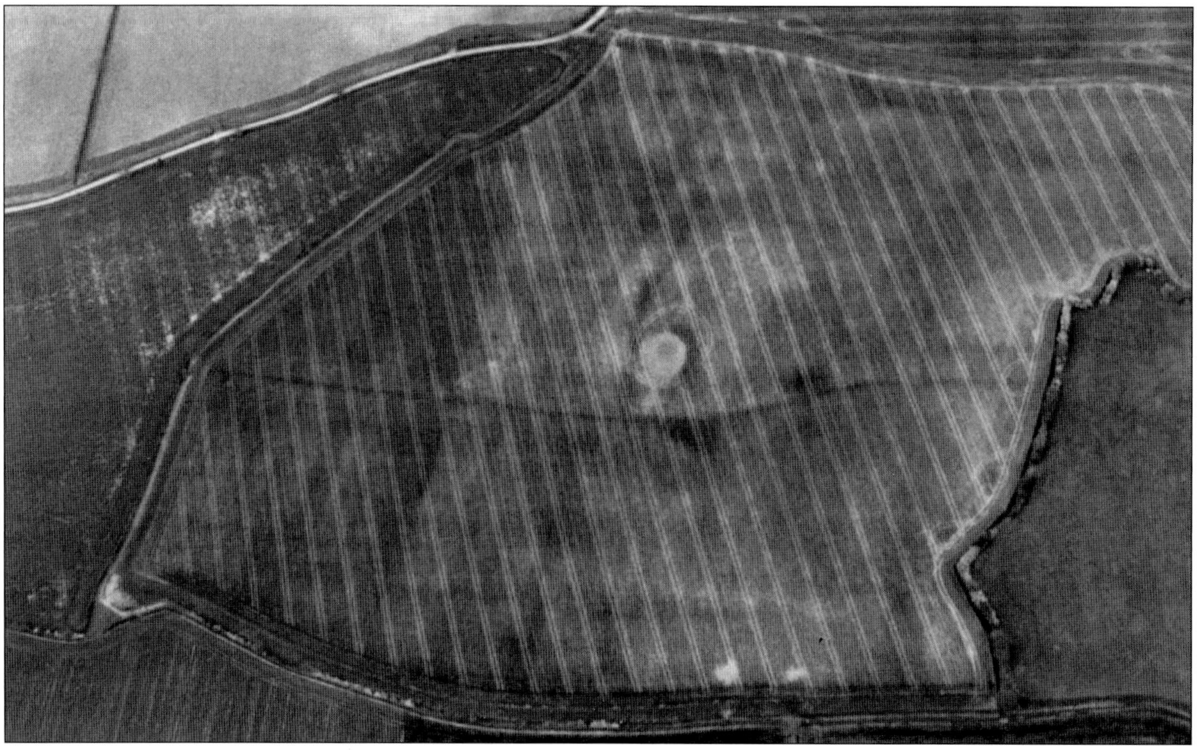

Above: *Ariel view of Stocklands showing crop marks, 1980s.*

Below: *North-east corner of Hempnall with archaeology and cropmarks.*

(ESTATE OF JAMES, VISCOUNT GRIMSTON 1767 NORFOLK RECORD OFFICE MC 607/1)

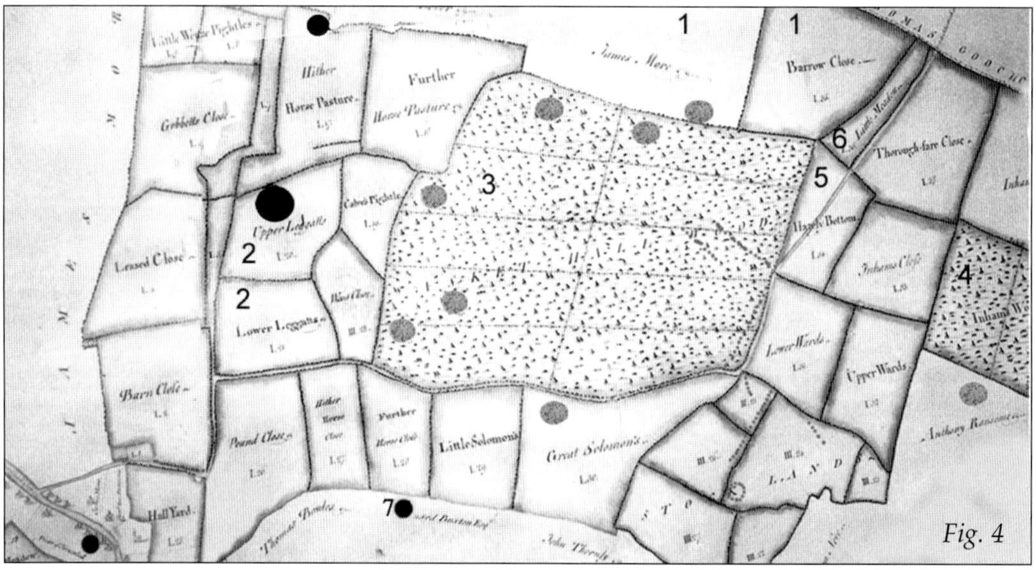

● *scatter of Roman sherds*

● *site of Romano-British farmstead*

● *burnt flints*

..........crop marks

1 *barrow fields*
2 *Leggatts*
3 *Street Wood/Asket Hall Wood/Askethawe Wood*
4 *Little Wood/Inham's Wood/Easthawe Wood*
5 *Hazley Bottom/Harseley/The Harrow*
6 *Haresleygate*
7 *The Walls*

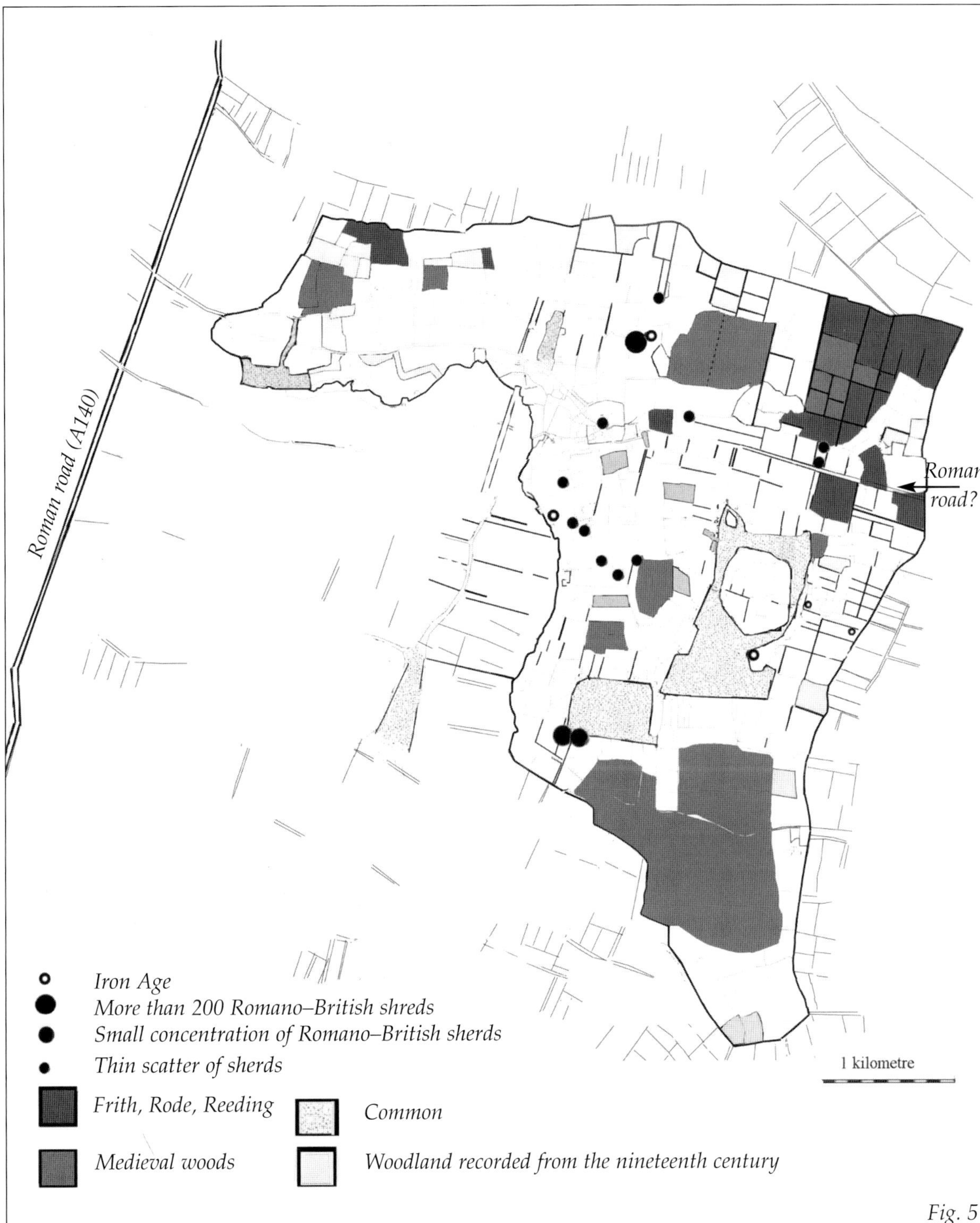

Alignment of a rectilinear field system at Hempnall with a Roman road.

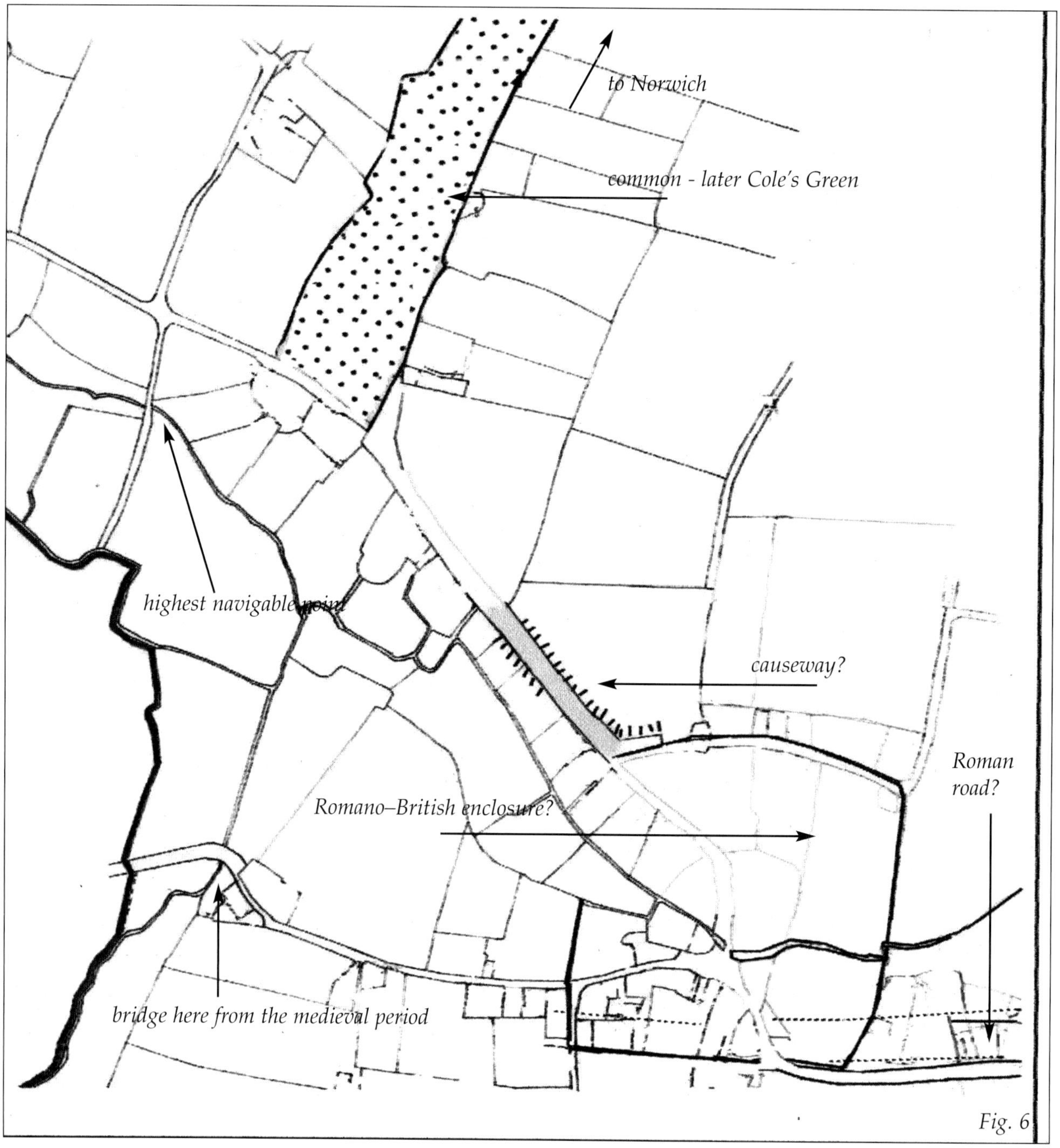

The village centre with ancient features.

of the Iceni tribe. At this time the climate was warmer than today, the sea level higher and the river deeper and navigable.

After Boudicca's rebellion in AD61, Iceni land became Roman property and the first planned organisation of the landscape began. Two farmsteads were constructed in the Roman fashion and occupied from the second to the fourth centuries. One of these farmsteads utilised the north-east area, probably because it was already partially cleared of trees, and perhaps with the intension of curtailing pagan rituals. The rectilinear fields adjoining this farm, if they survived from this period, perhaps remained preserved because of the ancient woodland that must have developed after the departure of the Romans. Moreover, these fields are parallel to the Roman road from Venta Icenorum to Colchester. The later parish boundary appears to have formed a triangular shape, half of an almost square piece of territory constructed to the east and parallel to the local section of this great Roman highway (Fig. 5).

This larger farmstead was constructed on heavy, chalky boulder clay close to the site of the present village centre. Artefacts include pieces of amphora, samian ware, a lead steelyard weight and a restamped Roman denarius. This coin, first minted to pay the soldiers after the Battle of Actium in 32BC, was restamped during the reign of Marcus Aurelius

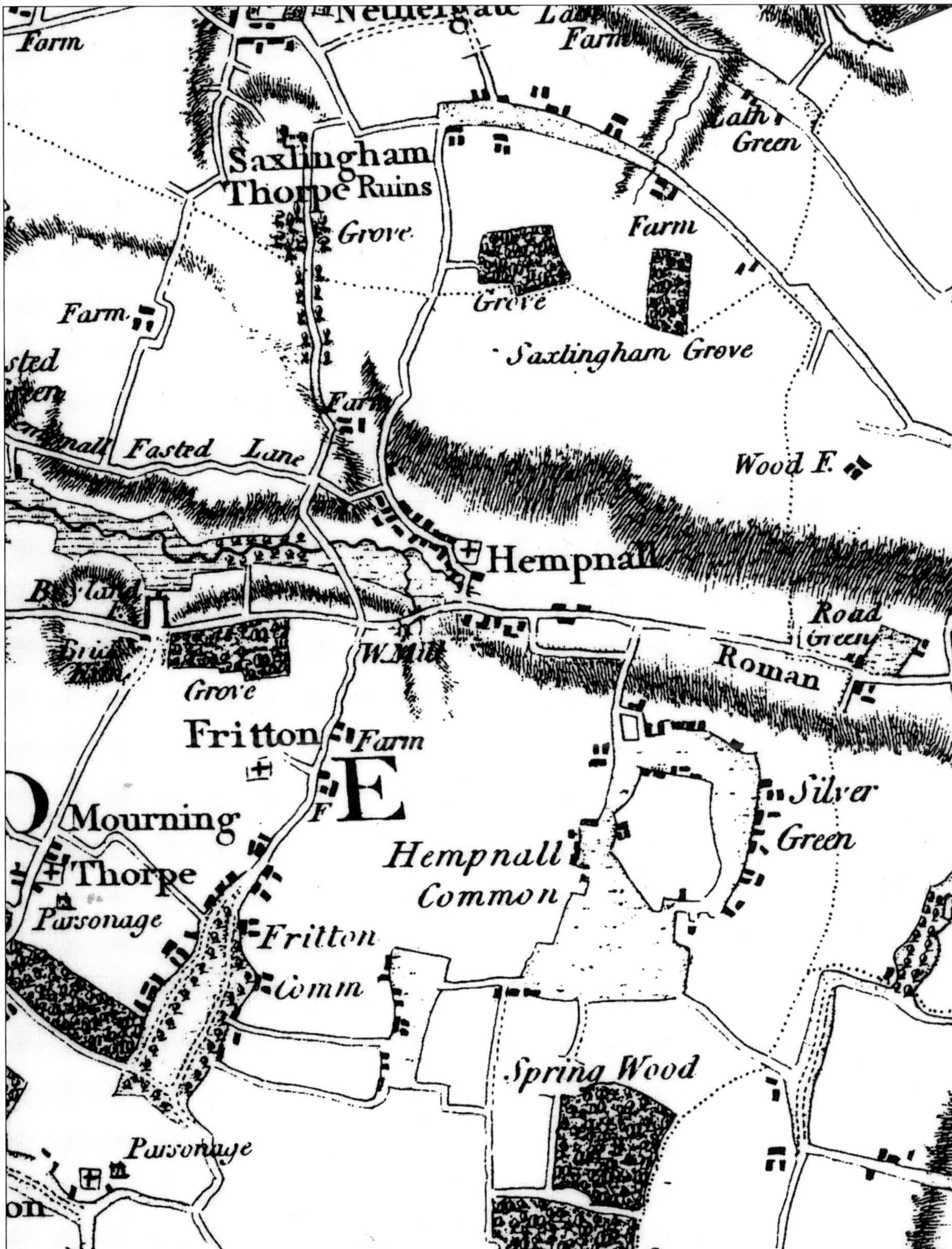

Part of Faden's map of Norfolk, 1797. (NORFOLK COUNTY COUNCIL LIBRARY AND INFORMATION SERVICE)

(AD161–180). It features a Roman galley on one side and the eagle standard of the Twentieth Legion on the other. It was probably one of many that came to Britain as a souvenir and was later brought back into use.

Pottery sherds have been found scattered where both farmsteads once stood, but only a few sherds are scattered on adjoining fields. If the land was used for arable, then more pottery would have been spread about with manure. The land provided good pastures and meadows, so perhaps the farmers were operating a cattle-rearing business, supplying meat to the local Roman town of Venta Icenorum a few miles north. This could account for fields divided by deep ditches. Indeed, many years later, Hempnall was unusual in that it rendered six cows as part of the Domesday tax.

The owners of the farms must have required a considerable workforce. Dr Tom Williamson, in *Shaping Medieval Landscapes: Settlement, Society, Environment*, argues that successful cultivation of heavy soil and hay cutting require access to a labour force at short notice. This argument applies to any period prior to the invention of heavy machinery.[2] The area of the present-day village centre would have met the requirements. Hempnall Street heads west from the village along a possible causeway towards the highest navigable point (Fig. 6).

It is possible that a network of Roman tracks developed, gradually widening, becoming waste and finally common land in later periods. Woodward, an historian particularly interested in Roman roads, recorded the existence of a 'massive' Roman road going through Hempnall.[3] This is likely to be that going towards Bungay, shown as Roman on Faden's map of Norfolk, published in 1797. An encroachment in 1683 confirms that this highway had been at least 6ft wider in some parts.[4] Allotments were made along the south side at the Inclosure of 1818, shrinking the road to its present width. Street Meadow and Street Close are adjacent north and south, close to the village centre. 'Street' names are often associated with Roman roads.

To the south of the larger farmstead and east of the main village, a burial place for cremated remains was established in a field now called 'the Walls'. There must have been a marker stone over each grave, as over 40 urns, each about 12ins in height, were buried at regular distances of 10–12ft in rows running from north to south. They contained a mixture of bones, wood, ashes and pieces of pottery. Most were of coarse manufacture. A few feet from the deposits of urns, a mass of black soil containing fragments of dark pottery of a superior character, some with a distinct flange and apparently turned, were unearthed. These were identified at the time as Romano–British.[5] None of these urns has apparently survived, so modern identification cannot be applied (Fig. 7). However, their orderly interment suggests that they were Roman. By AD410 most of the regular Roman Army units in Britain had been recalled to Italy as raids along the coast by Angles or Saxons multiplied. Since the pots found at the Walls were of poor manufacture, perhaps they were the work of the indigenous population, who remained after the Romans left and tried to carry on the Roman tradition without the skills of Roman craftsmen.

In conclusion, evidence suggests that the area developed from a few isolated farmsteads into a thriving Romano–British community, within a planned landscape with good communications – perhaps part of a planned Roman estate.

References

[1] Mesolithic flint axe at Lundy Green, 1992

[2] T. Williamson (2003) *Shaping Medieval Landscapes: Settlement, Society, Environment* (Macclesfield)

[3] S. Woodward (1831) 'A descriptive outline of Roman Remains in Norfolk' Society of Antiquaries pp.358–73. NRU SMR 13652 Woodward records the existence of a 'massive' Roman road going through Hempnall (1824–26)

[4] Manor of Hempnall Court Book A 9, May 1683. Encroachment measuring 80ft x 9ft x 6ft. Barningham Hall 'Hempnall'

[5] V.S.W. King (1859) 'Examination of an Ancient Cemetery', NA Vol. V, pp. 49–52 (Norwich)

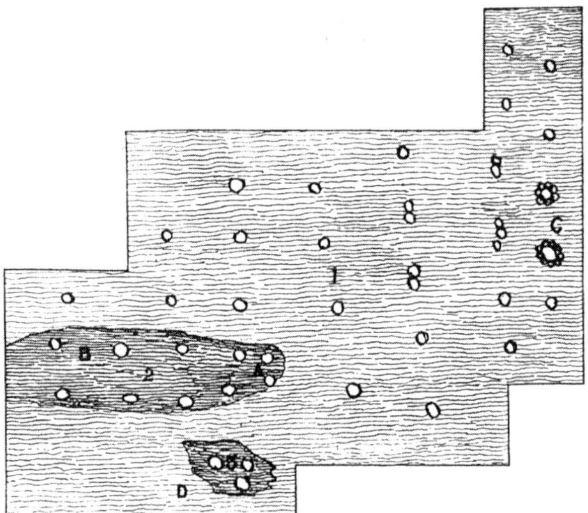

Fig. 7

1 *soil disturbed*
2 *gravel pit*
3 *black earth & ashes*
A *first urn found*
B *broken urns 12–18 inches below surface in poor condition*
C *2 circles of smooth stones without bones or ash*
D *black soil & Ashes with dark pottery, turned with distinct flange*

Plan of an excavation at the Walls in 1854 from a plan drawn by Revd Samuel W. King.

✦ CHAPTER 2 ✦

Boundaries c.410–1199

For about 300 years, following the end of Roman occupation, the area appears to have been somewhat neglected. Despite extensive field-walking over a period of 30 years, no pagan Saxon pottery has been found. During that time woodland regenerated, perhaps fossilising the Roman rectilinear field pattern in the north-east and south. When the first Anglo-Saxons arrived, they apparently neglected much of the land in the north-east corner at a time when tumuli would have been more prominent.

By the middle-Saxon period, about 700, there is evidence of activity near the site of the Town Field and close to the highest navigable point of the River Tas, or Rucham, as it was anciently called in the village. During the late-Saxon period, woods were cut down and the areas of land given names such as frith, reading and rode, indicating tree clearance. The commons and strip field systems were juxtaposed on the landscape. The earliest routes followed streams or ridges. The parish boundary, established during

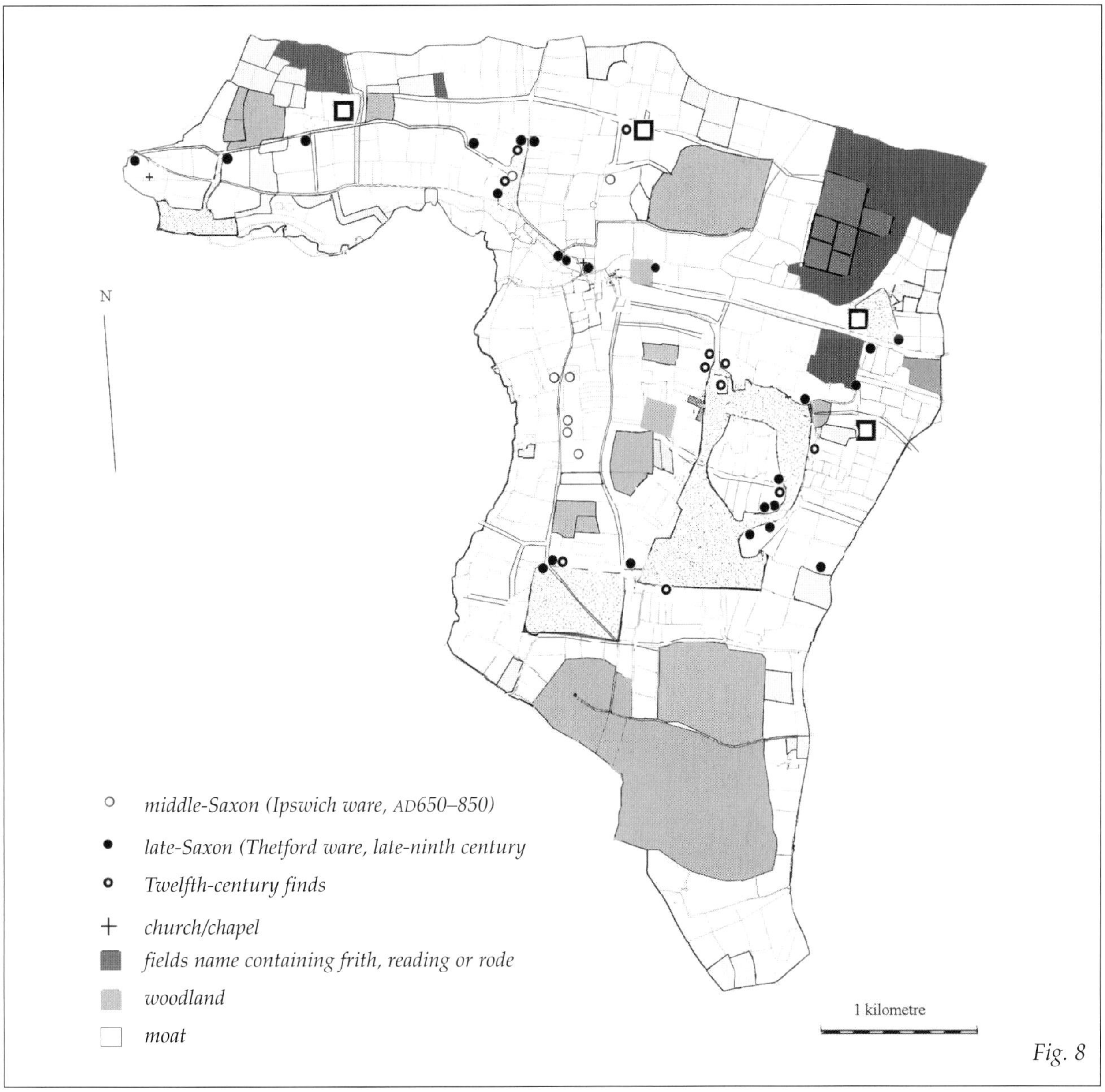

Saxon archaeology.

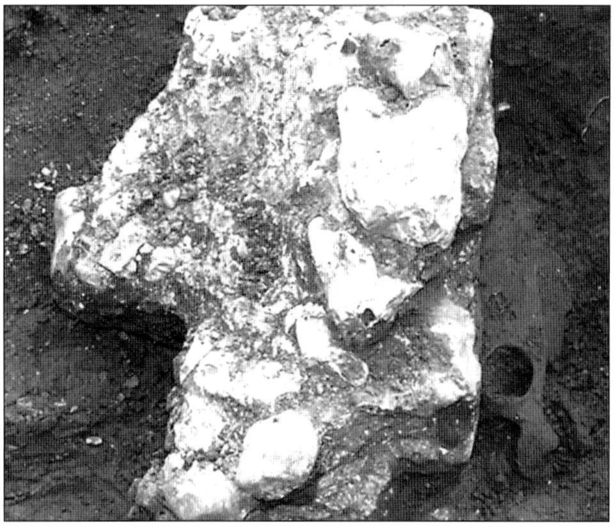

The corner of a building with a horse burial, possibly part of a former watermill.

the Saxon period, was defined by the river in the west and ridges in the north and east. The northern boundary was probably indicated by the line of barrows. Other objects, such as trees or stones, would have marked the circumference at certain points to guide inhabitants on their annual perambulation of the boundary (Fig. 8).

By the late-Saxon period, the present-day village centre was inhabited and a small hamlet was established in the western corner of the parish adjoining Tasburgh, perhaps called 'Weston', judging by the number of fields with this name in the area. Linking this community, a track later named Westgate Street skirted the south side of cleared woodland. Habitation along its length dates from the late-Saxon period. Another route, overlooking the Tas valley and later named Fairstead Lane, appears to have crossed the West Field towards Tasburgh.

About the year 800, Viking raids occurred in coastal regions, and in 869 the Saxons were defeated in East Anglia.

The Norman Conquest in 1066 had a powerful effect on the lives of the inhabitants of Hempnall. Thorn, a Dane, had owned Hamehala or Hemenhala then, but by the Domesday Survey of 1086, Lord Bainard, one of the barons who came with William the Conqueror, was the owner.

In 1066 there were fifty-four villains, forty-one borders, seven slaves, a priest and three freemen. By 1086, there were thirty-four villeins, fifty-eight borders, four villagers, four smallholders a priest and three freemen. No women were counted in the Survey, so allowing for a wife and family, it can be estimated that there were about five hundred people living on the manor. There were two churches and a wood supporting two hundred swine. The deer park, belonging to Lord Bainard, contained an enclosure called Schieteshaga that belonged to the Abbot of St. Benet at Holme. There were two watermills. It is

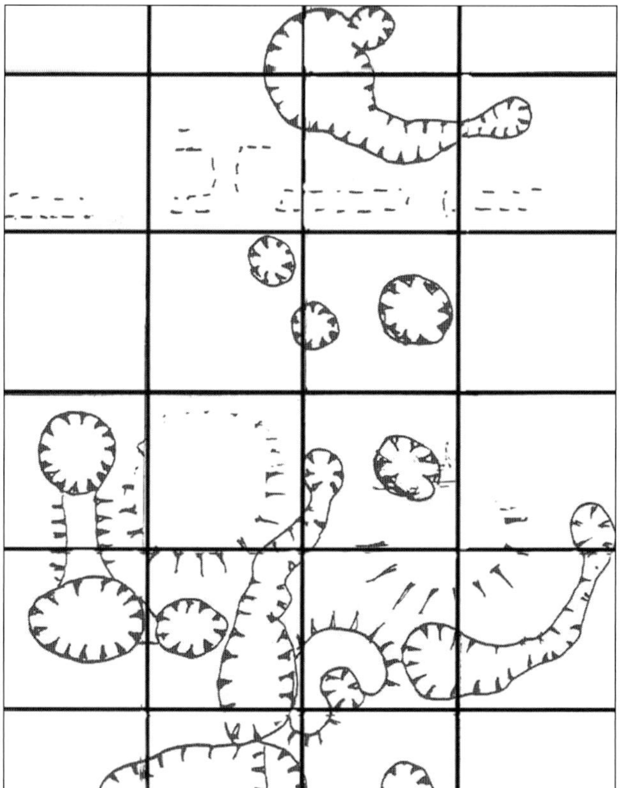

Fig 9.

Excavations in 1980. Large quantities of pottery and building material found in the pits dated from Roman to post-medieval times.

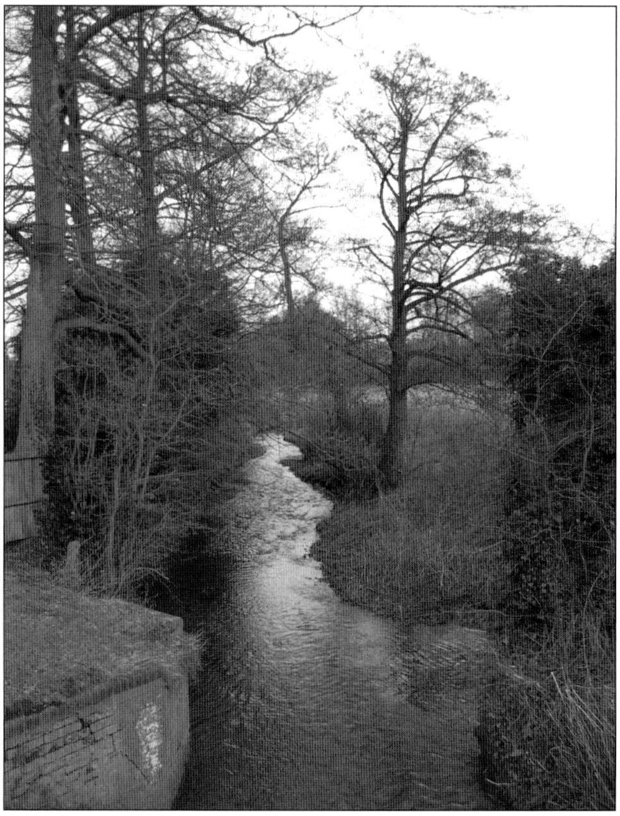

The site of the Bury Bridge/Long Bridge/Red Bridge on the Bungay Road at a spot known as Revell's Watering.

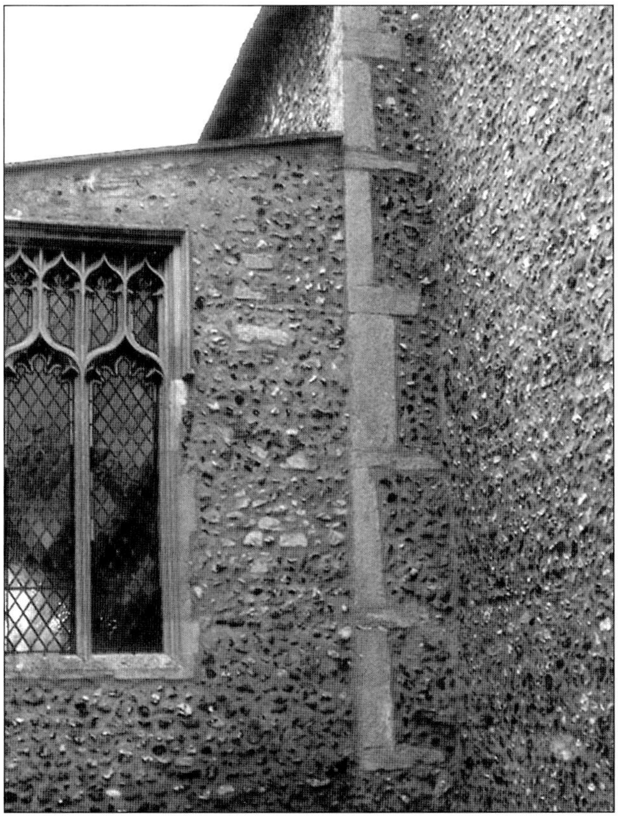

The north-west corner of the church, showing quoins: Saxon long and short work

interesting to note that although the population was the highest in the Hundred of Depwade, there were very few freemen.[1]

The first watermill, belonging to the lord of the manor, may relate to a discovery by the river bank not far from the Town Bridge of the corner of a flint building, with the bones of a horse criss-crossed beneath. Pits excavated on the opposite bank may have stored grain (Fig. 9). Artefacts found during this excavation include Thetford Ware, St Neot's Ware (both late-Saxon), medieval pottery, a shaped antler from a roe deer, a twelfth-century curfew sherd, used for damping a fire at the time of the curfew, and pieces of a bellarmine jar (1500–1700), which were often buried under doorsteps to keep witches at bay. The Abbot of Bury St Edmunds owned the second mill, established after 1086 and named Piper Mill, or 'Twa-grind', on Long Bridge. This bridge, which spanned the river between Hempnall and Fritton, was later variously called Bury Bridge and the Red Bridge.

Remains of Saxon 'long and short work' can be found against the north aisle of the existing church, now dedicated to St Margaret. A drawing made prior to the restoration in 1857 shows three narrow, round-headed windows in what was originally the north wall.[2] Wall paintings were discovered behind the plaster on this wall during a Victorian restoration.[3] A second church, dedicated to St Andrew, was estab-

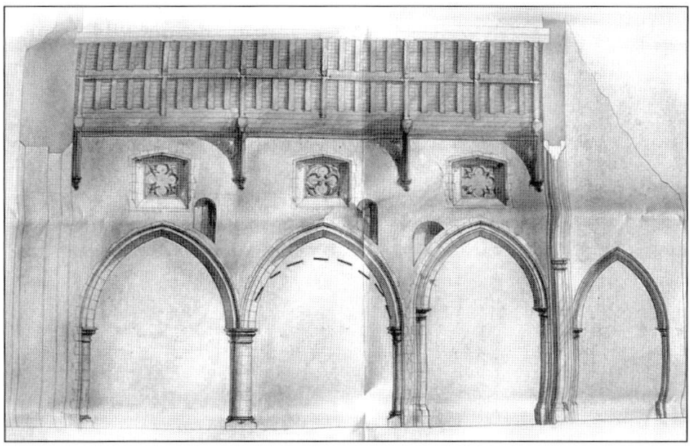

Blocked Saxon/Norman windows in the north arcade of St Margaret's Church. A central arch was changed to perpendicular style from description.

(FACULTY PAPERS 1857 NORFOLK RECORD OFFICE DN/CON/138)

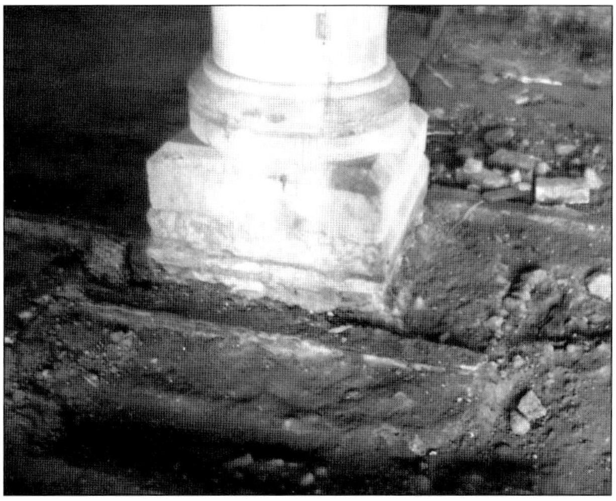

Pillar in the north arcade of the church during building work, showing that the original base was much larger.

lished at 'Weston'. The village became grouped with about 20 others to form a hundred, an administrative unit of land. The north and east boundaries became the boundary of the hundred of Depwade.

It has been suggested that, before the establishment of the parochial system in the tenth to the twelfth centuries, Hempnall was once the centre of an Anglo-Saxon estate.[4] These very large estates were served by a 'minster' church, from which a small group of priests could support several outlying communities. In support of this argument it is notable that, in a large population, there were but three freemen at Domesday, suggesting a dominating authority. The 'long and short' work of the original church indicates a lofty building. Hempnall manor was formerly called Hempnall Rex, suggesting that the king once owned it, another indication of its importance.[5] The manor owned land in several other parishes, and in 1327, on the death of Robert Fitzwalter, it was noted that £6.19s. was paid yearly to Hempnall manor for Castle Guard, or Castle Ward, from Wheatacre, Chedgrave, Langley, Hales, Kirkley,

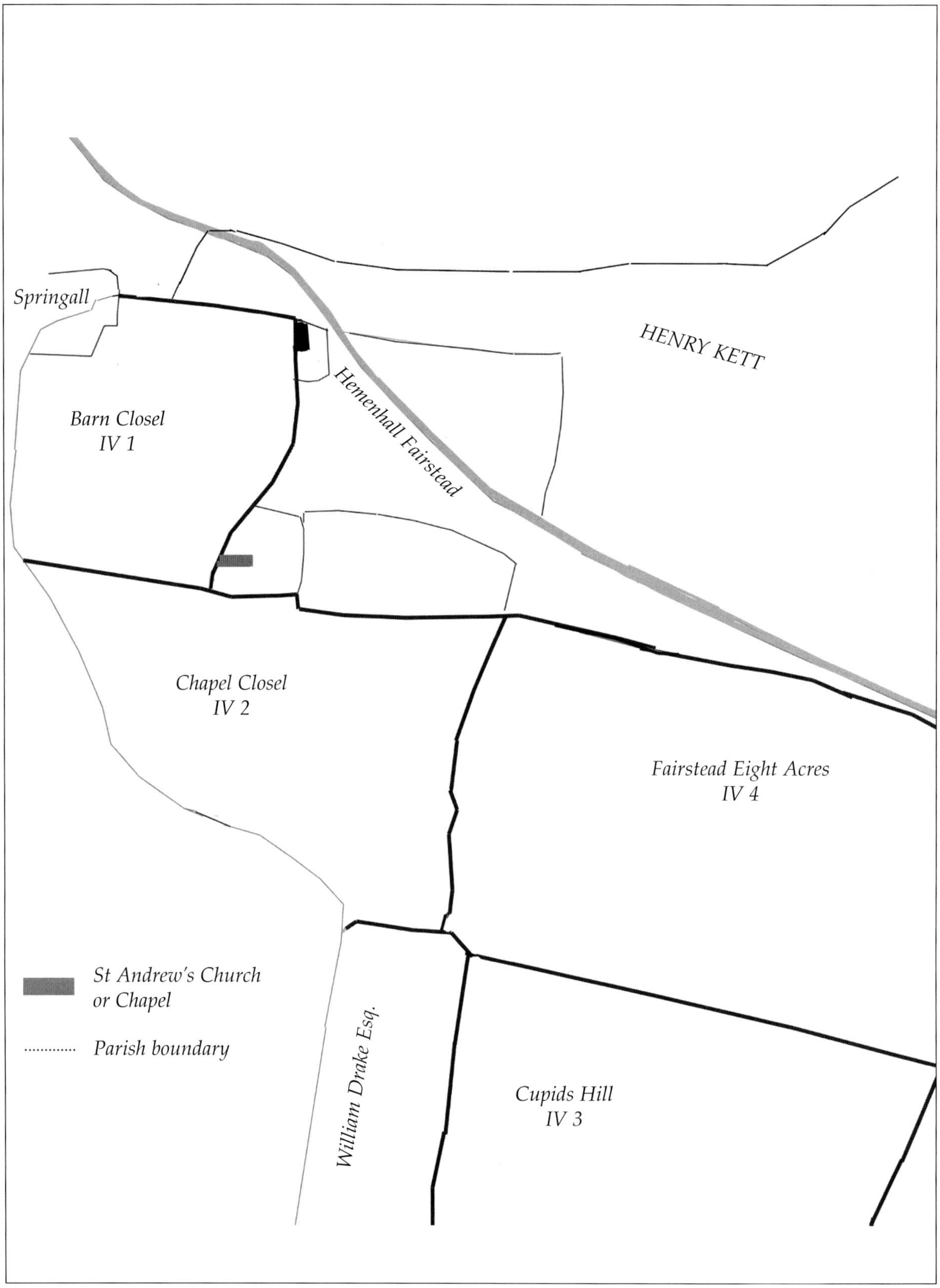

The site of St Andrew's Church and the fairstead after the Grimston map of 1767 (original map inset opposite).

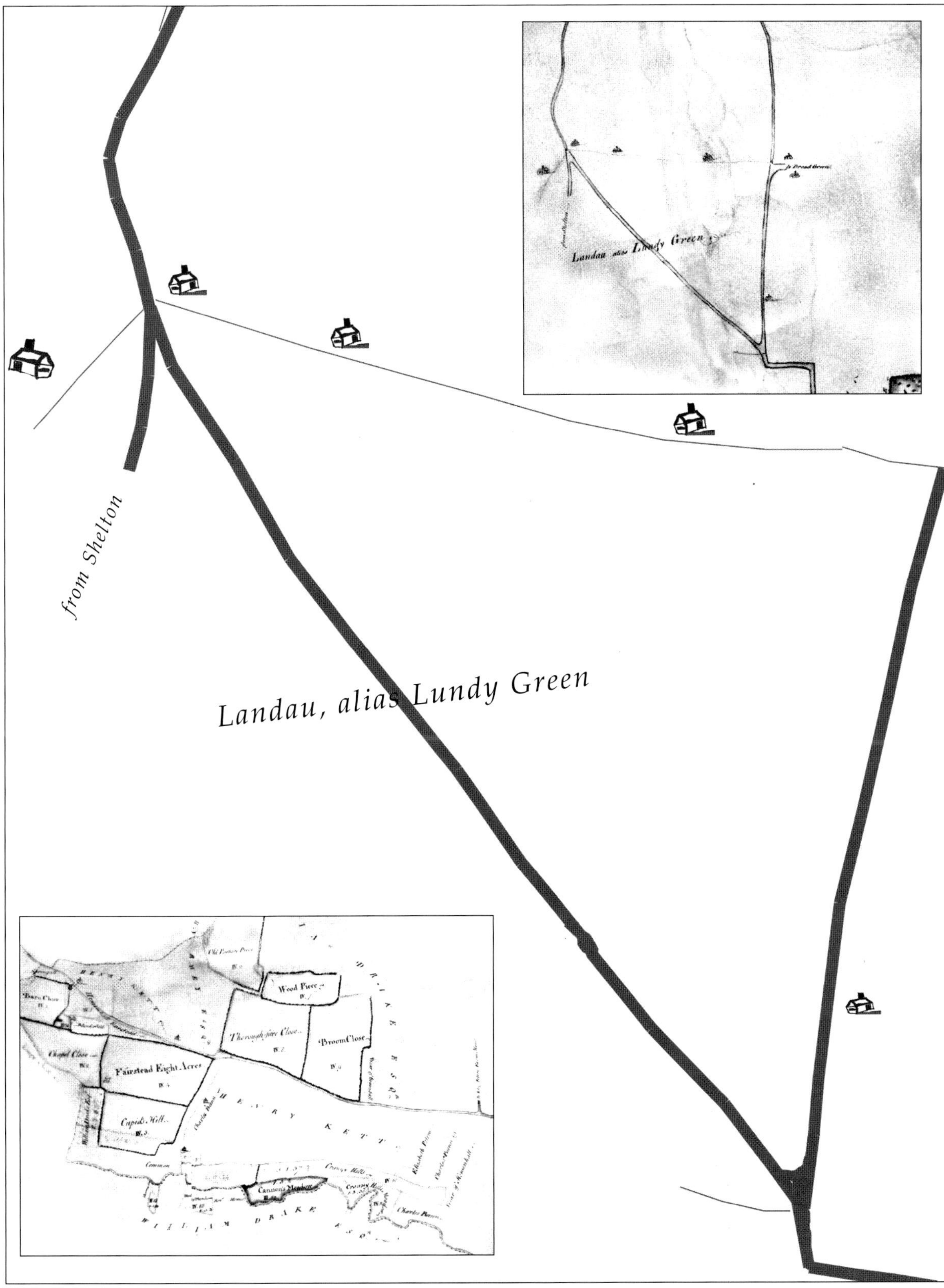

Lundy Green after the Grimston map of 1767 (original map inset top right).

Broome, Barton, Stadsett, Tittleshall, Holme Hales and Wicklewood. These parishes are scattered all over Norfolk.

Faden's map of 1797 shows Great Green to be almost rectangular, nibbled away by earlier encroachments. There were two enclosures within this common. The first, a small area in the north-west corner, was later named Plum Pudding Piece, suggesting, from this description, the site of a barrow. The larger, almost circular enclosure, later le Ox croft or Oscroft, is partly defined by streams. Habitation around Great Green dates from the late-Saxon period. Lundy Green, linked at its north-east corner with Great Green, earlier named Lundhaugh/ Lundaw/London, is likely to have originated in Viking times, Lundr being the Danish name for a grove. Pottery sherds reinforce this theory. Rode Green (now Road Green) was created partly over a Roman road.

All the commons and greens in Hempnall appear to be part of a communication system. Were they routes before becoming commons or, as commons, were they found to be useful as routes? The Romans appear to have settled next to Lundy Green, but it could not have been a common then, nor is it likely to have been woodland. As part of a route system it could have joined the south side of Great Green and headed east towards Topcroft Street and north following a former stream. A map of 1767 marks a diagonal way across the green.[6]

Hamehala had become the property of Lord Bainard, one of the barons who came with William the Conqueror and a wealthy landowner with a castle in London.[7] At some point he built a country residence at Little Dunmow, in Essex. In 1104 Lady Juba, his sister, founded an Augustinian priory there. The monks were commonly called the 'black canons' because of the black habits they wore. Geoffrey Baynard, Lord Bainard's son, gave land in Hempnall to the canons and this is probably the origin of the manor of Hempnall Cannons.[8]

William Bainard, Lord Bainard's descendent, forfeited his lands and manors in 1111 because of his involvement in a rebellion against Henry I. The king bestowed his estates on Robert Fitz Richard, the ancestor of the barons Fitz Walter, to whom the advowson of the priory belonged until the Dissolution.

By the twelfth century, the parish was more commonly called Hemenhale. A charter of 1177 records that Walter Fitzwalter, the lord of the manor, had given the advowson of the church at Hemenhale to the priory of Little Dunmow, whilst retaining ownership of the Chapel of St Andrew at the west of the parish.[9] From then, until the Dissolution of the Monasteries, the priors were responsible for the appointment of the vicars.

Archaeological evidence indicates that the population was increasing around Great Green and Lundy Green. Four likely moated enclosures were established from the twelfth century, symbols of control, power and dominance.

Two interesting coins have been discovered, the earlier minted during the reign of Aethelred II (the Unready, 978–1016). The moneyer was Godwine.[10] The second, a halfpenny minted in 1109 during the reign of Henry I, was discovered at a common edge. It would have bought the equivalent of two loaves of bread. Halfpennies were an experiment that proved unpopular and they were recalled for melting down, but this particular coin must have been lost, making it a rare find.[11]

This period gave Hempnall its first true identity. Middle and late Saxon peoples established fixed boundaries, a village centre and a hamlet in the west. They built two churches, created the open fields and eventually, with an increased population, began to build dwellings around the commons.

References

1 VCH p.23 (f.249) ref. 6

2 NRO DNCON/138 faculty papers 1857

3 Bryant, *Norfolk Churches: Depwade*, p.111

4 Dr Adam Longcroft, University of East Anglia, verbally

5 NRO [PHIL/166 577X2] PHILLIPPS 31170. Deeds referring to a chantry 1400–1541. Copies of Court Roll of the Manor of Hempnall Rex being the surrender by John Roper to the use of John Sporle of a messuage called Quintyns with a curtilege annexed

6 NRO MC 607/1 (MS 33540). Estate of James, Viscount Grimston, 1767

7 Baynard's Castle, London

8 Bryant, *Norfolk Churches: Depwade*, p.107

9 R.E. Levy (1965) 'The Cartulary of Little Dunmow Priory. (MA dissertation, University of Virginia, USA)

10 Fitzwilliam Museum, Cambridge. EMC No. 1989. 0082 (Ref: CR 1989:82 *British Numismatic Journal* 59 (1989) No. 82. coin

11 Fitzwilliam Museum, Cambridge. NCirc 1990, 198–99. coin

CHAPTER 3

Expansion 1200–1320

The Saxon Church of St Mary in the main settlement had almost doubled its original size with the addition of a newly completed north aisle. The north wall had been pierced by three arcades, leaving the ancient narrow windows partly filled by the new stonework. The church tower was completed during the fourteenth century, further dominating the thatched cottages, with their crude walls of wattle and daub, clustered in groups close to the river or straggled along the street.[1]

For the peasants, the village was their world, and their struggle for survival was dominated by the feudal system. They had few rights. Fees were paid at the manor court when they moved house and when a daughter married. They paid rents for their houses in money and services. They were forbidden to grind their own corn or bake their own bread.

As it was not possible for the lord of the manor to oversee the activities of the manor, the bailiff, reeve and steward would have been responsible for its smooth running, including discipline. Robert Fitzwalter was the most notable lord during the thirteenth century. He owned many other manors and was heavily involved in politics. He was the leader of the belligerent barons who forced King John to sign the Magna Carta at Runnymede in 1215. He harboured a particular grudge because of the king's behaviour towards Matilda, Fitzwalter's daughter, who was supposedly poisoned after she refused the king's unwelcome attentions.[2]

The manor was not the only institution to dominate the lives of the peasants. The prior of Little Dunmow in Essex exercised considerable influence on the local population. Over 30 grants of land and houses in Hemenhale were made to the priory at Little Dunmow during the twelfth and thirteenth centuries, enough to incur a tax problem. Several acres were therefore sold between 1208 and 1234, including, in 1209, 21 acres of land in the North Field belonging to St Mary's Church in Hemenhale.[3] This church changed its dedication to St Margaret in the sixteenth century.

The wealthier villagers used their money to buy influence with the prior or to ensure their path to heaven. About the year 1248, Walter, son of William of Brusingham, gave to the prior and the convent a serf and a piece of land between the garden and the land of the canons of Hemenhale. For the grant, Geoffrey the prior of Dunmow and the canons allowed him and Adam, the vicar of Hemenhale, to build a chapel in his courtyard in the village. William Fige and Richard the freeman gave their woods in Easthowloch. Alan the smith gave all his lands to the priory. In 1256 Roger, son of Henry, granted the prior permission to make a road from the meadow called Branelsmere to Oldcroft, for transporting and driving stock. In 1234 the prior sold some of his lands to Roger de Hemenhale. Sir Ralph de Hemenhale had bought Curpeil's manor from the Fitwalters by 1307 and subsequently it became known as Sir Ralph's manor.[4]

The vicar, appointed by the prior of Little Dunmow, was responsible for St Mary's Church as well as for St Andrew's Chapel, perhaps aided by a monk from the priory. The vicarage house was opposite the church and the tithe barn adjoining was the store for one-tenth of the produce harvested on the manor. The vicarage lands, called glebe, were scattered about the parish to take advantage of meadows, woods and arable. These holdings are indicative of the open field system (Fig. 10).

On 2 May 1225 Robert Fitzwalter, a minor, was granted a weekly market each Monday until his coming of age.[5] No reference is made to a fair, which the historian Blomefield claimed was on the same deed. However, according to later records there was

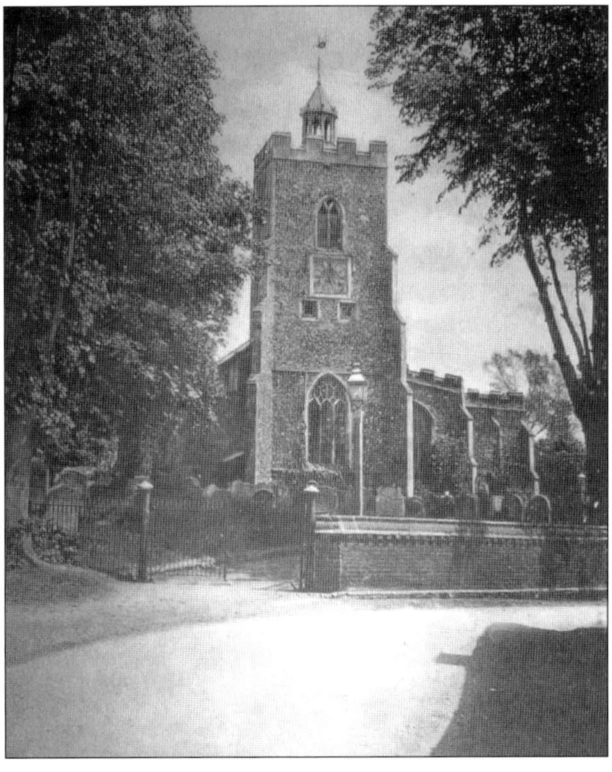

St Margaret's Church, formerly St Mary's.

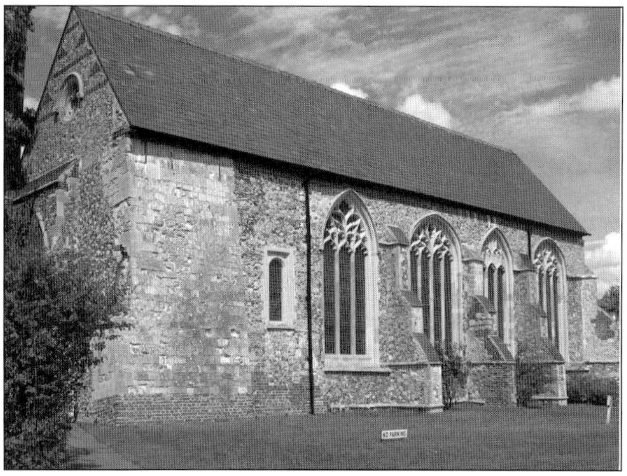

St Mary's Church, Little Dunmow, Essex, formerly part of a priory.

another fair that was always held on Whit Monday near to the village centre.

It could be argued that this first market was held at the highest navigable point near a green, later called Cole's Green, an obvious focal point, being the convergence of several radiating routes. The Tithe Map of 1842 records 'Market Hole' as a field nearby. Later documents refer to the market place as being opposite the church. Meanwhile, the population was rapidly expanding, as can be seen from archaeological evidence, rendering the village the most highly taxed in the hundred of Depwade, as shown by the Norwich Diocese Taxation of 1254. It was still the wealthiest in 1291 at the taxation of Pope Nicholas.[6]

According to Blomefield, another Robert Fitzwalter was granted a pillory, ducking stool and assize of bread in 1286, but no reference was given and no such grant can be found at the Public Record Office.

The division between rich and poor probably increased during this period. John Bressingham, a freeman, owned a messuage (house) and 100 acres. Anastasia Croune had several servants and sufficient possessions to attract the attentions of local thieves, who broke into her house, assaulted her, carried away her goods and ill-treated her servants.[7]

Although no manorial documents exist for Hemenhale manor for this period, some local names occur in registers kept of prisoners delivered from gaol to stand trial at Quarter Sessions. Walter Atthirne, also known as Walter in the Hirne, was accused of two robberies at Tasburgh in 1312. He was acquitted, but was found guilty two years later of a double murder and a robbery at Marsham. His ten acres, worth 6s.8d., were seized for the king and he was hanged, perhaps on Gallows Hill in the village. John de Rode was burgled in 1313. His horse, valued at 20s., was stolen. Woollen and linen cloth, a brass vessel and a half mark of silver, together valued at 60s., were also taken. Two locals set alight Henry Olbarlik's house, which was valued at 60s. and its contents at 20s.[8]

When a person of some importance committed a crime, the king himself might give judgement. The case of Nicholas de Hemenhale was brought before Edward II in 1319 at York after he was involved in a fight in which John Press was killed. The king pardoned de Hemenhale for the murder and for his outlawry when a witness testified that the killing was in self-defence and that the defendant had fought bravely for the king in Ireland.[9] There used to be a boundary stone, Baron Duel, where the parishes of Hempnall, Topcroft and Bedingham met, perhaps the site of this deadly conflict.[10]

This period saw a further increase in population. The establishment of the market and fairs, a financial

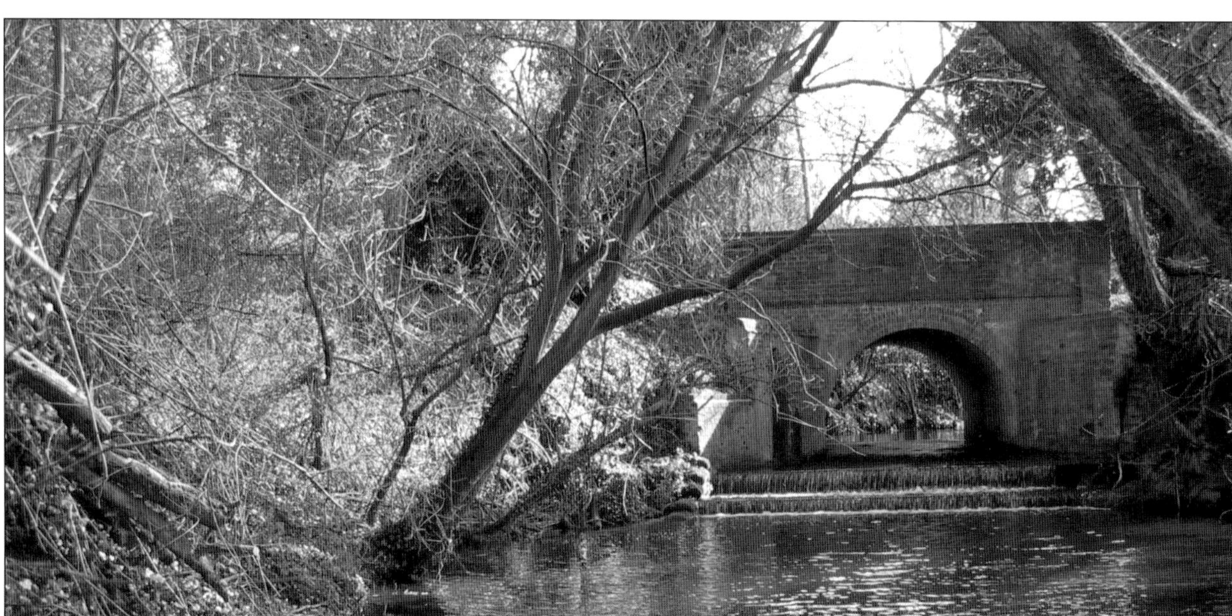

The bridge on the Rons, or Krons, at the highest navigable point.

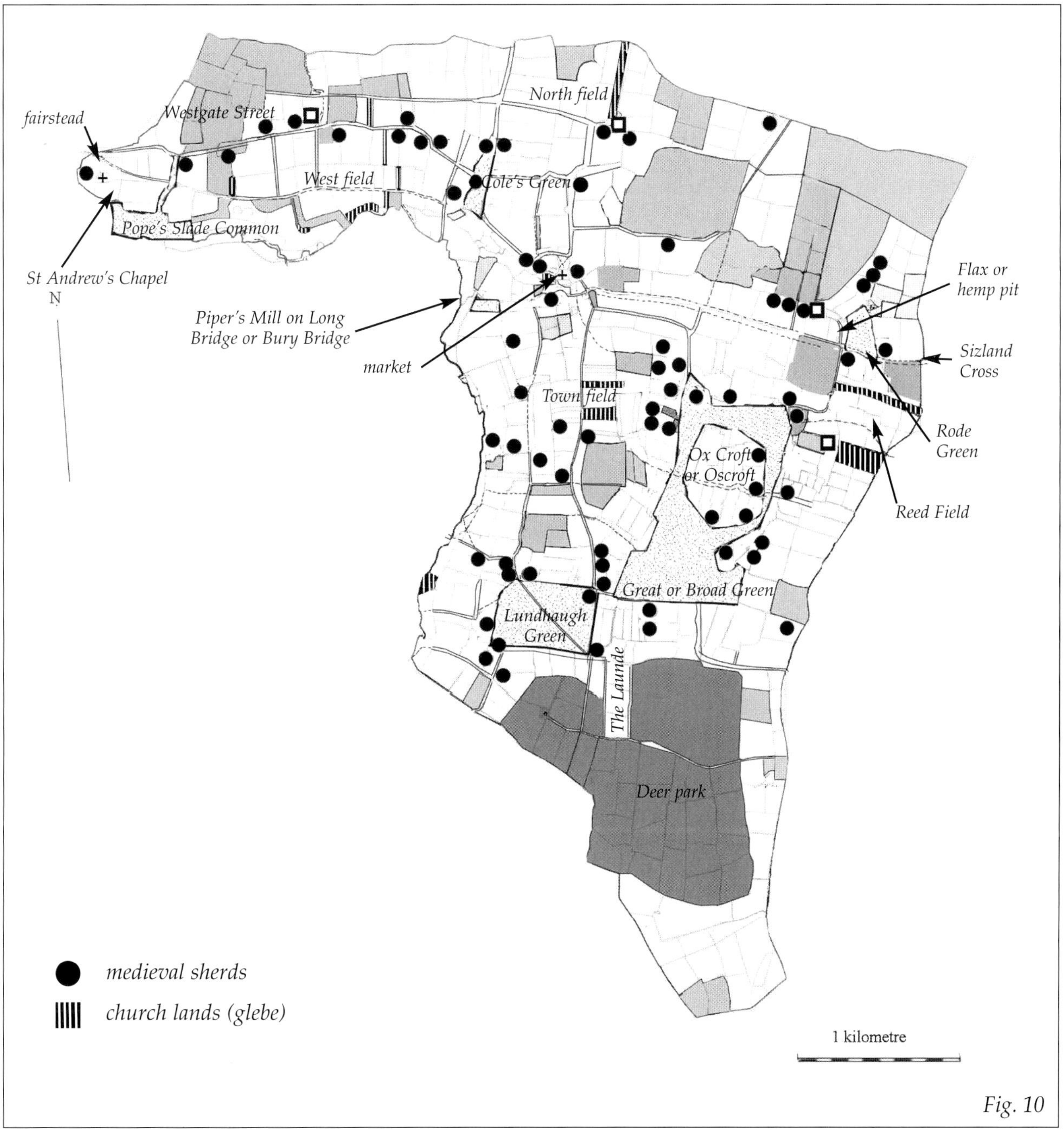

Medieval archaeology.

benefit to the lord of the manor, must also have increased the wealth of some of the population. Probably about this time a planned development took place along the Street towards Cole's Green (the war memorial now stands on a remnant of this green), each plot being approximately half an acre. Brewing and tanning industries were established in this area.

References

[1] N. Pevsner (1962) *The Buildings of England: North-West and South Norfolk* p.192 (Middlesex)

[2] Bryant (1915) *Norfolk Churches. The Hundred of Diss* p.90 (Norwich)

[3] CFF King John, 5 January 1209, No. 368. [case 154, File 27. No. 368]

[4] Bryant, *Norfolk Churches, Depwade* p.111. Arms of the Hemenhales were formerly in the windows on the south side of the nave.

[5] CCR 10 Henry III, m. 19

[6] Revd W. Hudson, FSA, 'The "Norwich Taxation" of 1254, so far as relates to the Diocese of Norwich, collated with the Taxation of Pope Nicholas in 1291', *NA* Vol. 17 p. 108

[7] CPR June 25 1309

[8] B. Hanawalt PhD, 'Crime in East Anglia in the 14th century. Norfolk Gaol Delivery Rolls 1307–16. *NRS* Vol. 44, Nos. 365, 311, 437

[9] CPR 14 July 1319, York

[10] NAU SMR 16115

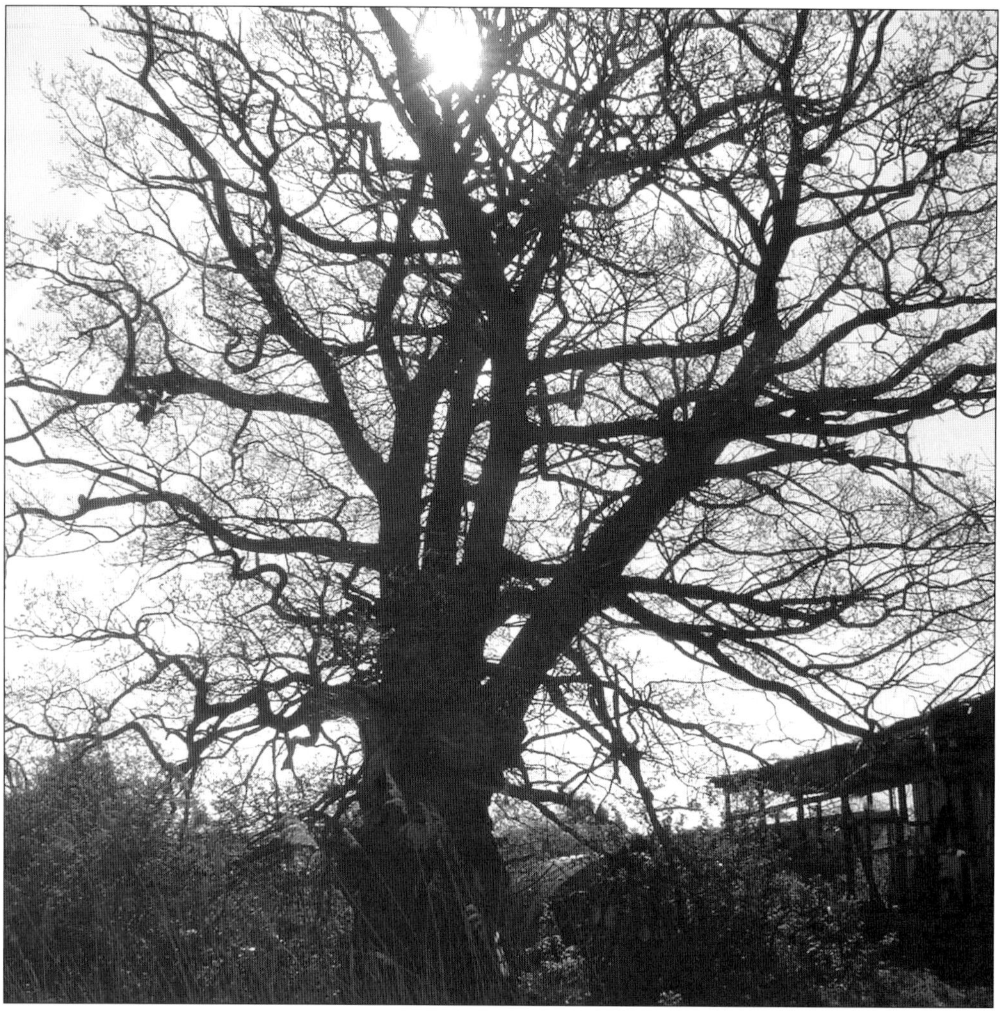

Ancient oak at Lundy Green. 860cm in girth, the second largest recorded tree in Norfolk.

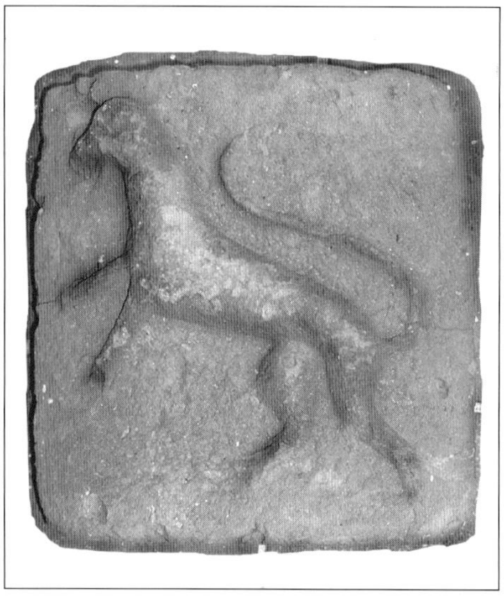

Sixteenth century moulded brick found with medieval pottery sherds not far from the church.

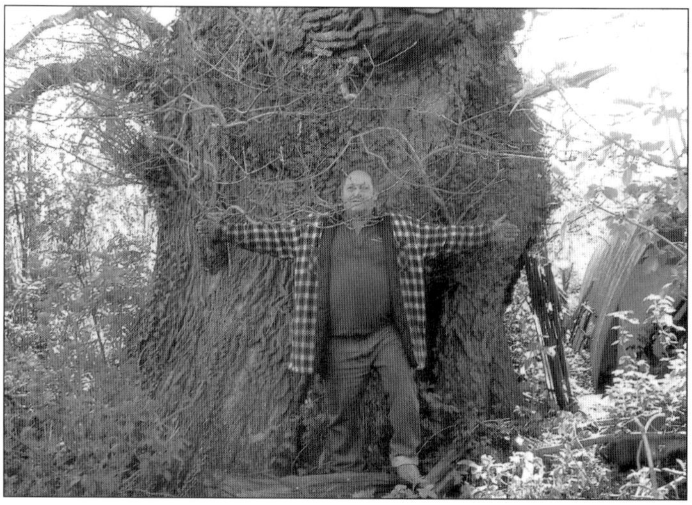

John MacRae by the oak in his garden at Lundy Green.

CHAPTER 4

Lords and Peasants 1327–99

The manor house, set within yards and gardens of six and a half acres, occupied a site adjoining St Mary's Church and was surrounded by features emphasising the power of the manorial system. There were fish ponds, dovecots, woods and a deer park of 240 acres. The estate amounted to 539 acres valued at £48.1s.10¾d.[1] Privileged guests would have been impressed by moated hunting lodges and the 'launde', a long clearing within the park where huntsmen could enjoy the chase without the problem of trees. The peasants would have been left in no doubt as to their place in society.

The de Hemenhale family, who resided in the village, held their land from the Fitzwalters and probably kept an eye on the Hemenhale manor. Sir Ralph had a younger brother, Thomas, who was elected Bishop of Norwich in 1336. The Pope vetoed the appointment and Thomas was later consecrated Bishop of Worcester.[2] In 1365 another Sir Ralph de Hemenhale was granted free warren in Hardwick, Shelton, Freton (Fritton) and Hemenhale on 8 October 1367.[3] The arms of the de Hemenhale family were set in the south aisle of St Mary's Church, an extension built in the fourteenth century.[4]

The organisation of the manor depended on administrators and manual workers. The steward was the most powerful and appeared from time to time to preside over the manor courts. The bailiff may have lived at the manor house, where he could supervise the running of the manor. Surveys and rentals ensured that such rents and services as were owed were duly collected from the serfs.

The population in general was seriously diminished by the Black Death of 1349, enabling those local peasants who survived to gain some power as a smaller workforce. Some made a bid for freedom following the 1381 Peasants' Revolt. In 1388 Anna Galyon was in Bongheye (Bungay), John Park in Tasburgh, John Galion in Beccles and the Coppyng sisters were living in Norwich. The steward, Simon Waynyld, knew where they were and the bailiff, Thomas ate Thorne, was instructed to bring them back, but they were still missing in 1393. The whereabouts of seven other absconders was unknown.

The local economy was boosted in 1380 by a charter granted to Walter Fitzwalter enabling him to hold a weekly market every Friday to replace the Monday market and to hold a fair on St Andrew's day, the fairground being next to the chapel there.[5] In 1387 John Sherwyn surrendered a messuage in the market place to Robert Larke, the vicar, and Thomas Baker bought a messuage with a curtilege in the market place. Ten years later he was buying a cottage called Ploumanstenement, with space on the west side to build a house with entry and exit to the quay without hindrance, another indication that the river was navigable for small boats. Tracing these records forwards, the Friday market place can be placed close to today's church.

Various court proceedings for the manors of Hemenhale, Dunmow Priory, Boyland and the rectory of Hemenhale manor begin in 1327.[6] However, it is not until 1387, when Philippa, the widow of Walter Fitzwalter, inherited, that the rolls become really interesting. The king apparently tried to interfere, as recorded in the Calendar of Close Rolls: 'Order to remove the king's hand and meddle no further with the manors of Hemenhall and Diss… Delivery to Philippa late wife of Walter Fitz-Walter, knight.'[7] She married secondly Sir John Golafre, who died in 1396, and then Edward, 2nd Duke of York, who was killed at Agincourt in 1414. She died in 1431.[8]

The first Leet Court of Philippa Fitzwalter was held in June 1387. There were 24 members of the homage present, both copyholders and freemen. Several tenants were accused of fighting, and much blood was spilt. Robert Baker was fined 2s.6d. for baking short-weight loaves and selling them against the statute. A long list of trespassers had caused damage in the lady's meadow, corn, barley, oats and woods, with oxen, bullocks, horses, cows, sheep and pigs. A few had hunted in the warren with dogs, taking hares and rabbits. Thomas Knopping, the bailiff of Topcroft, was fined 20s. for hunting in the warren with a greyhound. Bartholomew Kyte, the shepherd, allowed the lady's sheep to trespass in her wheat at le Wesoe.

Robert Baxter was a troublesome fellow, fined for attacking Walter Leece on the highway, assaulting John Bocheler, trespassing in the lady's meadow at 'Le Pond' with three pigs, overturning the lady's tumbrill and drawing blood from Margery, a member of his household. Baxter was a miller renting a watermill grinding malt and wheat for 16s.8d. annually.

Roger Broun of Aldeburgh was fined 3s.4d. for attacking Richard Pynsthorpe, the hayward. Broun later came at night with his family, and, perhaps in revenge, smashed the fence and drove 20 cows and 160 sheep on to the lady's meadow.

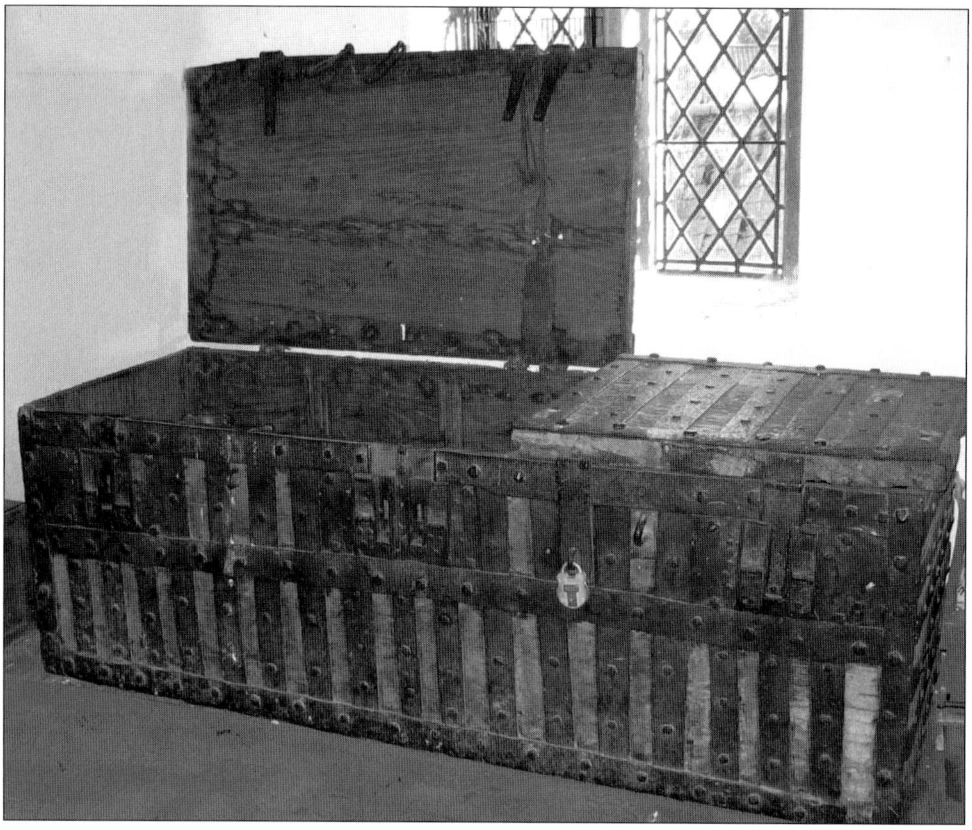

The fourteenth-century church chest in the parvis above the porch

The bailiff, who was supposed to be above reproach, caused bad and useless wheat to be sown in 80 acres and was fined 26s.8d. His inefficiency allowed six peasants to evade autumn boonwork for several years without paying a fine. John Barbour had not performed this work for five years.

Wet weather might have contributed to the cattle disease recorded from 1386 – 81 lambs, 32 ewes and a goose died. In 1388 it was noted by the inspector of carcasses that 11 old ewes had died of disease before shearing and lambing and that nine lambs in the care of shepherd Bartholomew Kyte had died of disease. Thomas Shepherde was responsible for 44 wethers and 12 ewes that had died of disease and not of neglect. On 12 September 1388 signs of madness were noted in cows, pigs and lambs. In 1390 skins were ruined in tanning and the pelts taken to the bailiff. Lists of diseased animals continue to the year 1396.

Very few closes, crofts or gardens are mentioned in the rolls, indicating that the landscape probably lacked hedges, but there was an abundance of woods and meadows. A few roads and paths are mentioned when property adjoined them. There was a highway at Sissegraves, common lanes at Glandhaugh, Cardokes, Chyrchwaye, Rodeway and Brahamseweye, sometimes called Berghamswey. There are 25 different houses or cottages recorded, with such interesting names as Cotones, Crowes, Eylwards, Hirnygg, Fullers, Hoghous, Sarbalds, Skippers, Sowyston, Schelhokes, Stylhous, Walsshes and Wynters, and two gardens called Boddy's and Hipperesyard.

Tradition says that about the year 1390 the parish church caught fire.[9] Somehow a fine iron-bound chest, almost nine feet long, survived. Robert Larke, described in his will of 1398 as vicar of Hempnall St Mary, left bequests to Brother Sumford (probably a monk), to his own brother, to Margaret Wyse and for the repair of the church. His executors were John Spens, chaplain, perhaps responsible for St Andrew's chapel, and William de Hemenhale. He was the first person from the village to make a recorded will.[10]

References

[1] 1327 Inquisition Post Mortem on the death of Robert Fitzwalter

[2] C. Harper-Bill (1996) 'The Medieval Church and the Wider World', *Norwich Cathedral, Church, City and Diocese, 1096–1996* (London) p. 290

[3] CChR 8 October 1367

[4] Bryant, *Norfolk Churches: Depwade* p. 111

[5] CChR, May 4, 10 1380

[6] NRO MC 1862/MS 35032 Hemenhall Court Roll 1327–98

[7] CCR 2 March 1387

[8] Philippa died on 17 July 1431. Buried in St Nicholas's Chapel, Westminster Abbey

[9] Bryant, *Norfolk Churches: Depwade* p.111

[10] NCC 1398 f.247 Harsyk

CHAPTER 5

Alterations and Altercations 1400–1539

The sight of the ruined church must have been unavoidable, stark against the sky, overshadowing the market place. Imagination sees a picture of a roofless church, debris and blackened windowless walls. The sight would have been devastating to the parishioners, for church services, ceremonies and festivals were integral to medieval life. Fortunately, from the surviving architecture, it seems that the tower and some of the walls were repairable.

Between 1437 and 1505, 11 wills record bequests, ranging from 12d. to £8 for the repair of St Mary's Church. Some people made specific bequests; for example, Walter Lessy gave 20d. for the painting of the rood over the rood screen in 1437, and William Baxter bequeathed 28s. for a new font in 1438.[1] Robert Redgrave gave two coombs of malt and 6s.8d. after the sale of his house.[2] William Passhelewe of Shelton bequeathed 3s.4d. to the hallowing of Hempnall Church in 1504, and in 1505 John Carentyn gave 12d. towards the repair of the steeple and John Halle 3s.4d. for the repair of the bell frame.[3] No wills mention St Mary's after 1505. Thereafter, the church seems to have changed its dedication to St Margaret.

The exterior probably looked similar to that of today, except that the chancel was much longer and there were two narrow windows in the tower, of which traces can be seen in the flintwork now partly obscured by the clock. The faint remains of a scratch or mass dial, perhaps from this period, can be found on a buttress against the south aisle. The furnishings, however, would have been very different. Churches at that time were often dark and cluttered, containing a number of altars cordoned off with screens. There were no pews, only benches round the outside walls for the weaker members of the congregation. The chancel was the holy part of the church, intended for the clergy and containing the high altar of stone and perhaps several chantry altars. Robert Andrew, in his will of 1486, requested that an honest priest be paid to sing for his soul and those of his friends for two years at the altar of St John the Baptist in Hempnall.[4] John Sporle gave 1s. in 1460 for the maintenance of the light of St John.[5]

The Guilds of St John and the Holy Trinity no doubt played an important part in the community and were mentioned in bequests. There was once a guildhall in the village, somewhere near the church, originally called Thatchers, alias the Guildhall, and Cowpers, Sowters and Wrights or the Guildhall by the seventeenth century. As all these names are of trades, these were probably secular gilds.

About the year 1487 money was being raised for bells. John Verdon was heard to say to his son John that he was dying and wished to provide a tenor bell for the church. Apparently, the son promised to perform the request when he had 'received the fruits of his lands for two years, but urged his father not to put the legacy in his will.' Since this promise, 15 years had passed, and in the year 1502 several of the parishioners gathered in the church to discuss the matter. John Bowring and Robert Goldsmith testified that Ralph Severby, William Sporle, Geoffrey Goldsmith were there at the time of the promise. There were arguments and then Ralph Severby and Geoffrey Goldsmith promised money towards a treble bell but suddenly John Verdon burst out: 'Keep your money in your purses, for by the will of my father I am bound to give a tenor bell, and his will I will perform.'[6] John Verdon, the son, sold one of the dwellings he owned, called Cottons, to Robert Sporle some time before his death in 1536. His will does not mention a bell, but he did give 50s. to the high altar of Hemenhale Church. He bequeathed his coat of violet and other colours and his doublet of worstead with fustian sleeves to Robert Sewell.[7]

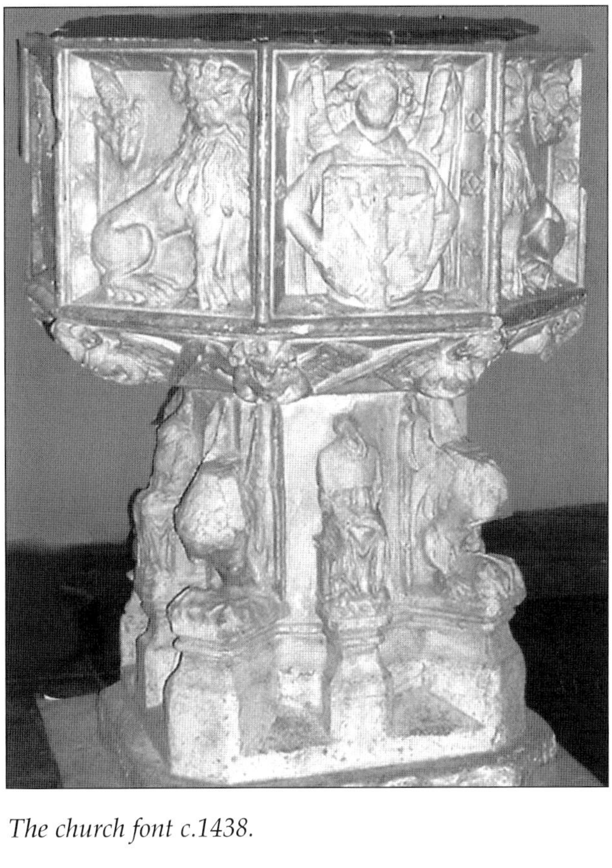

The church font c.1438.

In the autumn of 1527 there was an altercation in the church between Ambrose Molle and Alice Cammel. At the Consistory Court the following year, Hempnall residents William Weston and John Barbor were called as witnesses. John Barbor testified that 'Molle's reputation had been in no way injured'. A fortnight later the two parties were again in court. This time Richard Hoker deposed that Molle had said things which damaged Alice Cammel's reputation. Present were John Brown and also John Bowring, who had appeared in the case of John Verdon.[8]

In 1449, as in 1334, Hempnall was paying the highest tax in the hundred of Depwade and therefore is likely to have had residents with money to spend on altering and extending their dwellings.[9] The parish was fortunate in having a plentiful supply of wood for building. During the reign of Henry IV (1399–1413), for example, a new timber bridge was framed in the Hemenhall Park for the Carmelites at Norwich.[10] It is possible that some timber-framed buildings, identified as 'hall houses' may exist from this period, some extended upwards after the addition of a chimney. A number of owners inserted a door in the tie beam. Lime Tree Cottage (formerly Toftys, Toftes or Toffees) and Wodehouse Farm (formerly Albutlers) are good examples. It seems likely that some of the copyhold names of houses came from the original fourteenth-century owners.

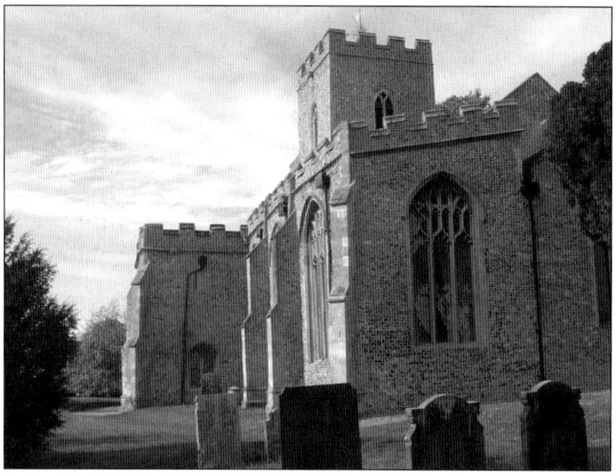

The church from the east end.

Evidence from wills indicates the subtle changes of spelling of the village name. The 'p' insertion appears from 1469, after which spellings vary from Hempnale to Hemphale to Hempnhall. After 1505 the 'p' and the 'h' were occasionally dropped and the name was spelled Hemnall. The present-day name, Hempnall, was generally in use after 1540.

Perhaps the old spelling lingered on as long as the de Hemenhale family resided in the village. Sir Robert de Hemenhale, lord of the manor of Ralphs, or Raffes, had died before 1406, and his arms were displayed in a window of the Austin Friars Church in Norwich. His son William was dead some time before 1419 without children. John, his uncle, brother of Sir Robert, inherited but also died without issue. The manor and lands went to Joan, daughter of John de la Pole and widow of Sir Robert.[11] By this time she had married her fourth husband, Sir John Oldcastle, who was outlawed in 1418 and then put to death for treason and felony.[12] The manor descended to Sir Thomas Brooke of Somerset, who was a son by Joan's second husband. The last of the family to live in the village seems to have been Ralph de Hemenhale,

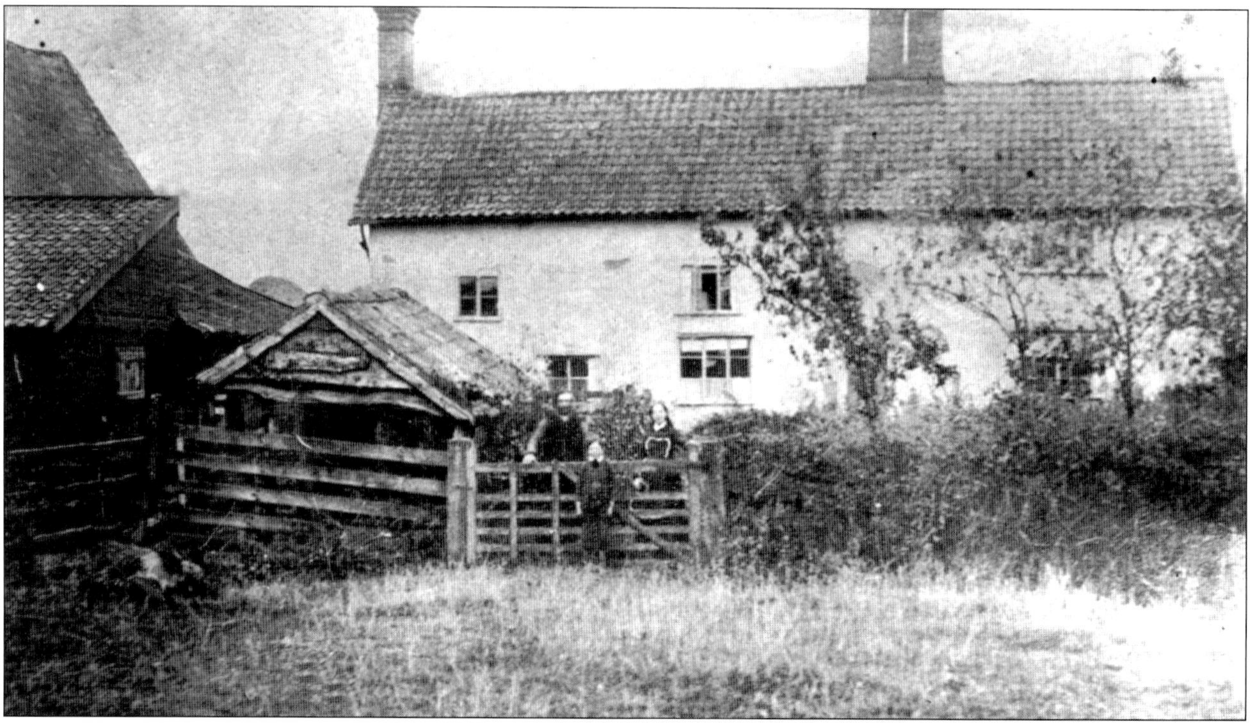

Silver Green Farm, owned by John Verdon some time in the fifteenth century (copyhold name Cottons).

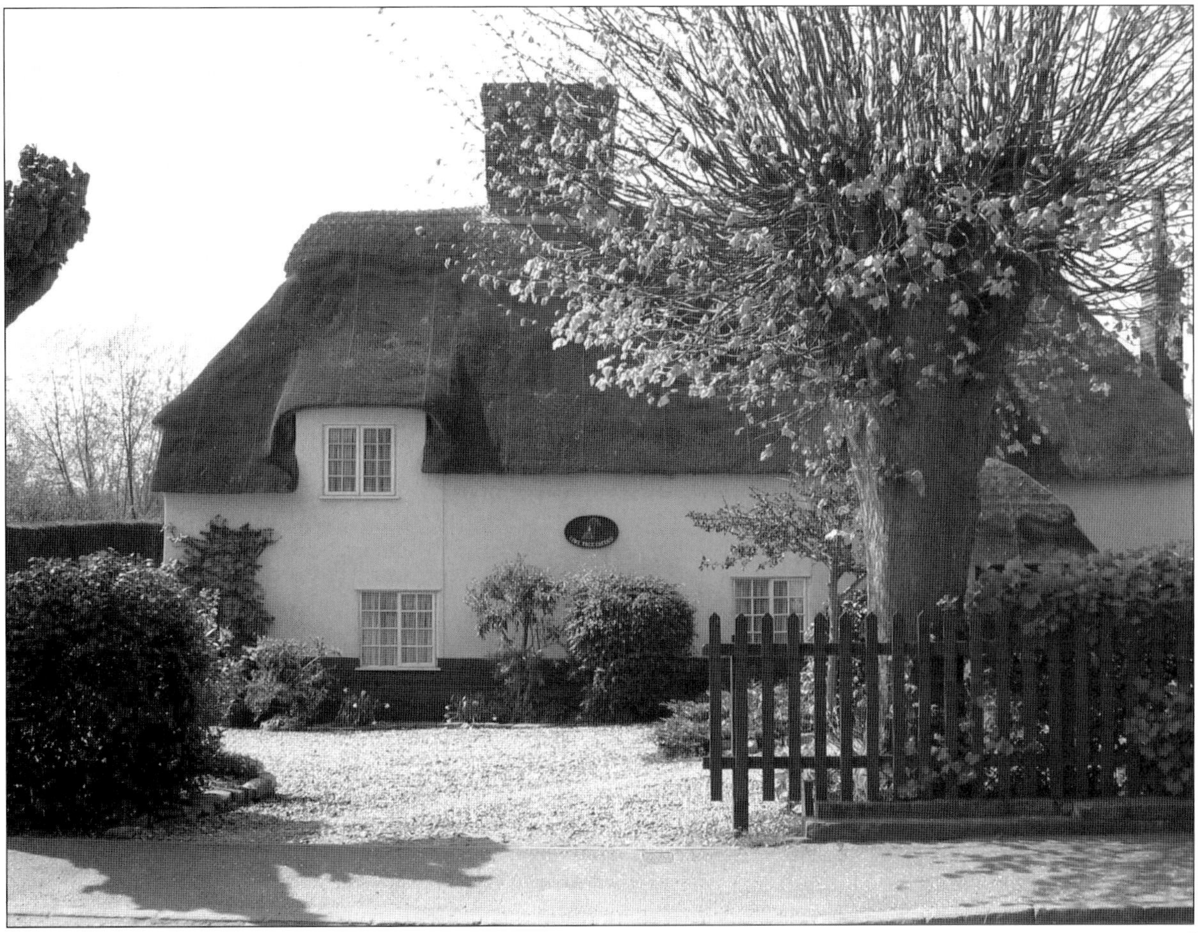

Lime Tree Cottage, earliest known date 1573/74. Copyhold description: Toftys, Toftes or Toffees. Timber-framed hall house.

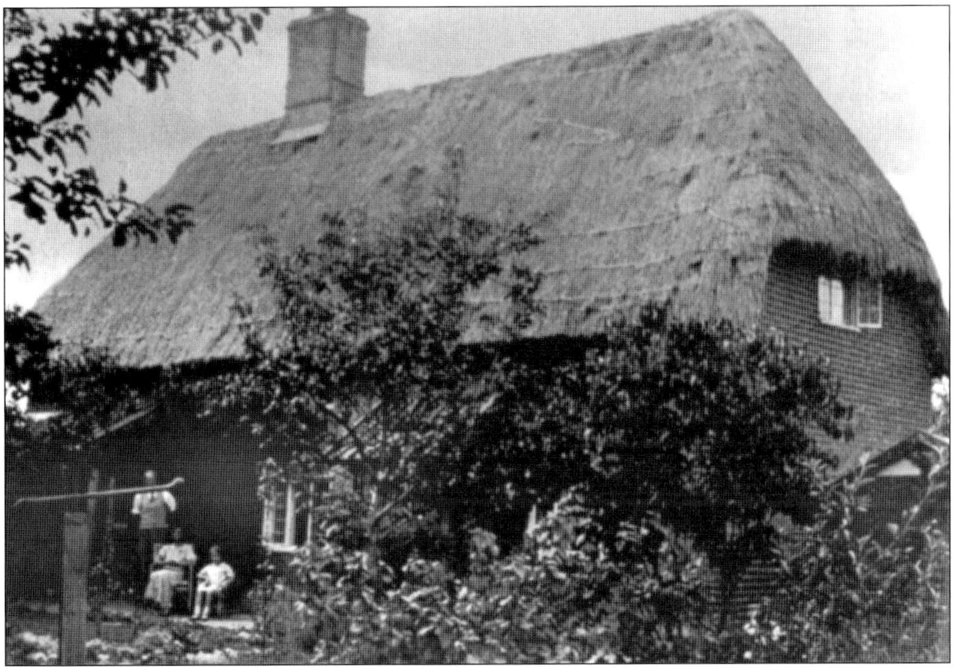

Wodehouse Farm, formerly the Haven, earliest known date 1651. Copyhold description: Albutlers. Timber-framed hall house

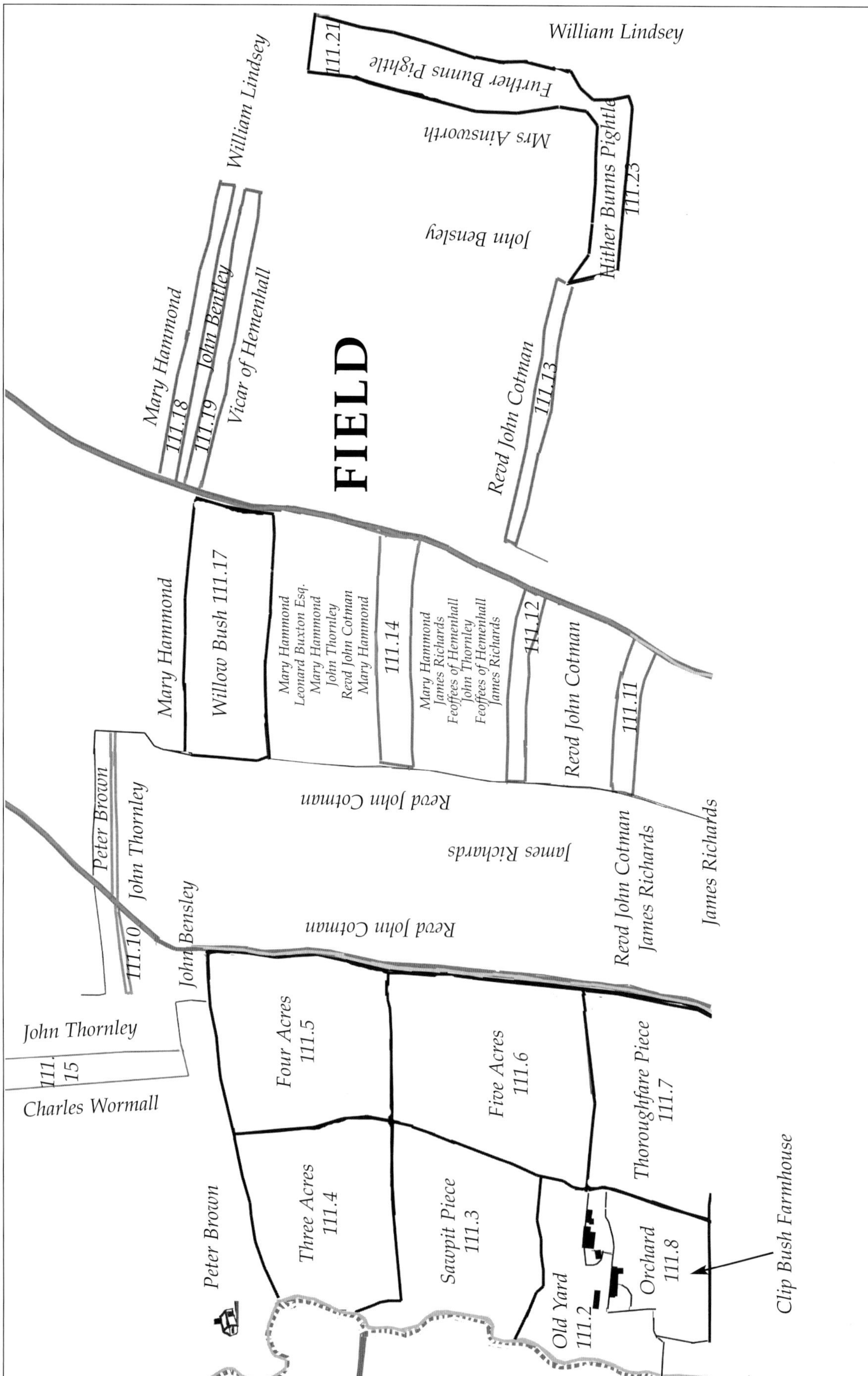

Clip Bush Farm and part of the Town Field. The numbers 111 refer to the land belonging to this farm, formerly likely to have once belonged to Little Dunmow Priory.

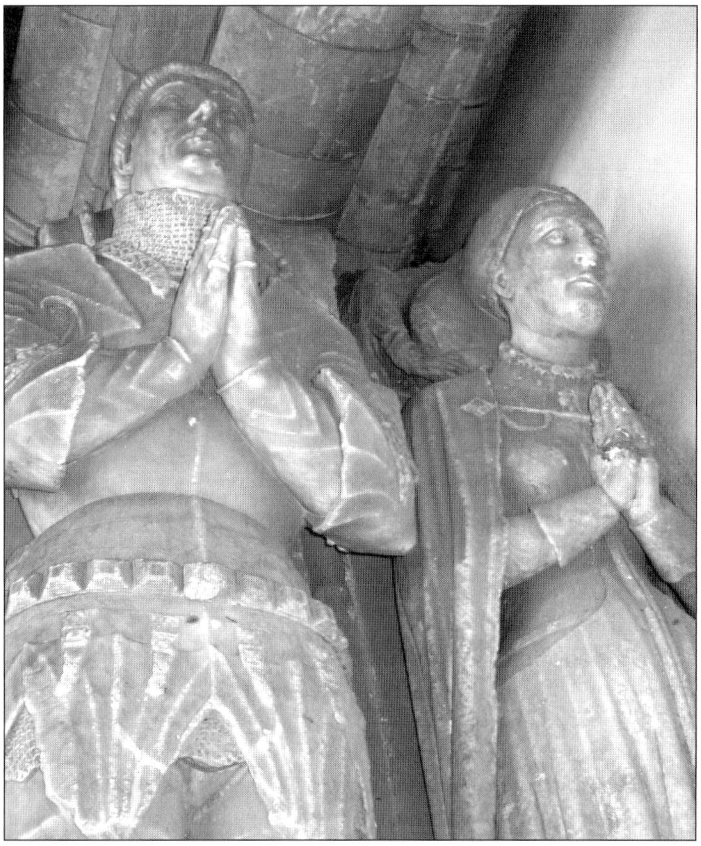

Walter Fitzwalter and his wife Elizabeth (née Devereux) in Little Dunmow Church.

described in 1422 as being of 'Hemenale County Norfolk, gentilman'. He failed to appear before Justices regarding a debt of eight marks owed to John West of Dounham, Suffolk.[13] The family eventually moved to Suffolk. Raffes Manor had passed to Richard Bromvle, or Blundevyle, by 1490 and disappeared as a manor some time after 1612.

Phillippa, the widow of Robert Fitzwalter, having died in 1431, Walter Fitzwalter, who had married Elizabeth Devereux then inherited Hempnall Manor. He died in 1432, leaving his widow to inherit. One of her daughters married John Radcliff, who took the title Lord Fitz-Walter in the right of his wife. In 1493 he was accused of treason for supporting the pretender Perkin Warbeck against Henry VII and his manors were confiscated. Henry VIII restored all to his son Robert in 1525 and in 1529 conferred on him the title of Earl of Sussex.

The Dissolution of the Monasteries in 1535 undoubtedly had a huge impact on the life of the church. The living at Hempnall, a rectory belonging to the priory of Little Dunmow in Essex, had a vicarage endowed. After 1535 the right to appoint the vicar was given by Henry VII to Robert, Earl of Sussex. St Andrew's Church became redundant.

This was another period of change. Land formerly belonging to Little Dunmow Priory was sold. The de Hemenhale family were no longer an influence and the village gradually changed its name. The inhabitants again showed their ability to co-operate and gilds were formed for the support and encouragement of those in trades.

References

[1] NCC 1437 24 Doke MF 25, NRO NCC 1438 74

[2] NCC 1485 f. 241 A. Caston

[3] NCC 1504 Popy 522 . NFK 1504 Davy 53 NCC 1505 Ryxe 302

[4] NCC 1486 f. 286 A. Caston. Will of Robert Andreu

[5] ANF 1460 f. 23 Grey Will of John Sporle of Hempnall

[6] E.D. Stone, calendared, 'Norwich Consistory Court Depositions, 1499–1512 and 1518–1530' *NRS* Vol. 10 No. 38 fo. 60

[7] NCC 153 6 MF43 HYLL

[8] E.D. Stone, 'Norwich Consistory Court Depositions, 1499–1512 and 1518–30' *NRS* Vol. 10 December 1502 No. 202 fo. 51b fo. 52 fo. 52b

[9] William Hudson 'The Assessment of the Townships of the County of Norfolk for the King's Tenths and Fifteenths as settled in 1334 and 1449' Depwade *NA* Vol. 12. Hemenhale paid £6.10s. Carltone Rode £6 Stratton £5.16s.8d.

[10] Blomefield, Norfolk p.250

[11] Bryant, *Norfolk Churches: Depwade* p.110. Bryant gives no references

[12] CCR 22 November 1418, Westminster

[13] CPR 6 February 1422

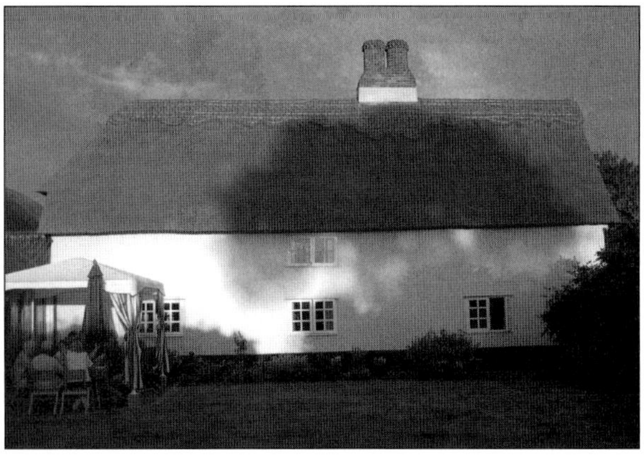

Home Farm, Silver Green. Earliest known record 1600s. (Messuage or tenement the common east. Timber-framed.)

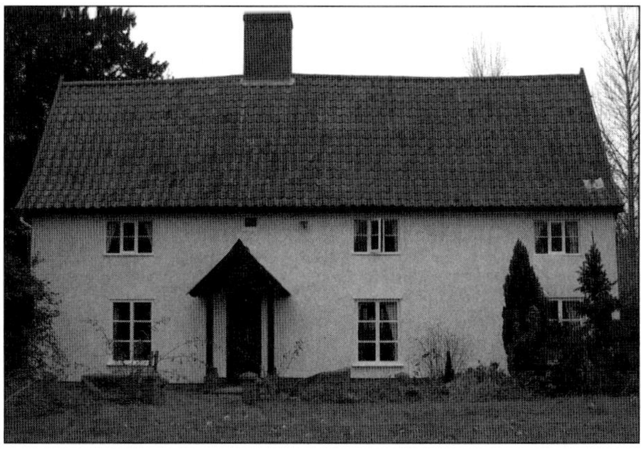

Yew Tree Cottage, Silver Green. Earliest known record from 1724, but probably much older. Timber-framed. (Copyhold description: Messuage with an orchard and garden on the south side of the common pasture called Long Green.)

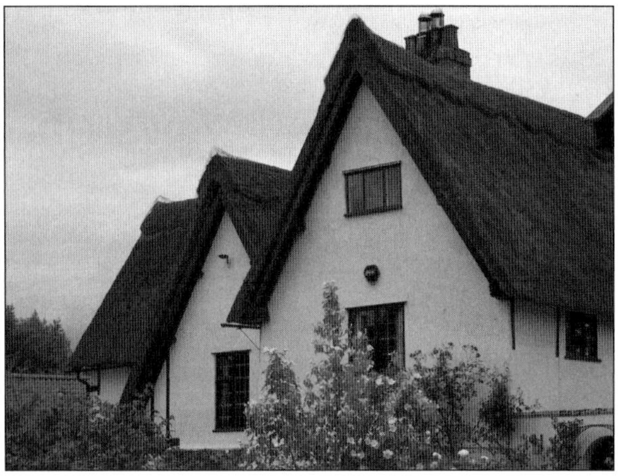

The Thatched House in the Street. Timber-framed (freehold).

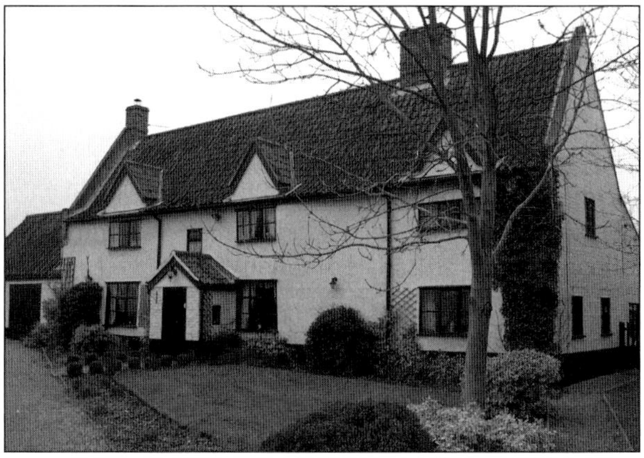

Meadow Farm, Silver Green. Earliest known date 1559. Timber-framed. (Copyhold description: Messuage called Thornes with a garden and Close).

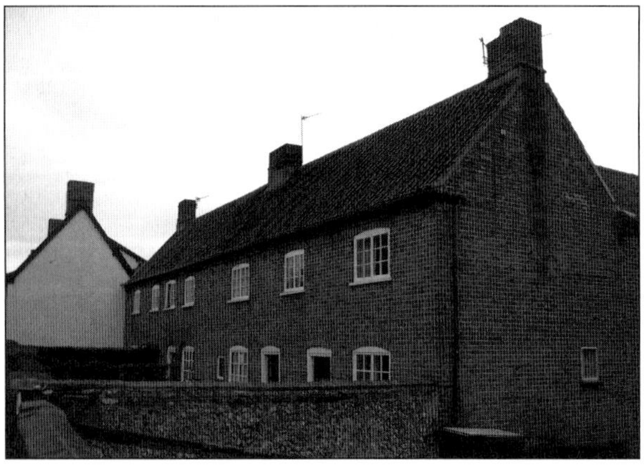

Manor Cottages. Earliest known record 1558. Once one house, it was given a brick skin in 1771 after it was bought by William Thrower in 1770 (copyhold name Shepherds).

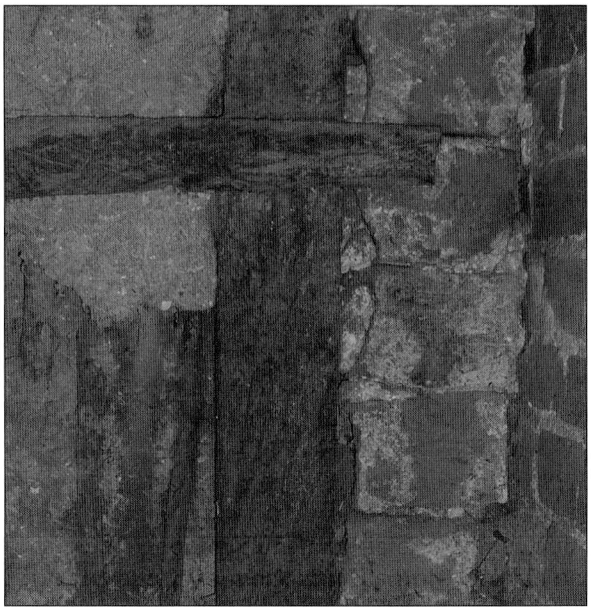

Right: *Timber frame with wattle and daub infilling within a cupboard at Manor Cottages.*

CHAPTER 6

The Tudor Village 1540–99

Before their final dissolution by Henry VIII in 1547, the monasteries provided assistance to the poor. The Elizabethan Poor Law of 1572 made poverty the responsibility of local communities. A Poor Rate was collected weekly from those who owned land to help the 'deserving poor'.

At Hempnall, though no individual was allowed to take a poor person into his or her own home, many villagers had ignored or were ignorant of the rule. In 1574 William Dowe had 'harboured and supported within his tenement a certain impoverished man called Asshe'. William Myngaye had 'harboured and supported an impoverished woman in his tenement' and was ordered to remove the woman or face a fine of 10s. Widow Graye illegally kept a 'feeble girl called a lame wench'. (Elizabeth Graye was a descendant of Robert de Grey, once lord of the manor of Littlehall in Hempnall, whose memorial brass was in the church. She was destined to live to be over 100.) Richard Bylong kept a 'certain Agnes Jermyn, widow, late the wife of Robert Jermyn, who is ill of fame'. John Ellys and Thomas Dymys had also taken in poor people. At the end of the court came a solemn warning:

No inhabitant of the township of Hempnall shall harbour nor support, nor in their houses have living those who are impoverished who can be discharged from the township, without the consent of Edward Jermyn, John Turnour, Ralph Robbe, Richard Chettleburgh, John Halles and John Sporle.[1]

It was still acceptable to bequeath money for the poor. Lawrence Halls died in 1569 bequeathing 4d. apiece to the poor householders of Hempnall, whom he named individually. His wife Marjorie had firm instructions to make no claim into any part of his lands and tenements: '... for if she do then I will that all my saide gift to her before bequeathed to be utterly voyde from her and her assigns for ever.'[2]

In 1575 the less fortunate were fined for not keeping their dwellings in good repair. John Meek was fined 3s.4d. for neglecting roofing and plasterwork in his tenement. Richard Jermyn allowed waste in his house, called 'a carthouse' because of neglect.

Between 1548 and 1551 the churchwardens, John Robard and William Myngey, with the permission of the inhabitants, sold a few items belonging to the church, including a cope and vestment of crimson velvet, a black velvet hearse, cloth and linen. The money raised was used to repair windows, stonework and the roof and to help 'impotent and bed-ridden persons'. This sale may indicate a move towards Puritanism, for during the short reign of Edward VI the 1549 prayerbook changed the way services were conducted and the arrangement of furniture within the church. After 1551, high altars of stone were demolished and a table was used for the Eucharist. A table, being movable, could be set up 'tablewise', that is with the narrower side facing the nave so that parishioners could gather round it to receive communion. However, an inventory of church possessions taken in 1552 shows the church still owned some fine possessions. There were five altar cloths, some of silk, three copes, one of crimson velvet, five vestments, two great and four small laten candlesticks, a chalice and a paten of silver gilt. One bell hung in the tower.[3]

St Margaret's Church, dominating the village centre, witnessed a bustle of activity each Friday. Stalls were set up in the market, the vendors turning up on foot or by donkey. It was the beginning of a more permanent shopping centre. The village shop of today is on the site of a 'little cottage or shop' rented by William Reynolds in 1578. There was a row of cottages on the north side of the churchyard, one called the Cocke Shopp (cook shop), belonging to Margaret Warde.[4] Opposite the church was Kitchens (the Bull Inn), both names indicating food providers.

The population was expanding and, on the whole, after the succession of Queen Elizabeth I, the people were enjoying a more secure life. A few of the wealthier inhabitants left wills revealing the style and contents of their dwellings and illuminating the lives of those who lived in them. Andrew Dowe left his wife Margaret his dwelling with the 'lytell parlor in the north end... with the chamber above the same'. She was allowed access at all 'convenyent tymes so long as she shall kepe unmarryed'.[5] She died a few months later, bequeathing to their daughters a posted bed, feather bedding, bolsters, sheets, her new little kettle, pewter dishes, her gown and a herd of swine.[6] John Pytte made good provision for his son, ensuring he had 'siffient meat, drinke and clothes by all the hole terme of his liff'. He left money for the repair of the churches at Bedingham, Topcroft and Hempnall, and 34s.4d. 'to have an honest pryst to praye for me and all my good friends in the churche of Hempnall'.[7]

The years 1570–1640 are often called the 'Great Rebuilding', when, traditionally, new houses were springing up all over England. A timber-framed

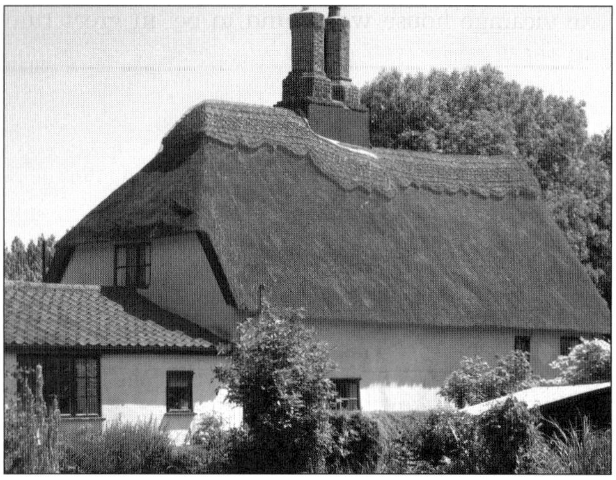

Poacher's Cottage, Silver Green. Timber-framed. Earliest known record 1664, but much earlier. (Copyhold description: The messuage formerly belonging to John Wesson).

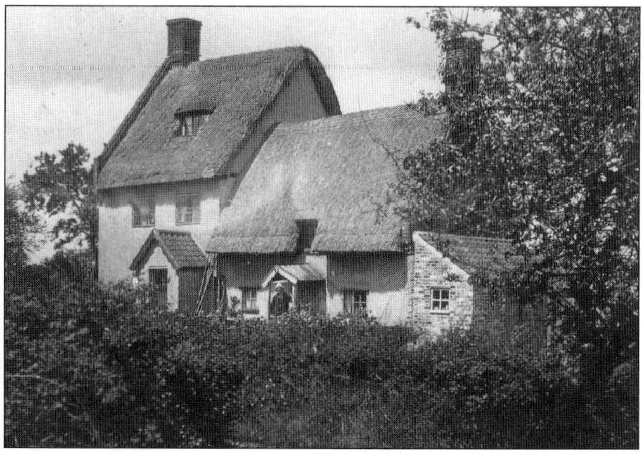

Chestnut Tree Farm, Silver Green. Timber-framed. Earliest known record 1615. (Copyhold description: A tenement with 5 acres of bond land).

house can contain wood from about 300 trees, mostly oaks. The most practical length of wood was 20ft, thus dictating the average width of the houses.

With timber in great demand it is likely that the lord of the manor, now the Earl of Sussex, was making a profit from the sale of oaks from his deer park. By 1573 most of the former park had become wood pasture enclosed in blocks of between 20 and 42 acres, subdivided into smaller fields of between 10 and 20 acres and were let.[8]

Manorial rolls from the sixteenth century for Hempnall manors have only survived from 1573 to 1590, but even within this limited period there is evidence that several new buildings were being erected. In 1573 Nicholas Dowe built a house without licence and George and Margaret Stanger owned a piece of land with a tenement newly built. Robert Eastowe took over a parcel of wasteland 'lately built upon once called St. Andrew's Chapel'. Robert and Margaret Ashe bought a bond tenement, newly built, with a garden, and John Sherdlowe had built a messuage part of the Paynfrith. Thomas and Ann Downing were selling a half rood of land 'with a messuage now built upon it in Westgatestrete'.[9] Older houses were being improved. John Bird, in his will of 1593, made provision for his wife, Alice, to have his house called 'The Plot' with a chamber over, and Philip Jermyn, his nephew, was allowed 'at his owne coste to build up a chymney in the parlor… to his use for the time being.'[10]

Some of the demesne (manorial) land belonging to Hempnall Manor was sold to members of the developing middle class. Robert Sporle, William Reynolds, William Dowe and Thomas Warde were admitted to several acres 'late the site of the manor'. Doffehouse (Dovehouse) Close, bought by Thomas Warde, would have been an important acquisition, since dovehouses were considered a symbol of affluence and power. Thomas Turner took over a further part of the site of the manor with gardens, buildings, houses, orchards, fishing rights, a piece of pasture called Peacock Acre, the Harsley and an enclosure called Newffayrplace (new fair place).[11]

Manorial documents have hitherto provided the best evidence for the lives of the ordinary villager, but only those owning copyhold property or accused of misdemeanours would have appeared in these records. However, after 1538, every parish was instructed to purchase a secure chest in which to keep a register containing a record of every baptism, marriage and burial that had taken place in the church. Hempnall registers begin in 1560. Almost every year there were substantially more baptisms than burials, indicating an expanding population. Almost none of the surnames recorded were the same as those from the fourteenth century.

John Kyrke was a tanner who had lately built a house at Longbridge 'with a newly made ditch, moat or embankment'. On 1 June 1572 he absconded, leaving his wife, Alice, and their three small children and owing money. The Queen's Commissioners held an enquiry and arranged for Kyrke's creditors to be recompensed. Edward Robberdes took some of Kyrke's bond land and his tenement Parkes (opposite the Chequers). Alice Kyrke's mother had left her a tenement, called Toftes, provided she kept and maintained a young boy called Andrew Burrye until he was ten years old. This she had not done, nor did she attend the manor court to explain why she had not kept to the terms of the will.[12] It seems that her father, William Reynolds, took pity on her. The cottage reverted to him and he agreed to share ownership with Reginald Kyrke, his grandson, Alice's eldest son.

In 1580 the queen's coffers were somewhat depleted and in order to obtain money, parliament granted her a subsidy. The Lay Subsidy was a tax of 2s.8d. in the pound on goods and chattels. In Hempnall, 37 paid this tax.[13] Most of these people wrote wills. All the men, apart from one, were described as yeoman. Henry Bullen or Bulleyn, the biggest taxpayer, moved away to Suffolk. He was related to the Bulleyn family of Shelton, who claimed a relationship with the Bulleyns of Blickling Hall and thus could boast a small connection with Elizabeth I.

With the prospect of invasion from Spain, the queen ordered a compilation of men over 16 who were fit and able to fight for England in the event of attack. In Hempnall, over 70 men were deemed to satisfy the criteria and were recorded in a muster. There were 19 householders, 25 cottagers, 21 artificers, four labourers and one gentleman.[14] They may have practised archery skills at 'The Butts', a meadow running between the Street and the river.

A number of minor offences were recorded in the court rolls, mostly about failing to clear ditches and allowing branches and thorns to overhang the common ways. Robert Goldsmith had illegally dug a ditch in the 'processional way' (the parish boundary) to the nuisance of everyone. James Woodyarde had illegally entered the warren belonging to the lord and taken partridges, and John Randolphe of Topcroft had taken payment from strangers, who grazed stray pigs on the manor and allowed them to wander at large in the field and close of Hempnall.' Usually, stray animals were kept in a pound. One was situated to the east of the churchyard and the other was near St Andrew's fairground.[15]

Taverns and alehouses were popular venues for entertainment, but not all brewers and sellers kept orderly premises. In 1575 Henry Harrys, Henry Sporle and Thomas Knytes were accused of 'supporting and allowing bad control within their houses and of keeping taverns without licence'. At Bishop Redman's visitation in 1597, Geoffrey Sendall and his wife were reported for 'suffering divers persons to eat and drink in time of divine service and sermons'. When Mary Stracke caused disharmony and strife in the village, only the vicar, George Skynner, came to her defence. The report described her as:

> *... a common drunkard and a sower of discord between neighbours and a breaker of the Christian charity, she hath three children and is very poor. When she spoke for her reelefe – they say she skoldethe and Mr Skynner certified that he have not knowne her ever drunkard but busy with her tongue.*

The vicarage house was found to be 'in great ruin and decay and part of the roof fallen in'.[16]

It appears to have been a period when the division between rich and poor was becoming more evident. The more affluent could afford to build new houses or modernise old ones. The North Field was probably enclosed during the Tudor period and farmed by members of the rising middle class. The field name 'Newffayrplace' suggests that the Whitsun fair had moved to a new venue close to the Town Field. A field in this area was scattered with hundreds of buttons, some from this period. However, the pit near the village centre is called 'the Fairstead' on the 1842 Tithe Award Map, so perhaps by the nineteenth century gravel extraction had ceased.

References

[1] NRO MC 1862/65, 863X1

[2] NRO NCC 147 Pouder Will of Lawrence Halls

[3] H.B. Walters FSA (1941) 'Inventories of Norfolk Church Goods' *NA* Vol. 27 (Norwich) p.129 1548–51

[4] NRO NAC 183 Sherwood. 1583/84 Will of Margaret Warde

[5] NRO NCC 251 Ingold 1558 Will of Andrew Dowe

[6] NRO NCC 206 Ingold Will of Margaret Dowe

[7] NRO NCC NRO 88-91 Wlylfoplt, 1 August 1543. Will of John Pytte

[8] NRO MC 1862/65, 863X1 1573–90 Thursday 1 April 16 Elizabeth (1573–74) Court roll of the Manor of Hempnall

[9] NRO MC 1862/65, 863X1 1573–90 Thursday 1 April 16 Elizabeth (1573–74) Court roll of the Manor of Hempnall

[10] NRO NCC 230 Clearke 22 May 1593 Will of John Bird

[11] NRO MC 1862/5, 863X1 1573–90 Thursday 1 April 16 Elizabeth (1573–34) Court roll of the Manor of Hempnall

[12] NRO MC 1862/65, 863X1 1573–90. Court rolls of the Manor of Hempnall 12 October 1576. Tofftes now Lime Tree Cottage

[13] Revd E.D. Stone MA (1944) trans. P. Williams SSA ed., 'Lay Subsidy of 1581 Assessors Certificates for the Norfolk Hundred of Depwade' *NRS* Vol. 18 (NRS) p.103

[14] NRO AYL 186 Muster

[15] NRO MC 1862/65, 863X1 1573–90 Court roll of the Manor of Hempnall 19 May 1575

[16] J.F. Williams MA FSA (ed.) (1946) 'Bishop Redman's Visitations 1597. ' *NRS* Vol. 18 p.104

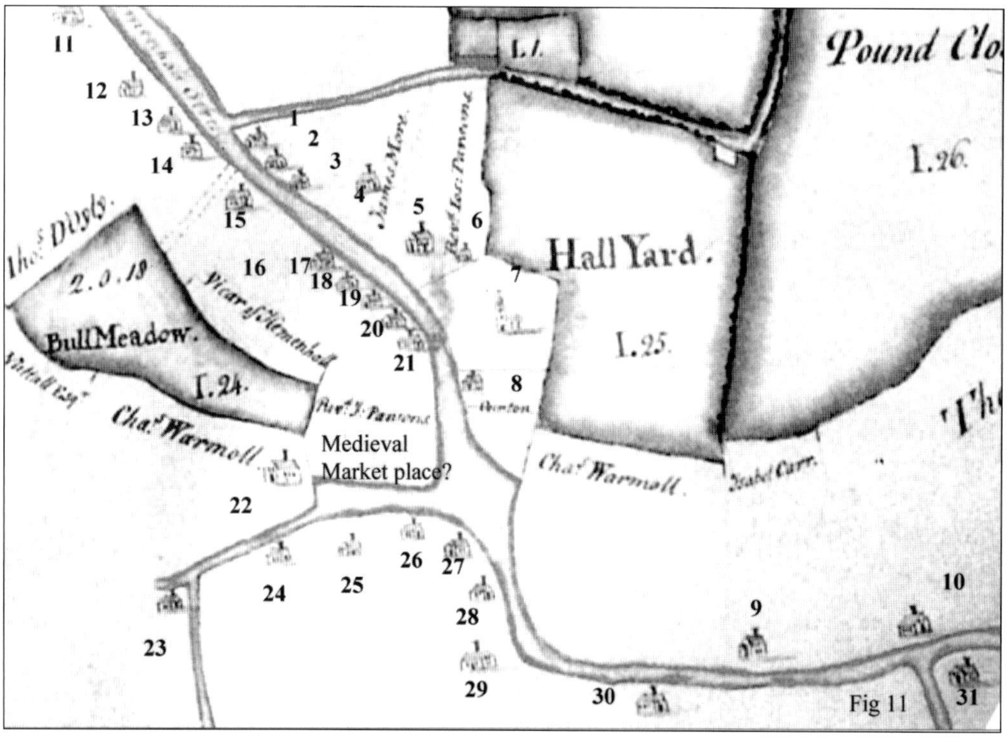

The village centre from the Grimston map 1767. Some houses were ruined or empty in the seventeenth century.

Earliest known printed date & description	**2008**
1. & 2..? 1559 Coopers, Sowters and Wrights alias the Guildhall	*Demolished after 1842*
3. 1632 Parcell of land with a tenement void with part of a well.	*Rebuilt after a fire in 1788.*
4. 1650 messuage & tenement wasted with 2 acres.	*Rebuilt. Manor Farm*
5. Old manor house.	*The Old Vicarage*
6. 1584 messuage formerly of Edward Knights adjoining the Cockshop with another cottage	*Demolished*
7. Saxon St. Margaret's church	
8. 1558 A bond tenement with a kiln or hut.	*The Longhouse*
9. a) 1502 Cottage in the Street.	*unidentified*
b) 1646 Messuage and one tenement belonging called the Stall. New built.in 1805	*Willow Cottage*
10. 1659 Messuage	*Tye's Cottage*
11. 1633. Messuage with a yard. Later The Swan	*Pevensey House*
12. 1573/4 Toftees/Toftys	*Lime Tree Cottage*
13. 1558 Messuage Sheppards. Rebuilt 1770 gable end.)	*Manor Cottages (WT 1770*
14. 1688 Messuage inhabited by William Moore	*Forge Cottage*
15. a) 1340 Messuage & 4 acres of the tenement Eylwards/Aylwards 1650 Edwards with bakehouse	*part of the present shop*
b) 1642 A parcel of a tenement with a little house or shop.	*Connaught House and shop*
16.1597 already ruined. The vicarage house	*Demolished 1744*
17. 18. 19. Two cottages belonging to the vicarage, built after 1731 1649 poor house	*Wilfred's Cottage Conway House*
20. 1393 Cottage once belonging to Robert Lark, vicar. Divided after 1653	*Priory Cottage*
21. 1606 Kychens/Kitchens/The Bull Inn.	*Demolished. Nelson on the site*
22.1564 Skynners alias Barbers/The Chequers or Falcon/Orchard House	*The Chequers*
23. 1787 Freehold . A shop	*Navestock Place*
24. 1633 The Horseshews.	*The Queen's Head*
25. 1576 Messuage Parkes	*Demolished*
26. 1642 Tenement Custons.	*The Poplars*
27. 1625 House with a smith's shop at the north end	*Demolished*
28. 1611 tenement Cutlers The Kings Head	*Thackery House,*
29. 1532 Mansion house called Coppings Street Farm	*Demolished*
30. Freehold	*Willow Farm*
31.1626. Tenement that Henry Fell inhabits	*Demolished*

CHAPTER 7

Turbulent Times 1600–99

The church caught fire again in about 1600, causing the chancel to fall. A note in the register in 1613 states: 'Here wants 15 years which some say was by the fier consumbed.'[1] It was the beginning of a dramatic period in the history of the village.

The Revd Thomas Porter, who became vicar in 1605 following the death of George Skinner, probably supported the trend towards Puritanism. Between 1603 and 1613 church plate was sold to the value of £25, an indication, perhaps, that these sacred objects were no longer as important.[2] Moreover, the chancel, the most sacred part of the church, was rebuilt to less than half its original length, despite the ruins surviving another 100 years.[3]

The shock of losing important documents may have prompted the gift of two new oak chests. The smaller, carved with the initials C.A., may have been given by George Allington, who inherited Sir Ralph's, or Curpel's, Manor in 1612. This chest was kept inside the larger one, which was about 10ft long. They were still in the church in 1845. Record keeping improved and church terriers, listing land and property, began in 1613.[4]

Thomas Porter died and was succeeded by the Revd William Barwick, in 1636.[5]

A Cambridge graduate and a Royalist opposed to Puritanism, Barwick was a supporter of Matthew Wren, Bishop of Norwich. Wren was concerned, as was William Laud, Archbishop of Canterbury, about the influence of the Puritans, and was particularly anxious to restore communion tables as sacred objects. Laud advocated that holy tables should be placed against the east wall of the chancel and separated from the rest of the church by a rail.[6] It was not until 1638, after the death of his wife Hannah and baby daughter, that Barwick began publishing his Royalist viewpoints and beliefs. He wrote subversive letters:

> *I will be for the Commission of Array, for that is set forth by the King, and if there be any disturbance in the country I have a gun at home, and powder and bullets, and will defend myself as well as I can.*

Parliament, in his view, was:

> *... but a company of factious Fellows and he knew of no good they did, except it were to destroy a kingdom... and were about to make apron elders, waistcoateers and petticoateers to be governors.*[7]

An entry in the baptismal register for 1641 notes:

> *All following to the yeare 1661 will be very defective many persons being not registered; by reason Register Books were not regarded, all things in this nation being in confusion.*[8]

When Edward Sporle was buried, the scribe wrote: 'Edward Sporle gent., the elder of this towne buried May 9, 1658. He kept away the Register book dureing his life.'[9] He owned the Longhouse near the church.

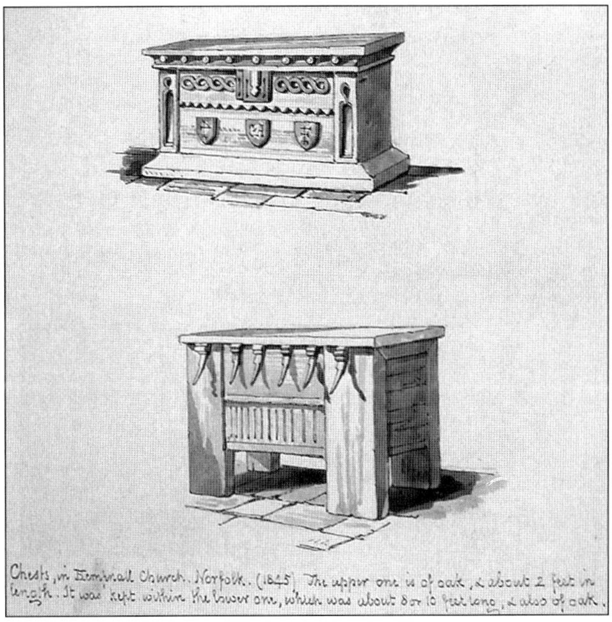

Church chests, from a drawing of 1845.

(REPRODUCED BY PERMISSION OF NORWICH CASTLE MUSEUM AND ART GALLERY)

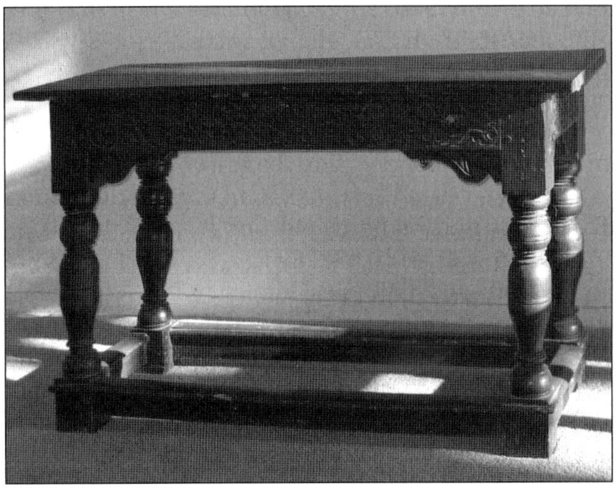

The Jacobean communion table.

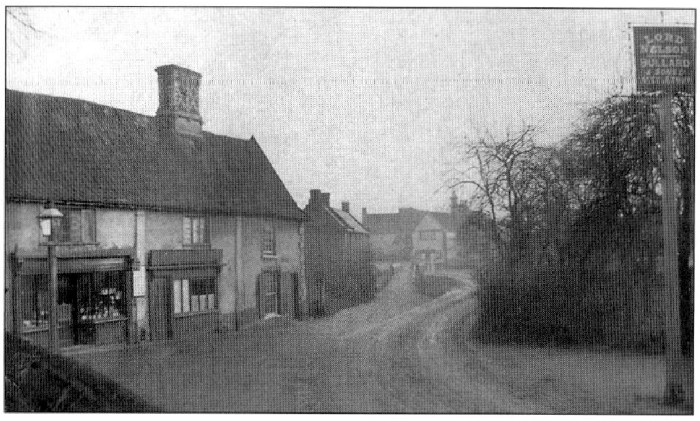

The Longhouse from the churchyard. Earliest known record 1558. (Copyhold description: A bond tenement with a kiln or hut one acre, the churchyard north, the stream south, the highway west.)

Barwick remarried and moved to Toftys Cottage (now Lime Tree Cottage) in the Street in 1643. That year Parliament and the Scottish Covenanters signed the Solemn League and Covenant, a military and religious alliance with the aim of defeating the Royalists on condition that Protestantism would be upheld and all signs of popery uprooted. In January 1644 all Englishmen over the age of 18 were required to sign this covenant. Barwick must have refused, and on 23 April 1644 was sequestered by the Earl of Manchester, accused of:

Opposing the Lectures of Godly Ministers in the Town, observing the Orders of the Church, declaring against the Parliament and rebellion, and swearing by his faith and troth.

From this time, we are told, 'several of the intruders kept possession [of the benefice] until 1649'.[10] Perhaps the Guildhall served as temporary barracks for soldiers, resulting in its partial ruin. Tradition has it that Cromwell's men damaged the figures on the font and stole the bells. However, it is possible that two bells were merely damaged, as in 1655 a new bell was cast from two old ones.[11] William Barwick was probably removed to Norwich Castle, but at some point he returned. He and his wife were obliged to sell their cottage to the broker Theophilis Braybourne in 1646, but they continued to live somewhere in the village.[12] Barwick was buried in Hempnall Church in 1649. He may have been reinstated as vicar, since John Potter, the next incumbent, was not appointed until after Barwick's death.

Perhaps the ruinous state of many houses near the church was a result of these turbulent times. Edward Sporle had 'suffered his copyhold house in the market place, sometimes used as a butcher's shop, to fall down for want of 'tymly repairs'.[13] On the opposite side of the road, next to the church, houses were empty or ruined. Here stood a 'voyd tenement with parcel of a well', two cottages 'voyd' called Sawters and Wrights and a tenement called Coopers otherwise the Guildhall, the site of the Cockshop and an empty messuage (Fig. 11). Other houses in the parish were also empty. Thomas Newman gained permission to demolish his malthouse, millhouse, brewhouse, house and barn in 1690.

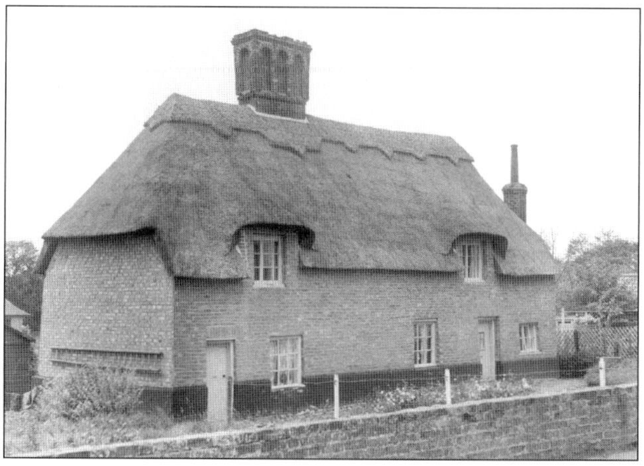

Lime Tree Cottage, formerly belonging to the Revd William Barwick, later converted into two dwellings and given a brick skin. (Eastern Daily Press)

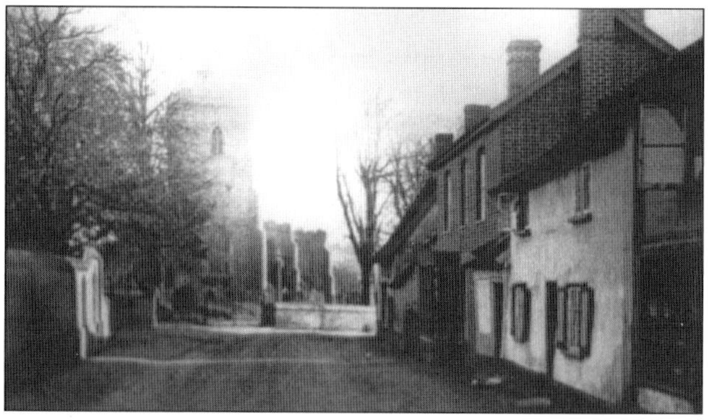

The properties on the right were once owned by the church. Several vicars lived in the house at the end opposite the church

On the flysheet of the first register book is written:

The 22nd Day of June 1649, I John Potter came into the parish of Hempnall and my first day of preaching in Hempnall Church was the Sunday following, it being midsummer day.[14]

He and his wife, Elizabeth, bought a house opposite the church once owned by Thomas Porter.

In 1603, the then vicar recorded that there were 400 communicants in Hempnall. Only a fifth of surnames occurring then matched names from the sixteenth-century parish. Of the 661 couples recorded in the baptismal and marriage registers between 1613 and 1699, 96 resided in the parish for more than ten years. These couples produced an average of four children who survived to maturity. During the year 1666 there were more deaths than usual, mostly in the summer months, when three families lost more than one member and 11 of the 24 burials were of children. It is likely a number of these deaths were as a result of the plague. A few cases of smallpox were recorded in the burial register between 1675 and 1691.

An indication of housing conditions can be found in the Hearth Tax, introduced in 1662.[15] Many of these records are in a poor condition. Of the Hempnall records, 79 hearths were assessed in 1664 but only 38 are legible.[16] In 1672 the hearths assessed numbered 222, of which 72 are readable.[17] Despite the lack of a complete list, it can be deduced that the majority of houses possessed one or two hearths, so no upper floor. Some were still lighting a fire on an open central hearth. Those receiving poor relief or living in houses worth less than 20s. a year were exempt. In 1672 there were 15 who were too poor to pay. However, nine householders possessed four hearths, three had five and three had six.

Clearly, Robert Gosling, the blacksmith, aged about 22 years, was not short of money, for in 1639 he was 'desireous to go to Holland to see the countrey and frinds and to retorne within 2 monthes'.[18]

The more affluent inhabitants regularly bequeathed money to the poor. William Sporle, who died in 1616, left £10 to be distributed over four years. The Feoffees of Hempnall were trustees of various charities. Robert Row bequeathed £10 to be paid out in bread and distributed to the poor on the first Sunday in Lent, while in 1691 Henry Bunn gave 3s.4d. to be paid annually to the poor. The Feoffees owned a cottage for the poor 'by the Red Bridge', given in 1634 by Edward Sporle. Two sisters gave a cottage by the Bull Inn in 1649.[19]

Parishes were responsible for supporting their own poor and if there was a chance of moving someone on to his or her place of birth, or getting another parish to contribute, the opportunity was not to be missed. Saxlingham applied to Quarter Sessions for relief when burdened with William Codman, a blind man with a wife and two children, one blind, one very young. By then, his mother was the wife of John Allen of Hempnall. Hempnall was ordered to contribute '12d. a week'.[20] Saxlingham petitioned Hempnall to accept Ann, wife of Robert Legate, who:

> *... came to her mother, widow Hellinge at Saxlingham and gave birth to a child likely to prove chargeable. Ordered Ann and her child to be put to the town of Hempnall.*[21]

Henry and William Carter were passed to Hempnall from Topcroft and were delivered to Fritton the next day and from thence to Yorkshire, 'where they said they were borne'. The constables of Hempnall noted that no 'roagues or beggars have suffered to passe through our parishe without punishment to our knowledge'.[22]

In 1635, 63 resident parishioners and another 30 who owned land in Hempnall but lived elsewhere, contributed towards the upkeep of the poor. John Backler and Ralph Jermyn paid the most, at 10s.6d. and 7s. respectively. Francis Johnson paid a penny, the least amount. Altogether, £15.10s. was collected and 31 people benefited during the year; for example, firewood was provided for Reade's wife and apparel for Thomas Bloomfeild.[23]

By the latter part of the century there is a hint of improvement to village life and money had been raised for church improvements. In 1683 the vicar recorded: 'the pulpit repaired, the women's seat backs mended, the men's seats coloured, a cover for the font and a new ally-way in the churchyard.'

Outsiders were investing in property and the more wealthy inhabitants were purchasing additional houses to let. Levels of comfort were improving as shown from inventories compiled after their decease. They owned more luxuries, such as musical instruments, warming pans, pictures, mirrors, books and portraits. Silver objects, curtains and carpets, however, were rare.

The vicar, John Potter, recorded details of the more dramatic occurrences in the village. In 1673 Margaret Wale was 'smothered in the setting cheese runeth or in the kettle where the cheese was set together in'. Samnell Garrard was 'slaine at the gravel pit' in 1674 and John Stanton was 'killed in a sand hole or pitt of earth caving upon him' in 1675.[24] In 1685 Potter noted the death of a local baker:

> *Israel Dunnet murdered by Abraham Bennet who stabbed him in the right legg about the gartering with a greate knife through a double boot and so his whole legg, of which stabb he immediately died and was buried 12 March.*[25]

Dunnet owned the Longhouse at that time. Abraham Bennet, who had married Elizabeth, sister of the murdered Israel, lived at Willow House. Bennet had previously been reported for belligerent behaviour, in October 1665, 'William Browne and Abraham Bennet began to argue in the house of Mr Bancroft,

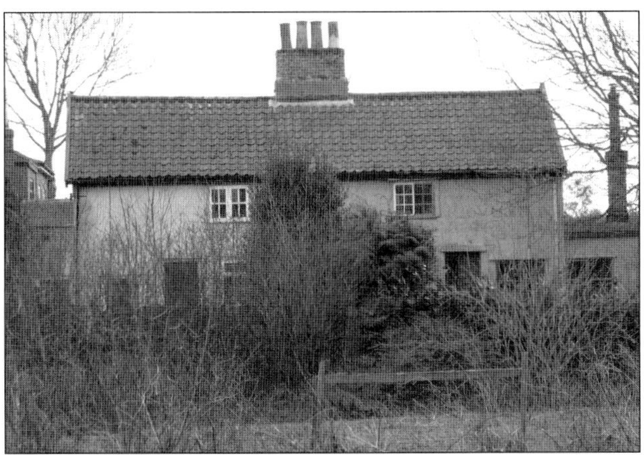

Once poor houses near the Red Bridge.

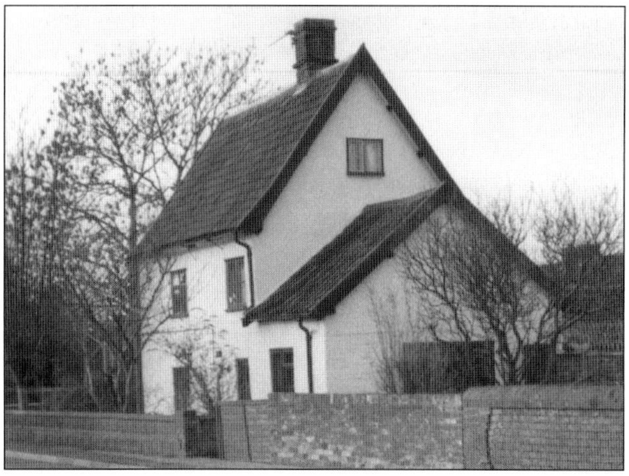

Willow House, Bungay Road, formerly occupied by Abraham Bennet, used as a shop from the 18th century. Earliest known record 1646. (Copyhold description: The Stall).

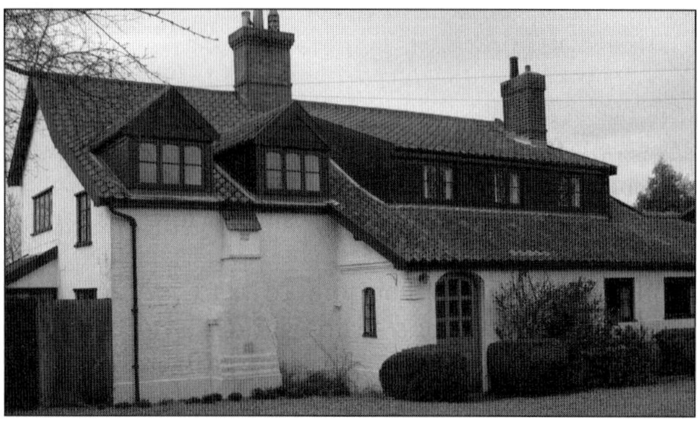

Hill House, Mill Road., Formerly belonging to Lewis Gedge the Quaker. Timber-framed. Earliest known date1669. (freehold, old description: Millgates).

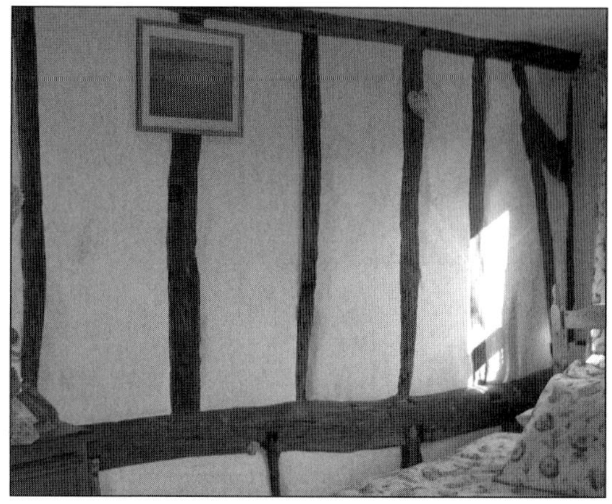

Willow House, internal timber-framing (freehold)

Heppenhale, Bennet calling Browne a "fexley bastard".'[26] At Quarter Sessions between 1688 and 1689 four Hempnall men were brought for trial. John Roberts and Simon Burlingham each appeared once, and Abraham Bennet twice, the second time with Roger Bennet, his son. Whether the Bennet appearances had anything to do with the death of Israel Dunnet is unclear.[27]

In 1676 the Compton Report was compiled from questionnaires given to each parish priest. John Potter returned that he had 380 parishioners who attended his church and four Quakers.[28]

Lewis Gedge, a Quaker, bought the house called Millgates with a brickyard and tannery (Hill House in Mill Road) from John Laurence, a prominent Quaker. Every two weeks about 40 Friends met for worship in Gedge's house. Among them were John Halls, John Goodman and John Brown, who were village residents. Gedge was eventually arrested for his faith and spent some years in Norwich Castle until his release in 1672.[29] Lewis Gedge was one of those listed in the 1672 Hearth Tax returns as owning just one hearth. An inventory made in 1699, shortly after his death, listed few worldly goods – his working clothes, a bed, chests, a coffer, linen and some old silver money. He possessed many books.[30]

Education and apprenticeship were becoming important during the seventeenth century. Thomas Moore, by will, instructed that his son be bound as an apprentice for seven years in 1634. Jeremy Brame, who died the same year, that money be used for the education of his children at a 'scole of good learneing'.[31] In 1674 John Turner gave £5 'towards the learning of Elizabeth my daughter' and £5 towards the 'binding out of my son as apprentise'. Roger Dunnet, a joiner, bequeathed 20s. to his apprentice Robert Pope in 1679. The first known schoolmaster, Thomas Stanton, bought a cottage adjoining the vicar's house in 1646, so beginning a long tradition of private tuition in the village that continued into the twentieth century.[32]

Records of Hempnall and Hempnall Cannons manors are complete between 1651 and 1922 (copyhold tenure was abolished in 1926). Thus it is possible, there having been more copyholds than freeholds, to trace the history of almost all the sites of ancient houses in the village and their owners. The sites of 67 different houses are recorded during the seventeenth century, of which eight were recorded in the previous century. Of the 67, 41 still exist on the same site, although a number received a brick skin in the eighteenth century, hiding their true age. The residences of those living outside the village are usually recorded, 39 occupiers of dwellings are named during this same century.

In 1662 a dispute arose concerning a footpath 'leading from the tenement of the lord of the manor, wherein Mary Pitt now dwelleth, to the church of Hempnall and Market Street there and back from them to the said tenement.' Several old inhabitants were called to give evidence about this route. William Dunnet aged over 60 years claimed that he knew the tenement and that 'the footpath leadeth from the said tenement over a meadow plot late Buskards now Robert Chettlebugh gent and from there over the land of Mr Chettlebugh's to Mr

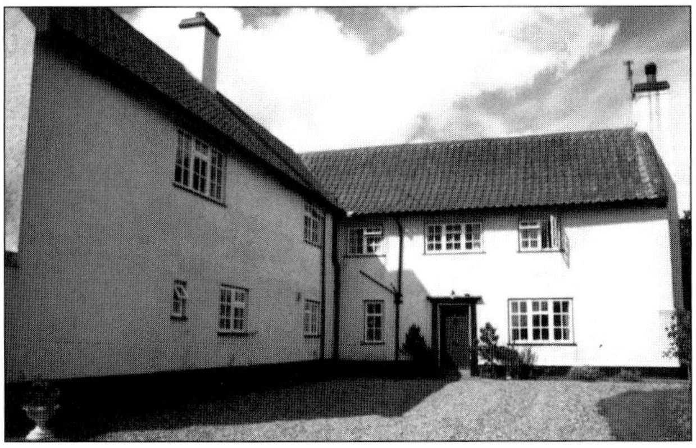

Willow Farm, Bungay Road (freehold).

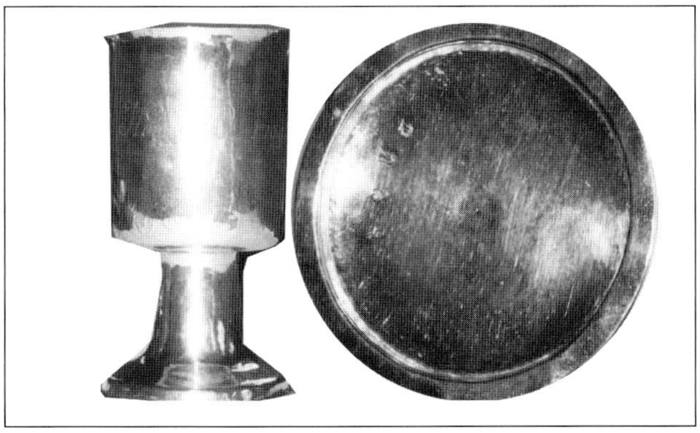

Church plate.

Randal's dyke row and so to Mr Randol's style near the highway called Roadway and so forward to Hempnall church and street aforesaid.' Ralph Jermyn, gent, Robert Sporle, William Brown and John Sendall supported the claim. All of them had used it for at least 30 years.

Robert Beane, who had been a witness in the Abraham Bennet case, lived to be over 80, a good age for the time, owned Willow Farm. He died in 1698 and his gravestone, the earliest recorded by Richard Hylton in 1860, sadly no longer exists.

The vicar, John Potter, who had served the village for 43 years, died in 1692. He was proud of his work in Hempnall and noted in the register: 'Midsomer day 1689 I John Potter have preached in Hempnall 40 years.' He was buried on 4 August 1692. John Smith, who succeeded him, died five years later. William Aggas was instituted in 1697. During his time a new chalice and paten were given, both inscribed: 'To the Towne of Hemnall in Norfolk 1704.'[33]

References

[1] NRO PD 435/1 1613 Hempnall church register

[2] T.F. Barton MA FSA transcribed, 'The Registrum of Anthony Harrison Pt 2 *NRS* Vol. 33 p.133

[3] NRO MSS. Rye No. 17 Vol. 2 Church Notes by Thomas Martin.

[4] Norfolk Museums and Archaeology Service NWHCM: 1958. 146. Vol. 2 p.291: F Drawings by A. Rolfe (attrib) 1845

[5] John Venn & J.A. Venn (1922) *Alumni Cantabrigienses: A Biographical list of all known Students, Graduates and holders of office at the University of Cambridge from the earliest times to 1900* (Cambridge) Pt 1 Vol. 1 p.102 William Barwick BA 1630–31 MA 1634. Priest Norwich 1632. 1636–44 sequestered.

[6] Archbishop Laud 1573–1645. Archbishop of Canterbury 1633. Imprisoned in the Tower of London 1641. Beheaded 1645

[7] W.R. Ketton-Cremer (1969) *Norfolk in the Civil War: A Portrait of a Society in Conflict* (London) p.242

[8] NRO PD 436/1 Hempnall Register. Baptisms 1567–98, 1613–1703

[9] NRO PD 436/1 (The only burial recorded between 1642 and 1662.)

[10] Blomefield, *Norfolk* Vol. 3 p.119

[11] Walter Rye *Index to Norfolk Topography*. MSS. No. 17 Vol. 2. Church Notes by Thomas Martin 1724–35

[12] Manor of Hempnall Book A. Court held 27 Oct 1652. Barningham Hall chest 'Hempnall'

[13] Court Book A of the Manor of Hempnall 1653. Barningham Hall

[14] NRO PD 436/1 First Hempnall Register 1561–1703

[15] M.S. Frankell and P.J. Seamam (translators) (1983) 'Norfolk Hearth Tax Assessment Michaelmas 1664' *Norfolk Genealogy* Vol. 15 pp.9, 10

[16] M.S. Frankel & P.J. Seaman, ibid., p.1. Residents paid 2s. per hearth. Tax was collected twice a year

[17] PRO: E179/154/697 rot. 9 1672–73 Hearth Tax

[18] Charles B. Jewson, 'Registers of Passengers from Great Yarmouth to Holland and New England 1637–39' *NRS* Vol. 25 p.82, July 19 1639.

[19] Original List of Feoffee property recorded by Richard Hylton, a nineteenth-century inhabitant

[20] D.E. Howell James (1955) 'Norfolk Sessions Order Book 1650–57' *NRS* Vol. 26 p.38 (244)

[21] D.E. Howell James ibid. p.57 (472)

[22] NRO NAS 1/1/2/154 Dec 4 1634 Constables Returns

[23] NRO NAS 1/1/2/152. Records of the overseers of the poor

[24] NRO PD 436/1 Burial Register 1560–98, 1613–42, 1662–1703

[25] NRO PD 436/1 Burial Register

[26] D. Peacock *Morals, Rituals and Gender Aspects of Social Relations in the Diocese of Norwich 1660–1703.* (PhD thesis, York University, Dec 1996) 106 NCD DN/DEP 47/51 1665 October

[27] NRO C/S1/10 1684–93 Quarter Sessions Roll 1

[28] NRO Compton Return for the Norwich Diocese 1676 No. 21489

[29] C.B. Jewson FSA (1965) 'Return of the Conventicles in Norwich Diocese 1669– Lambeth MS No. 639. Lists of conventicles or illegal religious societies in Norwich Depwade Deanery.' *NA* Vol. 33 (Norwich) No. 41

[30] NRO INV 66. Inventory of Lewis Gedge

[31] NRO NCC 1634 113. Playford Will of Jeremy Brame

[32] E.H. Carter OBE MA (1937) *The Norwich Subscription Books. A Study of the Subscription Books of the Diocese of Norwich 1637–1800* (London) p.167

[33] E.C. Hopper 'Church Plate' *NA* Vol. 15 p.257

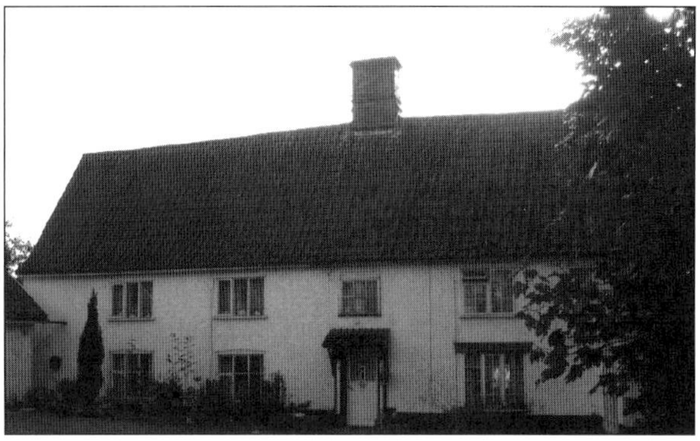

Pevensey House in the Street, formerly the Swan Inn. Earliest known record 1633. (Copyhold early description: tenement with five acres of bond land. First called The Swan in 1733).

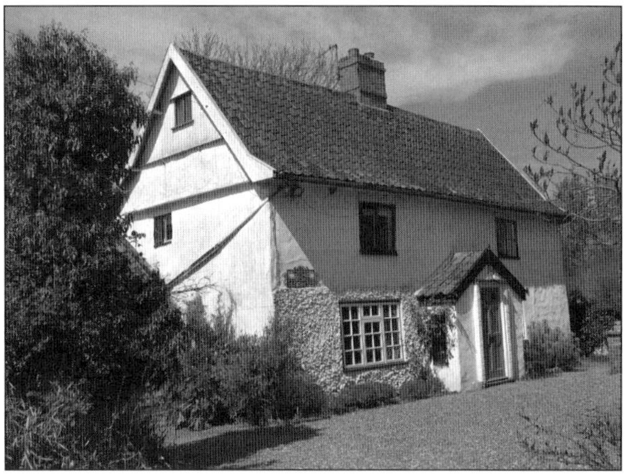

The Two Friends, now The Feathers, between Lundy Green and Silver Green. Timber-framed (freehold).

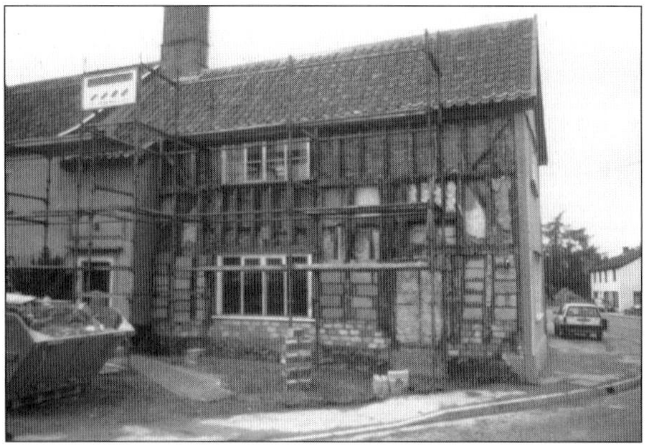

Above: *Thatchery House, with the timber frame revealed during repairs in the '80s.*

Right: *Thatchery House, formerly the King's Head, in the village centre. Earliest known date 1611. (Copyhold description: Cattlers or Cutlers).*

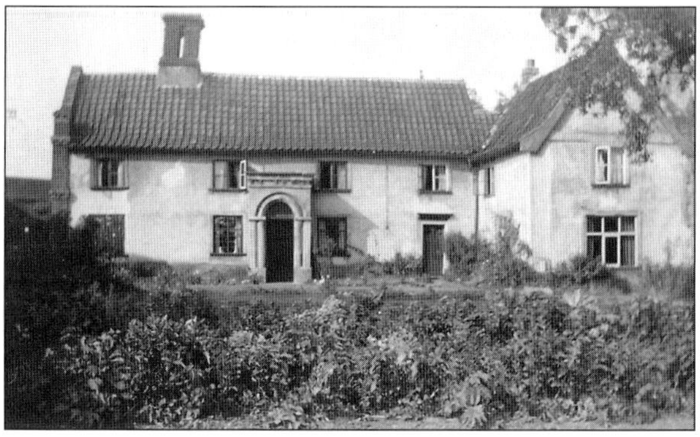

The Chequers or Falcon, in the village centre. Earliest known date 1564. (Copyhold description: Barbers, alias Skinners).

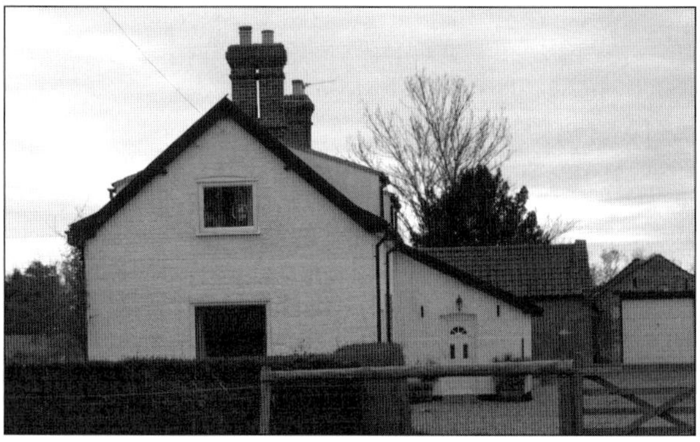

Formerly called the Chequer, next to the Fairstead on Fairstead Lane. Earliest known record 1677. (Copyhold description: Messuage at St. Andrew's Hill, commonly called the Chequer).

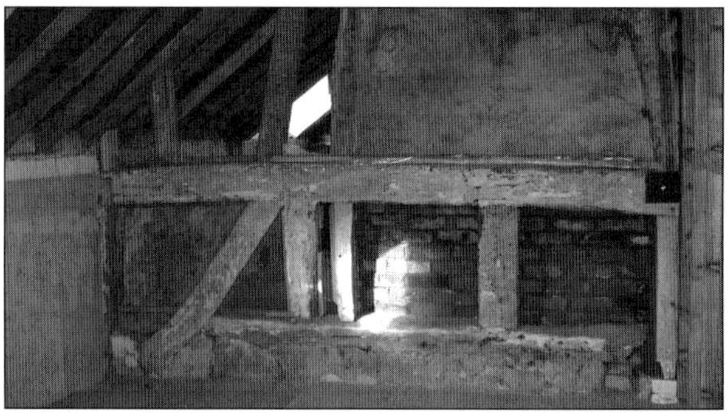

Timber frame inside the Chequer.

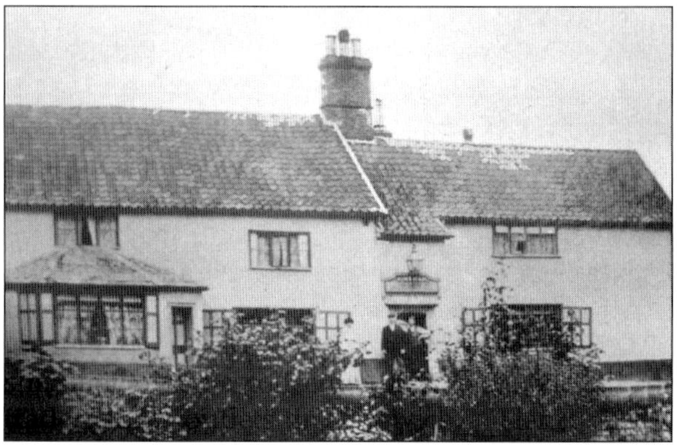

✦ CHAPTER 8 ✦

Famous and Infamous 1700–59

This was a time when gin and ale were cheap and taverns and alehouses were springing up about the parish, fulfilling customer demand for pleasure and entertainment. The inhabitants 'made themselves merry' in 1714 and then smashed an old bell with large hammers. It was recast to celebrate the coronation of George I.[1]

The Swan, a substantial building with a yard, was situated in the Street near a brewery and maltings.[2] The Two Friends was located between Lundy Green and Great Green, the Cock and Lion and the Hole in the Wall were also somewhere on the Greens and the Chequer adjoined the Fairstead, next to the redundant Church of St Andrew. Four other taverns or alehouses competed for customers near the market place: the Chequers, renamed the Falcon at this time, the Bull, the King's Head and the Horseshoes (now the Queen's Head). The King's Head was the venue for the Petty Sessions for hiring and retaining servants and the manor court was held at the Bull.

Roger Smith was the owner and landlord of the Falcon and overseer of the poor in the year 1727, when William Huby and his wife Mary absconded, leaving their three small children to be cared for by the parish. Huby was aged about 'twenty-five, about five foot high, and wore a blue thred-bare coat', and his wife was described as 'a low thin Wench, about the same age'.[3] Whether or not they were discovered is not known.

In 1733 the village celebrated the visit of the aspiring politician William Wodehouse. He was met:

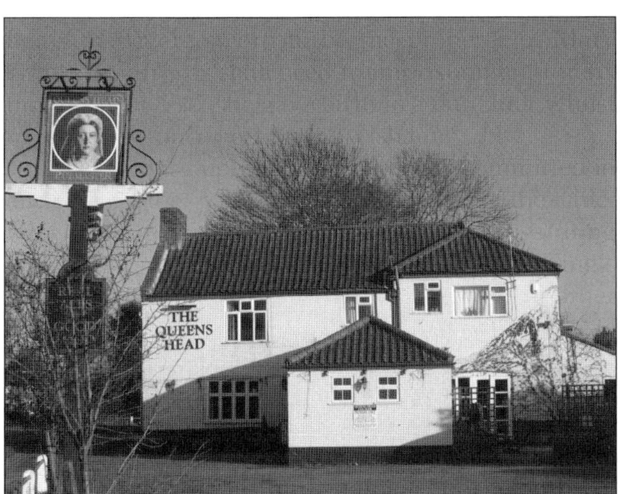

The Queen's Head, Mill Road, formerly the Horseshoes. Earliest known date 1633. (Copyhold description: Part of Parkes).

... by a very handsome Train of Coaches, and a great Number of Gentleman, Clergy, and Freeholders on Horseback, and welcomed in with Music, firing of Guns, and the loudest Acclamations of the people; and that the Appearance there was so very grand, that the like had never been seen in that Place before. There was a general Face of Joy appeared among them, and the constant cry was BACON and WODEHOUSE! There was a handsome Entertainment provided for the Company, and Mr Gunton the Chief Constable ordered Two Barrels of Strong Beer to the Populace in the Street.[4]

Elections at this time often involved bribery and bullying, as the ballot was not secret. Of Hempnall's residents, 12, the male freeholders, were entitled to vote. Roger Smith cast his vote in May 1734 for Tory candidates Sir Edmund Bacon and William Wodehouse, as did six others.

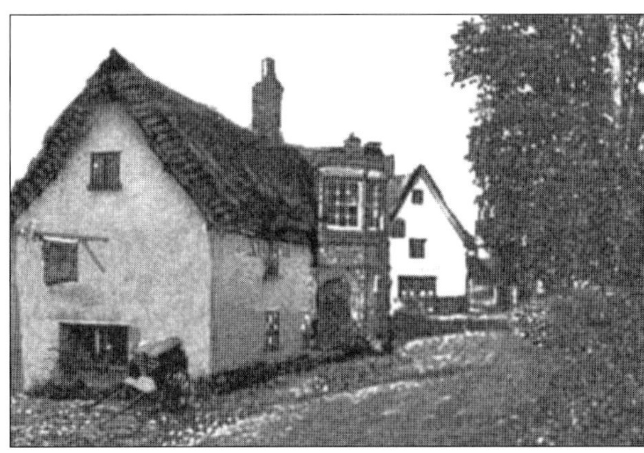

Impression of how the Bull might have looked. Earliest known date 1606 (copyhold name Kitchens).

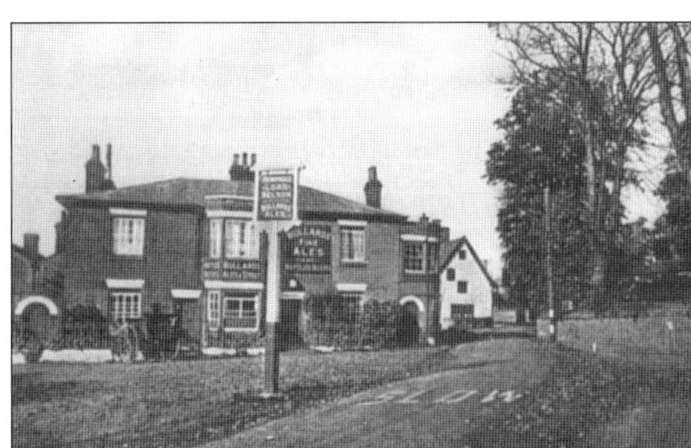

A view from the same position as the top picture showing the later Lord Nelson.

One evening in July 1736 Roger Smith was heading home from Norwich when he fell from his horse by the river at Lakenham, hit his head upon a sharp stone and bled to death immediately.[5] The inquest was held at the Red Lion at Lakenham. Witnesses reported that he was aged about 63 years old and:

... being so very much overcome by liquor riding last night between the hours of eleven and twelve... had the misfortune to fall from his horse. By the force of the fall fractured his skull in such a manner that he immediately expired.

The coroner's verdict was 'misfortune'.[6] After his death an inventory was complied of all his goods, making it possible to take a tour of the Falcon (previously and subsequently the Chequers). The 'little parlor chamber' was furnished with seven chairs, a table, three jointed stools, a desk and a clock, along with a few of his clothes with £3.16s.6d. in a pocket. The room could be heated in winter, for there were dog irons, a spit and a pair of tongs. Earthen pots and pans and a stone pitcher were stored in a closet adjoining. On the other side of the chimney was 'the hall'. Since medieval times halls had been the principal rooms, where cooking, eating and socialising took place. Here the furniture consisted of two small tables, nine chairs, two stools and a cupboard. There were beer measures, pewter dishes and plates, a basin, a porringer and beer glasses. Cooking was obviously done here on the open fire, the cook making use of two gridirons, a frying pan, two flesh forks, a brass kettle, a chopping knife and a cleaver.

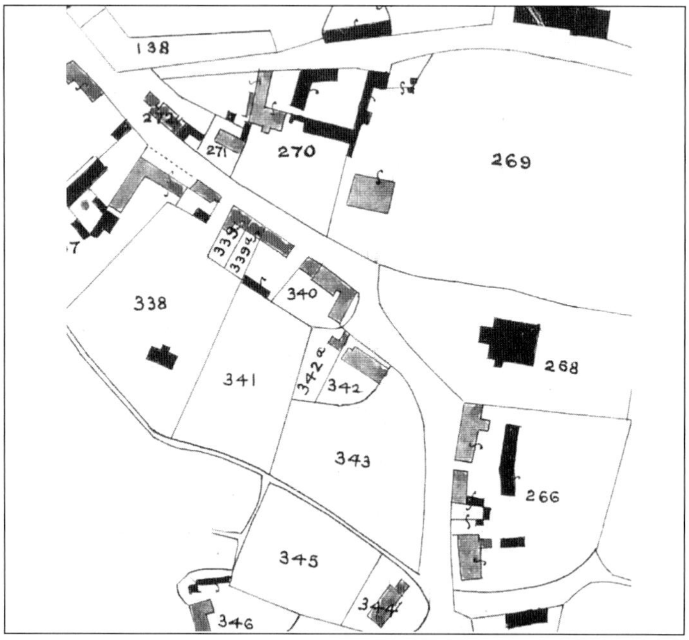

Part of the Tithe Map of 1842 showing The Bull (No. 342), Priory Cottage (No. 340), the Old Manor House (No. 269).

Number	*description*	*owner*	*occupier*
266	*houses & gardens*	*Roger Roberts*	*Robert Wyard & others*
268	*St. Margaret's Church*		
269	*houses premises & garden*	*John Thruston Mott*	*Revd. Robert Rolfe*
270	*farm house and premises*	*John Thruston Mott*	*Robert Riches*
271	*house & garden*	*John Thruston Mott*	*empty*
272	*house & premises occupied*	*John Thruston Mott*	*William Neave and others*
337	*house, premises & garden*	*Elizabeth Thirkettle*	*herself*
338	*vicarage yard, barn & pasture*	*glebe*	*Revd. Robert Rolfe*
339	*cottage & premises*	*George Warnes*	*William Leveritt*
339a	*cottage & premises*	*David Sheldrake*	*himself*
340	*house & premises*	*William Goose*	*Elizabeth Barham*
342a	*cottages & garden*	*Hempnall Feoffees*	*William Fryer and others*
342	*cottages & garden (formerly the Bull)*	*William Goose*	*Charles Townsend*
343	*Bull Meadow*	*William Goose*	*William Richards*
344	*cottages & garden*	*William Goose*	*John Flint*
345	*meadow*	*William Goose*	*William Richards*
346	*house & garden (the Chequers)*	*Benjamin Bullen*	*himself*

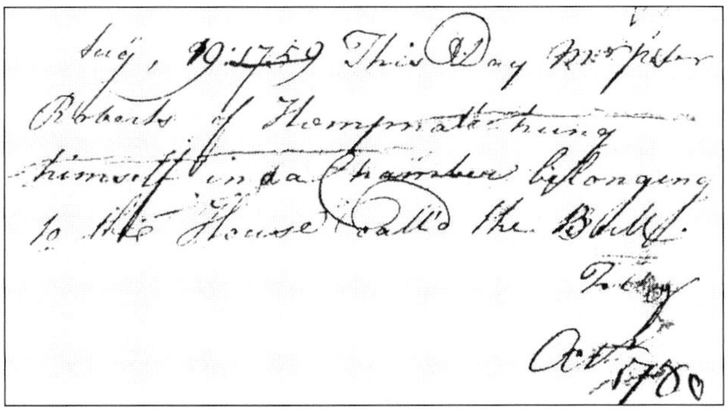
Aug, 19 1759 This Day Mr Peter
Roberts of Hempnall hung
himself in a Chamber belonging
to the House call'd the Bull.
Oct 1760

'Aug. 19 1759. This day Mr Peter Roberts of Hempnall hung himself in a chamber belonging to the House called the Bull. Oct 1760.'

Other useful culinary articles included a salt cellar, a pepperbox and an hourglass. A looking-glass hung on the wall and there were four candlesticks. Customers could congregate in 'the great chamber', which was probably in the wing of the house. This was furnished with 14 chairs, a small table and a cupboard. Four pictures adorned the wall. A pair of garden shears, a stone bottle and glass bottles comprised the small items in the room, and a pair of scales and pewter measures were stored in the closet. There were three upper rooms, each containing a bed and other furniture.

The Bull Inn stood opposite the church, overlooking the river. On 19 August 1738 two carpenters strode into a back room, where they accosted William Freer. The landlord, Roger Roberts, bolted the door behind them. Freer was attacked and murdered, his assailants apparently 'beating and misusing him in such a terrible manner, that even his Private Parts were bruised and torn to a most shocking Degree.' Thomas Freer of Morningthorpe, the father of the victim, placed an advertisement shortly afterwards in the *Gazette* offering a reward of two guineas. When there was no response, he doubled the reward in April the following year:

> *Whereas William Freer was barbarously murdered at the sign of the Bull at Hempnall... by one John Cotton of Beddingham... and one John Funnel jun. of Mulbarton, who immediately fled from justice... and whereas there is reason to believe they are still hiding in some place adjacent, concealed by some who would wickedly screen them from justice; this is to give notice that whoever apprehends the said John Cotton and John Funnell... shall receive four guineas reward upon conviction of either one of them. N.B. They are both carpenters... Cotton is a tall man and goes a little shaling, and Funnell is a low quaddy man; they are both very young, and wear wigs or caps.*[7]

A week after the murder it was reported that Roger Roberts, the landlord of the Bull, had been arrested and committed to the castle at Norwich on suspicion of being involved in the murder.[8] The full story will never be known, and it seems the carpenters were never caught. About 20 years later the death of Peter Roberts was noted in a book once belonging to the schoolmaster, Charles Warmoll, and copied by Richard Hylton.

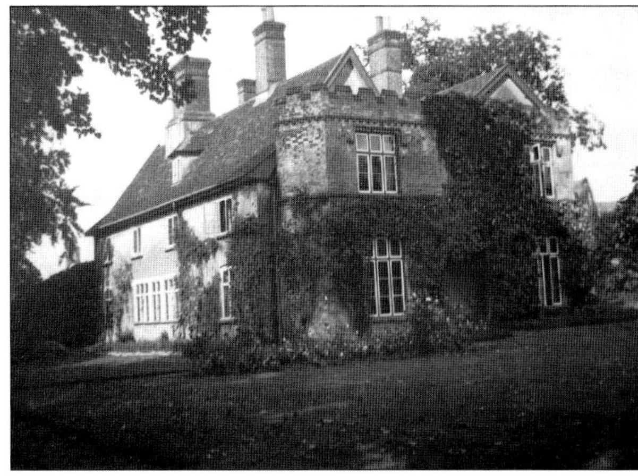

The Old Manor House, once owned by the Revd Joseph Parsons (freehold).

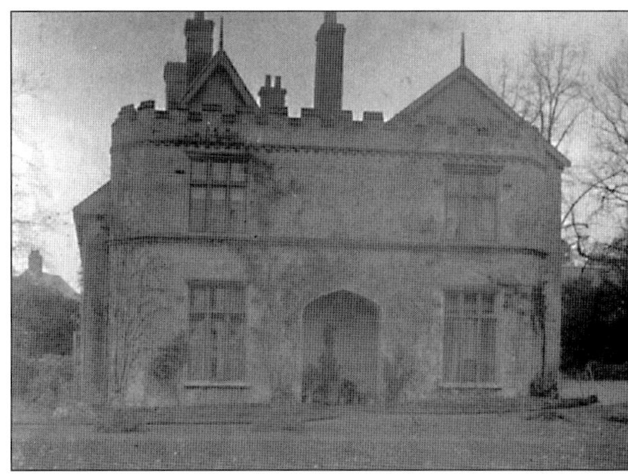

The Old Manor House, later the vicarage, from the east.

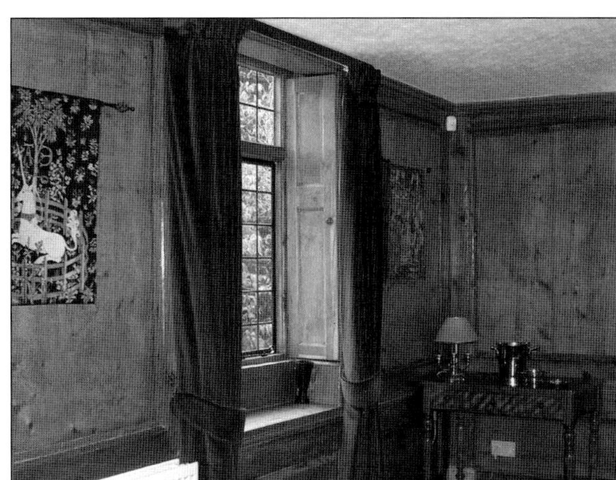

Panelled room within the Old Manor House, later The Vicarage

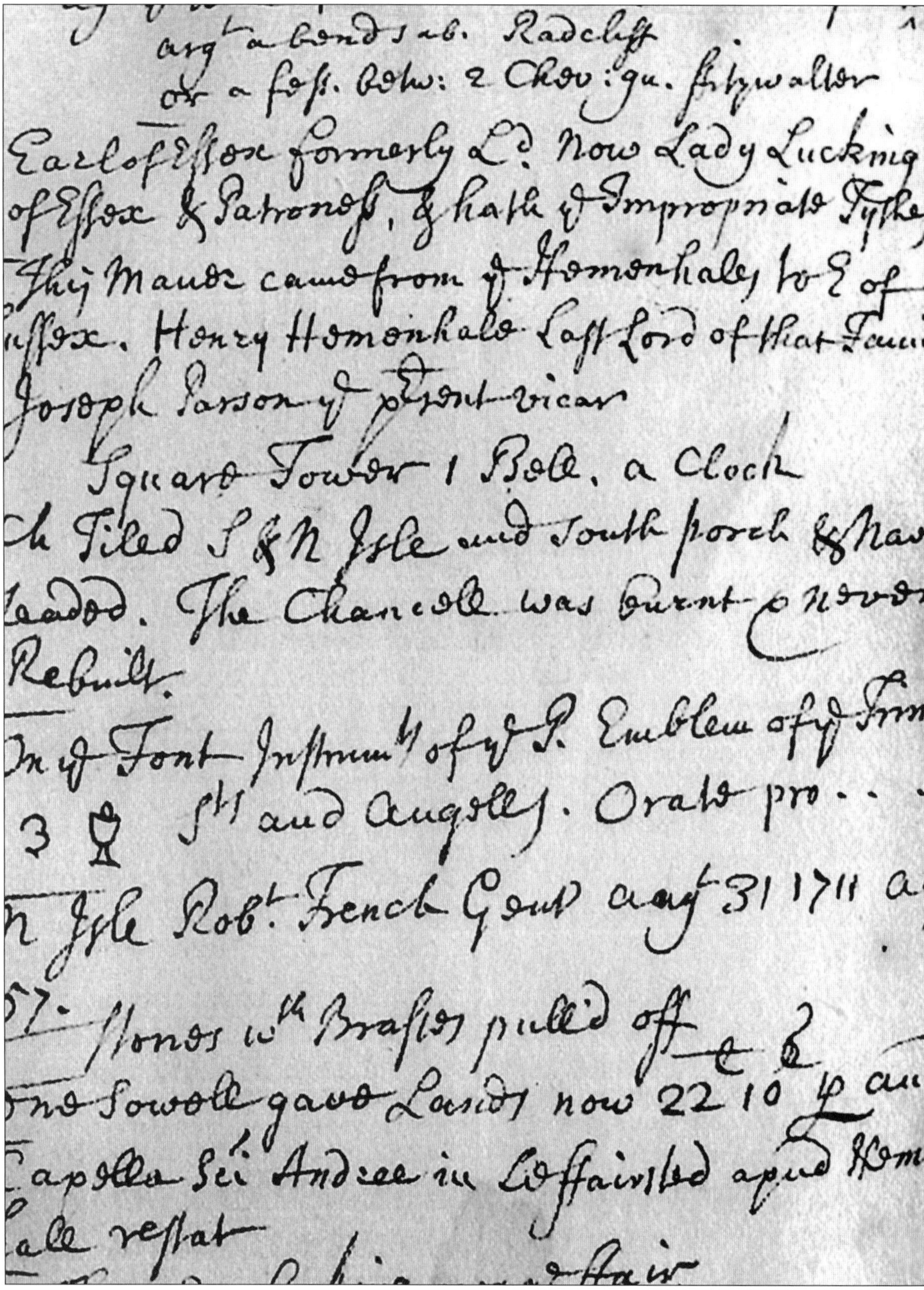
argt a bend sab. Radcliff
or a fess. betw: 2 Chev: gu. Fitzwalter
Earl of Essex formerly Ld. Now Lady Lucking
of Essex & Patroness, & hath ye Impropriate Tythes
This Manor came from ye Hemenhales to E. of
ussex. Henry Hemenhale last Lord of that Fami
Joseph Parson ye present Vicar
Square Tower 1 Bell. a Clock
ch Tiled S & N Isle and South porch & Nav
leaded. The Chancell was burnt & new
Rebuilt.
On ye Font Instrumts of ye P. Emblem of ye Trin
3 Sts and Angells. Orate pro . . .
N Isle Robt. French Gent augt 31 1711 ag
57 stones wth Brasses pulled off
ne Sewell gave Lands now 22 10 £ an
Capella Sci Andree in Wassfairsted apud Hem
hale restat

Notes made by Thomas Martin some time between 1724 and 1735. (Norfolk Record Office Rye 17/1)

Many crimes committed in the village appeared in the local newspapers. Several horses went missing and poachers destroyed game in the woods belonging to the lady of the manor.[9] The farmhouse of Mr Simon Goose was burgled and 'there was feloniously taken away a large copper that would boil off three Furkins...'.[10] Henry Roads was committed to Norwich Castle for 'harbouring and entertaining in his house Samuel Hager, otherwise Eager, an outlawed Smuggler under Sentence of Death in Newgate.'[11]

The Revd Joseph Parsons, the vicar, was to speak his mind on the subject on several occasions. In a sermon preached several years later, he said:

> *A further cause of iniquity... is men's fondness for amusements and diversions, and delighting to spend their time in alehouses and places of public entertainment; where they often meet with the worst of company...*[12]

Parsons had been appointed to the living in 1724.[13] The patron, Lady Mary Luckyn, was his mother-in-law, his wife being Elizabeth Luckyn, a daughter of Sir William Luckyn, who until his death was lord of the manors of Hempnall and Hempnall Cannons. Parsons was also rector of Bedingham and chose to reside there initially, perhaps because in Hempnall there was no accommodation suitable for the daughter of the lord of the manor. The vicarage house had been unfit for habitation since 1597 and was demolished in 1744, described as:

> *... so mean and incommodious as to be altogether unfit for the residence of any incumbent and hath been time out of mind by the account of the ancient inhabitants, there being but one ordinary room therein with two small lean-tos and the whole timber and materials thereof agreed not the value of £5.*[14]

Parsons's move to Hempnall was prompted by an argument with the Stone family of Bedingham some time after 1746:

> *Attack on the Lord's day after service in the churchyard from Mr Stone occasioned by his wanting to drive the coach in and I was warned to quit their house where I had resided and paid rent enough, for near 20 years.*[15]

In 1747 he bought a house opposite the church together with a coach house on the site of a shop that had been pulled down in 1710 and a garden plot in the market place.[16] This house must have been either Priory Cottage or an adjoining building. In 1750 he purchased a house next to the church and in 1759 bought the Bull Inn. The tithe barn, on the site of the old vicarage house, was in need of repair, the contents being part of Parson's income. He wrote in 1758: 'The vicarage barn repaired the porch made

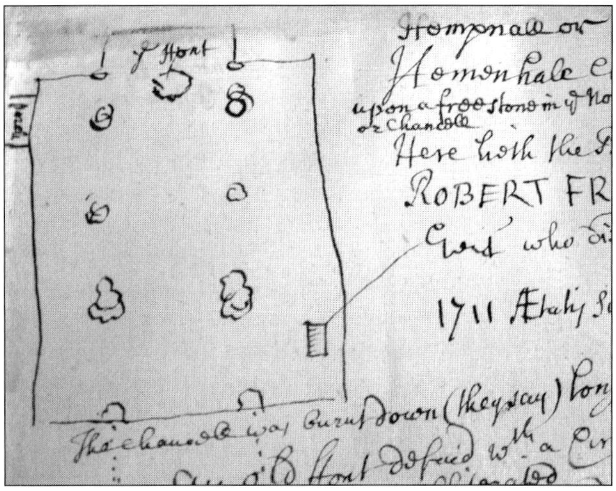

The interior of St Margaret's Church sketched by Thomas Martin between 1724 and 1735.

(NORFOLK RECORD OFFICE RYE 17/1)

with the great doors and part of the floor laid by the vicar.'

Some time between 1724 and 1735, Joseph Parsons was visited by the historian Thomas Martin.[17] Martin drew a rough plan of the church using a dotted line to mark the remains of the ruined chancel. Inside the church there were gravestones with the brasses pulled off. He mentioned the fair, St Andrew's chapel and that the arms of the Radcliff and Fitzwalter families were on a wall of an inn.

Jeremiah Fassett, the schoolmaster, undoubtedly supported Parsons in his fight against crime. His schoolroom was somewhere near Parsons' residence. On 7 June 1754, after 30 years of teaching, he advertised in the *Norwich Mercury* for an assistant to teach writing:

> *Any sober Person who writes well and comes properly recommended, may be treated with respect by Jeremiah Fassett, master of the said school: where youth are boarded, and taught reading, writing and arithmetick, both vulgar and decimal, at twelve pounds a year.*

Mr Charles Warmoll was appointed to the post and in 1754 he bought the Falcon, which then ceased trading as an inn.

Joseph Hallmark, a boarder from Yarmouth, was only ten when he died in 1755. Thereafter, for many years, his family chose to be buried at Hempnall. Their memorials were enclosed by a palisade on the north side of the church. Richard Hylton, who copied the inscriptions in 1860, noted: 'They had a son who came to a good school here where he died and was interred here. The family chose this spot for their resting place.'

Jeremiah Fassett had decided to retire at Christmas 1758, but intended to keep in touch by reserving 'to himself the liberty of taking four or five young boarders to read only'. Charles Warmoll,

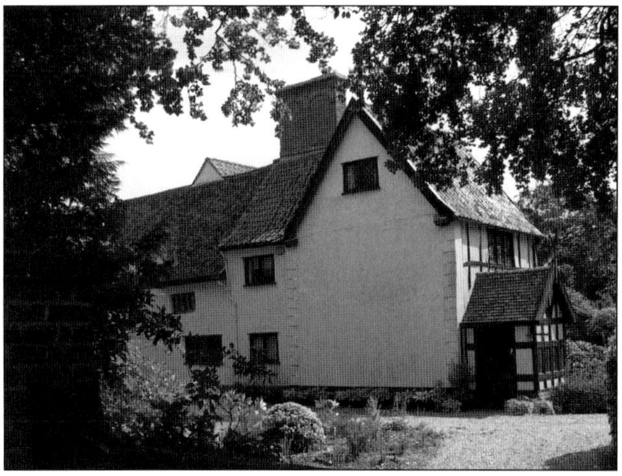

Krons Manor, the Street, formerly Fairstead House. Earliest known date 1454 (copyhold name Quintyns/ Quintens).

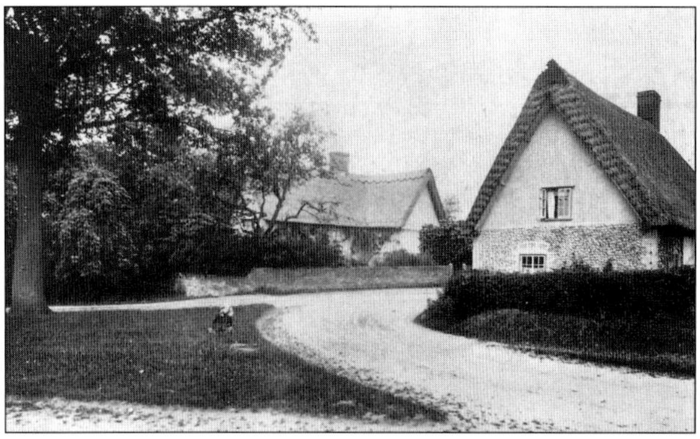

The site of Cole's Green. John Wesley preached here.

having taught as an assistant for several years, advertised that:

> *I now have a house very convenient for boarders and day-scholars... teaching them reading, writing and arithmetic, from the method so many years practised in Mr Fassett's school...*[18]

An inscription on a wall in the wing of the old Falcon begins: 'Say unto Wisdom, Thou art my Sister...' This may have been the new school house.[19] The following year Warmoll bought the Longhouse next to the church and this could have been a residence for the boarders.

Two of Mr Fassett's pupils were to make a mark in the wider world. Edward Thurlow was the eldest son of the Revd Thomas Thurlow, vicar of Tharston. The family were Hempnall residents and the Revd Thomas was one of those who made the survey of the vicarage house in 1744. Edward attended Fassett's school as a young lad. When Sarah, the widow of Jeremiah Fassett, died, the vicar wrote:

> *She was a faithful parental yoke-fellow training up members of both sexes the younger part of life very commendably and usefully who became worthy members of the common wealth to fill important stations – no less than Attorney General viz Edward Thurlowe.*[20]

Thurlow maintained a connection with the area as a young man, having a 'boy–girl affair' with a Miss Gooch from the local village of Shottesham. She would not have him and married the village doctor instead.[21] Edward became a lawyer and eventually, in 1778, Lord Chancellor of England. Clever and witty, he once inspired Charles Fox to remark 'No man could be so wise as Thurlow looked.'[22]

William D'Oyly was a contemporary of Edward Thurlow and at one time the Thurlows resided at William D'Oyly's father's house (now called Knons Manor). At 14 D'Oyly was apprenticed to a shopkeeper in Long Stratton. He moved to King's Lynn, then Tasburgh, but his desire was to enter the church. Encouraged and supported by the Revd Dr Copper of Great Yarmouth, he obtained a degree at Cambridge in 1778 and then returned to his father's house at Hempnall. He served as a curate at Gissing and Burston for about ten years, then at Stratton St Michael, Flordon and Hapton. His name appears in the Hempnall registers between 1784 and 1790, so he may have been the curate. He had two attempts at obtaining a living. The second time he approached Edward Thurlow, believing that as the chancellor's father had lived and died in his father's house, he would be shown some favour. 'This plea though lodged with the greatest modesty was treated with neglect and silence.'[23] Disappointed in his hopes of advancement in the church, William D'Oyly directed his energies towards improving a road for the public benefit, there being a dangerous hill at Tasburgh, a village adjoining Hempnall. He raised money in sixpences, shillings and half crowns by travelling to surrounding villages on an old grey pony. He caused further improvement to a dangerous corner of the turnpike at Newton Flotman. His next scheme was to improve Brigg Street in Norwich, so narrow that traffic from London found difficulty in reaching the market place. He had raised £450 towards this project before his death at Long Stratton in 1814. This work was completed in 1836, and a plaque once hung in Brigg Street, Norwich which recorded that: 'Revd William D'Oyly 1745-1815 In his old age rode 12,000 miles on horseback collecting subscriptions for the widening of this street.'

As a young boy, William D'Oyly may have witnessed the arrival of Revd John Wesley, who walked from Norwich to Hempnall on Tuesday, 4 September 1759 and preached under a great oak tree. Wesley was becoming famous, and wherever he preached, people came to listen, some out of curiosity, others to mock and disrupt. On this occasion a mob arrived and the ringleader began blowing a horn. Someone snatched it away from him and

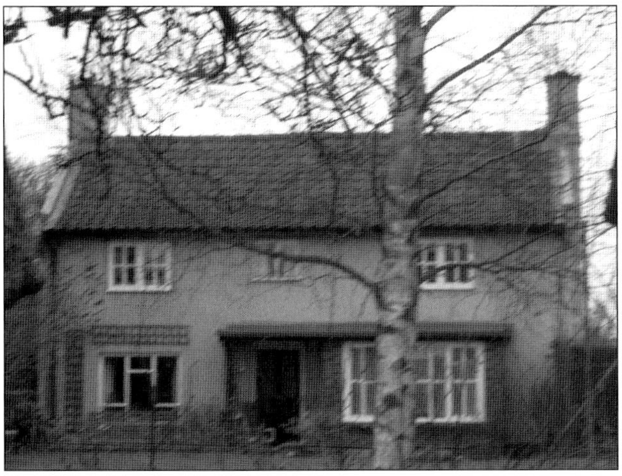

The former workhouse on Lundy Green.

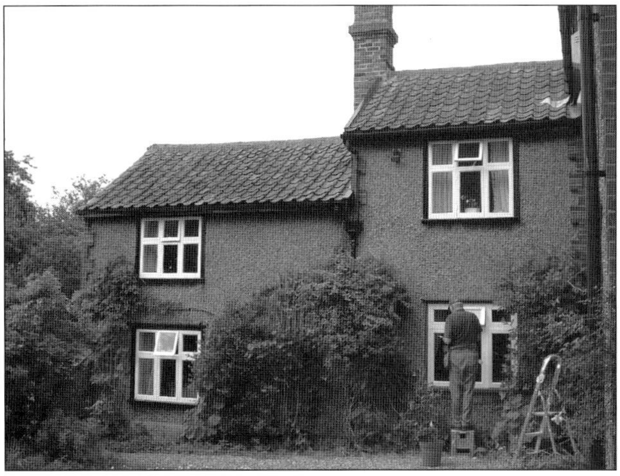

The house owned by John and Mary Scales, where converts of John Wesley may have met. Earliest known date 1691. (Copyhold description: Colls)

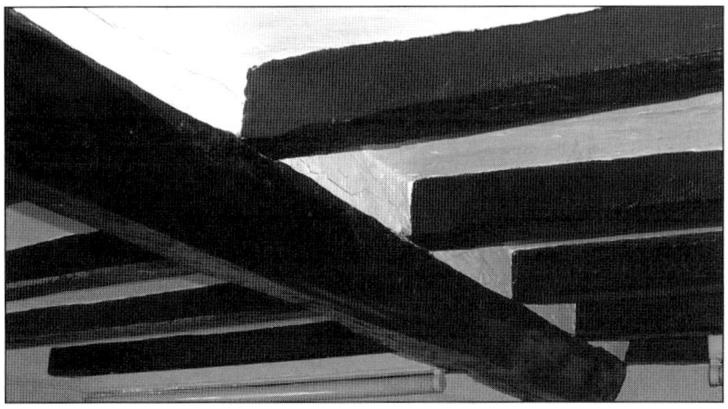

Beams inside John Scales's house.

before long he was deserted by his companions, who became absorbed by the message of the preacher.[24] There is a story that Sam Head, a higgler and innkeeper, on his way home from Woodton to Wicklewood, noticed people making their way along Hempnall Street to hear Wesley. He decided to follow and was so inspired by the preacher that he changed his life. He rented a few acres and became a smallholder, turning his alehouse into a Methodist chapel.[25]

Wesley travelled, mostly on horseback, between 4,000 and 5,000 miles a year, aiming to visit each society he had founded at least once a year, a mammoth task. Why, then, did he take the trouble to walk from Norwich to this village? There is a strong possibility that he was invited, as itinerant preachers regularly visited Hempnall.[26] In 1754 a group of dissenters, headed by James Wheatley and William Roberts, were meeting in the dwelling-house of John Fuller at Hempnall, who, in 1777, was living in 'The Cottage in the Street', opposite Willow Farm.[27] Wheatley had once been one of Wesley's preachers, but had been expelled for inappropriate behaviour towards various women. John Wesley would have nothing to do with the man. In 1755 John Bunn, Francis Osborn, John Pedgriest, Robert Poll, John Warns, Benjamin Legood and Edward Sendall requested permission to hold services in the house of John Scales, who in 1735 had a house on the east side of Cole's Green and who, in 1736, inherited a house opposite the school, now Forge Cottage.[28] There is no proof that either group were calling themselves 'Methodists', but it is a possibility.

It was inevitable that local the clergy would not take kindly to preaching without licence in their parishes. The Revd Joseph Parsons condemned:

> *... these new gospellers, instead of preaching the gospel, do in truth overturn it; by setting men at variance one against another... and encouraging the ignorant and the unlearned to advance themselves... some become mopish and melancholy, not knowing where to fix; others grow careless of their souls, and lie open to commit all iniquity with greediness.*[29]

However, neither Parsons nor the influence of John Wesley were to have much effect on the level of crime. There had been a rise in population and many inhabitants were doomed to live in overcrowded conditions, some in abject poverty. To add to their misery, the price of wheat was so high that, for example, in 1756 in Norwich, 12,000 poor people were sold bread at half price.[30]

Cattle distemper was particularly virulent between 1742 and 1760. On 23 April 1746, Joseph Parsons delivered a sermon at Bedingham on 'Preventing spreading of Distemper now raging among cattle'. His target was landowners: 'Thoughtless and vain people... amused into complacency and love of life through the satisfaction of honour, riches and splendour.' To the ordinary folk his message was: 'Lead a religious, good life, avoid whatever is offensive, do such things and duties as are pleasing to our Redeemer and maker.'[31]

Joseph Parsons recorded the distribution by the charity of the appropriately named Mr Bunn's bread at Hempnall Church in 1745, 1749 and 1751. In May 1757, 20s. worth of bread was distributed as part of another legacy to the poor. The same year the

Honourable Harbottle Luckyn, lord of the Hempnall manors, gave 5 guineas to the needy. In July five bushels of wheat were made into 85 loaves and distributed at a cost of £2.8s.9d., and in August 80 loaves were given away.

A workhouse, or house of industry, designed to alleviate the problem of poverty, was built near Lundy Green. The lane leading to it still called Workhouse Loke.

Hempnall must have been a place of some importance, with inhabitants of independent thought who would have listened to such political and religious figures as chose to visit. Weavers and spinners, still working independently from their own homes, were based at Lundy Green and Field Lane, and two weavers' shops were in the same yard as an 'old accustomed' butcher's shop near the Town Bridge.[32]

References

[1] Richard Hylton, 23 August 1860

[2] *NG* Saturday, 7 September 1728. Malting office and brewing office in Hempnall Street to be let

[3] *NG* Saturday, 12 August 1727

[4] *NG* Saturday, 20 October1733

[5] *NG* Saturday, 24 July 1736. *NM* Saturday, 17 July 1736

[6] NRO NCR case 6-16

[7] *NG* Saturday, 14 April 1739

[8] *NG* Saturday, 8 August 1738

[9] *NG* Saturday, 5 January 1734, *NG* Saturday, 19 November 1738, Saturday, 24 February 1739, Saturday, 23 May 1741.

[10] *NM* Saturday, 25 May 1745

[11] *NM* Saturday, 5 October 1751

[12] A published sermon printed at the Bible & Key near St Paul's, London, 1763, price 6d.

[13] NRO DN/REG 21 Book 29 1707/08 pp273 & 263 Norwich Diocesan Registers

[14] NRO DN/FBA/1 A. B Box 389, 11 Oct 1744 Faculty bond.

[15] Bedingham register

[16] NRO NRS 26671 149X2. Indenture messuage and land.

[17] NRO MSS. Rye No. 17 Vol. 2. Church Notes by Thomas Martin.

[18] *NM* Saturday, 9 December 1758

[19] Proverbs Chapter 7 verses 4 and 5

[20] NRO PD NRS 436/3, 27 January 1771

[21] R. Gore-Brown (1846) *Chancellor Thurlow. The Life and Times of an XVIIIth Century Lawyer* (London) p.16

[22] Lord Campbell (1846) *Lives of the Lord Chancellors*, Vol. 5 (London) p.661

[23] *NC* Saturday, 4 January 1817

[24] N. Curnock (ed.) (1938) *The Journal of the Revd John Wesley*, A.M. Vol. 4 (London)

[25] Elizabeth Chapman *Methodism in Hempnall* (1995)

[26] Revd Joseph Parsons. Published sermon, 1763, printed at the Bible & Key near St Paul's, London, price 6d.

[27] NRO DN DIS Register of meeting Houses 1751–1810

[28] NRO DN/FCB/2/2 p.32 16 March 1755. Faculty Book.

[29] Revd Joseph Parsons. Published sermon, 1763

[30] *NNR* p.15

[31] NRO FEL 787 555 X 7 sermon

[32] *NG* Saturday, 30 August 1718

✥ CHAPTER 9 ✥

Skulduggery 1760–99

On Tuesday, 1 March 1763, Susanna Sporle, an elderly widow of some means, was discovered murdered in her bed at her house on the edge of Lundhaw (Lundy) Green. Her skull was fractured, her jaw broken and one eye was gouged out. A pane of glass had been taken out of the kitchen window, cupboards and drawers were open and her belongings were scattered about the house, but, apparently, nothing was stolen. A rammer, such as carpenters used to ram posts with, was found clean but broken on the floor. The clock in her house had stopped at three minutes past midnight.[1]

Joseph Parsons wrote in the burial register: 'Susanna Sporle widow, found barbarously murdered in bed March 1 and buried the 4.' Parsons took the opportunity at her funeral to vent his anger against the 'evil of amusement and diversions' offered by the alehouses. He condemned the role of strolling teachers who preached 'pernicious doctrines'. He accused parents of keeping their girls at home 'till they are debauched and ruined, through want of better advice and better example.'[2]

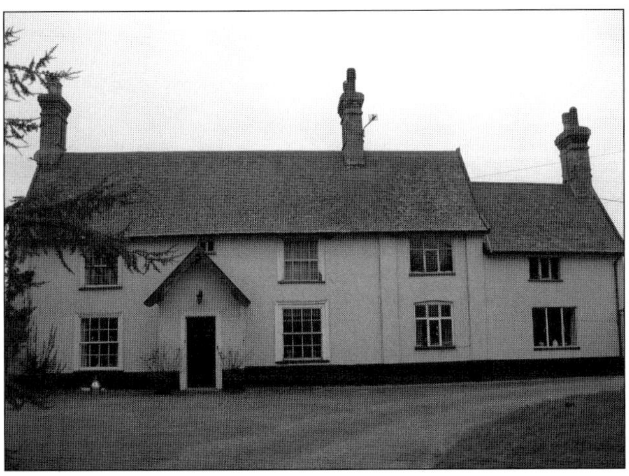

Grange Farm, Lundy Green, once owned by Susanna Sporle (freehold, old name Wrights).

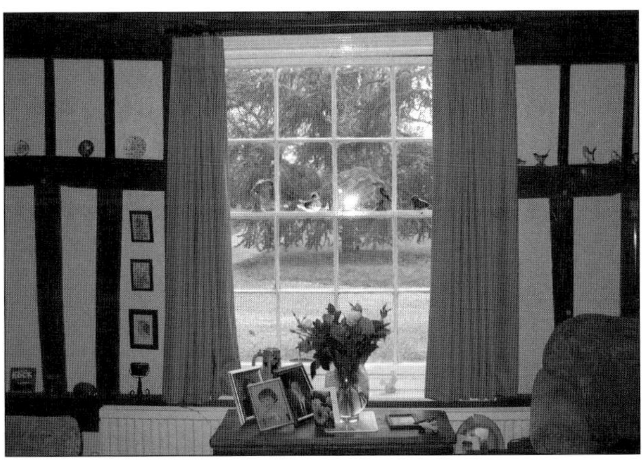

The interior of Grange Farm.

Robert Sporle of Shottesham, Susanna Sporle's son, and John Meadows of Hempnall, her son-in law, offered ten guineas reward for information. Suspicion may have fallen on highwaymen, who had hitherto lurked in woodland ready to exploit the unwary slow traveller; but who had found their efforts curtailed following the development of the turnpikes, the better main roads encouraging faster traffic. Consequently, they paid more attention to the old, rutted, winding lanes and roamed the countryside seeking areas where the rich might reside.

Fortunately, fairs were happy diversions. Stalls for the 1763 December fair were stored in the redundant Church of St Andrew. James Knights from Tivetshall bought four pairs of shoes and several pairs of stockings but wanted change from a guinea to pay for them. Being a very shabby fellow, the stallholder asked how he came to be in possession of such a coin. Knights replied that he had found it at the fair. This caused suspicion, as Knights was well-known for house-breaking. A warrant was obtained to search his lowly cottage adjoining Tivetshall common. 'A goose just killed' was discovered in his bed. 'A great quantity of sheep-skins, carpenters' tools... numbers of geese and turkeys' heads, with about three score goose wings' were found about the

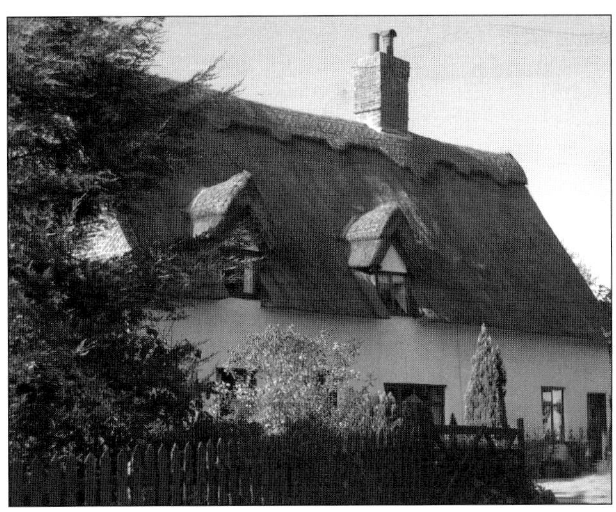

The Chestnuts, Lundy Green, once owned by Susanna Sporle. Earliest known date 1677 (copyhold name Ketteringhams).

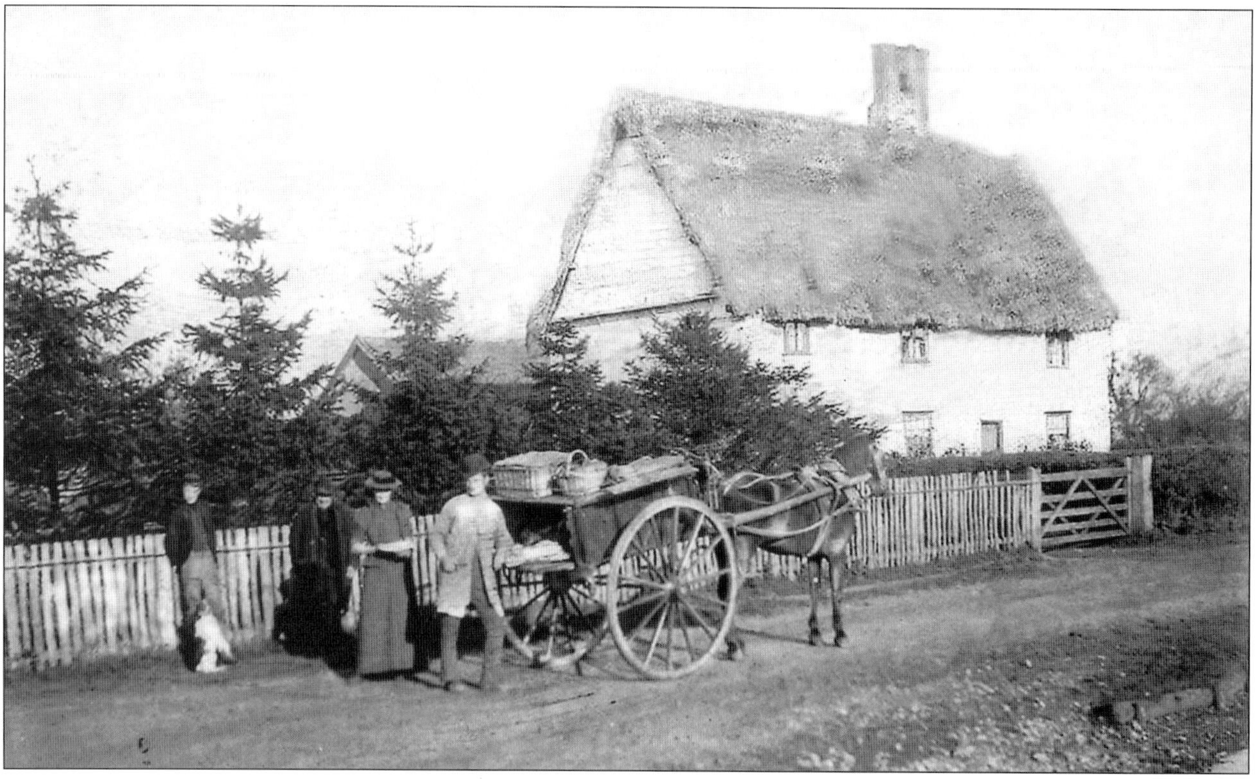

A cottage at Lundy Green, near Hugmore Pond, once owned by Susanna Sporle, since demolished.

house. The thatch, a favourite place for hiding stolen goods, was pulled off 'and out came £43.10s. in a box... with ten gold rings'. Knights was sentenced to transportation, but contracted gaol fever and died. His wife must have been furious, having slashed his leg to the bone some years before to prevent him being taken for a soldier.[3]

Over the next few years other incidents in the village may have overshadowed the mystery of the unsolved murder. In 1763 Mr Flint, a farmer from Saxlingham on a visit to Hempnall, went out of the house looking for the 'vault' (lavatory) in the dark, lost his way, walked into a ditch and was drowned.[4] John Gerard was killed by accident while tending his cow; a horn was thrust into the corner of his eye, and 'fractured his skull, is supposed'.[5] Daniel Meer fell from his horse and was trampled to death and John, son of Isaac and Susan L'Estrange, was killed when a cart overturned as he was going with his mother to Bungay.[6] Joseph Perfait was suffocated by the overthrow of a load of hay while going to Norwich in the night.[7]

In January 1766 a gang of robbers broke into the warehouse of Mr Watling, the Hempnall carrier. The warehouse had been recently stocked with goods from Norwich – wool, groceries, yarns, stockings and alcohol to the value of £20.[8] Three of the thieves were caught red-handed. At their trial, John Jermy, Thomas Baker and George Woodbine confessed to the Hempnall theft and several other burglaries. Hoping for leniency, they accused William Boulton, alias Baley, a blacksmith from Wymondham, of being with them in 1763 when they had broken into the house of Susanna Sporle and cited him as the murderer. They were hanged on the Castle Hill at Norwich. 'They died very penitent: After dangling the usual time, their bodies were carried away in a hearse to Wymondham to be buried.'[9]

Detailed information was now available of the supposed murderer. Handbills advertising a reward were 'dispersed to most parts of the kingdom'. Boulton, alias Baley, was described as:

> *... about 28 Years of Age, four feet five inches high, or thereabouts, swarthy complexion, short brown hair, sometimes tied up with a piece of string, walks stooping, had lately an old Fustian Frock, sometimes a Duffield coat, and an old red waistcoat. The first joint of the fore-finger of his right Hand is off... it is suspected that his hair is lately cut off.*[10]

It was fortuitous that about a year later, a butcher's boy who had been in London with his master recognised Boulton near Stratford and called a soldier, who immediately arrested the wanted man. When apprehended he had a loaded pistol, tinder-box, matches, and a very long knife in his pocket.[11] He was committed to Barking Bridewell in Essex. A search conducted a few days later at a house in Stratford, where he had been living with a local woman, uncovered 'large quantities of silver cutlery, a pair of doe-skin breeches, 20 silk handkerchiefs, several fine shirts and many pairs of stockings.' He was convicted at Hertford Assizes for a number of crimes. However, he would never admit to the murder of Susanna Sporle. At his trial he had the impudence to make a request for the return of his possessions. When the judge enquired as to the nature of this property, he replied:

That besides the plate... there was a bunch of pick- lock keys which belonged to his calling, and were of great service. The above keys were delivered to the High Sheriff and ordered to be knocked to pieces...[12]

Thus the notorious house-breaker and highwayman was executed and buried under the gallows without a coffin. However, the story does not end there for the following night his body was dug up and carried off – 'it is conjected; the body was recovered by some persons employed by the surgeons, in order for its being anatomised.'[13]

Local people, it seems, were never convinced that Widow Sporle was murdered by highwaymen, and 100 years later a villager wrote: 'It is asserted and quite believed that this person was murdered by her own son… a tragic account brought down by tradition to the present time.'[14]

The murder of Mrs Sporle probably sent shivers of apprehension through members of the respectable, genteel, 'polite society' of the village. The 12 male freeholders who voted in the 1768 election were resident and owned freeholds valued at more than 40s. a year. They and their families would perhaps represent the core of this society in the village.

In the register books Joseph Parsons gives a few insights into village life during this period. Mrs Fryer had obviously annoyed the congregation by elevating her position in church:

The seat in the church where Mrs Fryer and the vicar's servants now sit hath no connection with Mrs Fryer nor the house or farms now occupied by her husband. Her sitting there is by connivance, the original right seems to be in the Vicar, for his family. According to the best intelligence, the wife of Zachary Brown, who then occupied Lady Luckyn's Farm… was placed there on a debate relating to the opposite seat by Chettleborough and descendants.[15]

About glebe land in 1757, Parsons wrote:

The piece of ground fenced in contiguous to the two cottages in occupation of Mrs Townshend and John Nash, belongs to the vicarage, which occupiers of the said premises are to pay to the vicar yearly the sum of 5s.

The vicar made a point of recording in the burial register examples of good and bad behaviour:

Loami Cunningham as it seems of a broken heart from a false wife. Jeremiah Fassett… a useful, just and exemplary neighbour a diligent and faithful schoolmaster to both sexes…[16] *Joshua Gryms an honest and industrious man.*[17] *William Neeve an inoffensive quiet man who departed not from the Temple but diligently served the Lord… was just and friendly to many.*[18] *Isabell Carr... of approved conversation in Christ… doing good and giving no offence in private: A rare example!*[19] *Robert Meadows taken off suddenly and strangely had grossly offended his aunt. Aged 22.*[20] *Dorothy Pitts a sober well disposed young woman aged 17 – who kept clear from the taint of Methodism amidst contagion.*[21] *Mary wife of Philipo Pitcher, 'believed to have suffered much', died of terror 'being carried into the house of Industry.*[22]

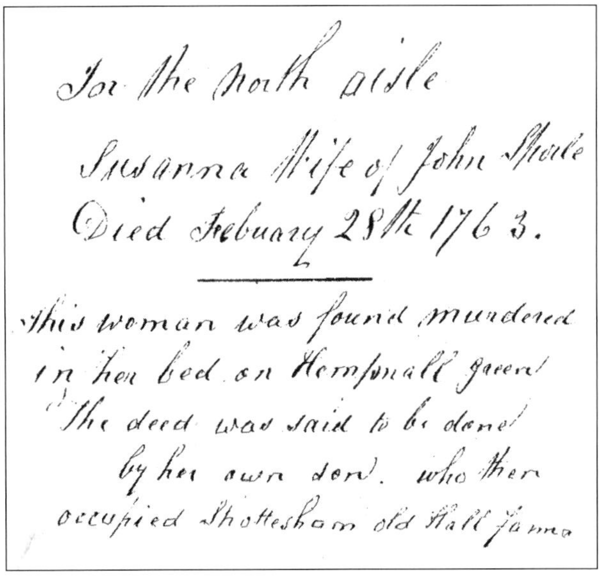
For the North aisle
Susanna Wife of John Sporle
Died Febuary 28th 1763.
This woman was found murdered
in her bed on Hempnall green
The deed was said to be done
by her own son. who then
occupied Shottesham old Hall farm

Note by Richard Hylton on the murder of Susanna Sporle.

It can be surmised that Joseph Parsons was financially fairly well off, owning a 'mansion house', several cottages and shops, employing his own coachmen and servants and apparently enjoying the income from both vicarial and rectorial tithes. However, in 1760 the manors of Hempnall devolved to the Grimston family following the death of Harbottle Luckyn. Lord Grimston employed 'one Delact, a man rash and ill advised', according to the vicar. There was a possibility of losing the income from the great tithes and his right to hay and clover. Parsons was outraged and visited a lawyer in London to recover his dues.

Joseph Parsons and his wife had no children. It seems that his wife's sister, Mary Tristram, Mrs Mary Cowper, a cousin and Daniel Parsons, brother of Joseph, shared their house or lived in other property belonging to the vicar. Mary Tristram died aged 84 'her end supposed hastened by a fall walking in her chamber'.[23] Joseph Parsons, 'Master of Arts, 50 years the indefatigable pastor…' died in 1774, aged 78, was buried in a vault under the communion table. In his will he directed that William Fellows of Shottesham

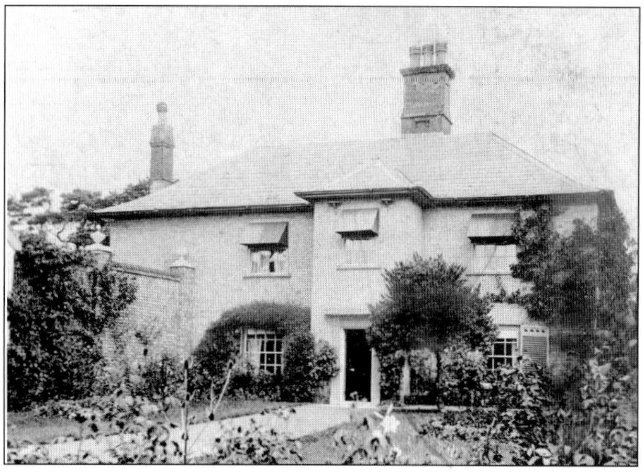

Manor Farm (freehold after 1812) Earliest known date 1650. (copyhold description: Messuage & tenement wasted with 2 acres. The tenement contained part of a well.) There is still a well inside Manor Farm.

Esq., Samuel Wegg Esq. of Middlesex and John Van Kamp gent., of Bungay, should be admitted to his copyholds provided that his wife and Miss Mildred Cowper could reside in his capital messuage or mansion house on condition they:

> *... permit and suffer his brother Daniel for life to dwell in the family with them and they provide for and allow him for life board and sufficient apparel and nessassaries in such manner as he had usually been provided for by the testator...*[24]

Thomas Short his coach driver, who died a few years later, so loved his master that he asked to be buried outside the church, at the feet of his master.

Improved roads had facilitated trade with more distant markets and enabled more people to seek work further afield, while cheaper and more varied manufactured goods could be purchased due to the effects of the Industrial Revolution. Large landowners became wealthier but many small traders lost their occupations. Unemployment continued to be a problem and the house of industry remained a real threat to liberty for many. The increased availability of alcohol, for there were no restrictions on opening times, may have encouraged disruptive behaviour and probably gambling.

Illegitimacy in the village rose dramatically during the eighteenth century. Some fathers were taken through the courts in order that the mother's parish was not landed with the expense of supporting bastards. In 1742 John Henery, yeoman (reputed father), and Richard Henery, his son, both of Hempnall, were ordered to pay £40 and then 20s. weekly towards the upkeep of the child of Elizabeth Dawdy of Bunwell. They were still paying in 1747. Daniel Meers, a glover, was ordered to pay 1s.6d. weekly for the child of Hannah Bunn of Tharston in 1796.[25]

Almost all the copyhold dwellings in the village centre were being rented by the end of the eighteenth century. Between 1783 and 1796, 71 paupers were buried. Those employed in the weaving industry were perhaps particularly at risk of pauperism, and some turned to crime as an alternative to the workhouse. A number of offenders were caught for short or false reeling yarn and embezzling wool.

The pit opposite the Swan Inn was being excavated for gravel in June 1779. John Durrant of Topcroft was at work when the ground above him gave way and a large quantity of gravel fell on him, wounding him dangerously. The editor of the *Chronicle* printed the warning: 'It is hoped this accident will be a caution to labourers in this season of mending roads, to be careful how they mine such a heavy body as gravel.'[26] James Adcock, who owned a shop opposite the present Queen's Head and also Forge Cottage, was robbed of four gowns and two petticoats. Susanna Whitehead was found guilty and privately whipped.[27] J. Pennywell of Bungay was visiting a tavern at Hempnall when he was invited to drink a dram. A bottle of 'corrosive sublimate being unguardedly where the liquor was generally kept, a glass of it was given him; he languished for a little time, and died.'[28] John Nobbs hanged himself by the side of a wood in Hempnall called Pope's Wood. He was suspected of murdering his son, whose skeleton was discovered in a ditch at Tasburgh. The verdict was 'self-murder and he was accordingly buried... in the King's highway at Hempnall'.[29] This spot, formerly Sizeland Cross, was renamed Nobbs' Corner and the path adjoining became Nobbs' Lane.

In 1777, in response to questions raised at the Bishop's Visitation, the Revd Coote Leicester, then vicar, declared that: 'there were upwards of 100 houses in the village and the chief inhabitants were in the middling station of life'. There were no Papists, Presbyterians, Independents or Baptists, but three or four families of Quakers attended meetings out of the parish. There was no chapel in the village. There was one service on Sunday and 'the sacrament' was administered four times a year to about 40 communicants. At the 1784 Visitation there were a few dissenters 'some styled Methodists who assemble occasionally in their own houses which are licensed.' There was one orderly Quaker family of shoemakers. He reported that there was 'no house belonging to the vicarage, nor any to be hired, but upon unreasonable terms' (the vicar lived at Shelton). There were two common day-schools and two or three houses for the accommodation of paupers. The last visitation of the century took place when the Revd John Johnson was vicar in 1794. Johnson of East Dereham was a friend and cousin of the poet William Cowper. There was a curate who lived in Morningthorpe.

The absence of a resident vicar may have contributed to a delay on 9 August 1787, when the church was discovered to be on fire. The flames 'burnt through a singing gallery and reached the

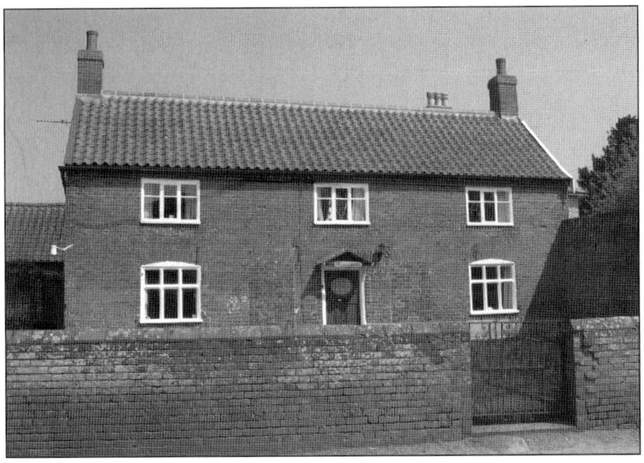

A cottage in the Street, rebuilt in 1788 after a fire.

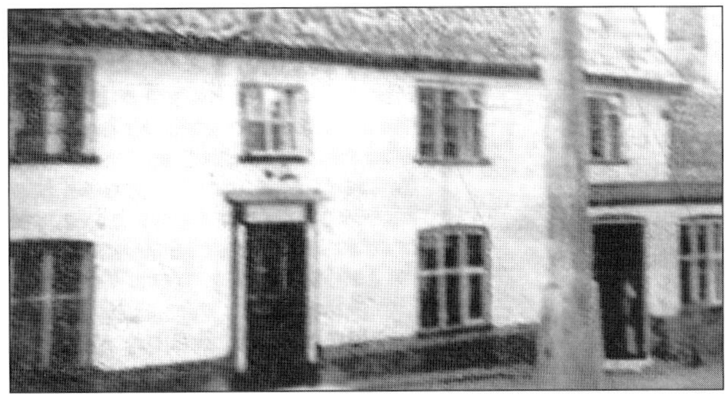

The Swan.

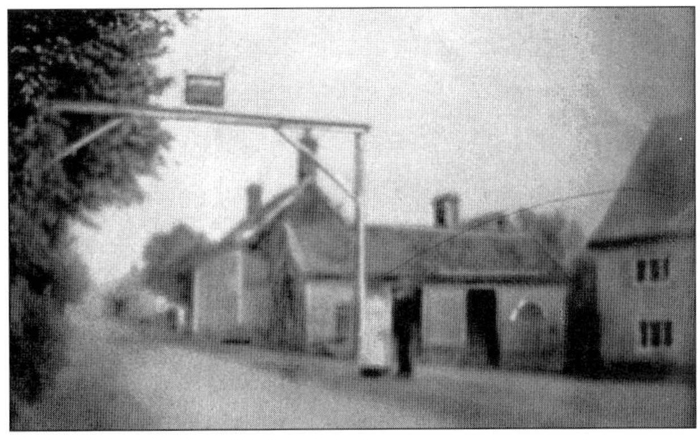

The Swan with the gantry over the road.

spars which support a lead roof'. That night there had been a:

> *... most awful and alarming tempest of lightening, thunder, rain and hail, the like not remembered in years... The tempest had fortunately called most of the parish from their beds, and thus this handsome structure was rescued from destruction.*[30]

The following year a house belonging to Mr Peter Brown was burnt down. Fortunately, owing to the calmness of the night, no other damage was done, although the house destroyed was situated near the church, and surrounded with thatched buildings at the distance of only a few feet.[31] The house was rebuilt with the date 1788 affixed to the façade.

During the last decade of the century the village or its inhabitants regularly appeared in the newspapers. Thomas Brundal, an old man, was found dead in his garden.[32] John Todd was killed through standing on the shafts of his master's cart with his hands on a ladder. As he attempted to whip the horses, the ladder gave way and he was thrown off and killed by the wheels going over him.[33] Elizabeth Buxton rented a newly built dwelling house in the Street and ran a boarding school for young ladies of under 12.[34] Elisha Tooke stole a coat from a horse standing outside the King's Head and sold it the next day at Ditchingham.[35] The following year he received three weeks' hard labour for stealing a greatcoat.[36] William King falsely accused William Goose, farmer and butcher, of having stolen a cow from Mr William Moore of Fritton. An apology was printed in the *Norfolk Chronicle* and the following year King left his farm.[37]

Eighteenth-century Hempnall life was not all misdeeds, misery and murder. There was the annual village outing of 'beating the bounds', a relic from the days when it was important that the inhabitants knew the boundaries of their parish. On one occasion a tree, which usually marked the boundary between Hempnall and Fritton, was found blown over and it was agreed that some other marker should be placed there. In June 1783 Carver the shoemaker took his wheel and found the circuit measured just over 14 miles.

John Nash, parish clerk and landlord of the Swan, introduced a 'Quarterly Club'. An advertisement for the event on Monday 16 June 1794 requested punctuality: 'Dinner on the table at three o'clock precisely'.[38] He was generous in form, weighing 24 stones in his 40s and generous by nature, giving a home to Peter Sewell for over 20 years.[39] Unfortunately in May 1795, Sewell fell down and broke his thigh and was taken to the Norfolk and Norwich Hospital.[40] He died in October and was 'handsomely interred' at the sole expense of John Nash.[41]

During August 1790 a young artist by the name of Henry Butter wandered into the village. John Nash, himself an amateur artist, encouraged him to complete several large works and then displayed them at the Swan 'in the manner of the paintings at the annual exhibition at Somerset-house, London'.[42] For two months this young artist roamed the village until he fell ill. Does a likeness of John Nash, or his inn, reside, dust-covered, in someone's attic? Sadly, Henry Butter died at the Swan aged 21, described as a 'self-taught genius in the art of painting'.[43] Nothing more can be found about this young man.

Hempnall must have been full of contrasting characters; the educated, illiterate, religious, dishonest, rich, poor and eccentric such as an old lady who married aged 80. The *Chronicle* reported that she had:

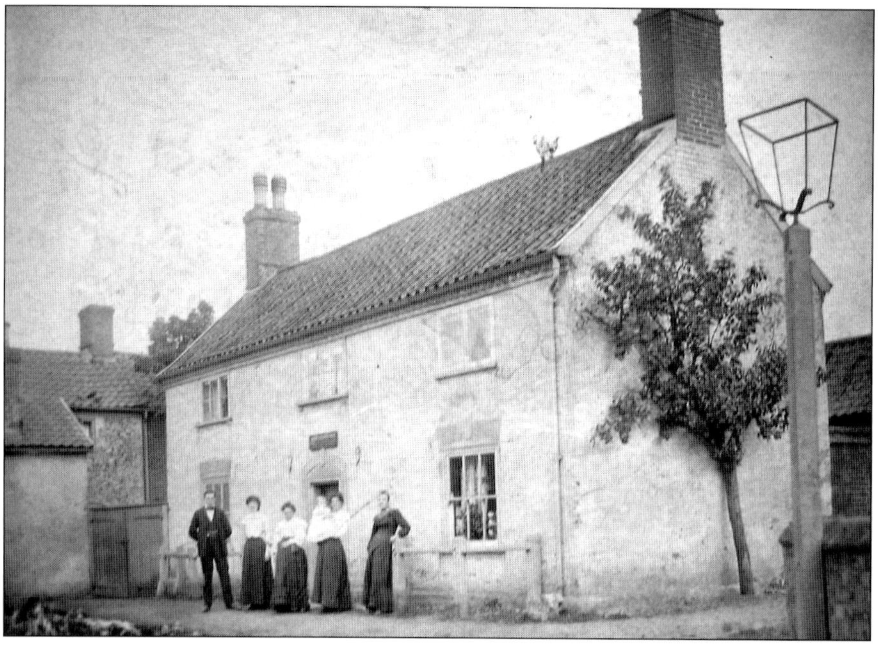

Left:
The Woodman. Built 1791 Left to right: Mr and Mrs Pegg, Esther Page, Ellen Sophia Page, wife of the landlord Harry George Page, James Raymond Page, babe in arms, Mrs Frances, landlady of the Nelson.

...for many years kept her coffin in her house, which she used every day to scour and in which she placed her tea-cups etc. We have not learned whether she means to convert it into a cradle.[44]

The Gin Act of 1751 stopped distillers and shop-keepers from retailing spirits and people returned to the more healthy drinking of beer. The Woodman opened to fulfil the new demand in about 1790. Tea became fashionable amongst the upper classes.

Although no known painting exists depicting the Georgian village scene, a map was made in 1767 of all the lands belonging to the lord of the manor, Lord Grimston. Not all the parish is represented, but some of the old strips in the open fields are shown. The church stands, in its almost circular graveyard, overlooking the market place, and many copyhold houses are shown as a representation according to size. The eighteenth-century village becomes imaginable.

References

1 *NG* Saturday, 5 March 1763
2 Sermon preached at the funeral of Susanna Sporle, 4 March 1763
3 *NM* Saturday, 15 June 1763; *NG* Saturday, 31 March 1764. James Knights died at Norwich Castle of an infected leg.
4 *NM* Saturday, 23 April 1763
5 NRO PD 436/3 1764 July 24
6 NRO PD 436/3 16 May 1765
7 NRO PD 436/3 4 Dec 1766
8 *NM* Saturday, 18 January 1766
9 *NM* Saturday, 11 April 1767
10 *NM* Saturday, 21 February 1767
11 *NM* Saturday, 18 June 1768
12 *NM* Saturday, 23 July 1768
13 *NM* Saturday, 20 August 1768
14 Richard Hylton, 1867
15 NRO 436/3, 1760 (no month or day)
16 NRO 436/3, 22 January1760
17 NRO 436/3, 17 November 1763
18 NRO 436/3, 21 February 1766
19 NRO 436/3, 25 May 1770
20 NRO 436/3, 27 January 1771
21 NRO 436/3, 18 July 1770
22 NRO PD 436/3, 1773 (unreadable date but after September)
23 NRO 436/3 7 May 1771
24 PRO PROB 1775, 316 PCC Probate 19 Aug
25 NRO PD 712/74/5; PD 708/101 Overseers Bastardy Warrants
26 *NC* Saturday, 12 June 1779
27 *NC* Saturday, 23 August 1783
28 *NC* Saturday, 3 January 1778
29 *NM* Saturday, 11 June 1785
30 *NC* Saturday, 11 August 1787
31 *NM* Saturday, 17 May 1788
32 *NC* Saturday, 27 March 1790
33 *NM* Saturday,28 Aug 1790
34 *NC* Saturday, 1 January 1792 (school); *NC* Saturday, 2 May 1795 (dwelling house to be sold)
35 *NC* Saturday, 22 December 1792
36 *NC* Saturday, 19 January 1793
37 *NC* Saturday, 20 February 1796; *NC* Saturday, 16 September 1797
38 *NC* Saturday, 7 June
39 Died in 1820 aged 84. Clerk to the parish for 56 years and landlord of the Swan for 35
40 *NM* Saturday, 16 May 1795
41 NRO PD 436/3. Burial register 25 October 1795
42 *NC* Saturday, 17 August 1790
43 *NC* Saturday, 2 October1790
44 *NC* Saturday, 15 October 1791

CHAPTER 10

War and Peace 1800–24

'Pitch dark with hoyl rayn with blustery wind from the south the mill going till 11 o'clock. Such a night I think I hardly new. Blow out at the Heavens...'[1] Thus wrote an unknown scribe in the church bible on a particularly unpleasant night. He noted at the same time that, on 5 January 1800, a benefactor had given 'nine plum coats to the deserving poor'. The writer may have been John Nash, the parish clerk, who could have viewed the mill from a back window of the Swan. It was reported in 1804 that during another terrible thunderstorm Mr Robert Thrower was returning from Norwich when he was struck by lightning and deprived of his sight for nearly an hour.[2]

A few years of poor harvests at the beginning of the nineteenth century, exacerbated by war with France, caused the price of wheat to spiral.

Many men were conscripted, but it was relatively easy to abscond at a time when few measures were taken to track down deserters. John Baker, a private in the 9th Regiment of Foot and a deserter, came from Hempnall. On 19 April 1800 he encountered Ann Peterson on her way home from Norwich market. It was reported at the trial that: 'he threw down the bundle that he carried under his arm and seizing her with violence, assaulted and ravished her.' She ran home and told her husband, who immediately gave pursuit. Baker was eventually discovered the next day, hiding in Hempnall woods. He was convicted at the next Assizes and sentenced to death, but this was commuted to transportation for life.[3]

The Treaty of Amiens, signed in May 1802, promised better prospects for the future. At Hempnall, the festivities began at noon on Tuesday, 8 June. The population feasted on beef, 1,500 plum cakes and penny loaves, cheese, and five barrels of strong beer. There were races with prizes and activities concluded at eight in the evening when '700 persons had finished the last barrel with enthusiastic expressions of heart-felt loyalty and thanks to their generous benefactors.'[4] The principal inhabitants had collected more than £30 for distribution amongst the poor, and a number of the more affluent inhabitants enjoyed a festive evening at the Swan.

The peace was short lived, and the Napoleonic Wars continued until 1815. In case of invasion, each parish appointed a respected person, such as a clergyman or principal farmer, to enlist a certain number of men for the militia by ballot. Henry Moore of Hempnall, a weaver, was drawn, but, not wanting to serve, absconded, leaving his wife and two children. Two guineas reward was offered for his capture. He

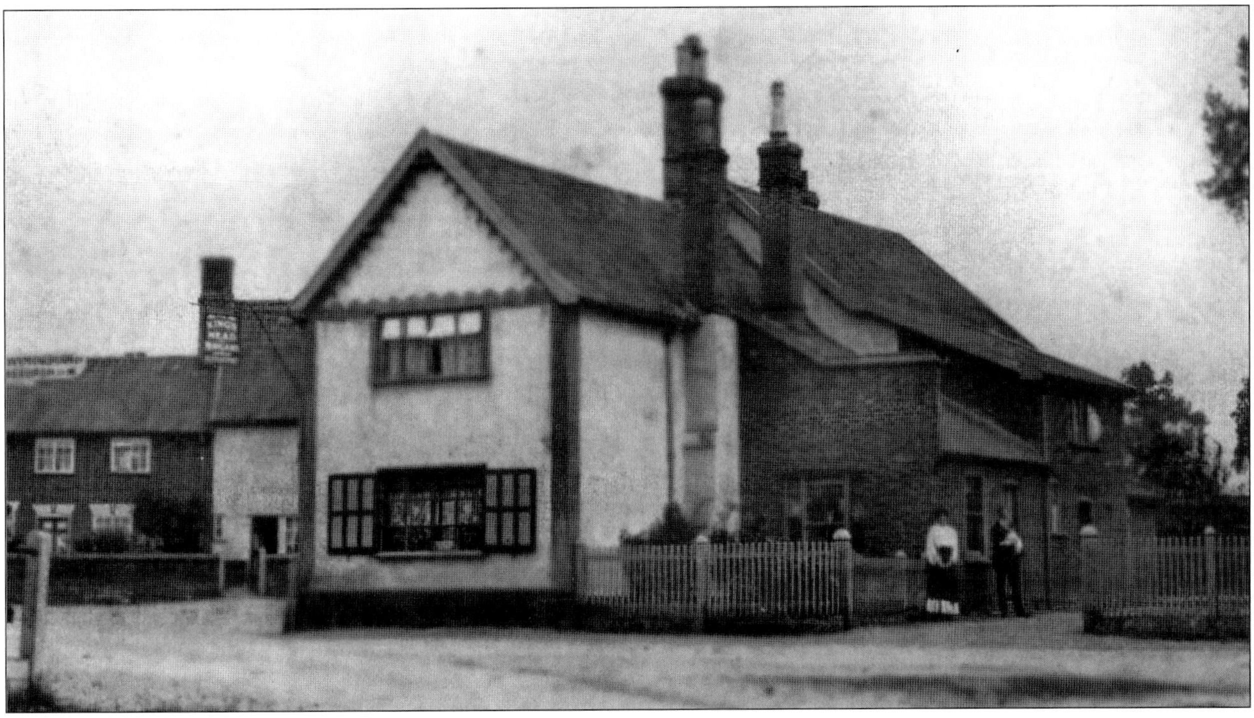

A view of the King's Head from the town bridge. The old blacksmith's forge was between the King's Head and the butcher's shop.

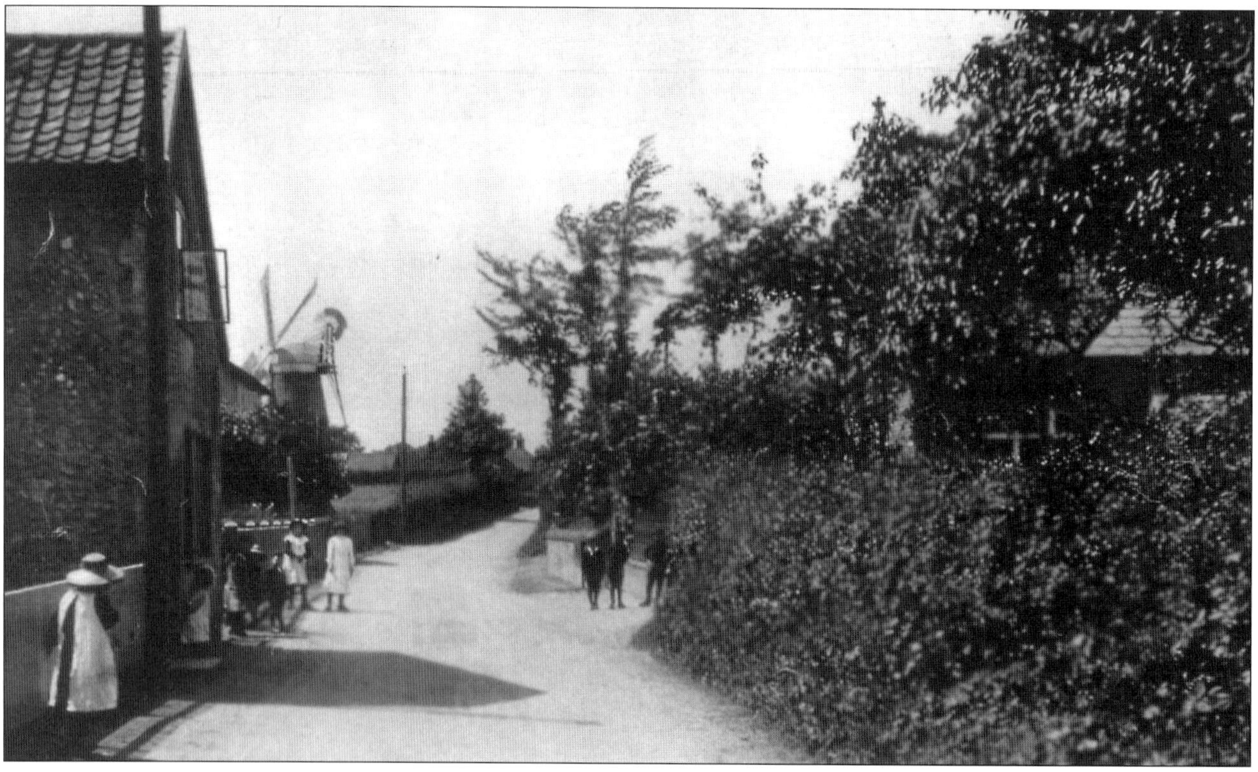

Mill Road with the mill in the distance

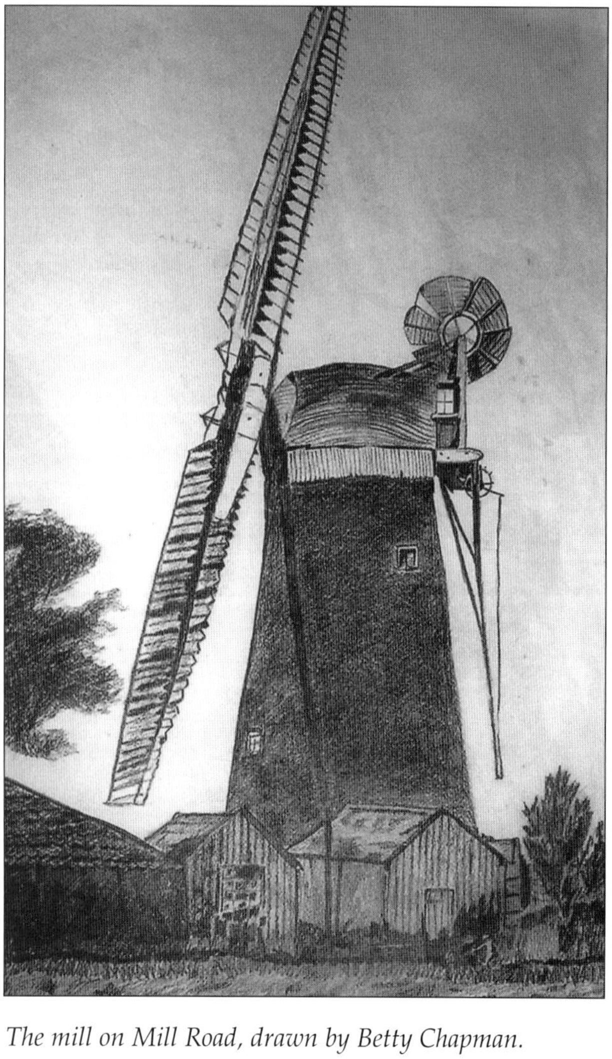

The mill on Mill Road, drawn by Betty Chapman.

was described as aged 21, five foot two inches tall, with light eyes and wearing a dark, straight coat, fustian frock and round hat.[5]

In October 1809 many villagers assembled at Great Green to witness the inspection of a squadron of Norwich Light Horse volunteers commanded by Major John Harvey. There followed a demonstration of manoeuvres. Afterwards the volunteers dined together at the King's Head.[6]

The capture of Madrid by the Marquis of Wellington, later the Duke of Wellington, in 1812 was a further excuse for celebration. A flag was hoisted on the church tower at Hempnall and 'guns fired to announce the glorious event'. A swivel gun was loaded and, on being fired:

> *... burst and flew to atoms, a part of which struck against a blacksmith's shop about 20 or 30 yards distant and recoiled near 16 feet. A man was at work in the shop at the time of the explosion, but providently neither he nor any of the bystanders received the least injury, except the person who fired the gun.*[7]

The smithy, at that time between the King's Head and the butcher's shop, appears in the copyhold records from 1625.

Hempnall market had probably ceased to function by the nineteenth century, as the turnpike road from Norwich to London had effectively isolated the village from main communication routes. The village still maintained a collection of little shops, and some traders had outlets in Norwich. Henry D'Oyly, brother of the Revd William D'Oyly, a hempen-cloth manufacturer, had a stall in Weaver's Lane on Saturdays.[8] James Chettleborough kept a shop in Hempnall and sold sheep in Norwich Market Place. He was charged with sheep-stealing in 1800. Three pigs were found alive, with parts of five dead sheep.[9]

James Carver, a miller, sold seeds in his son's shop near the Castle Ditches.[10] In April 1814, during a gale, one of his post mills on Gallows Hill took fire by 'friction of the gudgeon' and burned to the ground in less than an hour. The church fire-buckets were borrowed and John Elsey was paid 1s. for ensuring their safe return.[11] Carver was in the mill at the time and, though enveloped in smoke, escaped injury.[12] Undeterred, within a year he had built a tower seed mill and was advertising clover, suckling and trefoil seeds drawn and dressed.[13] In 1819 his new tower mill and his large post mill were put up for sale.

The church buckets were needed again in 1819, when a fire in a chandling office near the church endangered several thatched buildings:

> *Fortunately the activity of the neighbours and the wind being in a favourable direction, the devouring element was got under without further damage than the demolition of the premises which is commenced.*[14]

Weaving had long been a tradition in the village, but with cheaper manufactured cloth available, those who worked at home were in financial difficulties. Some were forced into dishonesty to survive. Mary Grint and Elizabeth Smith had been charged with false reeling on more than one occasion. They were sharing a room in the workhouse at Hempnall in August 1816. During the night, Smith helped herself to 'divers articles of wearing apparel, and 15 penny pieces' which Mary Grint said she kept in a box by her bedside. Rachael Basham, of Norwich, said that she had bought a child's petticoat and a lad's waistcoat for 2s.3d. off Elizabeth Smith. These articles were produced in court, along with several other items that were sworn to be the property of Mary Grint. Smith was sentenced to imprisonment for six months.[15] In 1817 she gave birth to a daughter whilst in the house of correction in Aylsham.[16]

'Numerous depredations' had been committed in and about the parish in 1812, spurring the chief inhabitants to begin an 'Association for Prosecuting Offenders'.[17] The first meeting was held at the King's Head in March 1812. Two years later, another meeting was announced at the same venue and 'all persons desirous of promoting the same' were requested to attend. The annual meeting of this association was to be held at the King's Head in January 1820.[18] However, in 1823 Thomas Garrard and John Roberts (woodman and gamekeeper), both of Hempnall, stole a silver watch, a musical snuff box, a necklace, a quantity of rings and other articles, together worth about £300, from a watchmaker in Norwich. George Barrett, a watchmaker, and Roger Roberts, both from Hempnall, were accused of receiving the stolen goods. Barrett removed the names and numbers from the watches before burying them in a pot in Hempnall Woods.[19]

The first census of the population of England was taken in 1801. Hempnall had 879 inhabitants. There were 114 houses occupied by 188 families and two houses empty. A total of 370 people were chiefly employed in agriculture and 223 in trade, manufacture or handicraft. Ten years later, 204 families were occupying 115 houses and 11 were empty.

Edward Finch bought the Horse Shoes in 1816, added an extension on the north side and renamed it the Queen's Head.[20] Charles Warmoll inherited the house called Chequers from his father, the schoolmaster, and became a surgeon.

John Sharpe, an auctioneer, bought the Longhouse and used part of the premises as a repository. His wife was running a boarding and day-school for young ladies in another part of the building.[21] She was involved in a serious accident one evening in 1819:

> *... occasioned by the very dangerous but too prevalent habit which women in the country have of flinging water on to the public road from the doors of their houses: a horse which Mrs Sharpe and Mrs Slipper of Hempnall were driving in a gig was frightened in this manner, and threw them both out with great violence...*[22]

The poor of the village continued to be supported by the Feoffees Trust and various other charities. When, in 1806, John Thruston Mott became lord of several manors, including Hempnall, he gave a splendid ball at the Assembly Rooms in Swaffham. The room was 'very elegantly illuminated with variegated lamps... the dancing was kept up with spirit to a late hour'. The poor of the various parishes each received a sixpenny loaf, a pound of beef and a pint of beer as part of the celebrations.[23]

Despite the generosity of the wealthy, many remained on the breadline. An impoverished man named Anger, found dead in a ditch in 1805, had been carrying home a loaf of bread, which was found under his arm, and a crust in his mouth.[24] In 1810:

> *... two women were delivered of two children which four persons (all sleeping in one bed) constituted three mothers, three daughters, one son, brother and sister and a niece.*[25] (Work that out!)

In 1814 the poor of Hempnall:

> *... to the number of 1200* [sic], *were made happy at Thanksgiving Day, by a good dinner of old English fare, roast beef and plum pudding; and in the afternoon about 250 females took tea.*[26]

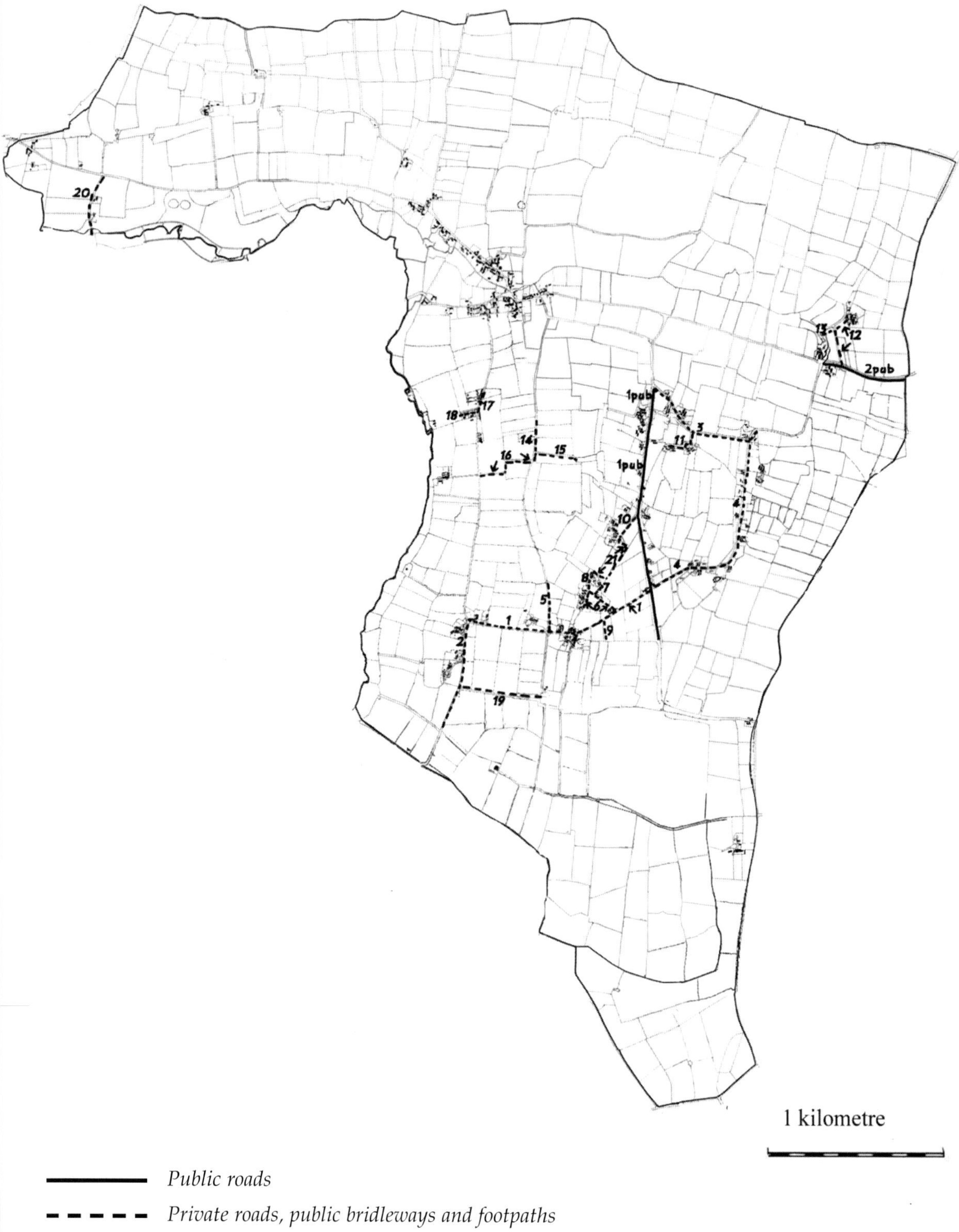

Fig. 12

Enclosure roads superimposed on the later Tithe Redemption map of 1842.

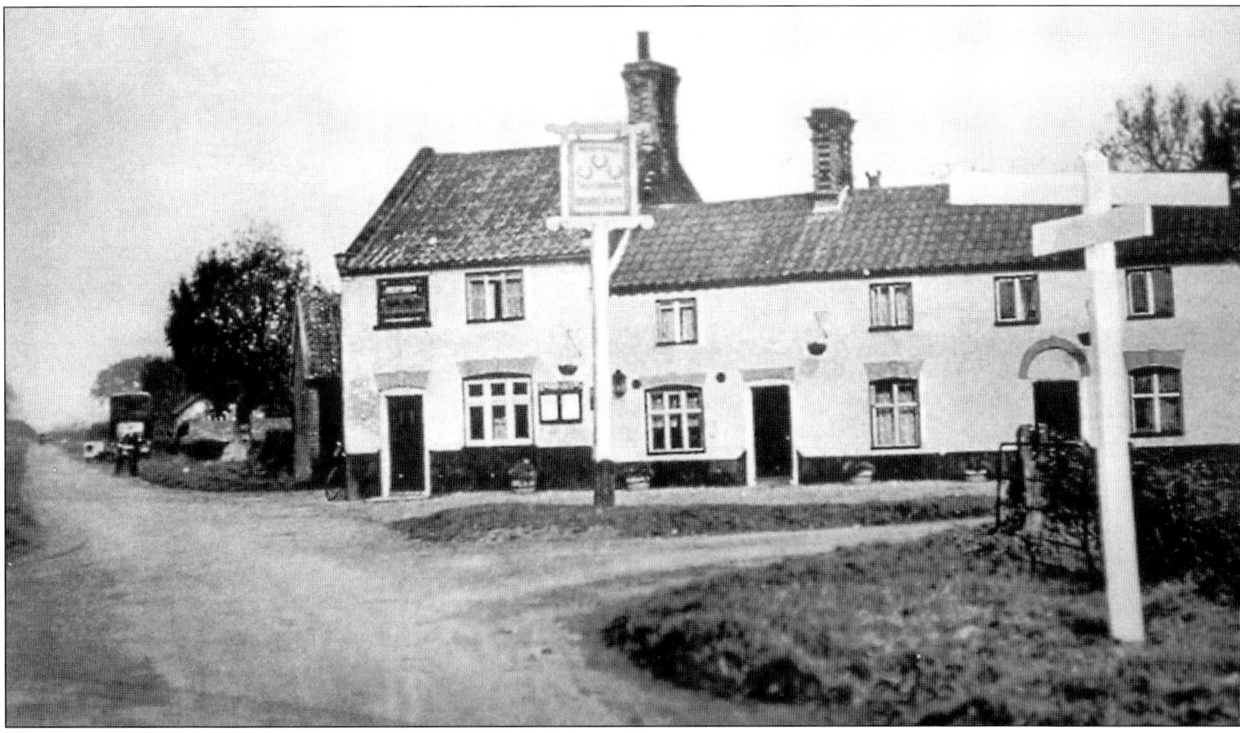

The Horseshoes, now the Three Horseshoes, on Silver Green, built after 1818.

With the institution of the Revd Castres Mott Donne in 1807, Hempnall once again had a resident vicar. Mott Donne noted at the visitation of 1813 that there were two Quaker families who assembled at Tasburgh and a few Methodists living quiet and orderly lives but with no place of meeting. Church of England services took place every Sunday and 'The Lord's Supper' four times a year attended by about 25 parishioners. There was a Sunday school for 112 children, supported by subscription, where children were taught to read and spell.

Eighteenth-century farming methods were becoming outdated, and turnips began to replace the hay crop as winter cattle feed. It made sense to put common land under the plough and to redistribute the old strips of land in the open fields to create larger closes. Through various Acts of Parliament commons, waste and open fields were gradually being enclosed all over England. On 23 May 1817 the Inclosure Act for Hempnall was passed. Those who owned land in an open field or had a cottage with a right of commonage were given an allotment or allotments. However, each allotment had to be fenced, and those who could not afford the expense were obliged to sell. Commons had been means of communication. With their disappearance it would be necessary to create new public roads across Great Green and Road Green. In all, 20 new private roads, which could also be used as public bridleways and footpaths, were planned (Fig. 12).

A meeting was held at the King's Head in June 1817 for members of the public to hear the proposals. In September there was an opportunity to buy 25 acres of former common and waste in 13 lots.[27] A detailed plan of the parish was produced showing the new roads and allotments. In addition, and unusually, all the copyhold plots were marked. Descriptions of the allotments and new roads were recorded in the Inclosure Award, together with an

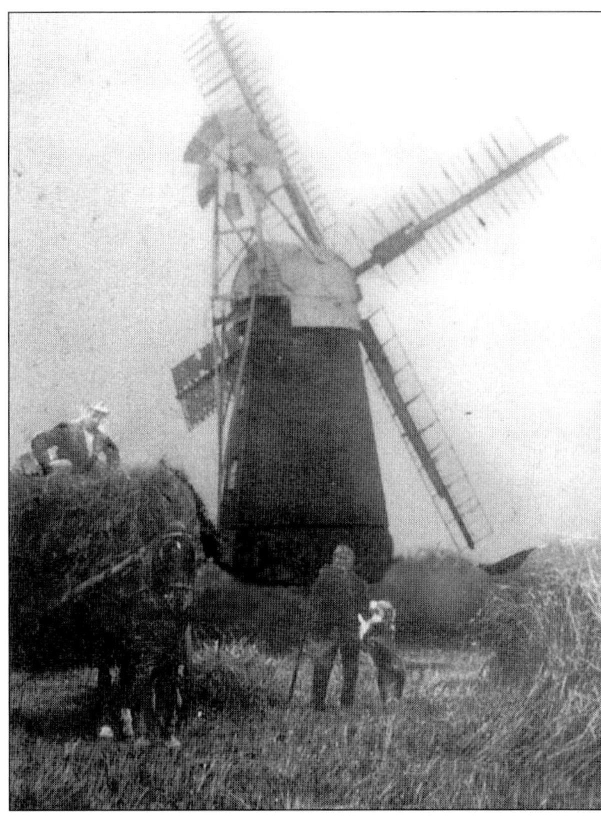

The smock mill at Silver Green, built after 1818.

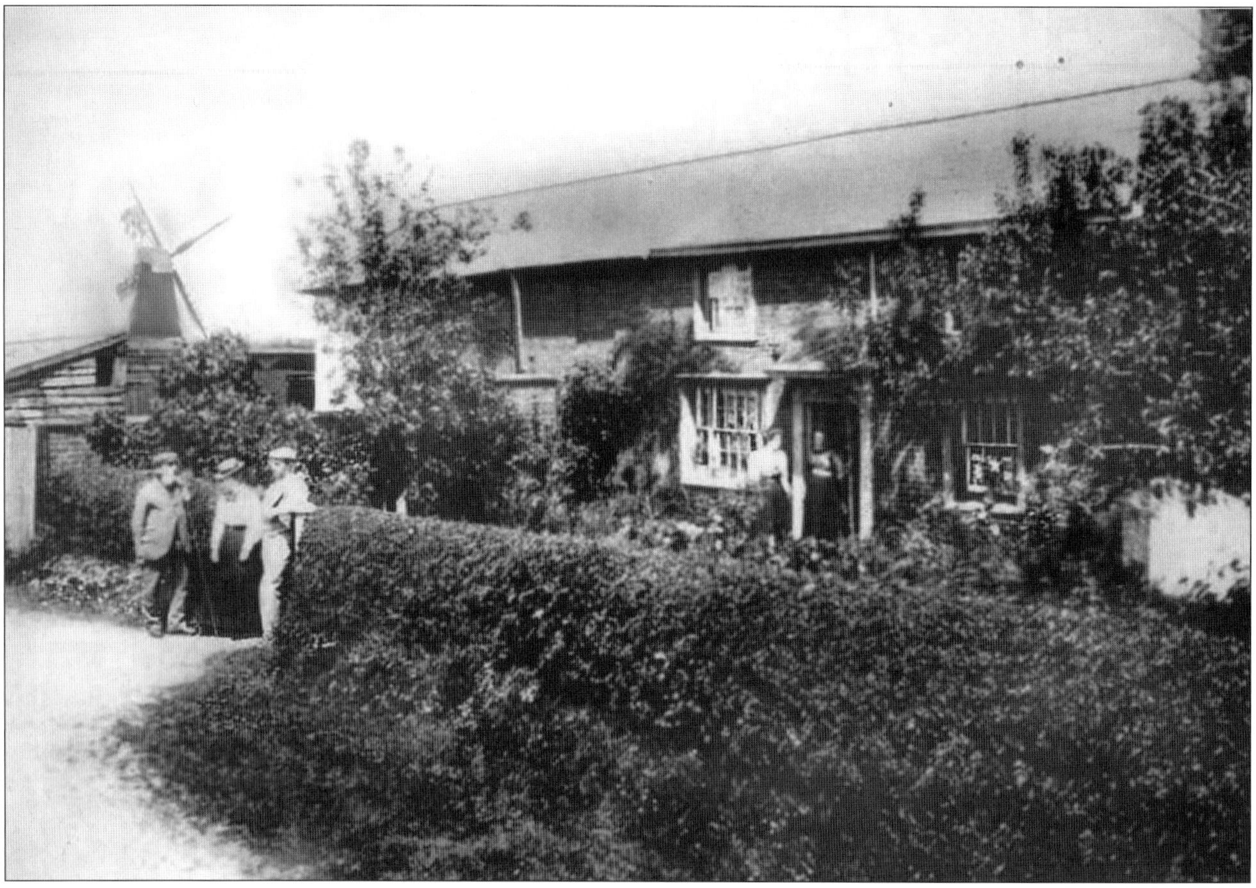

Richard Hylton's house and mill on Silver Green

updated description of copyhold property. Unfortunately, although three plans were made, none is known to have survived.

New buildings were constructed against the new roads. The Horseshoes was built at the new crossroads in the middle of the former Great Green. A smock mill was constructed nearby, adjoining the first public road, but its cap and four sails were blown off in a tremendous gale shortly after its erection.[28] In 1826 this windmill, a tenement, a dwelling-house, a baking office, a stable and an engine for grinding corn were sold and Richard Hylton, a man who contributed enormously to the history of the village through his meticulous note-taking of people and events, became the tenant.[29]

There were 1,014 people resident in 1821, inhabiting 224 houses, the majority employed in agriculture. It was noted that in Fritton, an adjoining parish, the younger people were employed at bombazine looms; 'but in Hempnall the effects of industry were thought to be injurious'.[30]

Between Hempnall and Saxlingham was a field called 'Camps', a name possibly derived from the Latin, 'campus', meaning field, which may be a reflection of its previous use as part of the North Field. However, it is just as likely to be a 'camping' ground. Camping was an ancient form of football, with few rules. A day of rural sports took place on Whit Monday 1820 with the usual foot races and

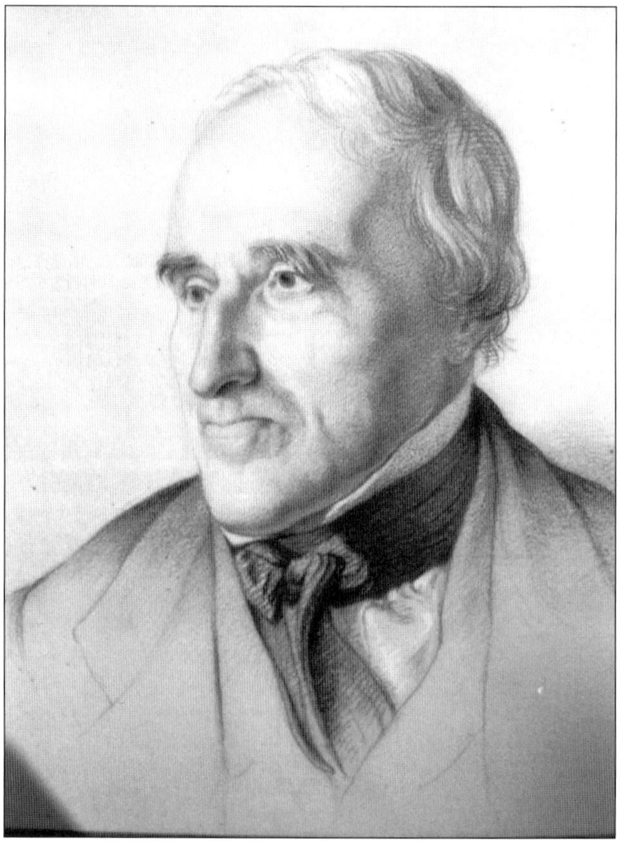

Richard Hylton, miller and collector of Hempnall memorabilia.

jumping in sacks, followed by a 'well-contested camping match'. The following day the 'Friendly Societies dined at their respective club rooms and paraded the village with bands of music and flags…'[31]

The winter fair at Hempnall was still continuing, although in 1821:

> *There was a good show of stock; but little business was done. Several persons had their pockets picked in a most dexterous manner; one poor man had the misfortune to have his purse taken out of his pocket with £14 in money.*[32]

The fair on 13 December 1824 was far more successful, an encouragement to those farmers who had taken the opportunity to expand at the Inclosure. In the *Norwich Mercury* it was reported that there was the:

> *... largest show of stock ever seen at that place, particularly of agricultural horses and ponies for which high prices were obtained. This and the unusual fineness of the day gave much spirit and gaiety to the fair, and more business was done than any former occasion.*

References

[1] Church bible, 23 January 1800
[2] *NC* Saturday, 11 August 1804
[3] *NC* Saturday, 9 August 1800
[4] *NC* Saturday, 12 June 1802
[5] *NC* Saturday, 6 May 1809
[6] *NC* Saturday, 21 October 1809
[7] *NC* Saturday, 12 September 1812
[8] Thomas Peck (1802) *The Norwich Directory* (Norwich)
[9] *NM* Saturday, 8 November 1800
[10] *NM* Saturday, 18 February 1815
[11] Richard Hylton notes
[12] *NC* Saturday, 4 April 1814
[13] *NM* Saturday, 18 February 1815
[14] *NM* Saturday, 13 March 1819
[15] *NM* Saturday, 17 August 1816
[16] NRO PD 602/4 Aylsham Registers Baptism of Ann, daughter of Elizabeth Smith of Hempnall, 26 January 1817
[17] *NC* Saturday, 14 March 1812
[18] *NM* Saturday, 29 January 1820
[19] *NC* Saturday, 9 August 1823
[20] Abstract of the deeds of the Queen's Head from 1743. First called the Horse Shoes in 1761. *NC* Saturday, 11 October 1806
[21] *NC* Saturday, 5 January 1805
[22] *NC* Saturday, 24 April 1819
[23] *NC* Saturday, 8 February 1806
[24] *NC* Saturday, 28 December 1805
[25] *NC* Saturday, 1 December 1810
[26] *NM* Saturday, 23 July 1814
[27] *NM* Saturday, 27 September 1817
[28] Norwich, Yarmouth and Lynn Courier. Saturday, 14 March 1818
[29] Indenture 13 November 1826
[30] 1821 Census Returns
[31] *NC* Saturday, 27 May 1820
[32] *NC* 22 December 1821
[33] *NM* Saturday 18 December1824

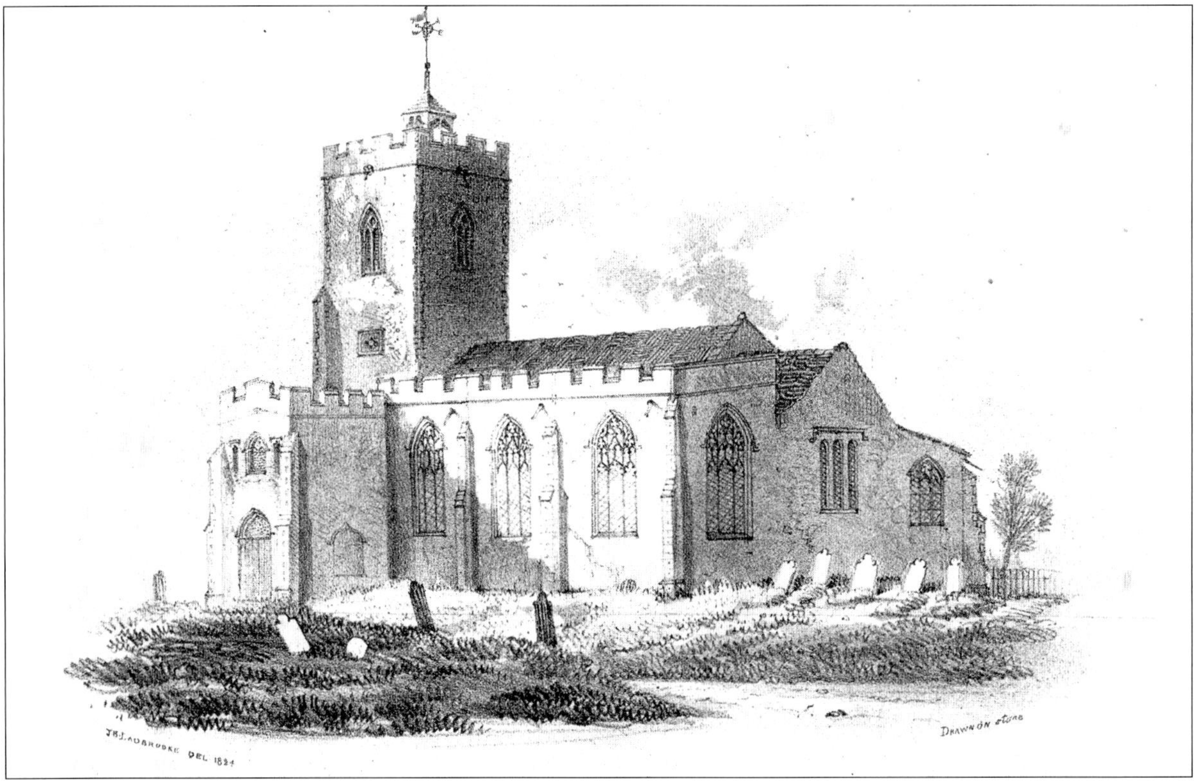

St Margaret's Church by J.B. Ladbrooke, 1824.

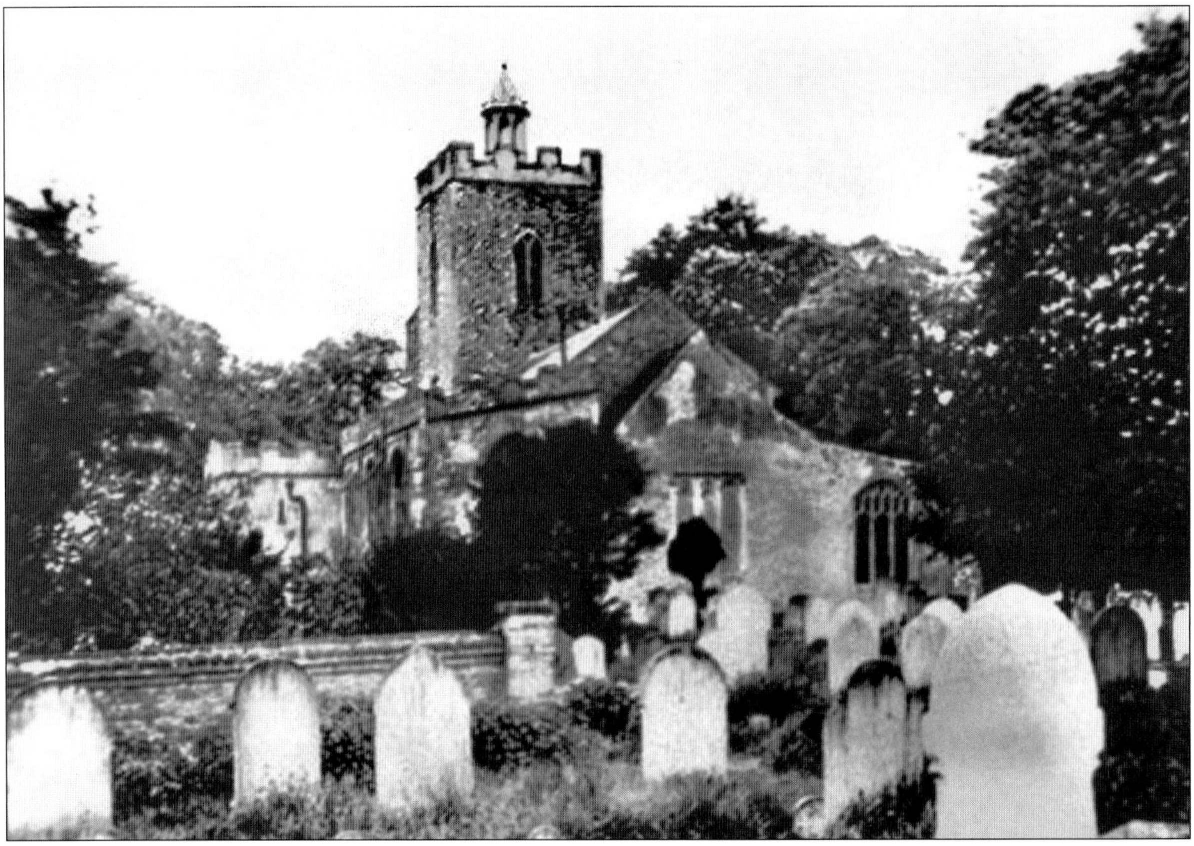

The church with a blocked east window in Tudor style

✦ CHAPTER 11 ✦

A Bridge in Time 1825–49

A noted missionary, Anna Martin was born at Hempnall in 1827. Her father, William Martin, a merchant by trade, rented a house opposite the church in 1826 and 1827.[1] Anna's mother died when she was five, and at 12 years of age she went to live at Lowestoft with her grandfather and an aunt. She married the Revd David Hinderer in 1852 and they were missionaries in Yoruba, West Africa, for 17 years. Eventually her health deteriorated and they returned to Norfolk, but she died in 1870. Her memoirs, published in 1872, were widely read.[2]

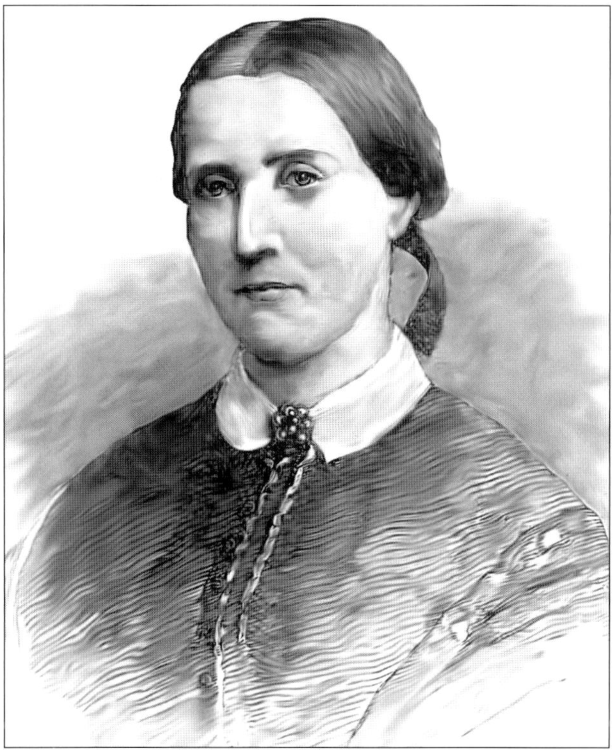

Anna Martin, missionary, born at Hempnall in 1827.

The artist J.B. Ladbrooke sketched St Margaret's Church in 1824 before the Victorian restoration. The east window, of Tudor design, records the rebuilding of the chancel after the fire of about 1600. The fence in the background marked the graveyard boundary before it was replaced by a wall in 1827.[3] John Thruston Mott, the lord of the manor, owned the house beyond the fence and rented it to the vicar, the Revd Robert Rolfe.

On a November day in 1829 a crowd gathered at the church to lay a carpet of flowers from the vicar's residence to the church porch to welcome Frances Rolfe on her wedding day. After the ceremony, several hundred villagers were entertained by a band on the vicar's lawn and: 'bountifully regaled with plum cakes and ale, racing, jumping in sacks and other rural sports, much enhanced by the beauty of the weather.'[4]

The Rolfes were not to reside in Hempnall for much longer. As was often then the case, clergymen were not incumbents of just one parish, and the Revd Robert Rolfe was rector of Cockley Cley and Thurgarton and also vicar of Yaxley, in Suffolk. By 1838 he was living in St Stephen's parish in Norwich. His departure thence may be attributed to a number of factors, but mainly, I suspect, to the convenience of living in a city, detached from parochial responsibilities at a time of economic decline, accompanied by increased poverty and crime.

A 'desperate gang of thieves', according to the local papers, had plagued the neighbourhood of Hempnall for some time. In February 1830 three of its members were discovered at the Lamb Inn at Norwich, quarrelling over the division of money for some stolen fowls. One of them attempted to sell a silver spoon to a member of the Norwich 'patrol', who, suspecting it was stolen, took the men into custody. They were committed to the castle for trial and the neighbourhood was rid of a gang that had 'been a terror to them for some time'. The three culprits, William Garrod, John Culling and James Melton, were found guilty of larceny and sentenced to seven years' transportation.[5]

As well as paying rent, farmers also had to pay tithes, a compulsory payment of one-tenth of the yearly produce of land or stock to the incumbent of the parish. When times were bad, tithes were distinctly unpopular, not only with farmers, but with those relying on them for employment. It was the time of the Swing Riots, when protesters burned hayricks and destroyed threshing machines in order to influence farmers to stop paying their tithes. In 1830 a threatening crowd gathered in Hempnall to protest.[6] The problem was alleviated for a short time by the Tithe Commutation Act of 1836, which stipulated that the payment of tithes in kind be converted into an annual rent.

Unemployment was high, particularly amongst weavers, and the Norwich weavers could be quite aggressive. One evening Mr Read, the Hempnall carrier, was returning from Norwich when a party of weavers stopped him near Lakenham Cock and a large quantity of yarn was taken from his cart.[7] In the villages there was little anyone could do, and many became paupers.

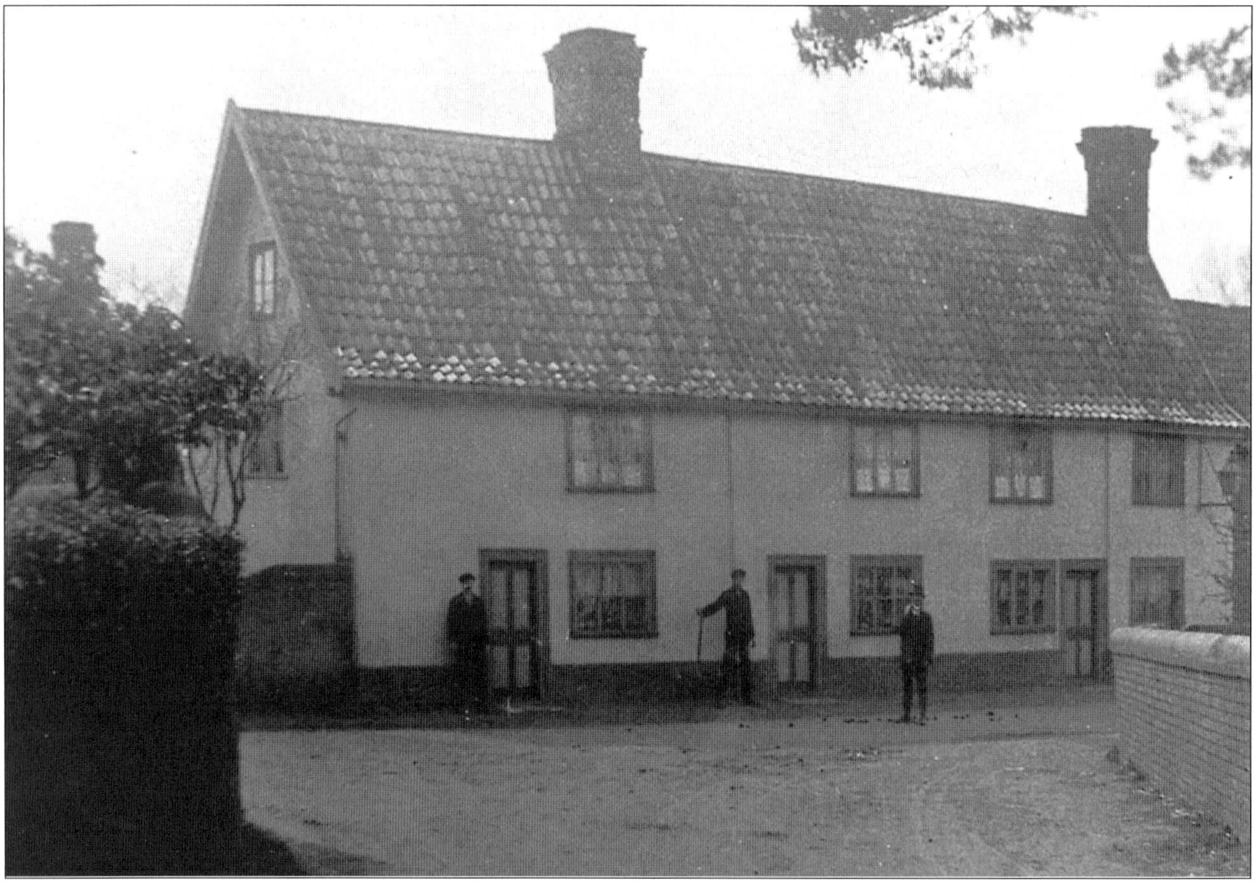

Forge Cottage opposite the school, occupied by John Elsey in the nineteenth century. Earliest known record 1642 (copyhold description: the house where William Moore formerly dwelt).

Until 1836 Hempnall had its own workhouse at Lundy Green and several poor houses. Under the Poor Law Act of 1834 the 22 parishes of Depwade hundred were united for the joint provision for their poor. The union workhouse was completed at Pulham St Mary by 1837. In 1838, 59 paupers from Hempnall were given support, enabling them to stay in their own homes; for example, Mary Grint was given 1s.9d. a week and Elizabeth Knights, a widow with four children, received 2s. and one stone of flour a week. It is possible that the Pulham workhouse was full, for several children were ordered to that at Diss, while 17 Hempnall paupers had moved to adjoining villages and 16 were living in Norwich.[8]

The population had swelled to 1,225 by 1831. More than 200 extra people in ten years had obviously led to more overcrowding and competition for jobs. Even those who had previously prospered were beginning to experience financial difficulties. The court books for the manor of Hempnall show a marked rise in the number of mortgages in the 1830s. John Gaze, tanner, John Elsey, carpenter, James Carver the younger and Mr Spurgeon, millers, and William Keeler Merrison, the clock maker, all went bankrupt.[9] William Hobart suffered declining business. Others emigrated in hope of a better life, William Pitts to America and Henry Thirkettle to Canada. Hempnall Cannon's manor court book records the names of those who had not paid quit rent. John Elsey had not paid a penny in 11 years and the steward noted: 'Elsey is a troublesome fellow, numerous approaches have been made.'

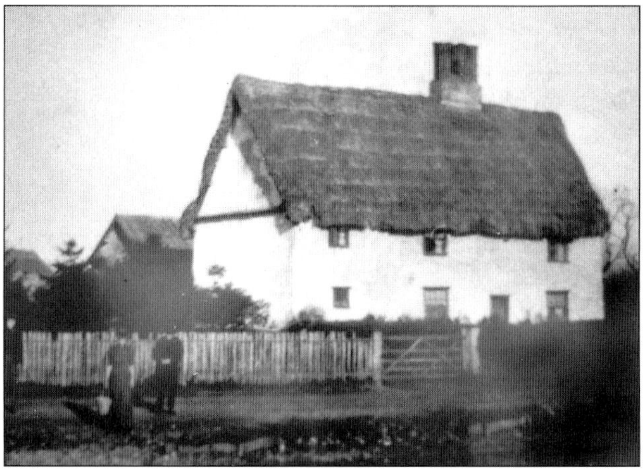

Cottage at Lundy Green, by Hugmore Pond occupied by John Page and Henry and William Sporle in 1837.

Drunken behaviour was frequently a problem. John Page and Henry and William Sporle, who shared a house at Lundy Green, stole 48 bottles of porter from a porter merchant at Hardwick one evening and drank a dozen of them that night.[10] The names of Henry Howlet, aged 24, and John Roberts

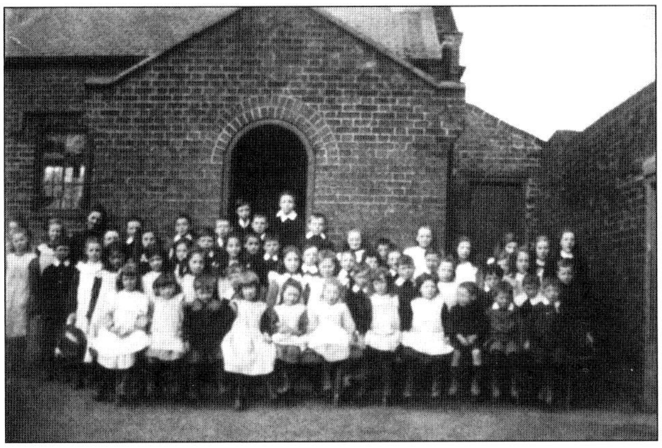

The Primitive Methodist Chapel, Silver Green.

were recorded in the Norwich Police charge book for being drunk and disorderly.[11]

There were a few who had called themselves Methodists since the day John Wesley preached under the oak at Cole's Green. Perhaps appalled by the effects of drink, they began to organise themselves. The Primitive Methodists built a chapel against the new road on Silver Green in 1837, and the Wesleyan Methodists built their chapel in Mill Road in 1839.[12]

Although the Methodists doubtless worked hard to discourage alcohol consumption, the inns and beer houses were still doing a roaring trade. In December 1837, John and Elizabeth Aldis were in the Queen's Head with their friend Charles Mortimer from Sprowston. By midnight they were drunk and John Aldis had begun flirting with Caroline Stone, who was with Esau Wade and Sam Carver. When Aldis tried to persuade Caroline to go home with him, Wade lost his temper and a fight ensued. At about half past midnight, they left the Queen's Head. Wade hit Aldis, who ran off, whereupon the attackers turned their attention to Mortimer, who was hit about the head. Mortimer, realising that Wade and Carver were heading for Aldis's house, climbed over the fence and went in the back door to warn him. Elizabeth Aldis was washing the blood off her husband's face when Wade and Carver burst in. After much taunting they made off with a purse containing a sovereign, two half-crowns and 5s. Entering the Woodman at about one o'clock in the morning, they encountered John Elsey and William Roberts, the landlord. Elsey and Roberts later testified at the assizes that Sam Carver and Esau Wade had been seen at the Woodman with a blood-stained 'wooden top'. They were sentenced to death.[13]

In 1838, on the occasion of Queen Victoria's coronation, the parish officials decided that no celebrations would be provided for the poor since this might lead to riot and disorder. Joseph Cator Webb, however, decided to give an excellent dinner to all his labourers and their wives and children. Over 100 enjoyed 15 stones of beef, 30 large plum puddings, two barrels of good old ale and the same quantity of cider, and the party kept it up for nearly two days.[14]

It fell to the Revd James Wenn, the curate, paid a salary of £150 a year, to support the parishioners and encourage moral behaviour. Sunday services took place at 11 in the morning and three in the afternoon. Most people attended the services respectfully, though a few individuals frequented inns and beer houses instead. Sunday-school children were taught the catechism every Sunday, and each child was heard to read twice. Each paid a penny once a fortnight and this money was doubled, according to the 1838 visitation, and used to buy clothes, which were distributed at Christmas.[15]

Charles Daines, a carpenter who lived with his wife, Hannah, and children on Field Lane, had 'formed an improper acquaintance' with widow Ann Lloyd from Tasburgh. One Monday morning, in March 1839, he left his home, having filled the kettle with water from the stream near the house and set it on the fire. After breakfast his wife and two of the children were violently sick. Elizabeth Mills, Mary Alexander and Sarah Rackham, neighbours, came to assist. Unfortunately, Elizabeth Mills drank some tea that was on the table and soon became very ill. Daines, who was working on a carpentry job at Mr Thirkettle's shop with his eldest son, was sent for. On his return he was seen to take the kettle off the fire, saying at the same time, 'Surely there is nothing in the water?' He then took it away, rinsed it in the stream near their house and filled it again, saying he thought they might need some warm water. A little later he returned to the shop and asked Elizabeth Thirkettle for castor oil for violent sickness. She told him to send for Mr Utting, the surgeon, and then demanded, 'Daines, have you laid any poison about the house for mice or anything?' Daines muttered something about fig powder that he had bought at Long Stratton, adding, 'And if it was poison the mice must have scraped it into the kettle.' The youngest

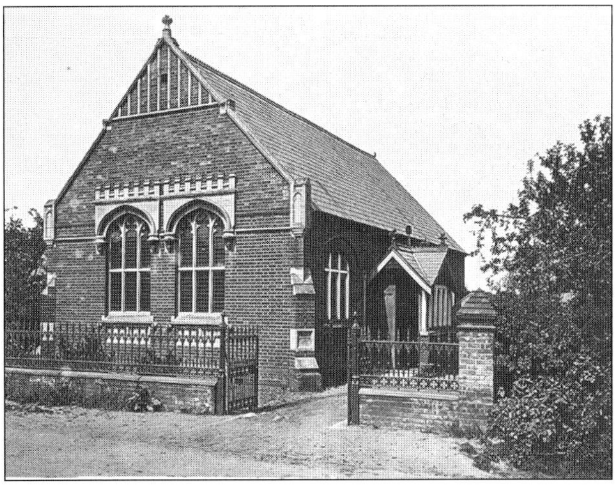

The Wesleyan Chapel in Mill Road, before the Sunday school was built.

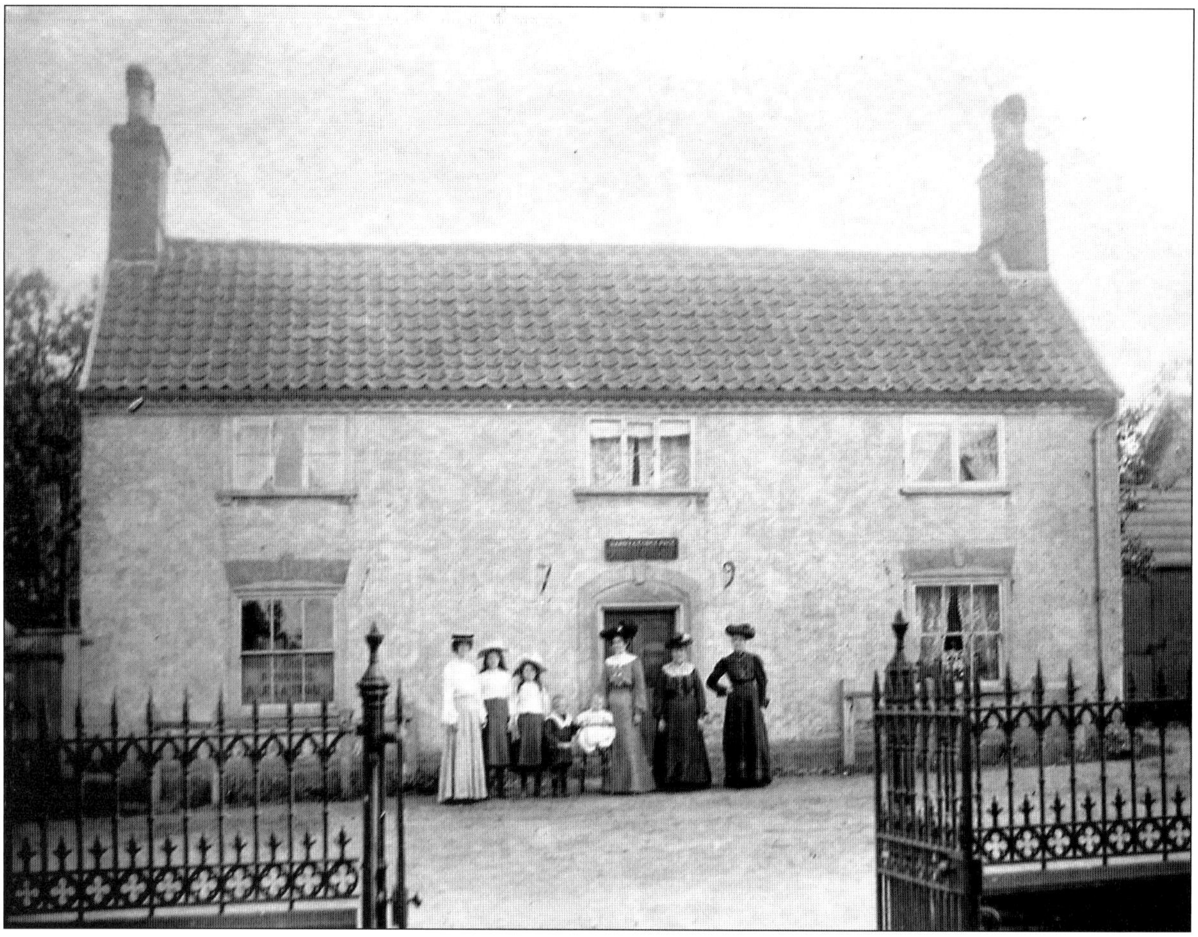

The Woodman as seen from the chapel gates.

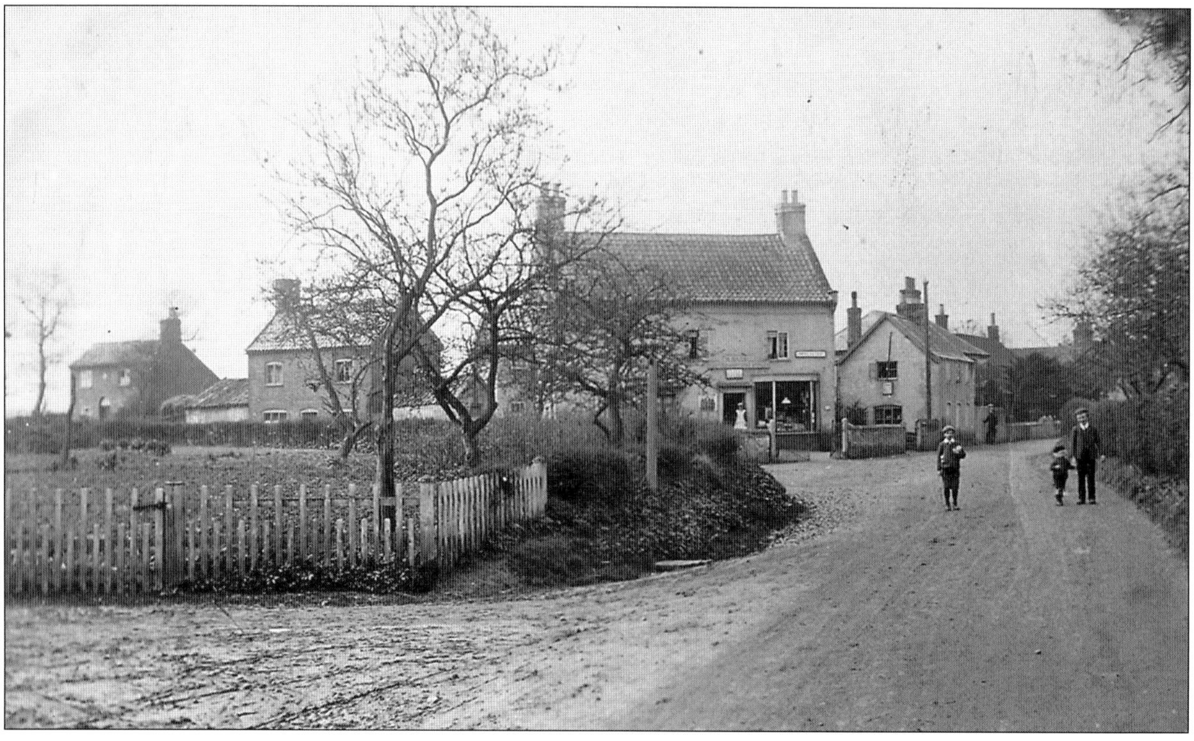

Mill Road with the houses on Field Lane on the left.

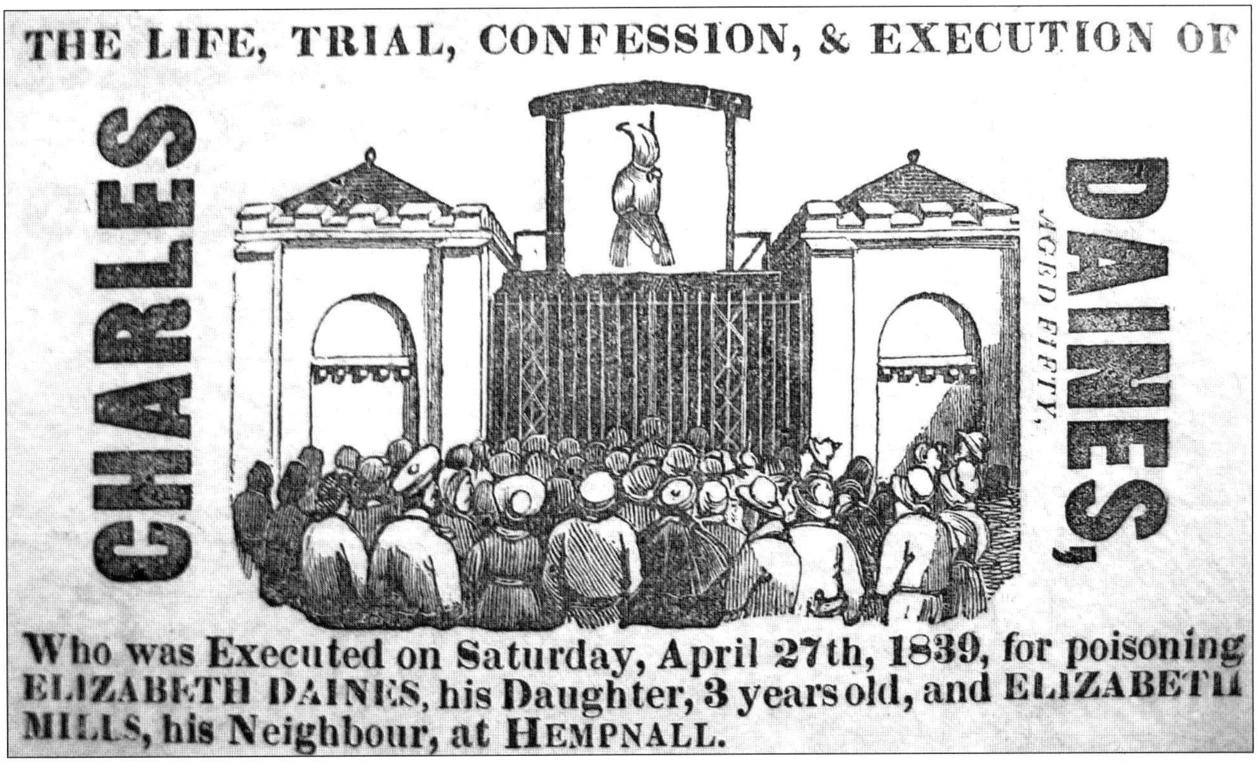
THE LIFE, TRIAL, CONFESSION, & EXECUTION OF
CHARLES DAINES,
AGED FIFTY,
Who was Executed on Saturday, April 27th, 1839, for poisoning ELIZABETH DAINES, his Daughter, 3 years old, and ELIZABETH MILLS, his Neighbour, at HEMPNALL.

Broadside 30129037775914. (NORFOLK COUNTY COUNCIL LIBRARY AND INFORMATION SERVICE.)

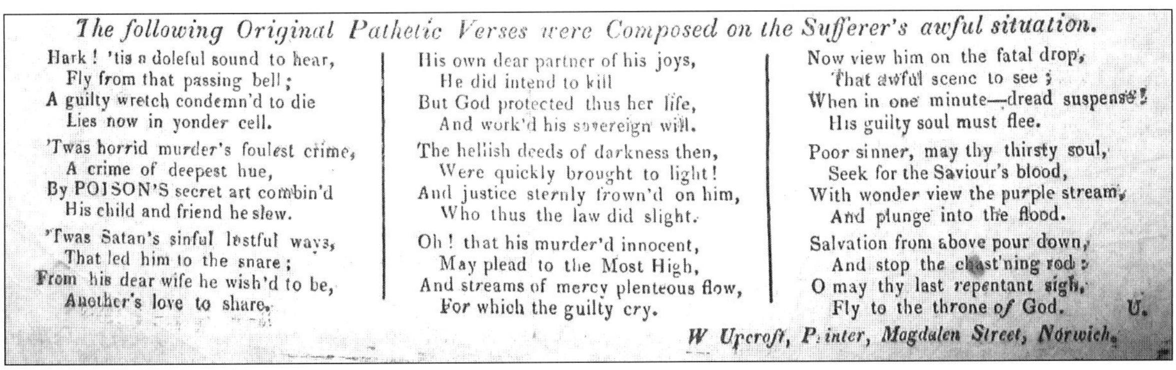
The following Original Pathetic Verses were Composed on the Sufferer's awful situation.

Hark ! 'tis a doleful sound to hear,
Fly from that passing bell ;
A guilty wretch condemn'd to die
Lies now in yonder cell.

'Twas horrid murder's foulest crime,
A crime of deepest hue,
By POISON'S secret art combin'd
His child and friend he slew.

'Twas Satan's sinful lustful ways,
That led him to the snare ;
From his dear wife he wish'd to be,
Another's love to share.

His own dear partner of his joys,
He did intend to kill
But God protected thus her life,
And work'd his sovereign will.

The hellish deeds of darkness then,
Were quickly brought to light !
And justice sternly frown'd on him,
Who thus the law did slight.

Oh ! that his murder'd innocent,
May plead to the Most High,
And streams of mercy plenteous flow,
For which the guilty cry.

Now view him on the fatal drop,
That awful scene to see ;
When in one minute—dread suspense !
His guilty soul must flee.

Poor sinner, may thy thirsty soul,
Seek for the Saviour's blood,
With wonder view the purple stream,
And plunge into the flood.

Salvation from above pour down,
And stop the chast'ning rod :
O may thy last repentant sigh,
Fly to the throne of God. U.

W Upcroft, Printer, Magdalen Street, Norwich.

Verses composed at the time of the trial of Charles Daines. (NORFOLK COUNTY COUNCIL LIBRARY AND INFORMATION SERVICE)

child died that morning and Elizabeth Mills was dead by the afternoon.[16] Daines was found guilty of murder and sentenced to death. He later confessed to the chaplain of the prison that he had made an attempt on his wife's life on two other occasions, once by putting arsenic on some fried potatoes and once by putting it in some pea soup.

The execution of Charles Daines attracted a huge crowd on Norwich Castle ditches, most of the spectators being women and children:

On the hill, levity and one might almost say, hilarity prevailed. The coarsest jokes and shouts of laughter were only broken by the cry of orange, nuts and ginger bread cakes, which were kept up to the moment of the fall of the drop. For one instance there was a hush, but then the din directly commenced...[17]

The Revd Samuel Hobson, from Kirstead, noted for his sermons, was invited to preach at Hempnall on the Sunday after the execution of Charles Daines. The title of his sermon was: 'Be sure your sins will find you out'. It was a lengthy homily, with no words minced over the sins of the murderer. After lecturing on the vices of Daines and the sins of men in general, he focused on the part played by Ann Lloyd:

Had this woman, as every virtuous female undoubtedly would have done, rejected his addresses with indignation and abhorrence, he might have checked the rising evil. By even listening to men's filthy conversation, a lady will soon lose her modesty and be led into the paths of vice and degradation.[18]

A very chastened crowd must have made their way home that day.

Two very important documents were compiled in the 1840s. The first was the Census Return for 1841,

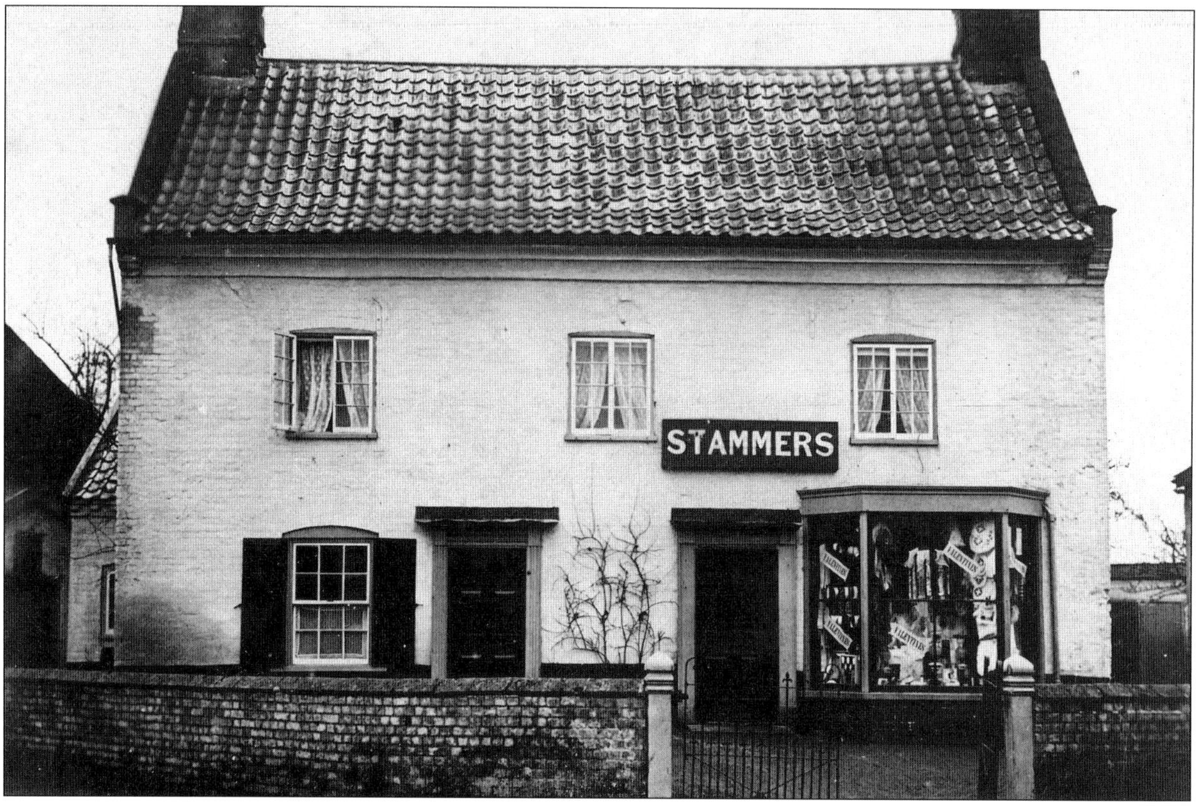

The shop occupied by the Stammers family, c.1880. Marked on the map of 1767. (NORFOLK COUNTY COUNCIL LIBRARY AND INFORMATION SERVICE)

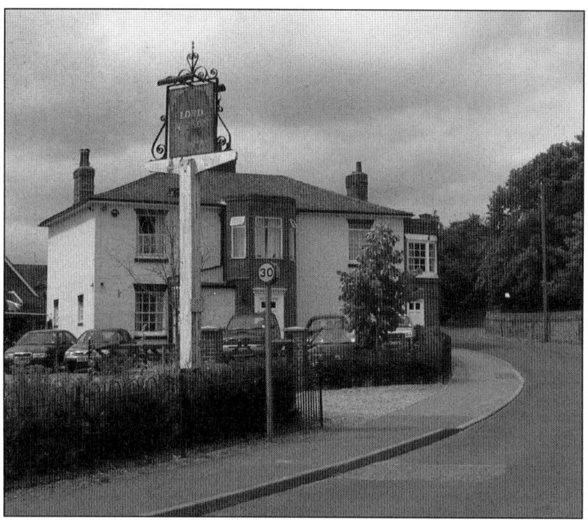

The Lord Nelson.

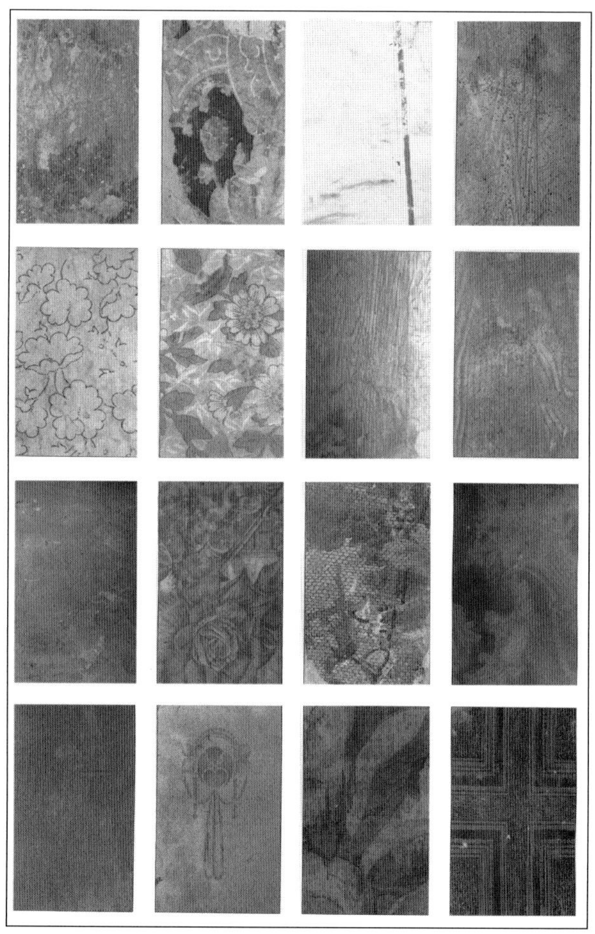

Right: *Examples of wallpaper from Connaught House, next to the Stammers's shop, earliest c.1840, latest 1938.*

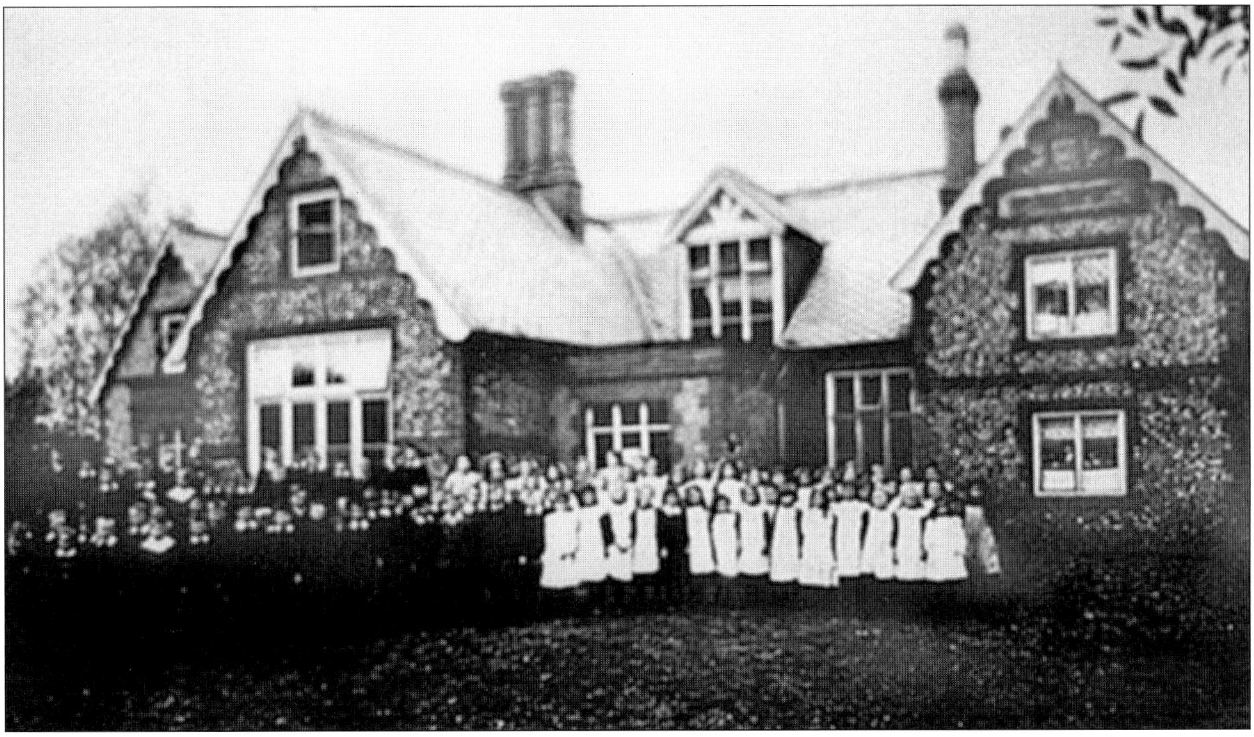

Hempnall School, c.1900.

which, unlike previous censuses, listed individuals together with their ages and occupations.[19] The second was the Tithe Redemption Award for Hempnall, made in 1842, which substituted an annual sum of money for payment of tithe in kind. The total sum for the parish was determined, apportioned among the properties in it and recorded in the Award with names of owners and occupiers, acreage and land use. The numbers given to each piece of land were shown on the map accompanying the Award. However, it is not easy to marry the Tithe and the census, since the census enumerators did not take a regular route and some houses were sub-let. For example, the Revd Robert Rolfe rented a house, as a vicarage, from John Thruston Mott, the lord of the manors of Hempnall, and his name appears on the Tithe Award as occupier. According to the census, however, the Revd Robert Rose Rolfe, his son, who had replaced Wenn as curate, was the occupant.

In 1841 there were 1,258 people living in the parish, occupying 273 houses with four houses standing empty. Adults living in the core of the village were employed in 33 different occupations.

The church, beer houses and shops probably constituted the focus of entertainment. The Bull Inn had ceased trading but was bought in 1844 by Roger Roberts, the woodman. The old part was demolished and a new building built on an existing extension. It opened with the name of the Red House, its sign showing the devil forking the vicar into a fire.[20] It was later renamed the Lord Nelson. The publicans, William and James Roberts, owners of the Woodman, were fined in 1846 for allowing beer to be consumed on Sundays. At the same court Charles Elvin was fined for threatening the police constable of the parish.[21]

William Stammers, the first of my ancestors to arrive in the village, took a shop opposite the Queen's Head in competition with Elvin Smith, whose shop was across the road in Field Lane. Elizabeth Barham's shop was opposite the church. Although she was called a grocer in the census, it is clear from the sale of her stock in 1842 that she was running a tallow-chandling business and vending a variety of items, including drapery, boots, shoes, bonnets, clogs, pattens, earthenware, glass and nails.[22] Phoebe Freston, grocer, and her husband, a shoemaker, lived in part of the Longhouse. Mary Laskey, also married to a shoemaker, had a shop in the Street. Elizabeth Thirkettle and her husband owned a general shop, part of the premises being a bakehouse. There had been a shop on this site since 1580, and the bakehouse dates from at least 1637. When my parents lived in the house, 19 layers of wallpaper were discovered pasted at the back of a cupboard, the oldest hand-printed in about 1840.

In the twenty-first century, only Mrs Thirkettle's shop remains, serving the whole of the parish; but in 1841 there were almost as many traders on the Greens as in the Street. In 1841 there were 351 children aged ten or younger. A few would have received a basic education at one of the two day-schools or attended the Sunday school. The majority would have been illiterate. By 1840 the need for a school was pressing. John Thomas Mott, then lord of the manors of Hempnall, gave part of a gravel pit for the use of the vicar and churchwardens as a school for: 'the education of children only of the labouring

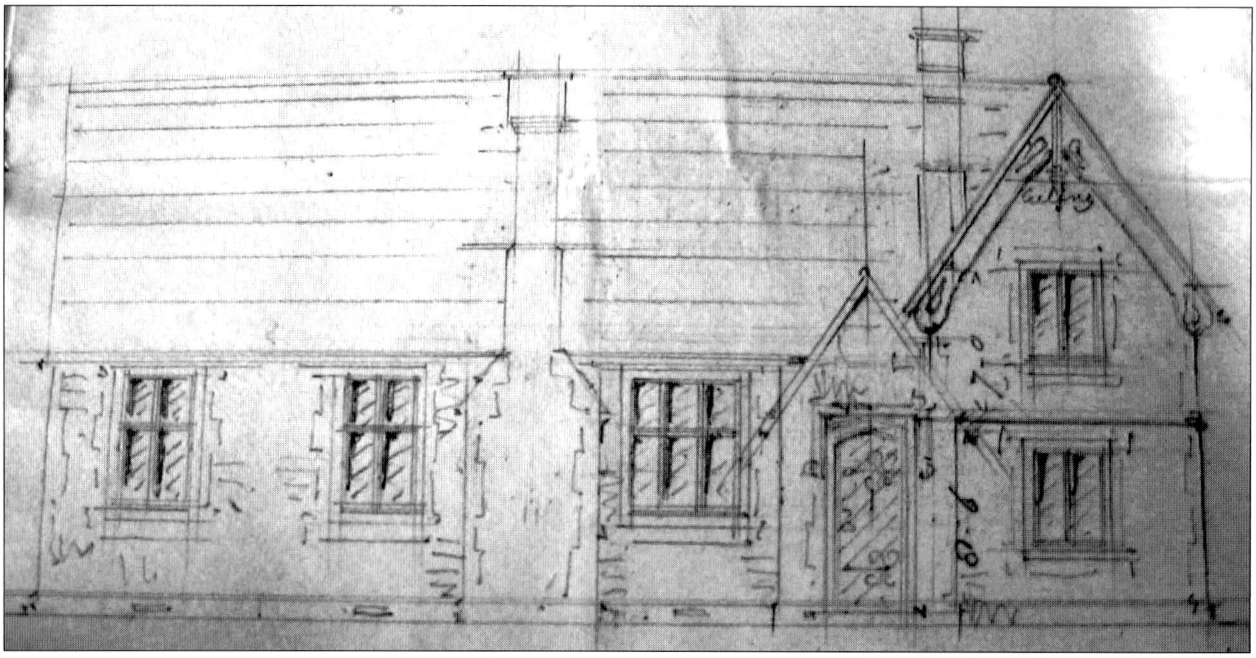

Proposal for the new school. (NORFOLK RECORD OFFICE P/BG/55/2 1847)

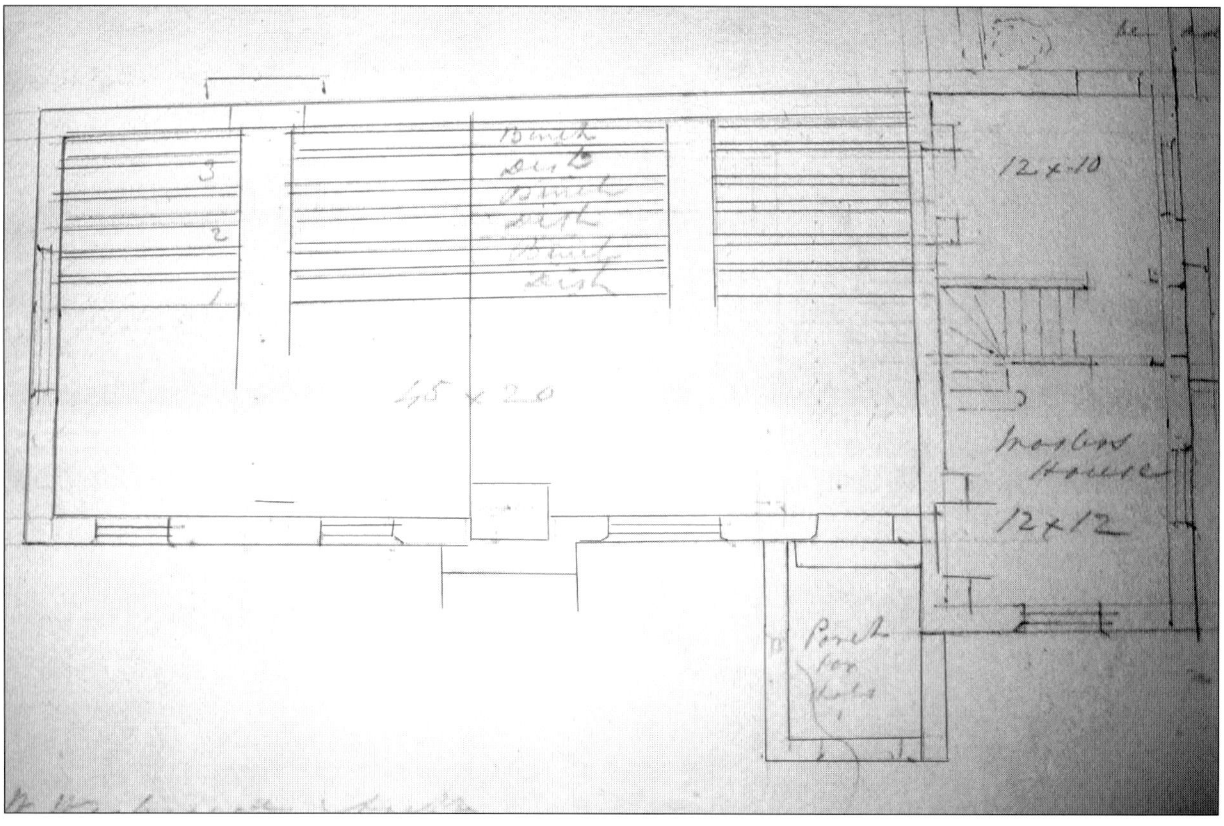

Plan of the the school, 1848. (NORFOLK RECORD OFFICE P/BG/55/1-2)

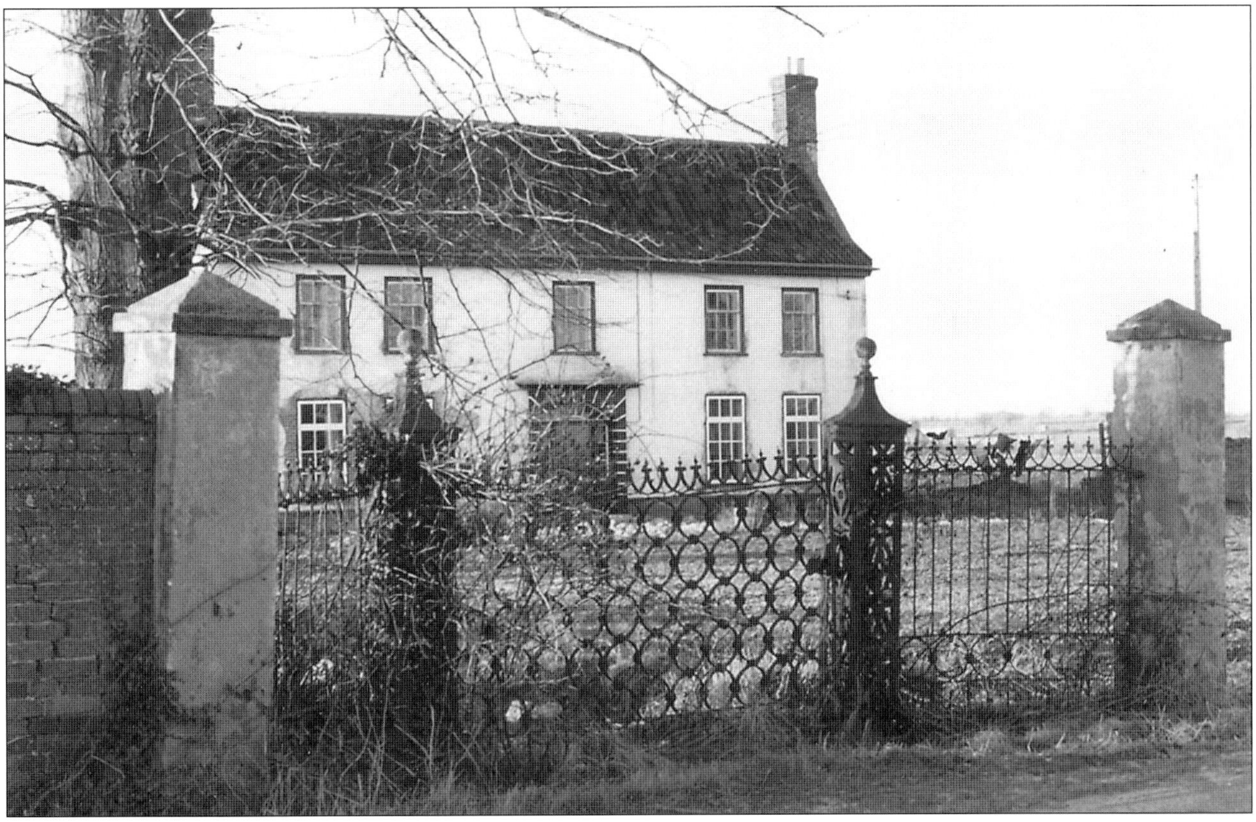

Villa Farm, 1985. Earliest record 1644 (copyhold description: Chattens).

manufacturing and other poorer classes in the parish of Hempnall… and as a residence for the teacher or teachers.' The vicar or curate was to have the 'superintendance of the moral and religious instruction of the scholars'. Eventually built as a public elementary school and completed in 1847 at a cost of £478.3s.4d., it was intended to accommodate 100 children. A sketch of the interior shows the master's house and one room for the children, taken up with rows of fixed benches.[23] Perhaps George Pitcher was one of the first pupils. Ten years old, he was regularly beaten by his parents. When his mother beat him for playing in some water it was the last straw, and he drowned himself in a nearby pond.[24]

The census record for the Greens begins with Joseph Cator Webb, a farmer aged 44. His son of the same name was aged 18. Joseph the elder died unexpectedly and the young Joseph Cator Webb inherited all at the tender age of 19. Clearly a sociable character, he chaired a meeting in 1848 at the Lord Nelson. A numerous and highly respectable party of gentlemen sat down to an excellent and substantial dinner to mark the respect with which Roger Roberts, the landlord, was regarded by his numerous friends. 'The company separated at a late hour, highly pleased at the cheerful evening.'[25] By 1849 he had married and was living at Villa Farm, employing several servants. He enjoyed an extravagant lifestyle, having accounts with numerous traders. He enjoyed cigars, brandy, horses, expensive clothes and travel-

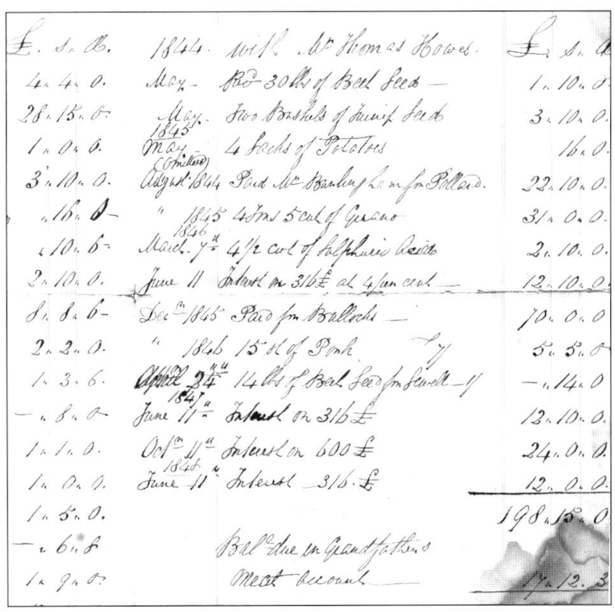

£. s. d.	1844. with Mr Thomas Howes.	£. s. d.
4. 4. 0.	May – Bo 30lbs of Beet Seed –	1. 10. 0.
28. 15. 6.	May. Two Bushels of Turnip Seed	3. 10. 0.
1. 0. 0.	1845 May 4 Sacks of Potatoes	16. 0.
3. 10. 0.	(Omitted) August 1844 Paid Mr Bowling [illegible] from Pollard.	22. 10. 0.
. 16. 0 –	" 1845 4 Tons 5 cwt of Guano	31. 0. 0.
. 10. 6.	1846 March 7th 4½ cwt of Sulphuric Acid	2. 10. 0.
2. 10. 0.	June 11 Interest on 316£ at 4 per cent –	12. 10. 0.
8. 8. 6 –	Decr 1845 Paid for Bullocks –	70. 0. 0
2. 2. 0.	" 1846 15 st of Pork	5. 5. 0
1. 3. 6.	April 24th 14 lbs of Beet Seed from Sewell	– . 14. 0
– . 8. 0	1847 June 11th Interest on 316£	12. 10. 0.
1. 1. 0.	Octr 11th Interest on 600£	24. 0. 0.
1. 0. 0.	1848 June 11th Interest 316 £	12. 0. 0.
1. 5. 0.		198. 15. 0
– . 6. 6	Bal due on Grandfather's	
1. 9. 0.	Meat Account –	17. 12. 3

Bill to Joseph Cator-Webb, 1844.

ling. Villa Farm was extended, remodelled and furnished in elegant style, the entrance hall being hung with paintings of hunting scenes. In the dining-room, which contained Kidderminster and Brussels carpets, the mahogany table, over six feet long, was surrounded by matching chairs with leather seats. The dinner service was blue and white oriental china. The contents of each room were listed in a catalogue in 1858 and every room gives the

133 Bee hive chair, covered in crimson and white damask
134 Mahogany framed sofa, with squab and two bolsters, stuffed in hair, and covered in crimson and white damask
135 A 6ft. mahogany sideboard, fitted with cellaret, three drawers and closets
136 Tea caddy
137 Draft board and men
138 Mahogany brass bound cellaret, on castors
139 Mahogany dining table, on turned legs and castors, *extreme length 9ft. 2in. by 4ft.*
140 Damask table cloth
141 Ditto
142 Barometer and thermometer, by "*Rossi*"
143 Pair of white tambour window curtains, and tassel holds
144 Pair of drab moreen window curtains
145 Pair of white tambour window curtains
146 Pair of drab moreen window curtains

BOOKS.

147 History of England, — vols.
148 Burns' Justice, 5 vols., and Supplement
149 The Lives of Eminent Englishmen, 4 vols.
150 Moore's Life of Byron, 3 vols.
151 Naval Chronicle, 5 vols.
152 Ditto, 5 vols.
153 Elements of Rigging, Seamanship, &c.
154 Pope's Works, 5 vols.
155 The Universal Songster
156 Theatrical Magazine and four other books
157 Guide to Paris and six other books
158 Various books
159 Ditto
160 Ditto
161 Ditto
162 Ditto
163 Journal of the Royal Agricultural Society of England

DRAWING ROOM.

LOT
164 A 3ft. 8in. cast-iron fender, with polished steel rail and standards
165 Set of fire irons
166 Pair of ottomans
167 Kidderminster carpet, 18ft. by 16ft.
168 A 5ft. 8in. hearth rug
169 Crumb cloth
170 Chimney glass, in gilt frame, plate 48in. by 42in.
171 Mahogany pole fire screen, with needlework slide
172 Wicker elbow chair
173 Six mahogany chairs, with turned legs, seats stuffed and covered in hair
174 Pair of elbow ditto
175 A 5ft. 6in. mahogany-framed couch, with squab and bolster stuffed and covered in hair
176 Mahogany card table, on turned legs and castors
177 Ditto
178 A 4ft. 3in. handsomely knotted oak loo table, on carved octagon pillar, triangular block, and castors
179 Green table cloth
180 "*Palmer's*" three-wick candle lamp
182 A 3ft. 8in. handsomely carved rosewood cheffioneer, with fretwork back, and fluted silk panel folding doors
183 Pair of white tambour window curtains and tassel holds
184 Pair of drab moreen ditto
185 Pair of white tambour window curtains
186 Pair of drab moreen ditto

STAIRCASE AND LANDING.

187 Fifteen brass rods
188 Two pieces of stair carpeting
189 Ditto

Sale of items belonging to Joesph Cator-Webb, 1858.

impression of affluence. Cleanliness was important, for in the main bedroom, beside the four-post bedstead was a double toilette set, a foot and hip bath and a mahogany corner washstand. Even the maid's room was made attractive with blue check furniture.[26]

In 1849 Maria Broughton, one of his servants, was accused of drowning her illegitimate child in the pond opposite the house. After a lengthy trial she was acquitted of murder but convicted of concealing a birth and committed to Wymondham Bridewell.[27]

Debts mounted and Webb became entangled with lawyers. Finally he was obliged to give up his residence and farm and move to Yarmouth, where he died shortly afterwards from a ruptured blood vessel, aged only 37. Richard Hylton wrote of him: 'He was gentlemanly in manners, affable, generous and open-hearted beyond his means, not without his faults, a kind neighbour and forgot not the poor.'[28]

References

[1] NRO Land Tax Returns

[2] Richard B. Hone (ed.) (1872) *Seventeen Years in Yoruba Country* (London)

[3] NRO Hempnall Glebe Terriers 2 June 1827

[4] *NM* Saturday, 14 November 1829

[5] *NM* 20 February 1830

[6] *NM* Saturday, 27 November 1830

[7] *NM* Saturday, 26 September 1829

[8] NRO C/aP 3/1 Records of Pulham Market Workhouse

[9] Clifford & Yvonne Bird (eds) (1996) *Norfolk and Norwich Clockmakers* (Chichester) James Merrison of Hempnall & Norwich, Clockmaker 1806–46, p.133

[10] *NM* Saturday, 2 July 1836

[11] NRO Norwich Police Charge Book 1836–38. Henry Howlett, 29 April 1837. John Roberts, 10 February 1838

[12] Janet Ede and Norma Virgo (eds) (1998) *Religious Worship in Norfolk. The 1851 Census of Accommodation and Attendance at Worship NRS* Vol. 62 (Cambridge) p.202. Primitive Methodist Chapel erected 1837; Wesleyan Methodist Chapel erected 1839

[13] *NM* Saturday, 8 April 1837

[14] *NC* 4 August 1838

[15] NRO VIS/65 Hempnall Visitation 1838

[16] *NM* Saturday, 16 March 1839; Saturday, 23 March; Saturday, 13 April; Saturday, 20 April

[17] *NC* Saturday, 4 May 1839

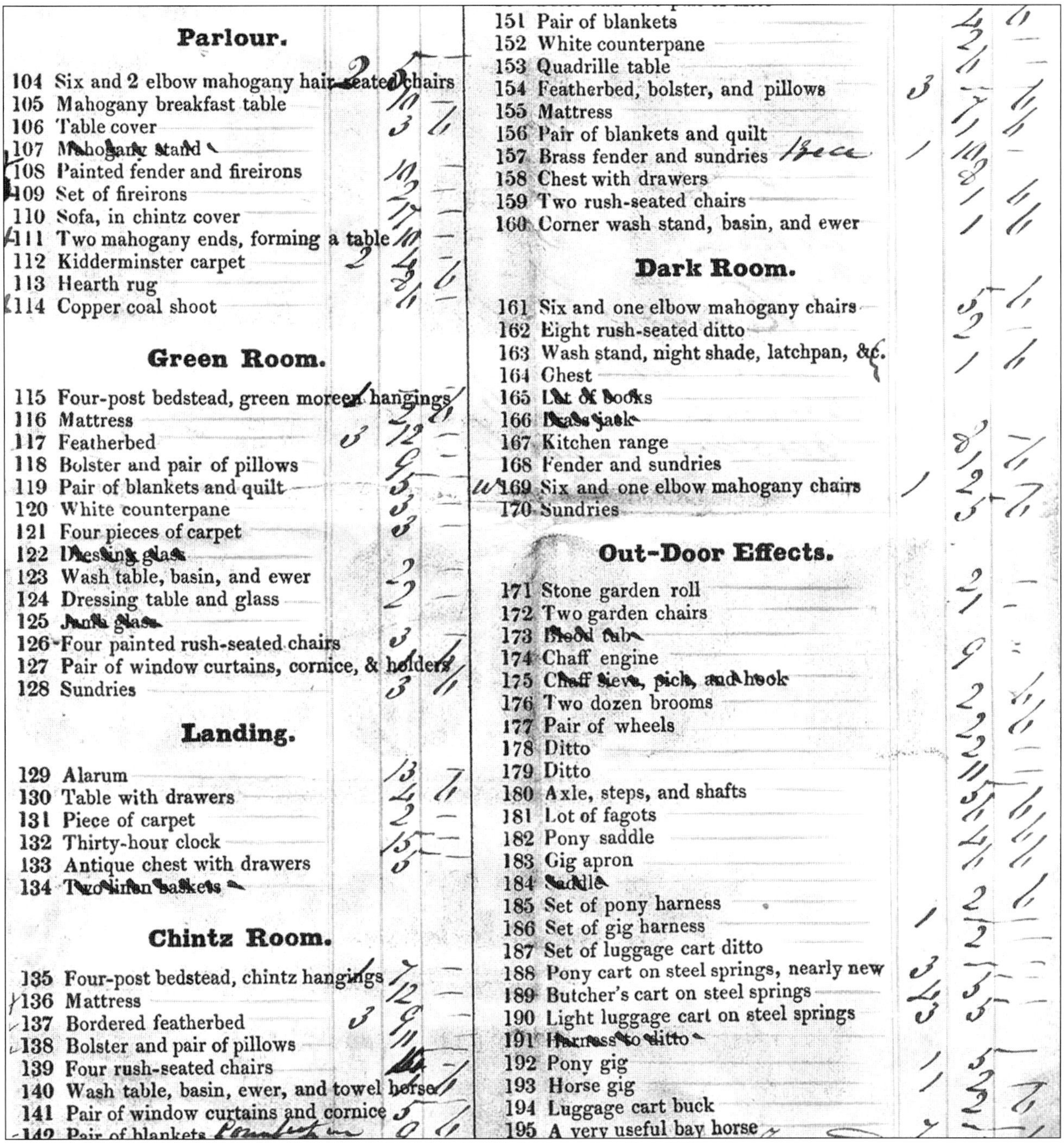

Parlour.

104 Six and 2 elbow mahogany hair-seated chairs
105 Mahogany breakfast table
106 Table cover
107 Mahogany stand
108 Painted fender and fireirons
109 Set of fireirons
110 Sofa, in chintz cover
111 Two mahogany ends, forming a table
112 Kidderminster carpet
113 Hearth rug
114 Copper coal shoot

Green Room.

115 Four-post bedstead, green moreen hangings
116 Mattress
117 Featherbed
118 Bolster and pair of pillows
119 Pair of blankets and quilt
120 White counterpane
121 Four pieces of carpet
122 Dressing glass
123 Wash table, basin, and ewer
124 Dressing table and glass
125 Jonta glass
126 Four painted rush-seated chairs
127 Pair of window curtains, cornice, & holders
128 Sundries

Landing.

129 Alarum
130 Table with drawers
131 Piece of carpet
132 Thirty-hour clock
133 Antique chest with drawers
134 Two linen baskets

Chintz Room.

135 Four-post bedstead, chintz hangings
136 Mattress
137 Bordered featherbed
138 Bolster and pair of pillows
139 Four rush-seated chairs
140 Wash table, basin, ewer, and towel horse
141 Pair of window curtains and cornice
142 Pair of blankets

151 Pair of blankets
152 White counterpane
153 Quadrille table
154 Featherbed, bolster, and pillows
155 Mattress
156 Pair of blankets and quilt
157 Brass fender and sundries
158 Chest with drawers
159 Two rush-seated chairs
160 Corner wash stand, basin, and ewer

Dark Room.

161 Six and one elbow mahogany chairs
162 Eight rush-seated ditto
163 Wash stand, night shade, latchpan, &c.
164 Chest
165 Lot of books
166 Brass jack
167 Kitchen range
168 Fender and sundries
169 Six and one elbow mahogany chairs
170 Sundries

Out-Door Effects.

171 Stone garden roll
172 Two garden chairs
173 Blood tub
174 Chaff engine
175 Chaff sieve, pick, and hook
176 Two dozen brooms
177 Pair of wheels
178 Ditto
179 Ditto
180 Axle, steps, and shafts
181 Lot of fagots
182 Pony saddle
183 Gig apron
184 Saddle
185 Set of pony harness
186 Set of gig harness
187 Set of luggage cart ditto
188 Pony cart on steel springs, nearly new
189 Butcher's cart on steel springs
190 Light luggage cart on steel springs
191 Harness to ditto
192 Pony gig
193 Horse gig
194 Luggage cart buck
195 A very useful bay horse

Valuation of items at Villa Farm, 1858.

[18] The Revd S. Hobson (1839) *Be Sure Your Sin Will Find You Out: Progress and Consequences of Sin Considered.* Printed sermon (Norwich)
[19] PRO HO 107/757/11 Census Returns 1841
[20] George Gerald Stammers (1986-89) *My Village* (Norwich) p.22
[21] *NC* Saturday, 29 August 1846
[22] *NC* Saturday, 17 September 1842
[23] NRO P/BG/55/2 Plans of Hempnall School
[24] *NC* Saturday, 4 August 1849
[25] *NM* Saturday, 2 December 1848
[26] A catalogue of household furniture, china and glass to be sold by auction on Tuesday, 19 October 1858, by Salter & Simpson
[27] *NM* Saturday 26 May 1849
[28] Richard Hylton, 2 August 1859 (Hempnall resident)

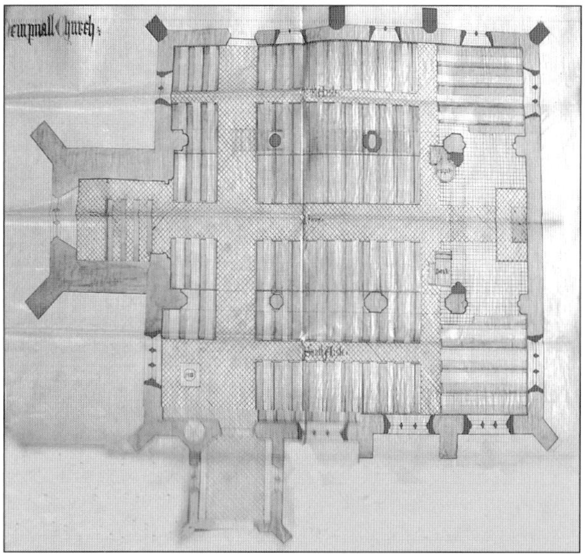

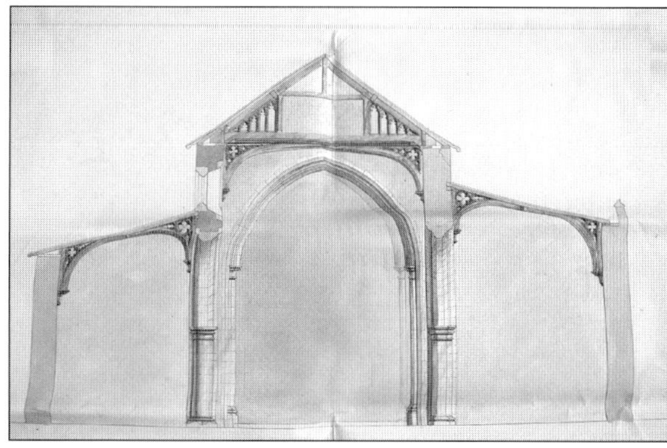

Above: *Church elevation 1857.*
(NRO FACULTY PAPERS DN/CON/138)

Left: *Church plan 1857.*
(NRO FACULTY PAPERS DN/CON/138)

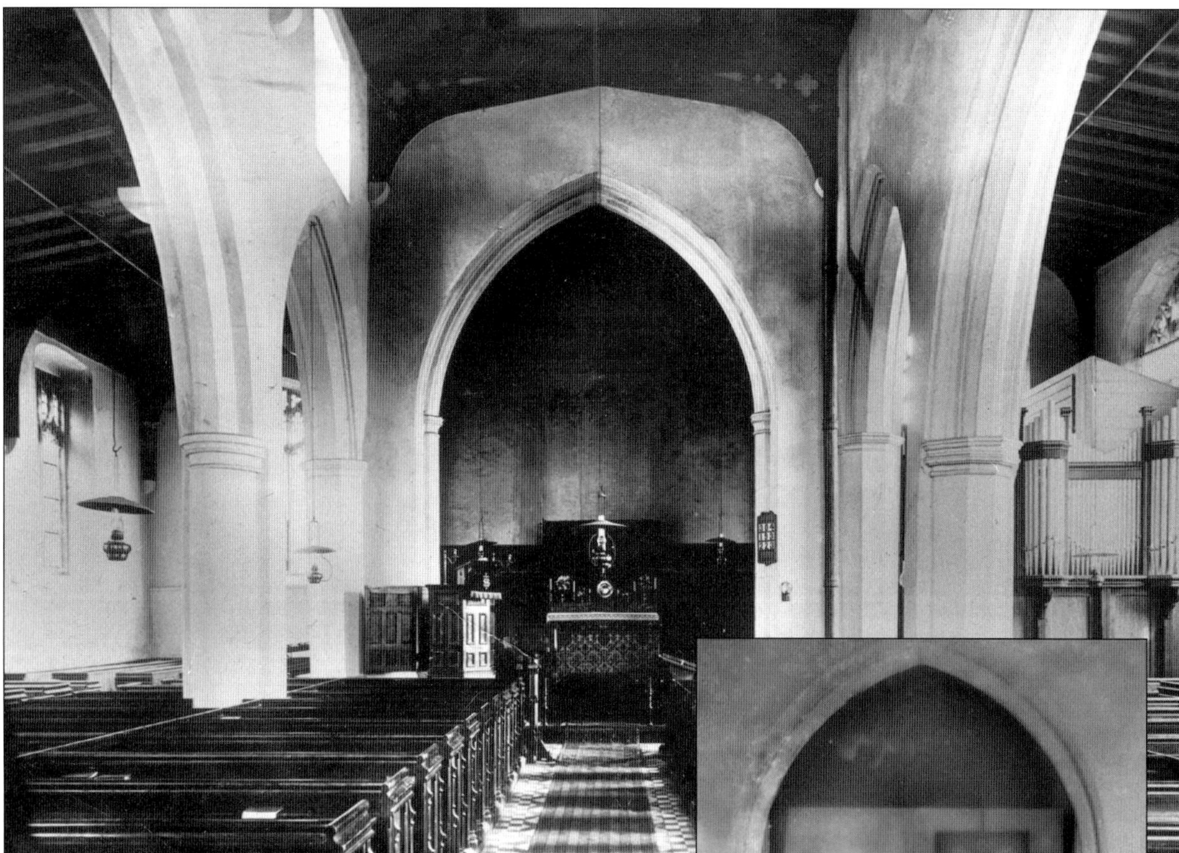

Above: *The interior of St Margaret's church with the blocked east window.*

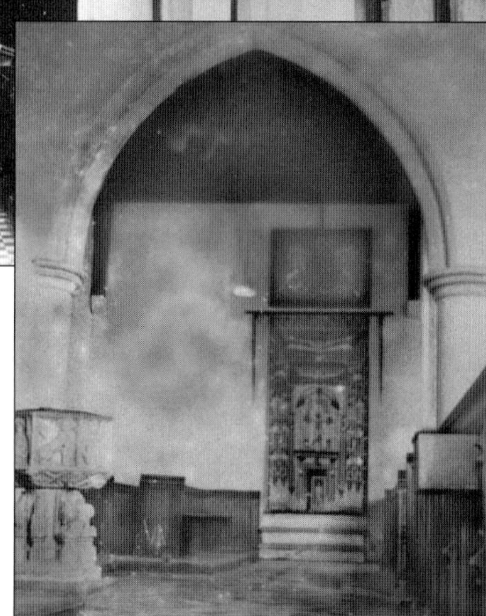

Right: *The north door of the church with the font in the old position at the west end of the nave.*

CHAPTER 12

Discoveries 1850–74

The church roof leaked, windows were crumbling and the north arcade was in danger of collapse when the Revd George Thomas Hall was installed at Christmas 1850.[1]

The village that he came to serve had seen an influx of newcomers, and by 1851 the population had rocketed to 1,258, the highest since records began.[2] Almost a third of these residents had not been born in the village. Most had come from elsewhere in Norfolk, but 50 had arrived from Suffolk and 12 from further-flung parts of the British Isles including London. There were 177 children aged 14 or younger; 77 were called 'scholars' and most who lived within walking distance attended the National School. Education, however, was not compulsory, and those living on the Greens were less likely to attend. Boys were frequently absent from early spring until late autumn, when they were needed on the farms. More women were in regular employment than in 1841, the majority in domestic occupations such as bonnet making, cooking, dressmaking, housekeeping, laundering and millinery. There were 22 resident paupers and 28 Hempnall-born persons were in the Depwade Union Workhouse at Pulham.

A farmer's labour account book for the years 1854 and 1855 provides an insight into employment on Walker's Farm, Silver Green, and Lundy Green Farm, both occupied by Henry Hylton. Three men with a range of skills were regularly employed throughout the year. Robert Hammond, the team man, was responsible for ploughing, drilling and horse shoeing. Other times he took barley to Norwich, and returned with coal. He collected sheep from the marsh using Reedham Ferry and took wheat either to Shottesham or Saxlingham mill. John Goose also looked after horses, journeyed to Norwich, worked on the bean, beet and turnip fields and mowed hay. James Lawn was an agricultural labourer, setting wheat, threshing and dressing barley. Others were specialists, employed only at certain times of the year. Isaac Roberts was paid £2.4d. for 22 days' work with his 'new machine', presumably for threshing. He threshed barley at 1s. per comb and set onion and beet seed. Thomas Gore housed two mares,

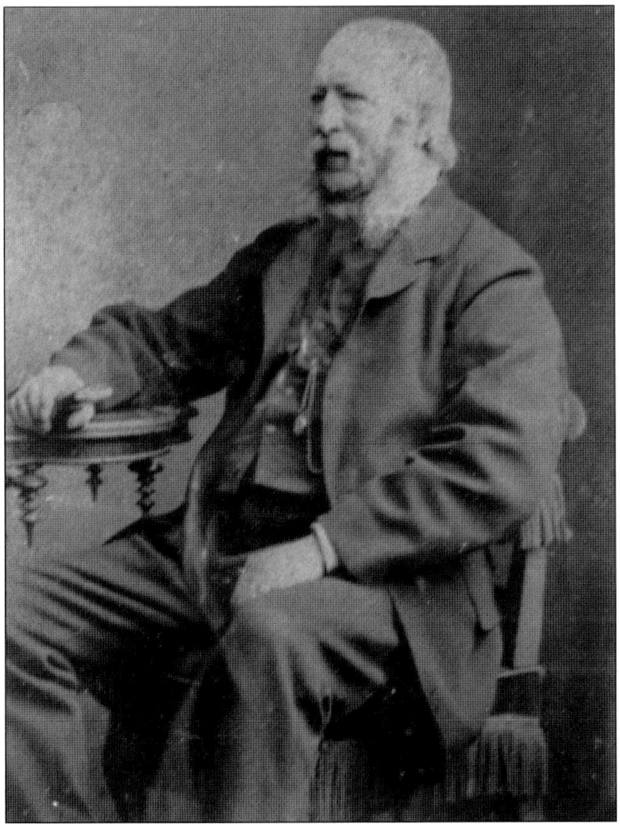

Revd George Thomas Hall, vicar of Hempnall for 35 years, died in 1885.

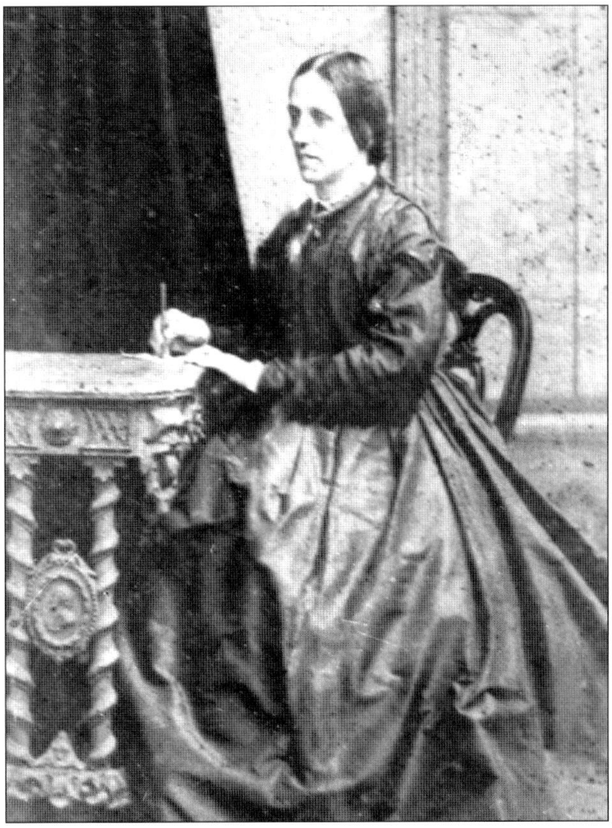

Mrs Annie Townsend Hall. Outliving her husband and eight of their children, she died at Hempnall in 1913.

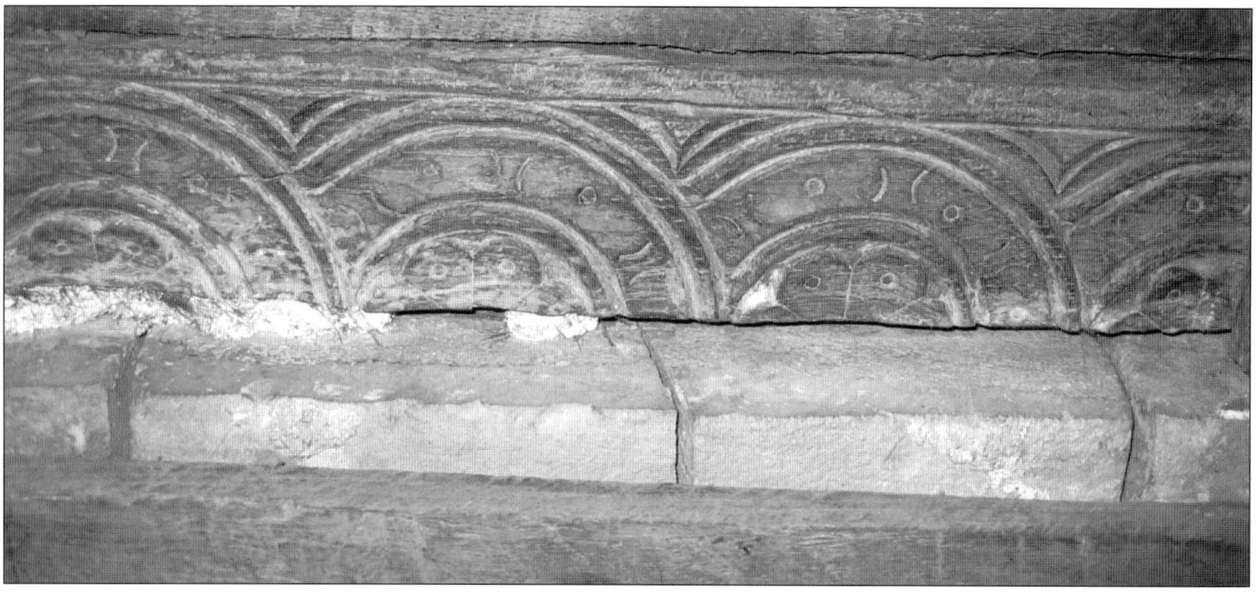

A carving found in Tye's Cottage, used to support a hearth in a room above..

hazarding half the money until it was certain they were in foal. Dade spent a day clipping sheep. Isaiah Tompson earned a shilling a day for 13 days putting stone on the roads. John Sporle earned 12s. for a year's work catching moles on Lundy Green. Harvesting beans and turnips earned 6d. an acre, whereas hoeing was only 3d. an acre. Threshing barley paid 11d. per comb and beans 8d. a comb. Men threshing wheat and barley were paid 7s. an acre. Wheat setting paid 8s.6d. an acre. Others were mainly employed at harvest but at other times of the year worked by jobbing about the yard, mending machinery, stopping up gaps and carting muck. Several woman and children were employed during harvest and on odd jobs at other times. 'Little Goose' was paid 5s.3d. for tending bullocks for three weeks. The girl Lawn earned 7s. for 28 days of crow scaring. Other jobs included picking docks, weeding and turning hay. In 1855 it was noted: 'Finished Harvest this day September 13th, detained two days late getting up the second crop of clover. All the corn up on the 11th inst. Harvest lasted 3 weeks exactly.' Henry Hyton left the farm and disappeared from Hempnall shortly afterwards. Only one of his workers was still in Hempnall in 1861.

Newspapers provide a few accounts of village activities. In 1850, 27 bottles of porter were stolen from the cellar of the Lord Nelson Inn. Roger Roberts, the landlord, found 17 bottles concealed in his hay loft. He kept watch and a few days later caught John Woods and John Revell stuffing their pockets with bottles. Although caught red-handed, the jury took a lenient view and acquitted both men.[3] In 1854 William Aldis stole a sovereign from Henry Todd at the Lord Nelson in the middle of the night. Aldis, although unemployed, was spending money in another public house the next day. He was arrested but insisted he had been lent the sovereign at the King's Head by Mr Moore, a local farmer. Aldis was found guilty and sentenced to six months' imprisonment and Mr Moore was reprimanded for aiding the offender.

Several minor crimes were considered news. Henry Hunt was convicted of stealing a rabbit trap in 1851.[4] Samuel Baldwin and Mary Ann Thrower were charged with stealing four tame rabbits from William Gourney, and Charles Tooke walked off with a hen in his pocket belonging to Henry French D'Oyly.[5] William Forster, landlord of the Swan Inn, was charged with stealing a Cochin China hen, the property of Mrs Elizabeth Thirkettle, miller and baker. Police Constable Pike searched Forster's premises and found a pie which Foster had had the audacity to have baked at Thirkettle's shop, telling her it was a meat pie. Still warm, it contained a feather from a Cochin China fowl.[6] In 1864 George Davy was indicted for stealing a brass candlestick, valued at a shilling, belonging to Roger Roberts, landlord of the Nelson. The incident occurred on Hempnall fair day, December 11. Mr Roberts had wiped the candlestick and some beer glasses that day and the next morning the candlestick was found in the prisoner's cart standing in the Street, but there was no proof that he had stolen the article and so he was acquitted.[7] In 1872 James Roberts and William Nash were fined for drunkenness; the latter was also accused of 'wantonly firing off a gun on the highway at Hempnall on the same day'.[8]

An inquest on the body of Martha Knights, an elderly woman of 63, took place at the Lord Nelson in August 1854. Her death was apparently accelerated by the violent conduct of her husband. A neighbour testified that, on the day of Martha's death, Knights, the worse for liquor, was put to bed in the afternoon by Mrs Elvin and Mrs Took. Martha Knights took the opportunity to take money out of her husband's pocket. Knights woke at seven, missed his money and shouted: 'If you don't give me the money I'll give you a rap.' He dealt her a slight blow across her head and then left the house. Martha Knights, having suffered with dropsy for some time and able only to hobble about with a stick, fell off her chair to the brick floor. Joseph Elvin sent for Mr Hardwicke, the surgeon, but Martha never recovered. The evidence was insufficient to prove murder, but the coroner expressed the opinion that Knights should be more sober in future.[9]

Perhaps the most interesting event of the period was the discovery during ploughing of several scalloped cinerary urns containing many small pieces of bone in a field called The Walls. A few farmers and tradesmen made a search on a small scale and found a few more specimens, which were put on display at the village Post Office.[10] The Revd Samuel W. King, from the adjoining village of Saxlingham Nethergate, a member of the Norfolk Archaeological Society, was invited to undertake an excavation. He discovered that the urns had all been deposited between 12 and 18 inches below the surface in parallel rows at regular intervals of 10–12 ft. Pottery of a superior quality was found nearby which King concluded, was Romano-British.[11] Some of the complete urns are supposed to have been given to the British Museum, but no record of them can be found.

In 1856 Revd George Hall and his wife entertained 250 people consisting of schoolchildren and members of the Adult Evening School and the church choir to a special Christmas feast at the school. After tea a magnificent Christmas tree was revealed, decorated with fruits and candles. The evening concluded with the distribution of oranges and presents.[12]

The Wesleyan and Primitive Methodists, and the Baptists and the Independents each held three Sunday services and one during the week.[13] The Zion Particular Baptist chapel was erected in October 1847 in a room taken out of a warehouse. This may have been the converted barn on the premises of the Longhouse, or in the grounds of the Chequers, as deeds from both houses refer to a chapel. The vicar, previously curate, was soon to formulate plans for the restoration of the church.

Early in 1857 he and the churchwardens agreed to sell the lead from the church roof to raise some of the capital. Thomas Jeckyll, architect, was employed to design the improvements. His plans involved rebuilding the nave roof, covering it with slate, renewing the chancel arch, demolishing the central arch of the north arcade and rebuilding it in Perpendicular style, replacing the clerestory windows, repairing the windows in the aisles, replacing the floor and substituting modern benches for the old box pews and benches. The chancel had been demolished in a fire in the seventeenth century, yet there were no plans to enlarge it to its former length, even though the foundations may still have been visible. It seems likely that the Revd George Hall did not want to elevate the chancel as a more sacred area and was probably of an evangelical inclination.

In October, as building work was nearing completion, there was a slight set-back. New lead for the aisles and chancel was lying in the churchyard and during the night half a ton was stolen; the marks of wagon wheels could be seen clearly the next day.[14]

The Bishop of Norwich was invited to preach at the reopening on Thursday, 25 March 1858. The *Norfolk Chronicle* reported that the 'unsightly assemblage of irregularly constructed pews and free-sittings' had been 'converted into well-arranged lines of accommodation for all classes of parishioners'.[15] A large congregation attended and the collection amounted to £46.6s.2d. A new patent barrel organ and a large harmonium provided the music.

Thanks to the vicar, we can begin to recreate the interior of the church as it was before 1857. He noted that there had been a screen in the south aisle as well as in the usual position at the end of the nave. The gilding was quite fresh on some of the woodwork and there was evidence of fire upon pieces of screen. During the restoration mural paintings, ancient painted glass and a piscina, used for the washing of communion vessels, were uncovered and subsequently destroyed. However, it was regretted that a quantity of good carved work had been stolen when the pine benches were substituted for the former old oak seating. 'And the tradition is', wrote Hall, 'that the said carved work was converted into articles of household furniture.'[16] Pieces of carved stone from the church windows, discarded at the time, can still be seen in the gardens of three Hempnall houses. A piece of carving, reused in a ceiling to support a fireplace above, can be seen in Tye Cottage.

By 1861 there had been a dramatic drop in population, from 1,258 in 1851 to 1,094, and 14 cottages were standing empty. Perhaps the railway was a factor. People had to travel to Flordon, and Hempnall was bypassed. The Eastern Counties Railway Co. had planned a route through Hempnall in 1835, but the line would have run through the Boyland Hall estate belonging to the Irby family, who objected, as did other landowners.[17] Many labourers were obliged to seek work outside the parish and found it more convenient to move than to travel. The families that remained rented from small proprietors who charged a high rent for rather poor clay lump dwellings, and those not employed on the land were increasingly likely to be involved in more than one trade.

The commissioners appointed by the government to enquire into the employment of children, young persons and women in agriculture, relied heavily on information supplied by the clergy. The Revd George Hall wrote of Hempnall in the report, published in 1867:

Many young girls seem to prefer work in the fields to domestic service. Farmers were never so much put to for dairy maids as they are now. Young girls will not go where there are cows to milk or a child or two to nurse. I have known girls thoroughly corrupted by a month's dibbing or stone picking. The married women are the corrupters of young girls. During gleaning the women forget all sense of propriety and decorum. I dread the approach of that blessed season almost as much as the annual fair. Often we see 100 waiting to enter a field about to be cleared. The conversation of some depraved ones is listened to and heard by all and much harm is done.[18]

Reporting on housing in the village, he wrote:

The worst hotbed of demoralisation is to be found in the crowded state of too many of our cottages and the consequent intermixture of the sexes. Very many cottages have only one room below and one above, in some instances where the families are large, they are crowded and generally the drainage and ventilation are very imperfect and a hole for slops and refuse of all kinds is the prevailing rule; often near the door, often no water supply and no privy. It is very difficult to make the cottagers see the benefit of ventilation. I have often found that they would not suffer a window to remain open when the stench was intolerable.

Hall counted himself an advocate of compulsory education, but found parents to be indifferent and farmers in opposition. The National School, he reported, was losing scholars to the private academies, as some parents considered them to be 'more genteel'. As many as 40 children were attending one of these alternative schools. Hall expressed the opinion that many children were growing up without proper discipline and education. An unsuccessful attempt had been made to start an evening school.

The Education Act of 1870 made the provision of schooling compulsory. Though the population had dropped to 1,005 by 1871, it was considered that 950 of these people had children who might be expected to attend the elementary school; but that the present building was inadequate for such an increased number. A special report was also made emphasising the decline of educational standards at the school. A boys' school under a master was strongly recomended, while girls and infants, it was thought, could be taught together. An extension of the building would be necessary. It was considered a problem that the small farmer might get a place for his child at the expense of the labourers. It was noted that there were some: 'pretentious small schools claiming to be "middle class" but inefficient in premises with little doubt in instruction too.'[19]

In March 1873 the School Board met and Samuel Read was appointed to make drawings and plans to add an extension to the schoolroom. Read recommended two coats of lime, repairs to the windows, uncovering a well, new desks and work tables, a gallery and a new window on the north side, in addition to the extension and repairs to the master's house. The cost was estimated to be £243.16s.6d. In 1874 the Board advertised:

Wanted for 1st October, a certificated master for the Board School with a wife or sister to undertake infants and sewing in a mixed school. Salary £60. A four roomed house, out houses and nice garden.

References

[1] *NM* Saturday, 7 December 1850
[2] PRO HO 107/1821/595 1851 Census Returns
[3] *NM* Saturday, 23 March 1850
[4] *NM* Saturday, 4 January 1851
[5] *NM* Saturday, 23 October 1852; *NM* Saturday, 20 November 1852
[6] *NC* Saturday, 18 February 1854
[7] *NA* Saturday, 9 January 1864
[8] *NM* Saturday, 10 February. District Police News.
[9] *NC* Saturday, 12 August 1854
[10] *NM* Saturday, 17 June 1854
[11] The Revd Samuel W. King 'Examination of an Ancient Cemetery at Hempnall Norfolk', *NA* pp.49–52
[12] *NM* Saturday, 27 December 1856
[13] Craven & Co. Commercial Directory of Norfolk (Nottingham 1856)
[14] *NC* Saturday, 4 July 1857
[15] *NC* Saturday, 3 April 1858
[16] George G. Plunkett 'Norfolk Church Screens – 1865 Survey', *NA* Vol. 37 Pt 2 p.183
[17] NRO C/Scf 1 /421 Railway plan 30 November 1835
[18] Commission on the Employment of Children, Young Persons and Women in Agriculture, 1867 pp.135, 140, 147, 151, 153. First Report of the Commissioners, with Appendix Pt 1 (London, 1868) pp.3–7, 13, 16, 19, 22, 23, 48
[19] PRO ED 2/317 School Board of Hempnall Abstract Vol. 49 p.68, 11 November 1871

✥ CHAPTER 13 ✥

Driving Forces 1875–99

Hempnall School was unable to shrug off a reputation for low achievement and poor discipline, and members of the School Board experienced much unpleasantness from those who were still unconvinced of the necessity of extending the school premises now the population was decreasing.

Education was not free, and funding came from county rates, a government grant and the children, who paid a few pence a week. The grant went towards payment of salaries, but was dependent on attendances and a satisfactory report from a school inspector. Members of the Hempnall School Board believed that Mr Hawes, the then headmaster, lacked discipline, and planned to replace him. Two advertisements were placed in local newspapers, but no applications were received. On 20 September 1875, Mr Hawes pre-empted them by announcing he had found a more lucrative position in another school. The School Board was unable to release him until a replacement could be found, so Mr Hawes offered to find some applicants himself. This time 15 applied for the post and Mr W. Alfred Marten, previously an assistant teacher at the Saxon Street Board School in London, was appointed on 30 September.[1]

Mr Marten was unpopular from the outset, particularly with the vicar. Two months after his appointment the School Board met to discuss allegations of dishonest and dishonourable conduct and of undue severity towards the boys. A copy of a letter sent to Mr Marten, accusing him of dishonesty, was produced, as was another from the headmaster of the Saxon Street School asking the board to give Marten a fair chance to retrieve his good name. The board decided that these letters were contradictory and took the matter no further. Mr Hipperson, however, was dissatisfied with this outcome and complained that his son had been unwilling to attend school because he was afraid of Mr Marten. Mr Marten was brought into the room to explain his behaviour, but before he could begin, Mr Henry Buck charged Marten with undue severity towards his son, explaining that he had been obliged to withdraw him from the establishment, and added that his niece had been taken away because: 'she did not know

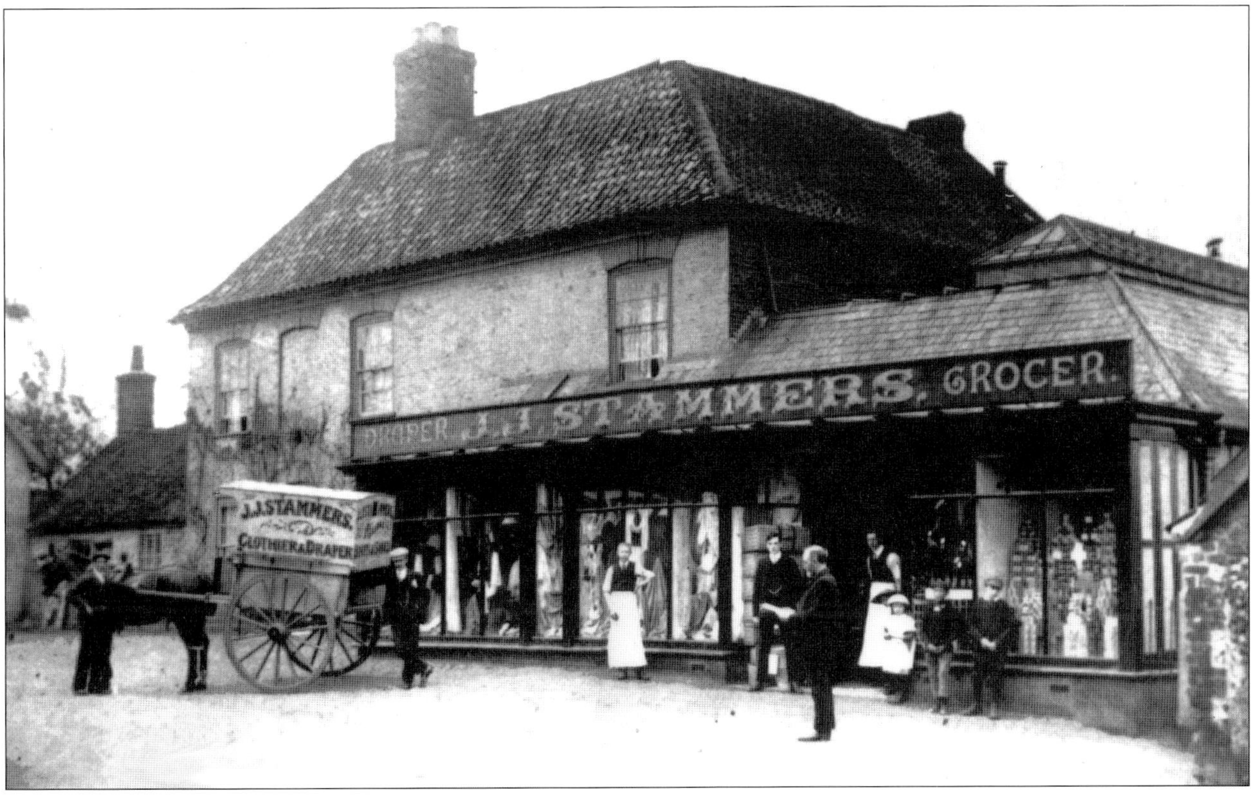

John Joseph Stammers outside his new shop, built in 1885. There had been a shop on the site from 1578 (copyhold name: 'Cottage or shop at the gate of the vicarage'. After 1701, when perhaps the house was given a brick skin: 'The house where John Brown formerly dwelt').

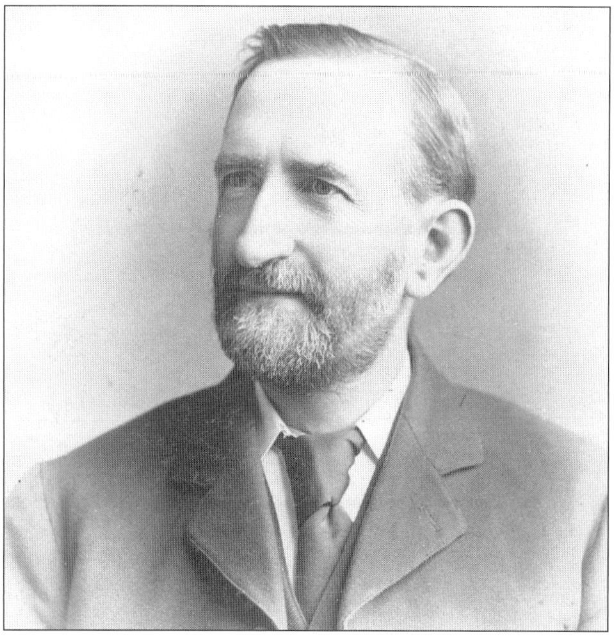

John Joseph Stammers.

anything and that quite 40 people objected to pay the school rate while Mr Marten remained master.' He also said that if the present board would not get rid of Mr Marten then the next board would. Mr Buck, when questioned by Mr Marten, said he was unwilling to mention any names. The matter was dropped. However, Mr Marten preferred to continue and produced a letter written by the chairman (the Revd George Hall) to Mr Peddle, accusing him (Mr Marten) of drunkenness, card sharping, insolence and incompetence, and asking Mr Peddle to assist him in getting rid of him (Mr Marten). Meanwhile,

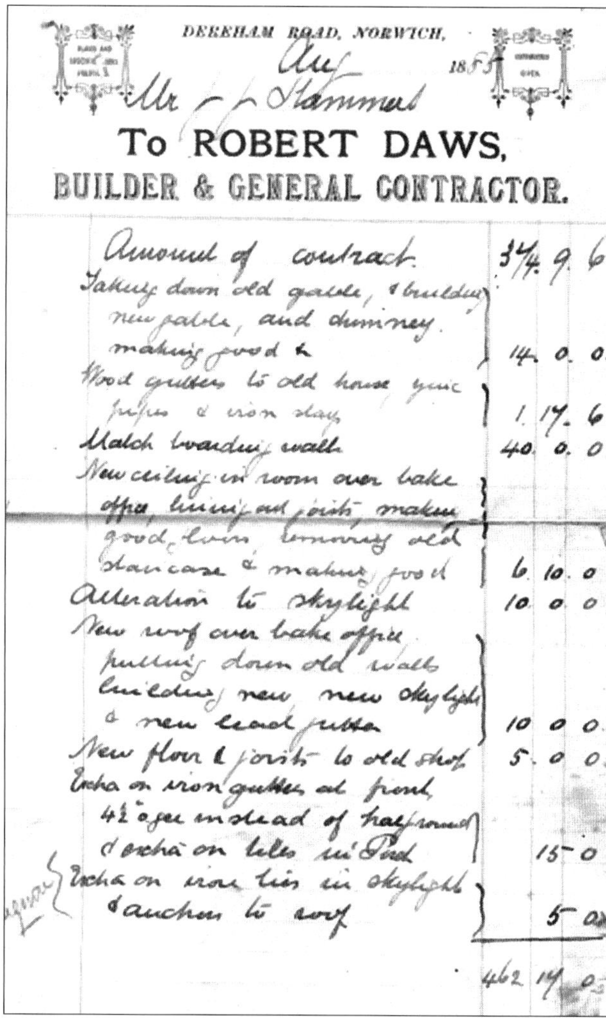

DEREHAM ROAD, NORWICH,
Aug 1885
Mr J. J. Stammers
To ROBERT DAWS,
BUILDER & GENERAL CONTRACTOR.

Amount of contract	374. 9. 6
Taking down old gable, & building new gable, and chimney, making good &	14. 0. 0.
Wood gutters to old house zinc pipes & iron stays	1. 17. 6
Match boarding wall	40. 0. 0
New ceiling in room over bake office, lining out joists, making good, removing old staircase & making good	6. 10. 0
Alteration to skylight	10. 0. 0
New roof over bake office pulling down old walls building new, new skylight & new lead gutter	10. 0. 0.
New floor & joists to old shop	5. 0. 0.
Extra on iron gutter at front, 4½ ogee instead of half round & extra on tiles in Yard	15. 0
Extra on iron ties in skylight & anchors to roof	5. 0
	462. 14. 0

A bill for repairs at Connaught House, 1885.

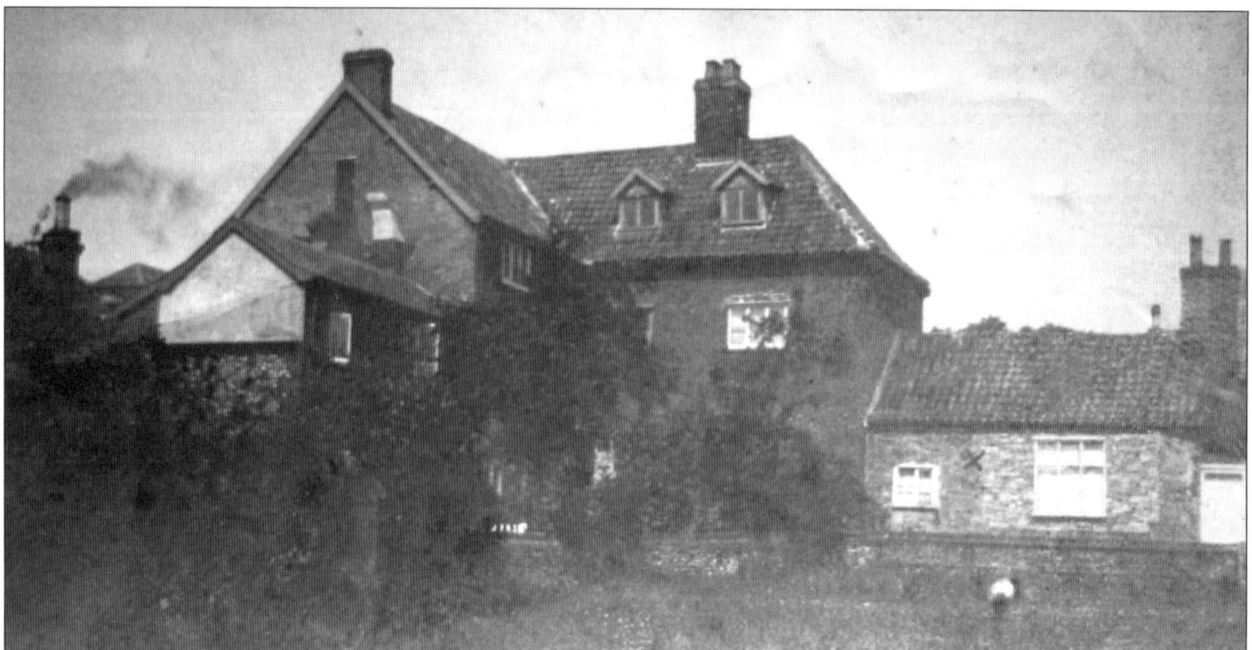

A rear view of the shop. The remains of the bakery chimney can be seen against the gable on the left. (Copyhold name Aylwards or Eylward, later Edwards. Earliest known date 1340.)

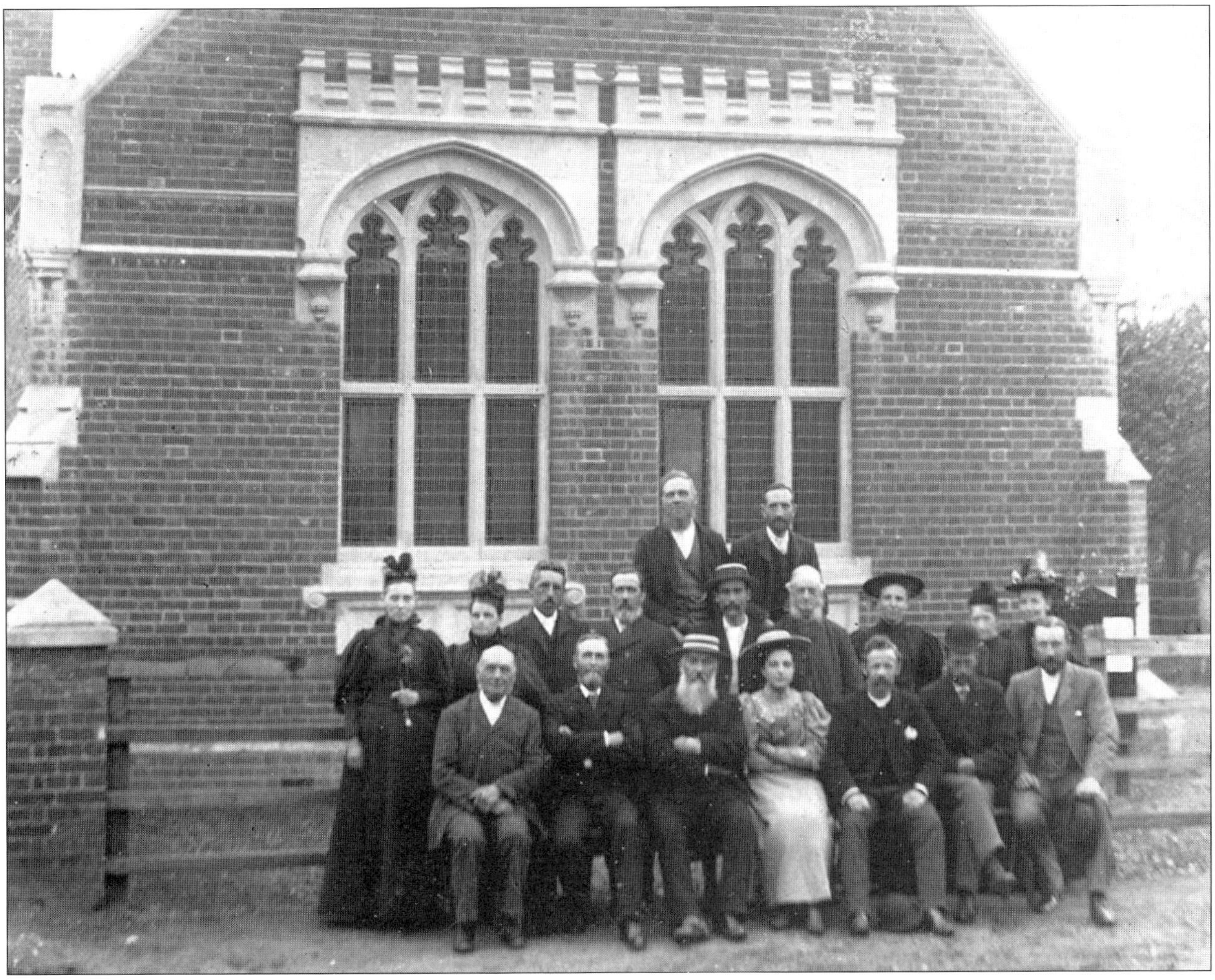

The Wesleyan Chapel, 1885.

as the assembled company grappled with the predicament in which they had been placed, Mrs William Knights, who rented the shop opposite the school previously owned by the Thirkettles, and who let a room to Miss Light, the pupil teacher, was brought in. She accused Miss Light of being absent during the evenings and of not coming home to meals. These accusations were dismissed as 'being unworthy of consideration', so she turned on Mr Marten and accused him of having caned Mr Leggett's and Mr Henry Roberts's sons so badly that their hands were swollen. In the absence of the aggrieved parties, however, the matter was ended. It only remained for the humiliated chairman to sign a cheque for the quarter's bills and salaries amounting to £63.10s.1d.

On 30 December 1875 the board recorded that Mr Buck's charges against Mr Marten were 'totally unfounded' and approved the change of Miss Light's residence. The clerk was instructed to obtain a book for the master to record the punishments inflicted on pupils and agreed to apply to Mr W.S. Read to draw up plans for enlarging the master's residence.

Poor attendance continued to concern the board, and in May the following year 21 children were regularly missing school. By then Mr William D'Oyly had taken over from the vicar as chairman. He offered to send a load of gravel to level the playground and proposed that a boys' urinal should be installed at the front of the school in the playground.

In June 1876 a school inspector expressed his dissatisfaction with the progress of the children. Mr Marten was forced to tender his resignation and vacate the schoolhouse while certain charges brought against him by Ephraim Gooderham, a pupil teacher, were investigated. Marten moved to a school at Belchford in Lincolnshire. A request from his new school for details of the circumstances of his departure came before the board. A testimonial was not supplied.

Advertisements were placed and this time there were 30 applicants. From a shortlist of five, Mr John Binley of Wylam-On-Tyne, Northumberland, was appointed in August. His salary was agreed at £80 a year and a regular supply of coal.

Mr Binley recouped £4.2s. in travel expenses and the term began on 11 September.[2] A new start was made – rewards were given for regularity, punctuality and for passing tests in reading, writing and arithmetic. Mr Binley, it seemed, could do no wrong.

When he complained that the schoolhouse was 'unsuitable for habitation' it was agreed he could hire rooms from Mr Roper at £8.10s. a year at the school's expense. George Elvin took the opportunity to offer to clean the school in lieu of rent for the schoolhouse, and this was agreed. Apart from a whooping cough epidemic, school attendance improved. The school began to be used for outside activities and with a library containing upwards of 500 books for the use of all parishioners.[3]

The School Board reported financial difficulties in 1885. To alleviate the problem the master's salary was reduced to £70 a year, the clerk offered to accept £10 a year instead of the £15 to which he was entitled and it was agreed to ask the ratepayers for £90. Mrs Roberts was sacked as assistant teacher and replaced by a monitor. Under the monitorial system, by then in decline, the master could teach a few older children who, in turn, were responsible for instructing small groups of pupils.

An epidemic of measles forced the school to close in May 1887. The education authority wrote towards the end of June to say that it had forgotten that Hempnall School was still closed and advised the board to open it the following day. That year John Joseph Stammers, my great-grandfather, was elected to the board. He proposed the introduction of English grammar, but was outvoted. However, geography was initiated and Mr Binley was instructed to procure copies of the *Royal Geographical Reader* from Messrs Jarrold & Sons. The school was under water in 1893, so it was decided to renew the drain. The financial situation appeared to improve at this time and the gallery was altered as suggested by an inspector.

My great-grandfather married Miss Ellen Lansdell, a blacksmith's daughter, in 1877. A shrewd businessman with an eye on market forces, in 1885 he bought the shop, previously occupied by Knights, in the Street. It was described as a capital messuage, general shop and bake office, with a warehouse, barn, stables, gighouse and sheds. Before long he was making major alterations, including removing a gable, a staircase and pulling down old walls. The old shop was absorbed into spacious premises and he was soon employing several assistants.

The editor of the *Norwich Mercury* was moved to write of a gale that swept Norfolk on Sunday, 24 March 1895:

> *The wind had been blowing briskly all morning and by noon had reached gale force, raising clouds of dust and rubbish which literally darkened the air... The howling winds were charged with dirt and the few pedestrians abroad soon began to acquire the complexion of people engaged in pulling down old buildings... strong men were compelled to cling to lampposts, wooden buildings in allotments sailed through the air... telegraph wires were broken... tiles and chimney pots were falling like leaves in autumn.*[4]

The Wesleyan Methodists at Hempnall, undeterred by the storm, attended the afternoon service just as the gale was at its height. My grandfather records that it was impossible to hear the minister's voice above the din. Someone advised the congregation to leave, for just then the whole roof was lifted off and carried away. Services were held in Mr Stammers' barn for the time being. With remarkable speed the Methodists began rebuilding. The entrance was moved to the side, as members of the congregation were tired of being jeered at by the clientele of the Woodman opposite. One of the foundation stones was laid by my great-grandfather and under it was placed a bottle containing coins of the realm, Wesleyan literature and a daily newspaper. A public tea for over 300 people was served afterwards in the Board School.[5] One old lady persuaded her son to take her to the event in a wheelbarrow.

Farmers suffered a series of problems in this period. Foot and mouth disease in cattle reached epidemic proportions in January 1875, putting several farmers out of business and accelerating the flow of population from rural to urban areas.[6] That summer was unusually wet and in July many cornfields in Norfolk were entirely under water, causing the wheat to be 'more twisted and broken down' than any crop since 1860.[7] The price of cereals rose and animal diseases were rife. In November 1895 Norfolk farmers were plagued by the problems of swine fever. They tried slaughter, cancelling markets and shutting off the countryside, but still pigs were being infected. It was a sore point that Suffolk did none of these things and yet had no more cases of swine fever than did Norfolk. To add to their difficulty, Lord Sandon's Act of 1876 stipulated that employers should not make use of children under ten, and children between ten and 14 were obliged to attend school at least half the time. This caused hardship for the smallholders, who had hitherto employed their own children on the land, often from the age of seven.

Three fires caused havoc during this period. A four-dweller cottage in Field Lane belonging to Thomas Ward burned down in 1881 and in May 1897 an overheated flue caused a fire at Clip Bush Farm. Isaac Ling, a man of over 80, was in bed at the time. When George Smith, Albert Took and William Catton attempted to rescue him, the door at the top of the stairs was found to be bolted and had to be broken down. The poor man was almost suffocated by the time they reached him. There was little time to spare, for the building was soon gutted. Later that year the heroes were presented with a certificate and a guinea each by the Royal Society for Protection of Life from Fire. Another fire in August took hold at a house belonging to a Mr Nash. Mrs Nash was alone in the house when a spark from a chimney set a cart shed alight and from there the fire spread to the thatch of the house. She had barely time to escape and all the

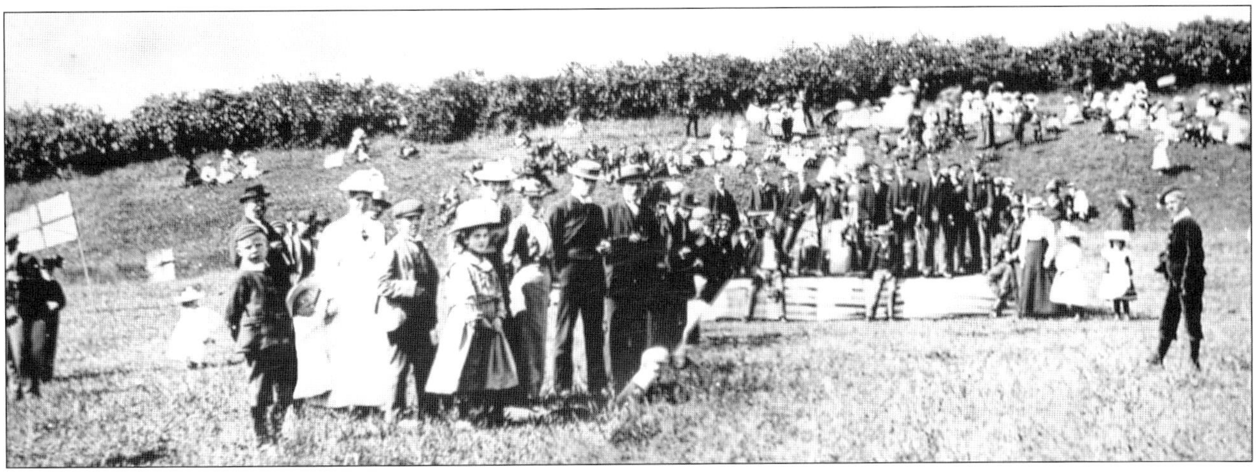

Celebrating Queen Victoria's Diamond Jubilee in the pit, 1889.

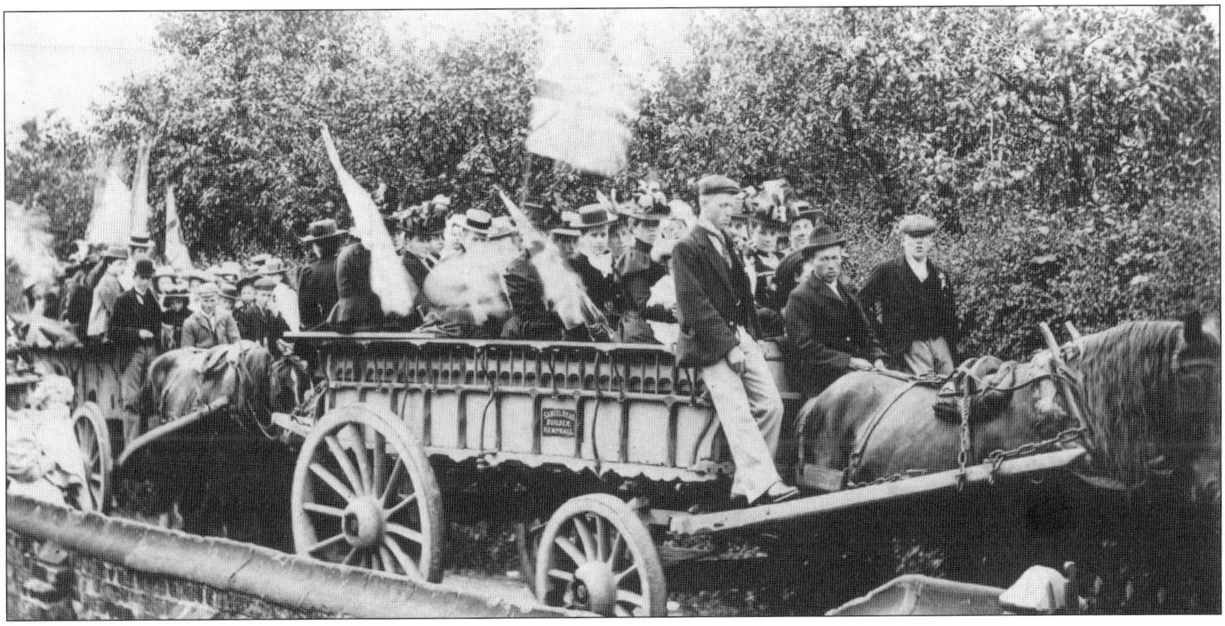

A village outing, possibly on the day of the Diamond Jubilee. Note the flags.

furniture was consumed. Long Stratton fire brigade arrived just too late to save the premises.[8]

Mr Stammers was intent on providing an independent reading room for the village and a meeting took place at the school on 10 June to further the scheme. In July the Norwich Church Army Mission came for a week. Later that month Mr Samuel Read took the people employed on his farm to Yarmouth, where a dinner was provided. When returning from Norwich on a dark night in September, Mr Moore was attacked by someone wielding a stick and a whip handle. A few days later Messrs Brown of Grove House gave a harvest supper for about 40 friends and employees to raise subscriptions towards the erection of a public room. Money was also raised for the Queen's Diamond Jubilee celebrations. In October a parish meeting was held to discuss the question of street lights for the village.[9]

After a long debate, the School Board agreed that Bible reading should be encouraged, and 100 Bibles were purchased in 1898. At about the same time a circular arrived for the teachers from the United Kingdom Band of Hope Union, hoping to arrange a series of lectures on temperance. The question of building a third classroom was on the agenda, but it was pointed out that if Standard 1 pupils were moved back into the infant room, with falling attendance, there might be fewer than 70 in a room originally designed to hold 72. A partition was considered, but finally they took the advice of a school inspector and a new room was added in November. Furniture was an additional expense, and three 12ft long desks, two easels and two blackboards were supplied. Mrs Elvin, the caretaker, demanded more money for cleaning during the building work but having received an extra 10s., she handed in her notice. Mrs Brown took her place and almost immediately complained about the state of the floor in the kitchen and wanted a new grate and wallpaper for two rooms. Two teachers resigned. Mrs Binley was appointed and the Binley's son, Percy, was engaged as a pupil teacher. Mr Binley had never been offered a return to his original salary after the cuts of 1885 and soon his supply of coal would also cease. The July report by an inspector was considered highly satisfactory, which may have alleviated some of the worries that had been plaguing the Binley household, for Mr Binley, through no fault of his own, was suffering financial difficulties, incurring debts amounting to £623 whilst acting as executor of Mrs D'Oyly.[10]

Many villagers were still living in poverty, and some accommodation had not improved much since the 1860s – 82 houses had four or fewer rooms in 1891.[11] Clothing large families was also a problem, so so two clubs, one for boots and shoes, another for more general clothing, were formed; the former distributed 1s 5d to each of its 51 members in 1897.

A New Year's tea had been held for 150 children, who were all sent home with a small gift.[12] In February, after heavy rain and snow, the main road in Hempnall was submerged, and a large stump with roots weighing several hundredweight was brought down by the stream to the centre of the village.[13]

With Queen Victoria's Diamond Jubilee approaching, in May 1897, a meeting at the school considered proposals to celebrate the occasion. Mr Stammers suggested a reading room, but the vicar, Revd Augustine Brutton, who had replaced Revd George T. Hall on his death in 1885, favoured a substantial dinner to be funded by public subscription, and this was decided upon.[14] The villagers assembled in the old gravel pit for the entertainment. My grandfather, as a boy of six, recorded the occasion:

The tables were set out in the school yard with large tarpaulins over the top. There were mountains of beef, huge stacks of hams, vegetables and home made bread, followed by plum puddings. I have never seen so much food devoured in such quantities in all my life.

Beer was provided for the adults and lemonade for the Board School children. The evening was rounded off with fireworks and the singing of the National Anthem.[15]

At the age of nine, my grandfather was taken to Norwich for a birthday treat. He wrote:

I was fascinated by everything I saw and heard. I went with him into several wholesale houses, and then when I was feeling exhausted and hungry, he took me down Davy Place and we entered Pike's Restaurant... so the day wore on until we stood at the edge of the market place waiting for a horse-drawn coach to take us up Earlham Road to an aunt to have tea. The fare for a small boy was one penny... We returned to the Lamb Inn in the Haymarket. All the purchases of the day were loaded, including one from a wholesale chemist in Magdalen Street to whom the order had been posted in Orford Place at 11a.m. and there, six hours later, it was already packed and loaded with the rest. Our horse knew we were on the homeward journey, for, with its head held high, we soon left the city behind. It was a heavy load and when we came to Skeets Hill, which was very steep, my father stopped the horse half way and drew him across the road to rest him. It was a good job there were no fast cars in those days.

In 1899 several young men had left the village for South Africa to fight in the Boer War. Mrs Hardy, Mrs Smith and the Misses Read, Roberts, Bussey and Stammers were the driving force behind the Transvaal War Fund Committee, which in 1900 raised £27.[16]

References

[1] NRO C/ED3/101 Minutes of Hempnall School Board
[2] The 'Harvest holiday' that year commenced on 11 August
[3] E.R. Kelly (ed.) (1879) *The Post Office Directory of the County of Norfolk* (London) p.322
[4] *NM* Saturday, 27 March 1895
[5] *NM* Saturday, 8 June 1895
[6] *NM* Saturday, 30 January and Saturday, 13 March 1875
[7] *NM* Saturday, 21 July 1875
[8] *NC* Saturday, 29 May 1897; *NC* Saturday, 16 October 1897; *NC* Saturday, 21August 1897
[9] *NC* Saturday, 10 June 1897; *NC* Saturday, 17 July 1897; *NC* Saturday, 31 July 1897; *NC* Saturday, 4 September 1897; *NC* Saturday, 18 September 1897; *NC* Saturday, 23 October 1897
[10] NRO C/ED3/102 Minutes of Hempnall School Board, 27 June 1901
[11] PRO RG 12/1891 Census Returns
[12] *NC* Saturday, 15 February 1897
[13] *NC* Saturday, 13 February 1897
[14] E.R. Kelly(ed.) (1879) *The Post Office Directory of the County of Norfolk* (London) p.322.
[15] *NC* Saturday, 22 May 1897
[16] *NC* Saturday, 10 February 1900

✦ CHAPTER 14 ✦

Community Spirit 1900–09

The roads were still dirt tracks and many houses were clay-lump hovels with a ladder to the upper floor. Neither electricity nor gas had arrived and plumbing was primitive. Schooling had improved, but 70 children were crammed into the infant class and Miss Wells, the teacher, broke the windows when the heat became oppressive. The outraged members of the School Board summoned her to appear at their next meeting. She was too fearful to explain, so 11s., the cost of repairs, was deducted from her salary.[1]

The school continued to have financial problems. In 1900 the board met to discuss the amount paid to Mrs Bingley, the wife of the schoolmaster, a temporary teacher. The vicar, the Revd Augustine Brutton, a member of the board, who had not attended a meeting for six months became incensed over the matter, calling his fellow committee members 'all fools'. Mr Joshua Bussey, a local farmer, reaching over the table, hit the vicar in the face, took hold of his coat and shouted, 'Scoundrel!' The vicar, being 'in such a state of passion', was asked to leave the room. Subsequently at Long Stratton Petty Sessions, the Bench were of the opinion that a technical assault had been committed, but under great provocation. Mr Bussey was fined a shilling and costs.[2]

Mr Edgar Bullen opened a bicycle shop in the Street. When Lizzie Roberts and George Sporle were married in 1901, they arrived at the church on decorated bicycles and then celebrated their marriage with a reception at the pit.

The horse, however, continued to be an important form of transport. In 1903 Peter Varney, the Hempnall carrier, who also kept the Queen's Head, was returning from Norwich via Long John Hill with his horse-drawn van, carrying five passengers and with household furniture piled on top, when the horses suddenly broke into a gallop, causing a wheel to break. Mr Varney was thrown out and the five passengers were obliged to return to Hempnall via the railway from Norwich Victoria Station. In 1906 Sydney Miles, the local butcher, had paused on his rounds at the Horse Shoes Inn when his horse bolted with the cart and continued up the road until it charged into a

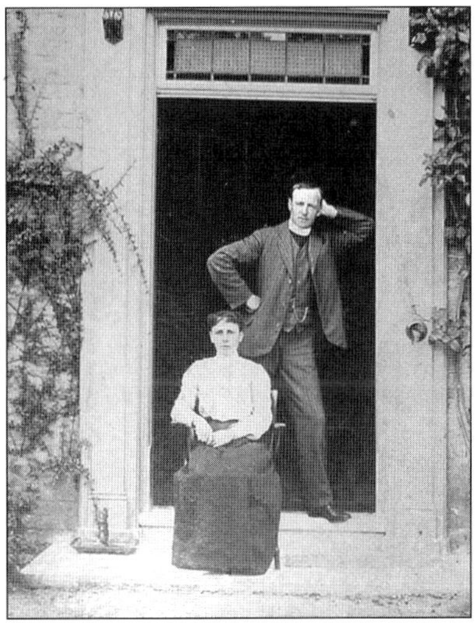

Left: *Revd Augustine Brutton and his wife outside Hempnall House.*

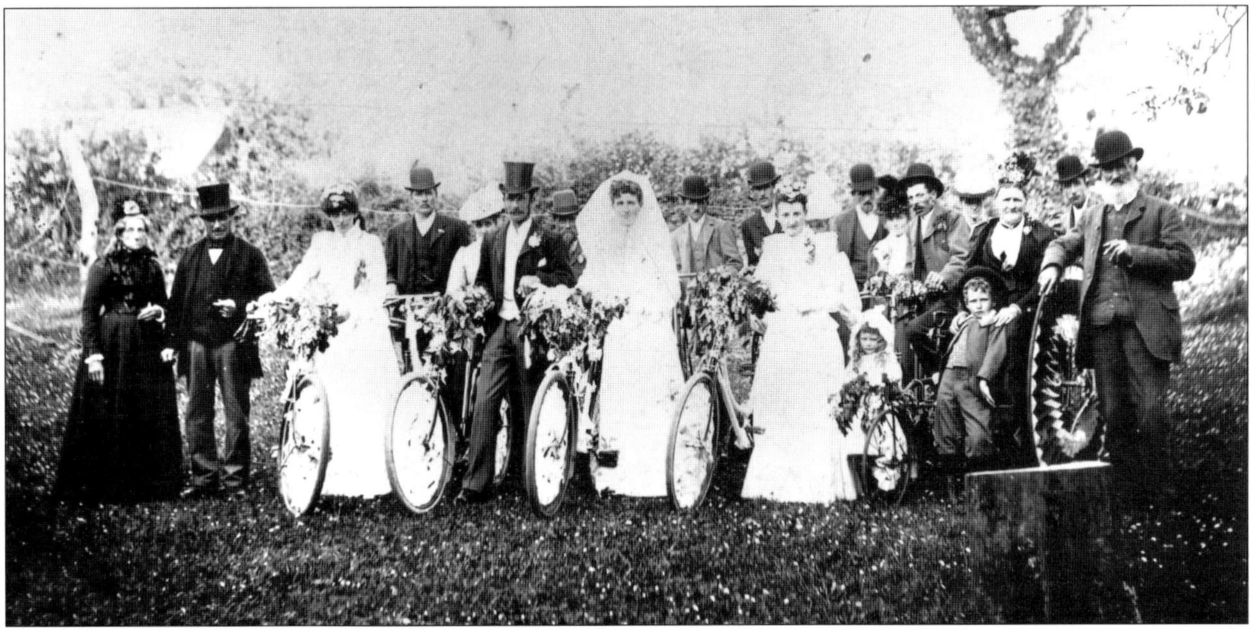

The wedding of Lizzie Roberts and George Sporle, 1901.

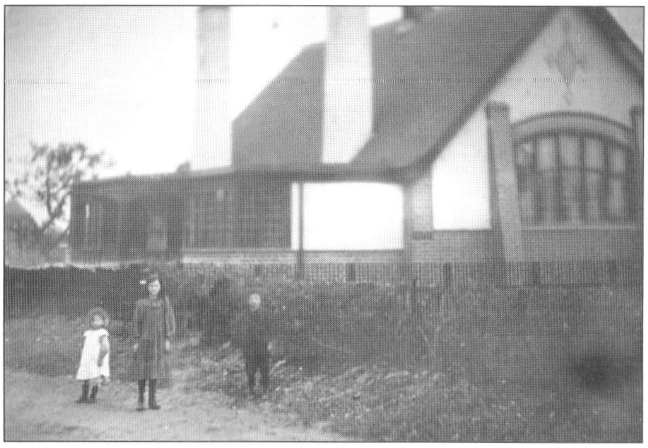

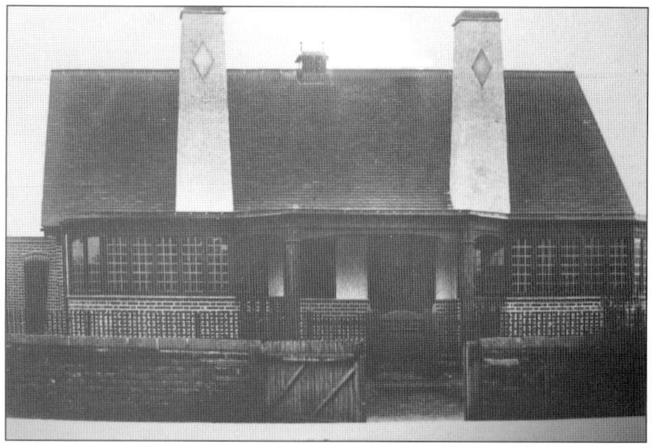

The Village Institute, built 1909.

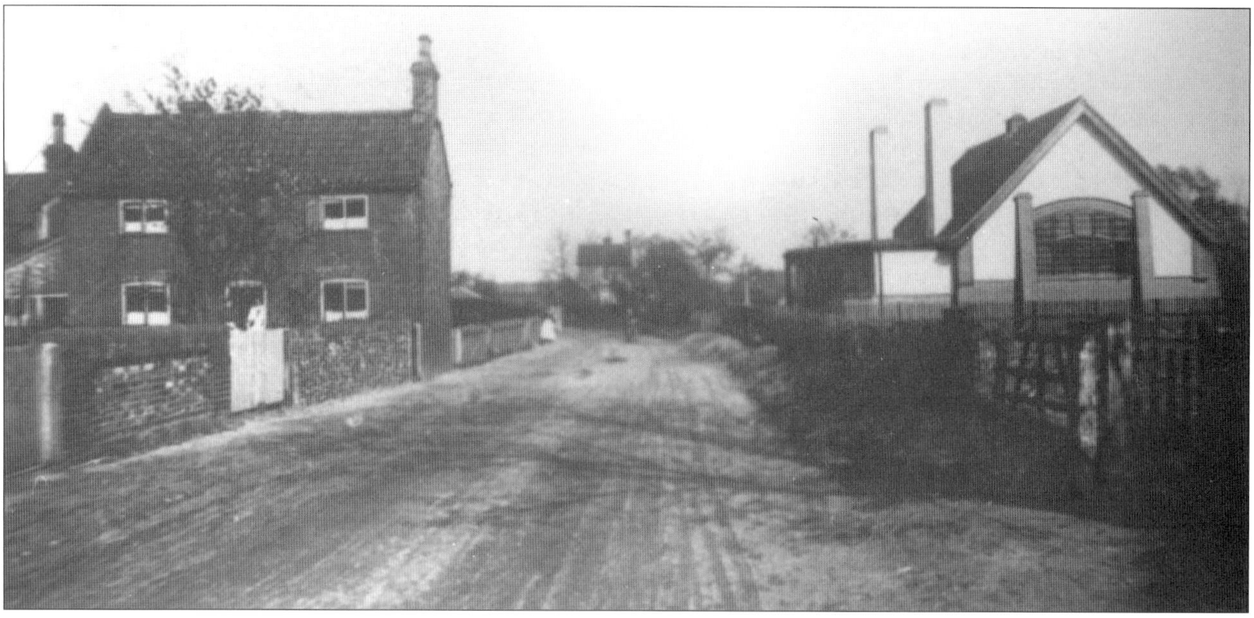

Bungay Road and the Village Institute.

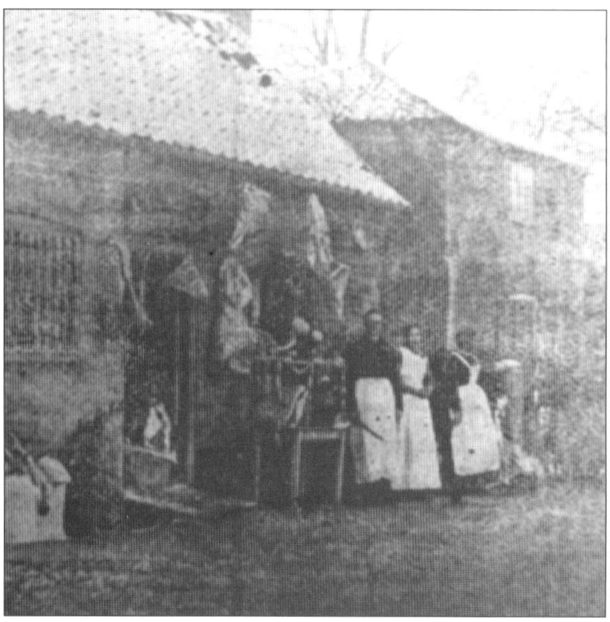

Sydney Miles outside his butcher's shop, c.1900.

heap of manure at Mr Tweeddale's farm. Mrs Elvin, the wife of Robert Elvin, had an accident returning from Fritton when her pony slipped, turning over her conveyance at the crossroads called the Rouans. This name seems to be the earliest known record for this part of Hempnall, called variously Runs, Rons and now the Krons.

The growth of mass consumerism encouraged the production of lively advertisements in the newspapers. Dr Williams' 'Pink Pills for Pale People', Sunlight Soap, California Syrup of Figs and 'Bile Beans for Biliousness' were some of the more eye-catching. For more serious reading there was Lord Kitchener's weekly report from South Africa on the state of the war against the Boers. In 1900 five men from the village were serving on the front and two more volunteers were awaiting orders at the Britannia Barracks in Norwich.[3] The Relief of Mafeking in 1902 heralded the end of the war, and peace celebrations took place all over the country. My grandfather told the story of one young soldier from Hempnall who overindulged during the celebrations and was obliged to answer charges of being drunk and disorderly. He borrowed a silk hat and frock coat and so impressed the magistrate that charges were dismissed.[4] Sadly, Private George Moore, once Chief Ranger of the Lodge of Foresters at Hempnall, died from fever, and George Gowing and Harry Moore were killed on active service.[5] Albert Sheldrake came back to the village a helpless invalid and died three years later.[6] Gunner Nash, of the Norfolk Regiment of Artillery, was one of the lucky survivors and received a medal for long service and good conduct.[7]

Hempnall had developed a strong community spirit, and the increase in leisure time encouraged social events and activities. The village sported cricket and football clubs, and there was a brass band with its own practice room near the church.[8] Concerts were a regular occurrence, usually to raise money for a good cause, and invariably included violin solos, choral singing and recitations. An amateur theatrical group produced short plays from time to time, and endless opportunities were presented by both church and chapel for community singing.[9] There were lectures on keeping poultry, home nursing and dairy produce, often illustrated with lantern slides.[10] There was a chance to understand the complexities of the 1902 Education Act, a talk on Queen Victoria and on politics and several opportunities to hear stirring lectures on temperance and missionary work. A group intent on forming a rifle club met in 1907 at the Nelson Hall, where it was proposed members should contribute 1s.6d. annually. Mr Joshua Bussey offered the use of sand holes for shooting practice.[11] Five months later the Hempnall Miniature Rifle Club was opened by Mrs Irby of Boyland Hall, who fired three shots, scoring a bull's eye and an inner.[12] A ladies' cricket club was begun in 1908. Mr William Ellis offered his meadow and the vicar's wife was chosen as captain.[13] For the more politically minded, there was the Long Stratton, Hempnall & District Unionist (Conservative) Society, which held smoking concerts, sports events and talks.[14] Many people joined the Agricultural Labourers & Small Holders' Union after a meeting at the Queen's Head in 1907.

Outings, teas and treats encouraged attendance at school, church and chapel. There was always a Christmas party at the school, where at least 100 children were given a present by the vicar.[15] Summer treats for the Sunday-school children included tea on a field near the vicarage.[16] The church choir enjoyed an annual New Year dinner at the Nelson, and in the summer the choir and friends were conveyed to Great Yarmouth.[17] On one occasion up to 40 attended, some travelling in a two-horse conveyance to Ditchingham Station to catch the train.[18] The anniversary celebrations at the Wesleyan Chapel always included a free tea.[19] Employees of Mr Bussey were treated to an annual supper at the Swan Hotel

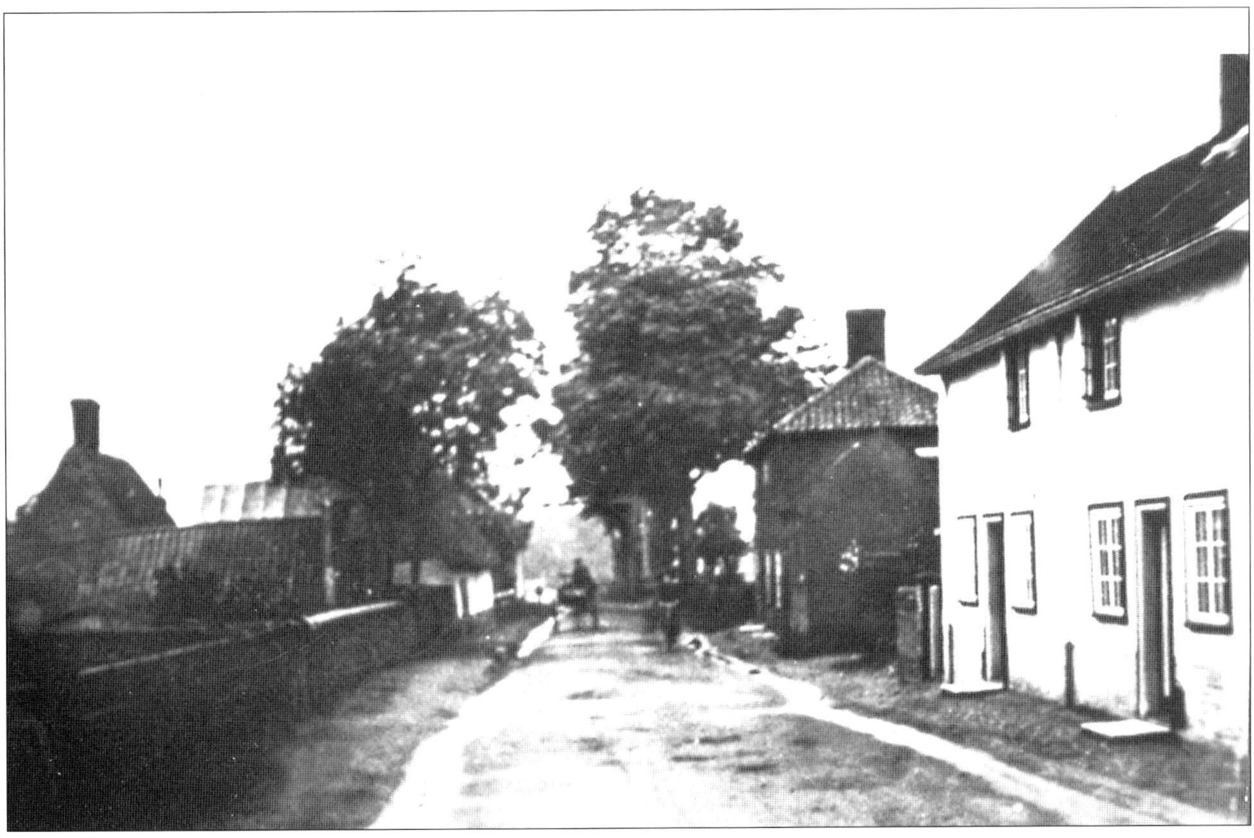

Hempnall Street with the Feoffees's coal store, a low building (on the right).

(formerly an inn) with the 'usual loyal toasts' and singing.[20]

Mr John Joseph Stammers, having bought two cottages adjoining his house, was happy to lend some space for a reading room until his plans were finalised for conversion to additional shop space.[21] He was thanked for his generosity in 1905, when it was proposed to begin raising funds to build a room for the purpose. In February 1909 it was reported that a gentleman had left money for the project and building work had begun.[22] By September the building, for a club and reading room, was complete and named the Village Institute. 'Men of sober, industrious disposition and of good character' living within three miles of the church were invited to join. Refreshments, no stronger than coffee, were permitted and the Sunday school, cricket, football and benefit clubs were invited to use the premises.[23] That year a whist drive and dance raised money for the cricket club and about 60 people attended in December.

The rise of friendly societies provided a form of insurance against sickness or unemployment for both men and women. At Hempnall the Ancient Order of Foresters (Court of the Poor Man's Friend) and the Independent Order of Oddfellows (the Loyal Woodman Lodge) both met at the Lord Nelson. Members were entitled to financial support in times of sickness providing they were not seen at any of the public houses. Members were expected to attend members' funerals. On 'Hospital Sunday' the groups usually joined forces and paraded in regalia, accompanied by the Hempnall brass band.[24] They attended the Wesleyan Chapel in the morning and the Parish Church in the evening, collections going to the Norfolk and Norwich Hospital.

The clothing and boot and shoe clubs were financed by concerts and generous individuals.[25] The Feoffees still provided money for the school and Parish Church and 100 cottage tenants were supplied with three hundredweight of coal at Christmas.[26] The villagers were up in arms in 1907 when the coal store in the Street was threatened with demolition. A deputation of ratepayers urged the council to save it.[27]

Pension schemes were rare, and folk either continued in work or relied on help from the younger generation. Henry Forder had been the Hempnall postman, but at 75, with failing health, he was obliged to retire. He received £5 compensation and then made a precarious living by hawking. Finally, attacked by paralysis and dependent on his son, he appealed to the Postmaster General, but was unsuccessful.[28]

There were still a number of people who, living on or below the poverty line, were faced with the ignominy of parish relief, but this was preferable to the workhouse. Esther Pymer was poor and she moved from Field Lane to Lundy Green after her husband died, taking in washing and working on the land to make ends meet. Parish relief had been withdrawn as she did not keep herself clean. She was last seen walking feebly, carrying sticks and a neighbour, concerned that she had not been seen for a day or two, looking in through a window saw her lying on the floor. Police Constable Hickling had to force the door, which was bolted and nailed up on the inside. She had been dead for two or three days. The house was almost empty – there was neither bed nor bedding and the only food was a few apples.

The Revd Charles Edward Hignett Wilford was inducted to the living in 1905.[29] His wife played the harmonium during services and may have suggested that an organ might be preferable. The new vicar must have set about raising money immediately, not just for an organ but for a set of tubular bells, there being but one bell in the tower. The tower needed repairs and these were paid for by Mrs Brutton, the widow of the Revd Augustine Brutton, the previous vicar. The organ supplied by Messrs Ingram & Co. of Hereford had originally stood in the Cathedral of St John's, Newfoundland. The dedication to which the choir and organist of St Andrew's Church, Norwich, had been invited took place in July, when £210 had been raised towards the cost. The Bishop of Norwich preached, but unfortunately, when Mr Harden, the organist from St Andrew's, Norwich, began playing, it became obvious that the organ was painfully out of tune.[30]

Various events were organised to reduce the £140 outstanding on the bells and organ. A jumble sale was held at the Nelson Hall and a children's concert at the school.[31] A garden fête held at Boyland Hall

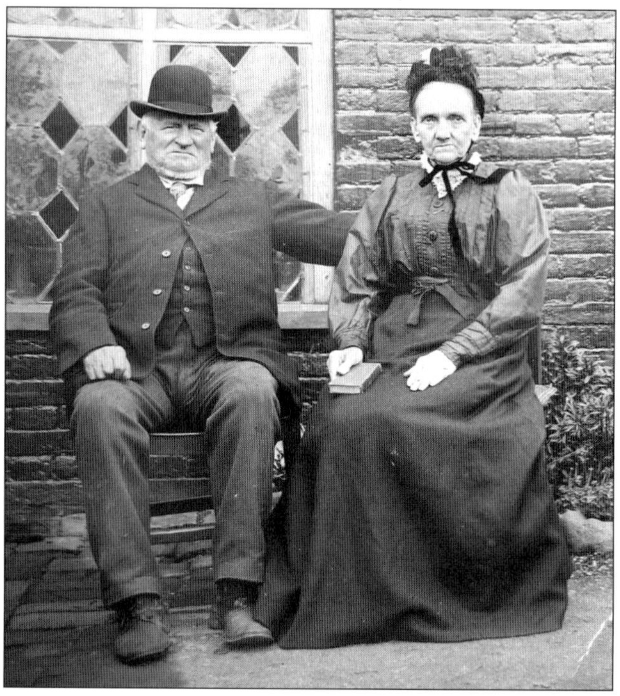

James and Mary Leggett outside Bridge Cottage, 1911. He was landlord of the King's Head for 30 years.

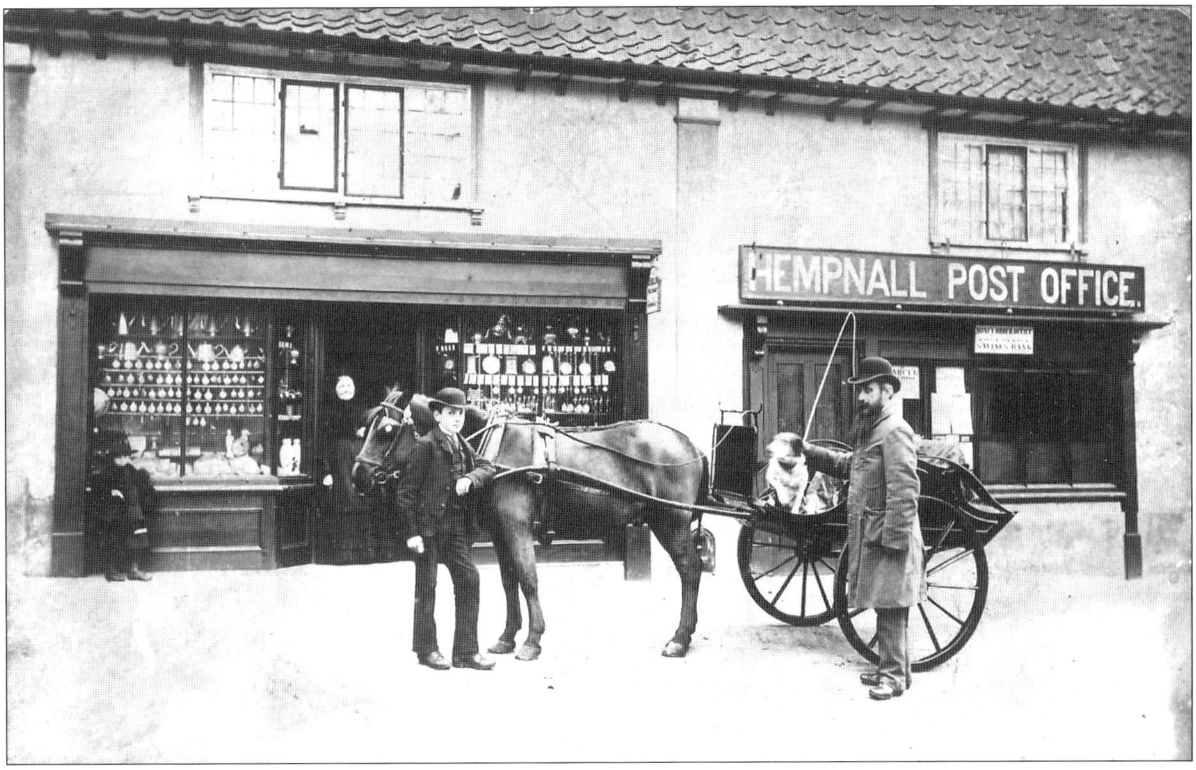

John Bullen, pictured outside the Longhouse, was sub-Postmaster, watchmaker and jeweller in 1888.

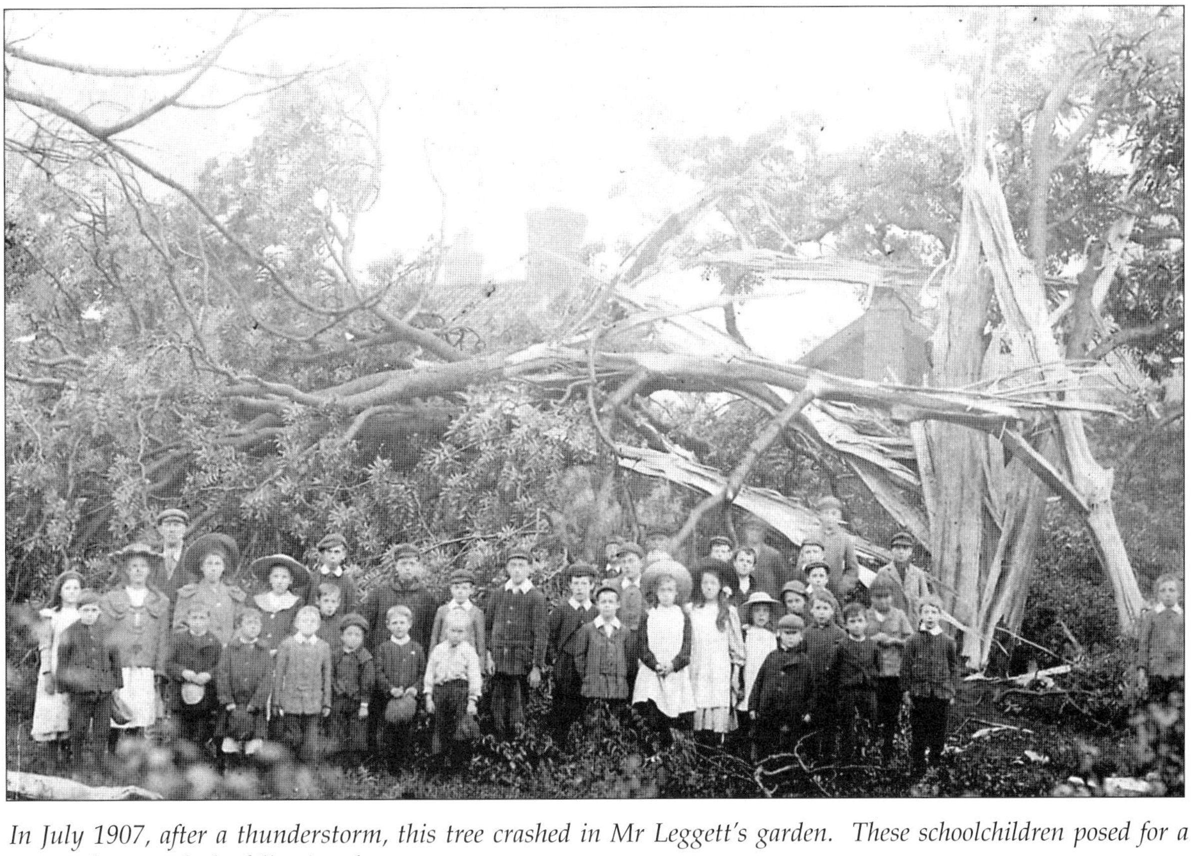

In July 1907, after a thunderstorm, this tree crashed in Mr Leggett's garden. These schoolchildren posed for a group photograph the following day.

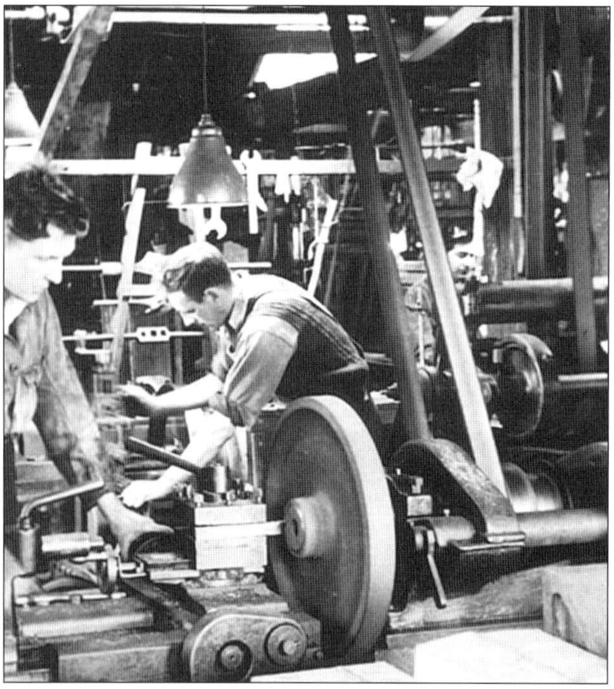

Lawrence Chapman (left) *and David Revell at work in Arnold's factory, 1957.* (EASTERN DAILY PRESS)

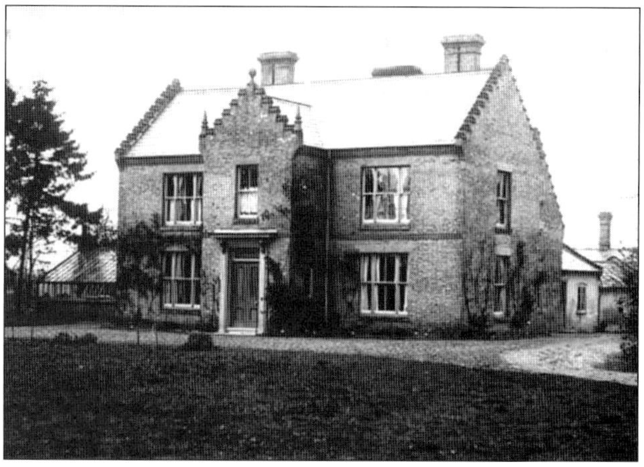

Hempnall House. Captain Frederick William Crawshay started a cider factory on the premises. Parts of the house are timber-framed. Earliest known date: 1661 (copyhold name: Old Barlick, or Old Bowleys).

included a concert by the Norwich Blind School band in a large marquee, with dancing in the evening.[32] A year later a bazaar was held at Boyland Hall. The stalls included plain, fancy, cheap jack, sweets and refreshments. A concert took place in the drawing-room, during the evening the grounds were illuminated with Chinese lanterns and the villagers were entertained by the Shotesham and Hempnall brass bands under bandmaster Boast.[33]

The Wesleyan Methodists began raising money for an organ and an extension of the chapel for their Sunday school.[34] The foundation stones were laid in November 1906. The chapel on the Greens was sold and reopened as a mission hall for the church.[35]

Although the population of England was on the increase, more people were moving to the towns and cities. The village population continued to decline and agriculture was still in difficulties. Swine fever was discovered at a Hempnall farm in 1907, making matters worse. William Ellis, the veterinary surgeon, lived for a few years at Fairsrtead House (now Krons Manor) and then moved in 1909 to Lynhurst in Broaden Lane. He concocted many of his medicines himself from herbs.

Arthur Arnold lived in an ancient cottage next to the Wesleyan Chapel. In 1905 he opened a tool making workshop in the Street, employing several men. He had begun his career in a grocer's shop, but after sending a photograph of a miniature steam engine, constructed in his spare time, to Savage & Co. of King's Lynn, he was invited to join the firm. He began his factory in Hempnall with a single forge and one lathe employing one assistant, Pip Vincent. Known as Arnold (Toolmakers) Ltd, the firm remained in the family until 1968, specialising in precision surface plates, guaranteed to 1/10,000 of an inch. In time, these were exported worldwide.

A young boy of three was blamed for a disaster in November 1906. Apparently he found some matches and set fire to a stack on the farm of the Misses Read. A total of 55 combs of barley were destroyed, the produce of five acres. Long Stratton Fire Brigade attended and laid a hose to a pond, thus saving three stacks of corn nearby.[36]

On Saturday, July 1907 a terrifying thunderstorm struck a huge ash tree near the Town Bridge, causing it to crash close to Mr James Leggett's house. 'All the branches were torn off and the trunk smashed to matchwood.' A photographer recorded the scene, with a crowd of children in the foreground.[37]

Captain Frederick William Crawshay opened a cider factory at Hempnall House, Lundy Green, in 1909. Bob Tweeddale used to work for him on Saturdays, picking apples and scrubbing out cider jars. Bob Moore fermented his own. His daughter, together with a friend, found a little hole in the cask

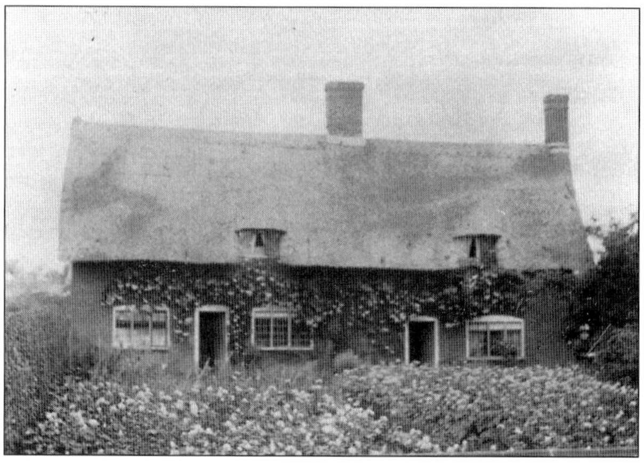

The cottage next to the chapel where Arthur Arnold was born (freehold).

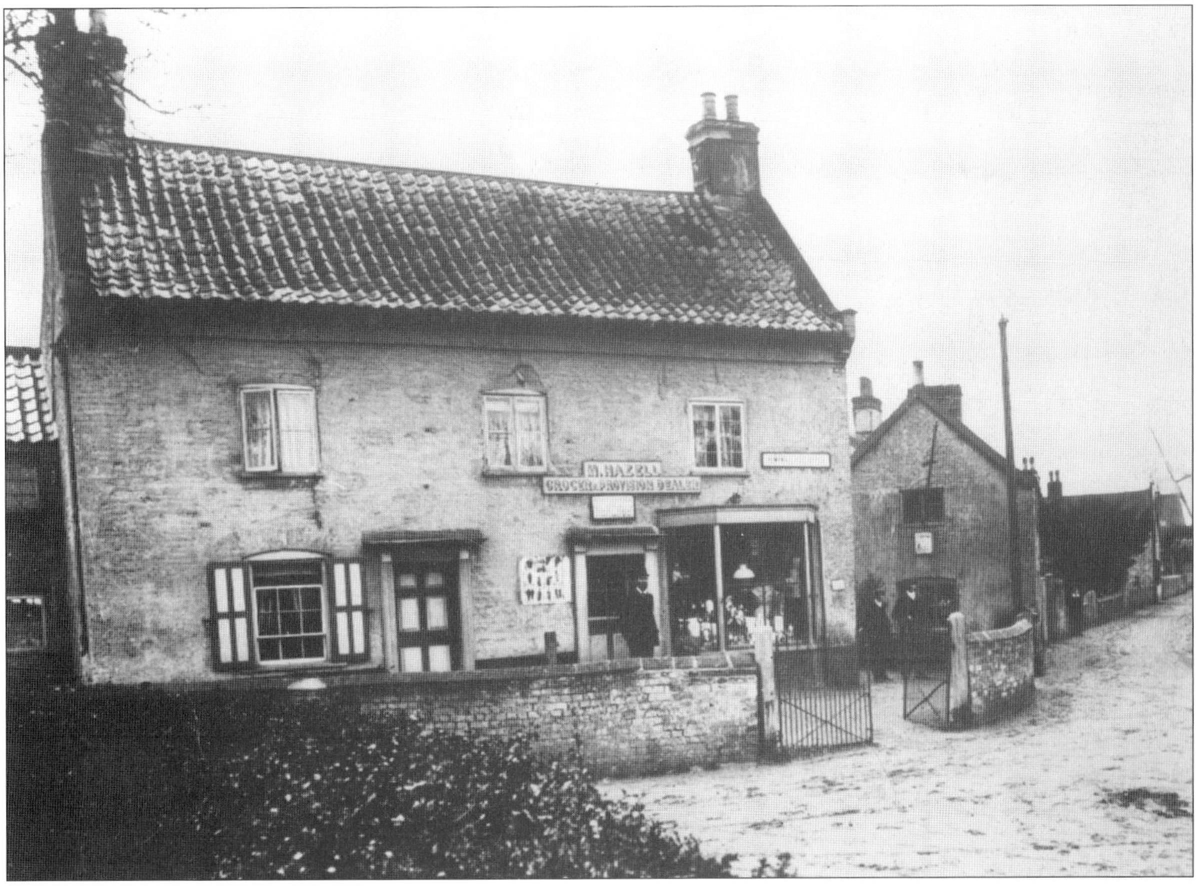

Hempnall Post Office on Mill Road. March Hazell as the sub-postmaster in 1908.

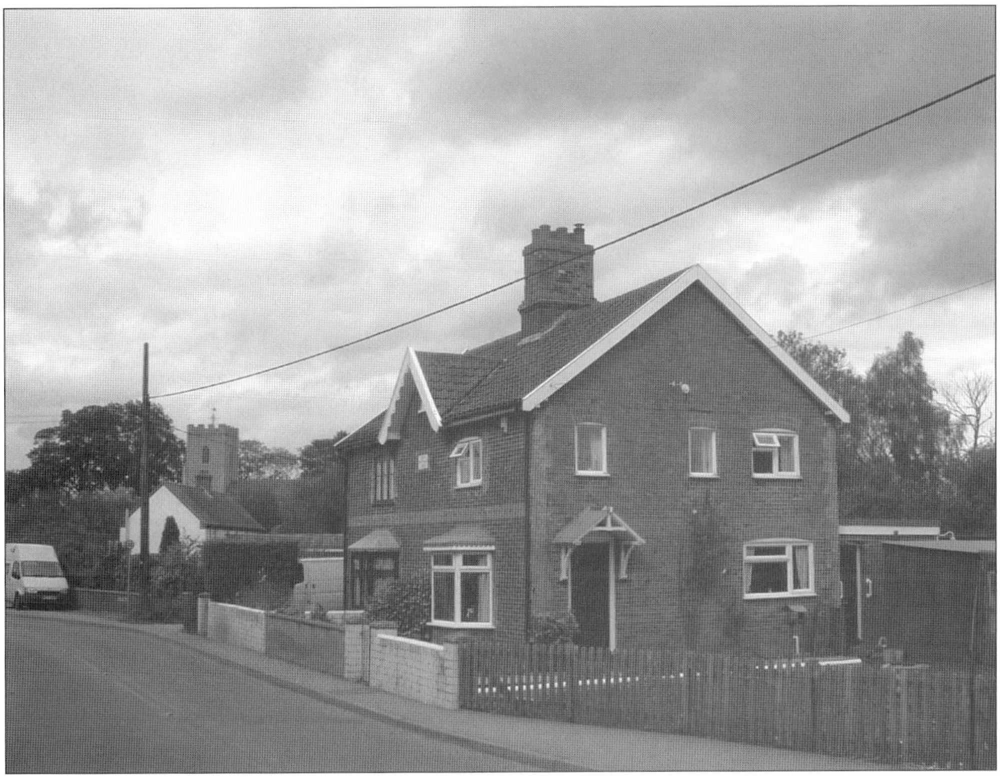

Bay Cottages. The house on the right was the village Police Station.

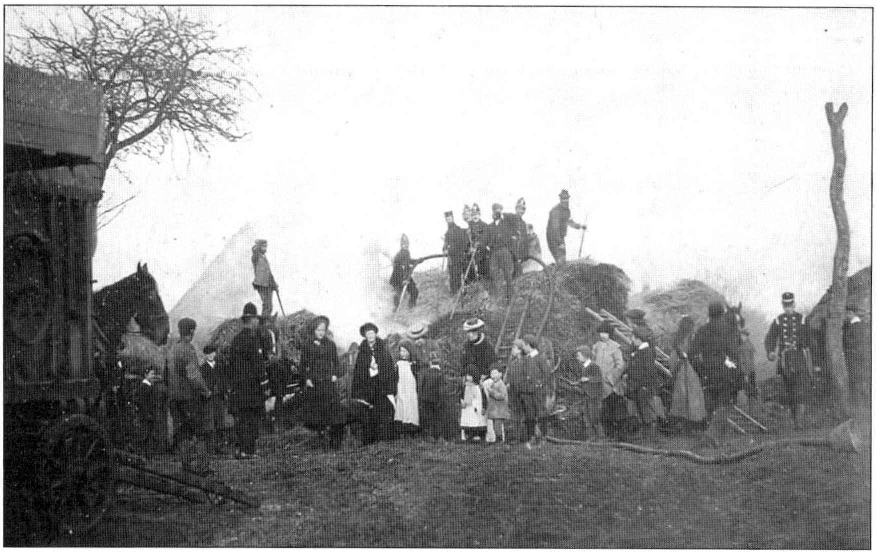

A haystack fire in November 1906.

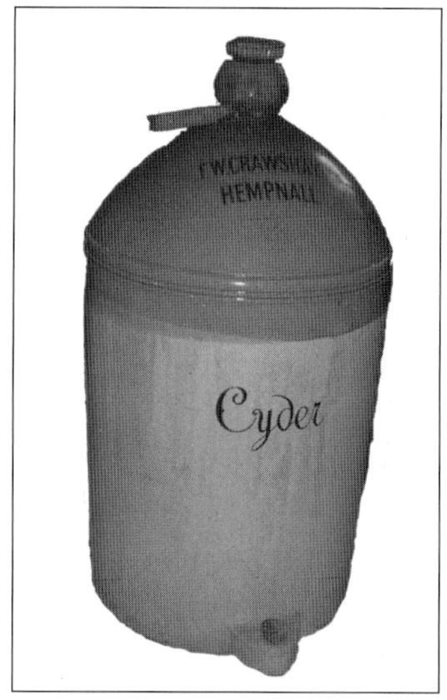

A Crawshay cider jar.

and the children poked straws through to sample the cider and were very ill as a consequence.

The inhabitants were deprived of modern amenities, but their social life might be considered enviable and some facilities were better than those offered today. In 1908 letters were received from Norwich at 7a.m. and 3p.m. and dispatched at 11.05 a.m. and 5.10 p.m. There was a Sunday collection and a postbox on the Greens. The postman walked the five miles to Flordon Station to collect the mail, took it to the post office for sorting, and then, still on foot, distributed it.

Hempnall had its own police station and a resident police officer and there was a variety of trades and little shops, making it unnecessary to make the journey to Norwich.

References

[1] NRO C/ED 3/101 Hempnall School Board
[2] *NM* Saturday, 13 January 1900
[3] *NC* Saturday, 10 February 1900
[4] G.G. Stammers (1969) *My Village* (Norwich) p.48
[5] *NM* Saturday, 18 January 1902
[6] *NC* Saturday, 4 July 1902
[7] *NM* 31 March 1906
[8] *NM* Saturday, 17 January 1903; *NM* Saturday, 5 August 1903. Mr L. Bussey, Captain
[9] *NM* Saturday, 16 February 1907 'A Happy Pair' and 'Little Toddlekins;' *NM* Saturday, 9 January 1909 'Babes in the Wood'
[10] *NM* Saturday, 4 March 1905; *NM* Saturday, 12 October 1907
[11] *NM* Saturday, 14 December 1907
[12] *NC* Saturday, 30 May 1908
[13] *NC* Saturday, 23 May 1908
[14] *NM* Saturday, 13 December 1902. Held at the Lord Nelson, 100 members present; *NM* Saturday, 21 January 1905. Held in the Society's Hall, Hempnall; *NM* Saturday, 19 November 1904
[15] *NM* Saturday, 4 January 1901; *NM* Saturday, 4 January 1902; *NM* Saturday, 10 January 1903; *NM* Saturday, 9 January 1904
[16] *NM* Saturday, 12 August 1905; *NM* Saturday, 7 August 1909. Outing to Dunston Park
[17] *NM* Saturday, 9 September 1905; *NC* Saturday, 8 August 1908
[18] *NM* Saturday, 17 August 1907
[19] *NM* Saturday, 13 January 1904
[20] *NM* Wednesday, 12 September 1906
[21] *NM* Saturday, 30 September 1905
[22] *NM* Saturday, 20 February 1909
[23] Indenture dated 30 September 1909
[24] *NM* Saturday 28 May 1904; *NM* Saturday 28 May 1905; *NM* Saturday 6 June 1906; *NM* Saturday 10 August 1907; *NC* Saturday 15 August 1908; *NM* Saturday 7 August 1909
[25] *NM* Saturday, 12 December 1906. A short cantata by the church choir to raise money for the Clothing Club; *NM* Saturday 30 December 1903. 19 children given funds; *NM* Saturday 24 December 1902. Friends of the Boot and Shoe Club raising money
[26] *NM* Saturday, 6 December 1905; *NC* Saturday, 19 December 1908
[27] *NM* Saturday, 28 December 1907
[28] *NM* Saturday, 3 January 1903
[29] *NM* Wednesday, 1 March 1905
[30] *EDP*, Friday, 21 July 1905
[31] *NM* Saturday, 30 September 1905; *NM* Saturday, 3 January 1906
[32] *NM* Saturday, 12 August 1905
[33] *NM* Wednesday, 8 August 1906
[34] *NM* Wednesday, 31 January 1906
[35] *NM* Saturday, 20 October 1906
[36] *NM* Saturday, 10 November 1906
[37] *EDP* Tuesday, 2 July 1907

✤ CHAPTER 15 ✤

Gathering Clouds 1910–19

The social life of the village was sustained by dances, concerts and a variety of events.[1] The Foresters enjoyed their annual parade, incorporating a service at the Wesleyan Chapel in the morning, another in the pit during the afternoon and concluding with a third at the Parish Church in the evening. In September 1913 about 600 people attended the service at the pit.[2] Mr and Mrs James Leggett celebrated their golden wedding in 1911. He had been landlord of the King's Head for 30 years and had run a mile in seven minutes when aged 70.[3] The cricket club thrived, captained by Mr Lee Bussey, and in 1910 played a charity match for which one side dressed as clowns.[4] A glorious victory over the Long Stratton Cricket Club was recorded in 1913.[5] Captain Frederick William Crawshay put Hempnall on the cider map by winning first and second awards at the Royal Show for the best exhibit in the bottled cider class, thereby bringing the Challenge Cup to Norfolk.[6]

The church and the Wesleyan Methodists organised the usual outings and were at the heart of village life for many people. Methodist services were sometimes disrupted by rowdy behaviour from the Woodman, but the wife of the policeman, who attended the chapel, would report the culprits and they would be beaten with his stick. Preachers often had stones thrown at them as they arrived for a meeting. However, the Woodman closed in 1909 and this may have alleviated the situation.

A gale in the spring of 1910 severely damaged the church tower window.[7] A friend of the vicar offered to pay for a new one and it was decided to erect a new screen within the tower at the same time.[8] The clock received a new face the following year.

A Boy Scout troop was initiated in 1910, encouraged by a visit from a detachment of Yarmouth Scouts who camped in a meadow in the village for a week. The troop marched to church on Sundays, the collection taken being in aid of the Hempnall Scouts'

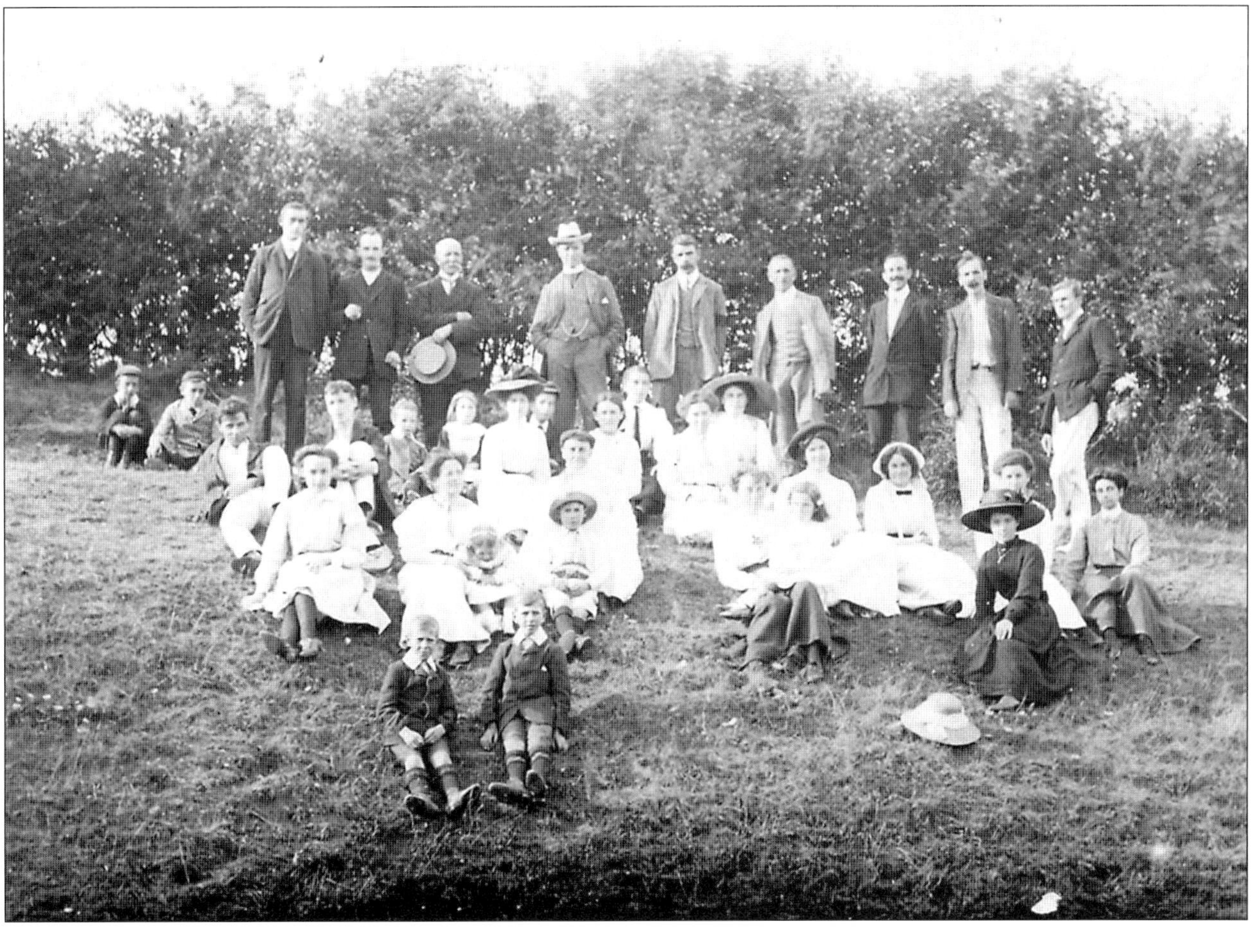

Spectators at a cricket match in the pit in 1911.

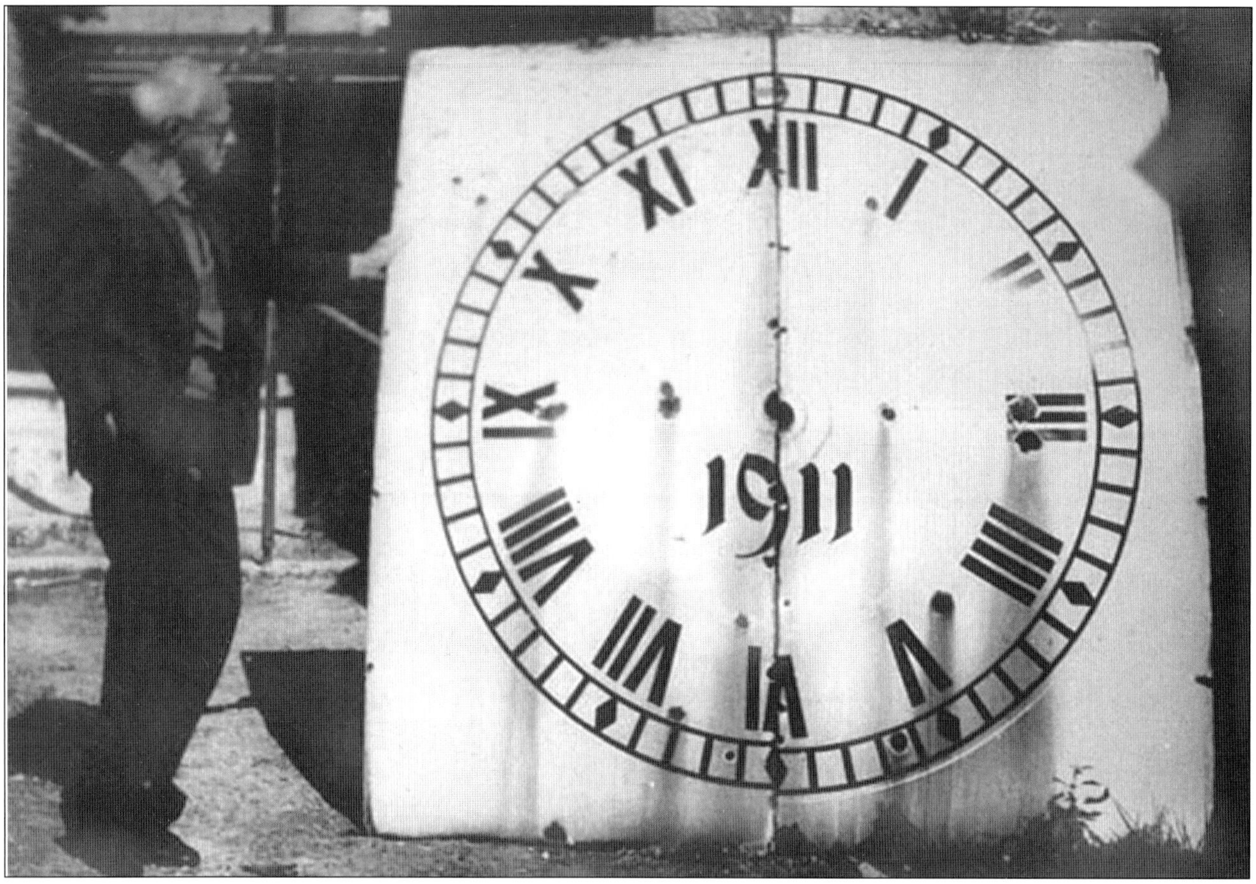

Mr Pechey with the church clock face, 1911.

kit.[9] A month later, fully kitted out and very smart, 15 Hempnall Scouts, led by the vicar's wife, marched to Saxlingham Nethergate followed by a small crowd.[10] In October they received tenderfoot badges and in December were entertained at the Village Institute with gramophone records. Money was raised for the Boy Scout movement the following year the boys put on a display and Scoutmaster J.B. Crabbe enthralled everyone with his demonstration of sword swinging.[11]

Charles Fairhead, a local farmer, had employed James Fryer in 1911 as a horseman, and as such Fryer had the use of a cottage rent free. After three months the employment was terminated as Fryer was unwell and he was ordered to leave the cottage. When Fryer refused the frustrated farmer removed all the doors and windows and forced the stove from the wall, setting fire to a mat. Fryer sued Fairhead for £50 damages and Fairhead came up with a counter-claim of £10 for holding possession of the cottage. The jury found for the farmer, but the judge ordered a fresh hearing as he felt the jury could not have been attending as the verdict was perverse and against the weight of evidence.[12] No record of the retrial seems to be in the newspapers, so perhaps the matter was settled out of court.

The old shop, being a room within the house, having become too small for the growing trade, needed further space. John Joseph Stammers took the opportunity to buy the shop-front of Buntings in Norwich when the building was demolished in 1912.[13] It was transported by horse and cart over two days. Shortly after the installation, someone vandalised the front and 5s. reward was offered to anyone who named the culprit. By this time Stammers was employing two maids, a housekeeper and five girls in the kitchen making bread, mincemeat and pork pies for sale in the shop. Female staff were accommodated in the attics of Connaught House initially, but, with a growing family, more space was required. He hired Ivy Cottage in the Street as a dormitory and installed a housekeeper. However, the girls used to climb out of the upstairs windows at night to meet their boyfriends and then raid the pantry on their return.

My grandfather, George Gerald Stammers, married Beatrice Betts in 1912. He had aspired to journalism, but the prospect of providing for a wife convinced him that financial security from the family business would be more practical, and he returned from Norwich to Hempnall. At first they lived at Meadow View in the Street. Then they decided to build and contacted Mr J.E. Burton, a Norwich architect, who took the train to Flordon and then cycled to Hempnall to discuss the plans. Two houses were built, the second being for Herbert Stammers, a

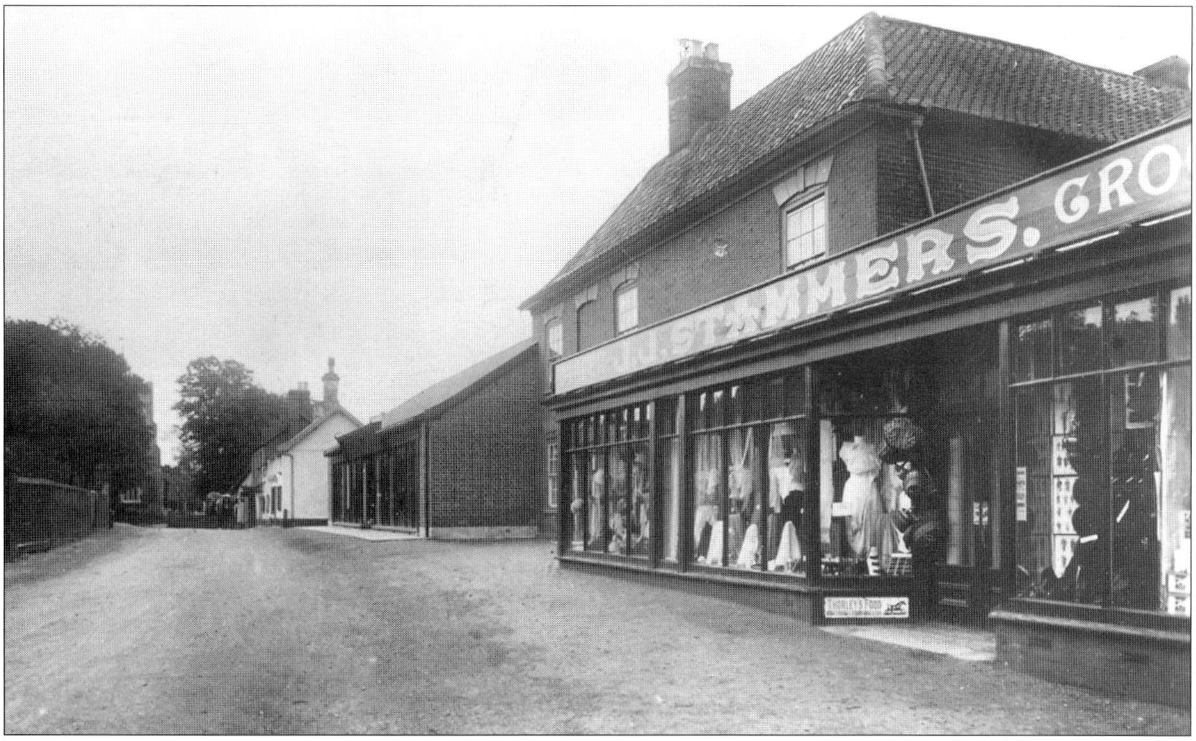

Stammers' shop after 1912, with the new furnishing department.

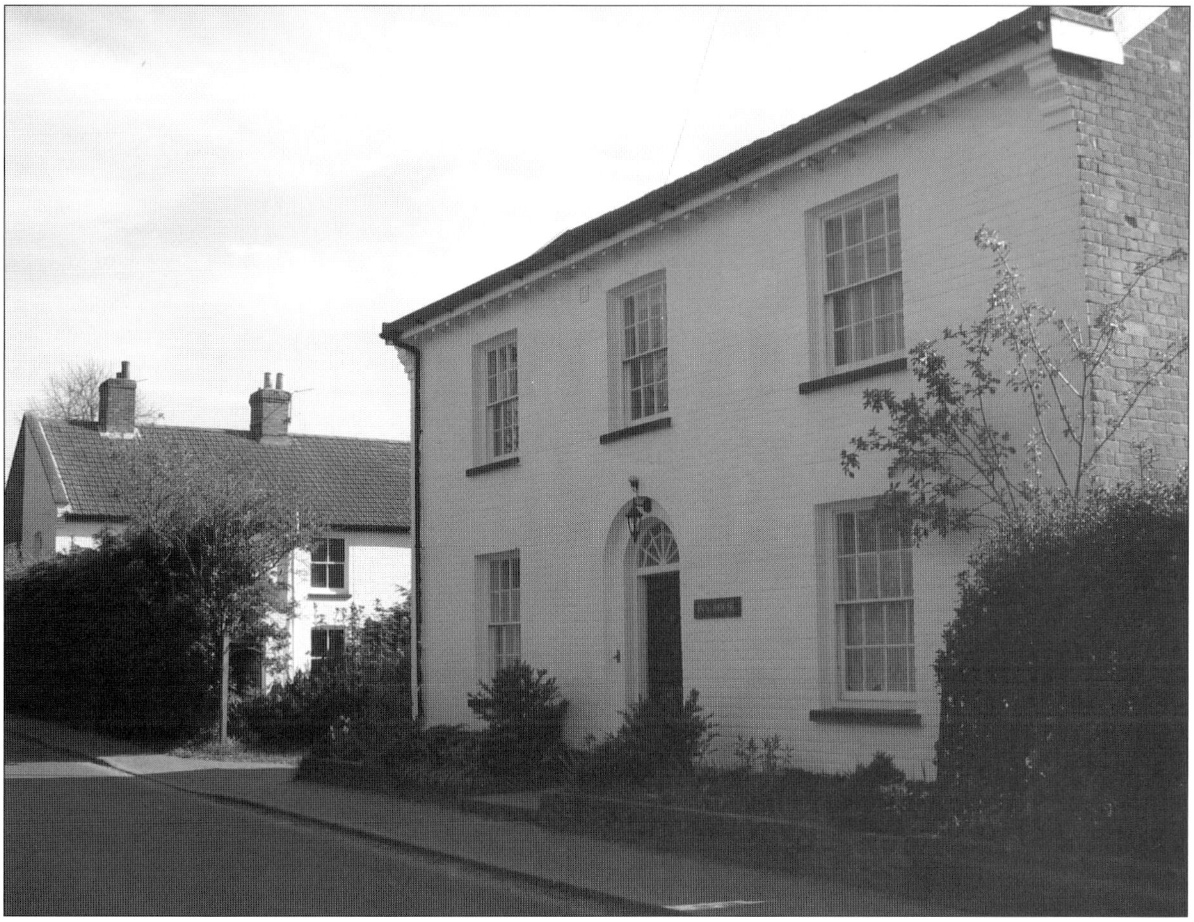

Meadow View (left) and Ivy Cottage.

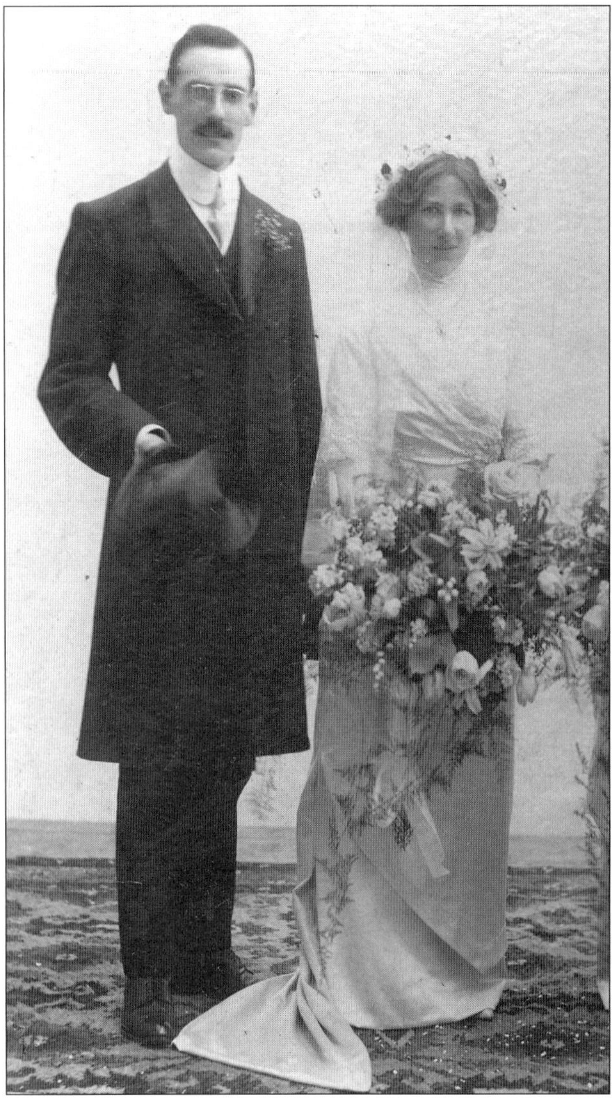

Gerald George Stammers and Beatrice Elfleda Betts on their wedding day in 1912.

cousin. Grandfather's house was called Rostrevor. The houses were built on the site of a pit that had been used as a dumping ground by the village, and it took 'Gobbler' (because he used to live at Turkey Row) Beckett, a one-legged man who lived in a gypsy caravan, all winter to fill it in. Gobbler is still remembered for his wooden leg, made from a table leg, and his ability to ride a bicycle with one pedal. Apparently, he lost his real leg falling out of a tree when working on a job. He was paid compensation, but his wife ran off with the money. His final days were spent in an old tin hut that still survives today.

The horse continued to be the primary mode of transport. In August 1912 Edward Hazell, a fowl dealer, was charged with driving furiously on the footpath through the Street and causing the local police officer and several others to jump out of the way.[14] Thomas Bullen was killed trying to stop a horse that was bolting.[15] Thomas Roberts, a journeyman wheelwright and carpenter, had been working at Costessy one Saturday and met his wife in Norwich in the evening. They left after dark in a pony and trap and stopped at Stoke Rummer for a drink and then again at the Queen Adelaide in Saxlingham. According to his wife, they gave a lift to a stranger, who took over the reins and caused the pony to fall. However, witnesses reported that the Roberts were the only passengers and that the pony stepped on a grating and fell, causing the pair to be tipped out. Mr Roberts died two days later, but his symptoms were consistent with shellfish poisoning. The jury decided that death was caused by accidental shock from having eaten unwholesome shellfish and from injuries suffered when thrown out of the cart which he was driving.[16]

Sidney Miles, the local butcher, asked James Townsend to sell an old horse for him. Townsend had it shod but it was still lame, a 'jibber', and 'junked' at the back. He later 'chopped it away' to a man called Francis and then offered to pay Miles a guinea, which he refused to accept. Miles took Townsend to court, believing that he had been robbed and should be paid at least £5 for the horse. The judge decided that a guinea was ample value.[17]

The old footbridge near the church was in need of repair in 1911. Plans had been submitted by a surveyor at a Rural District Council meeting in September. An amendment was proposed for a more substantial bridge, measuring 16ft across, for vehicles; but the motion was defeated by one vote.[18] The work was completed by April 1912, just before a ferocious storm that devastated Norfolk in August of that year, when 6.59ins of rain fell in 12 hours:

> *At Hempnall there were exciting scenes during the storm and pigs, ponies and donkeys were hastily removed to places of safety through the rapidly rising waters which were two or three feet deep. The water invaded many of the houses and the inmates had to go upstairs for safety and spent a weary night with water still in their dwellings.*

Mr Read's workshop was completely demolished.[19] At a School Board meeting it was recorded that the caretaker's house was under water, but nothing could be done until the water subsided as the roads were impassable.

The school, lying in a hollow, was often prone to flooding. In February 1913 the garden belonging to the caretaker's house was under water and plaster was falling down in all the rooms. At the back of the school grounds the drainage from the boys' urinal was floating out on the flood water. Sarah Brown was the unfortunate caretaker. She subsidised her income by taking in washing, and the boys would collect pebbles from the playground and use the bloomers on her line for target practice and she would come after them with the prop.[20] By 1914 Mrs Brown had had enough and resigned, having been caretaker for over 20 years.[21] The river water was

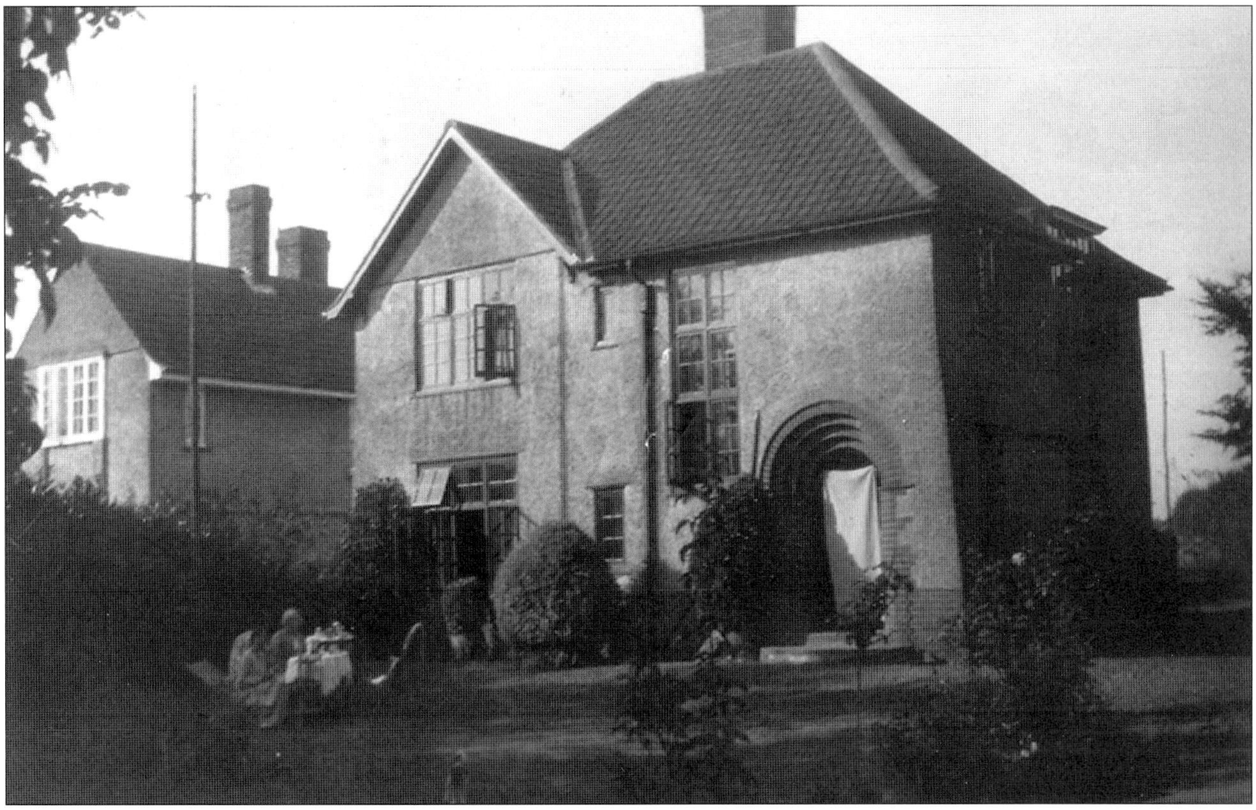

Rostrevor, now Rosewood, in the Street, built in 1912.

again high in September 1913, when Mabel and Clarence Lockwood and their friend, Annie Theviston, fell off a footbridge on the Swan Meadow. They were holding hands when Annie slipped in, pulling the other two with her. Police Sergeant Culley heard their cries and pulled Annie out. Mabel got out by herself and dragged out her brother.[22]

The villagers gathered at the Institute in 1913 to say farewell to the Revd Charles H. Wilford and his wife, who were about to depart for Stow Bardolph. The vicar was highly praised for the church improvements he had instigated, and his wife was thanked for training the choir and playing the organ. They were presented with a suite of dining-room chairs with commemorative brass plates and four plated flower vases.[23]

The Revd John Talbot Gardiner bought the Old Manor House next to the church, making major internal alterations. The Brutons had lived at Hempnall House and the Wilfords at the Villa Farm; now, at last, the village would have a resident clergyman in the centre of the village.[24]

As the threat of war with Germany drew near, the villagers may have heard rumours of the Naval airship base which was being established at Pulham Market a short distance away.[25] The grand procession that accompanied the funeral bier of Mr Samuel Read in July 1914 may have been the last recorded parade before war was declared.[26]

War was declared on 4 August 1914. Patriotism was the principal reason for young men to volunteer, but there were other factors, for the war presented an opportunity for adventure, to see the world outside the village and to leave the hard agrarian life. There was the prospect of great marches, battles and then, after a quick victory, a return home by Christmas. A crowd gathered at Thorpe Station on the 6 August to witness the departure of the 3rd Norfolks and the reservists of the 1st and 2nd Norfolk Regiment, some Hempnall men among them.

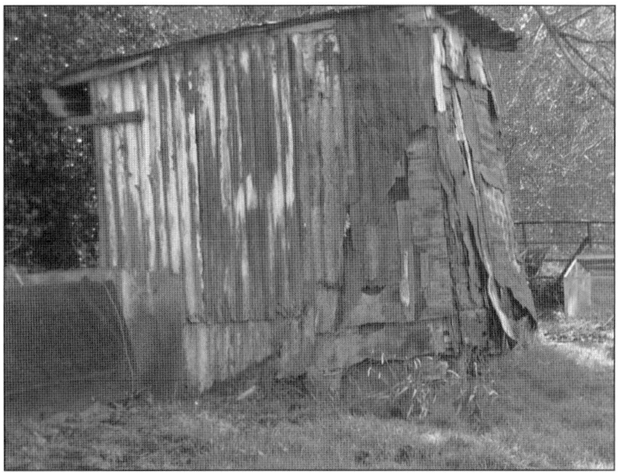

'Gobbler' Beckett's hut.

The first months of the war were rampant with rumours of spies and saboteurs. Hempnall had been visited just before the war by representatives of a German company who had taken photographs of the village and imposed them on various

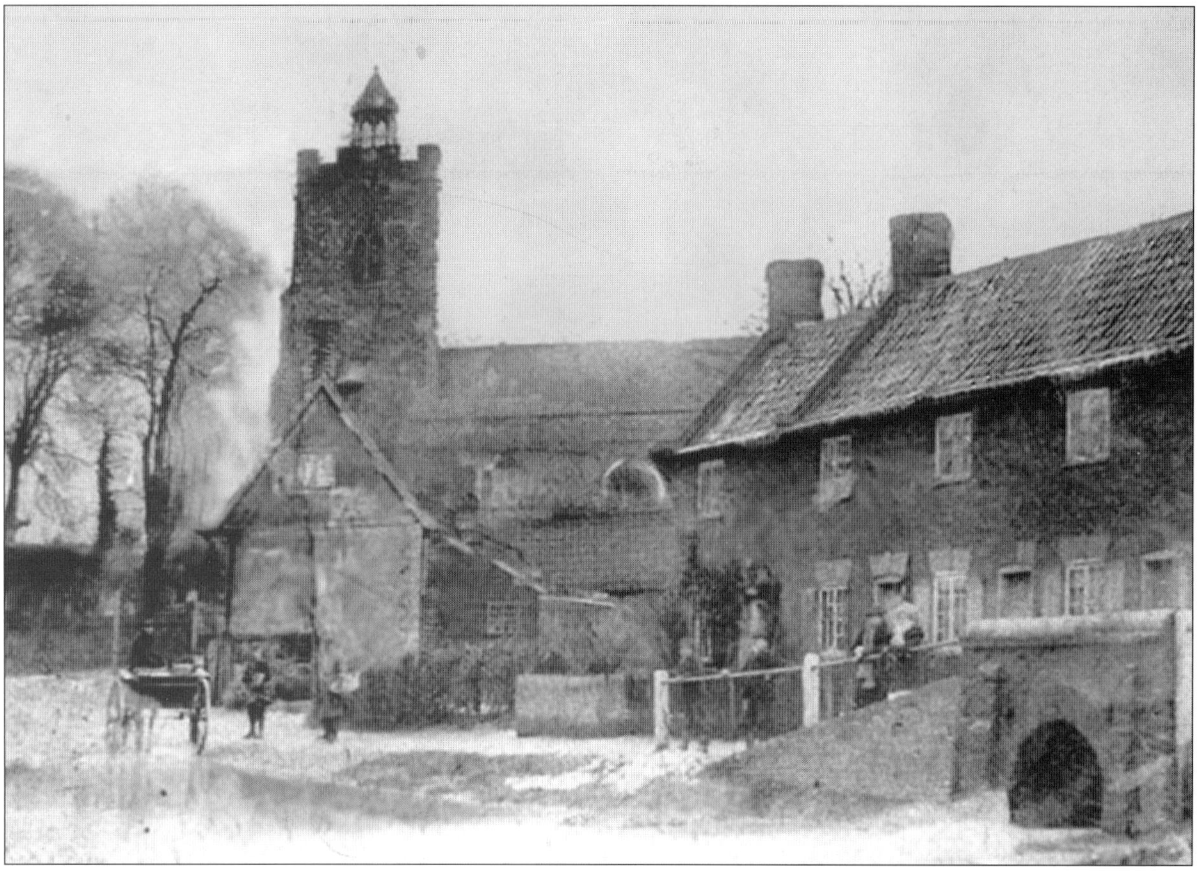

A flood at the town watering, c.1912

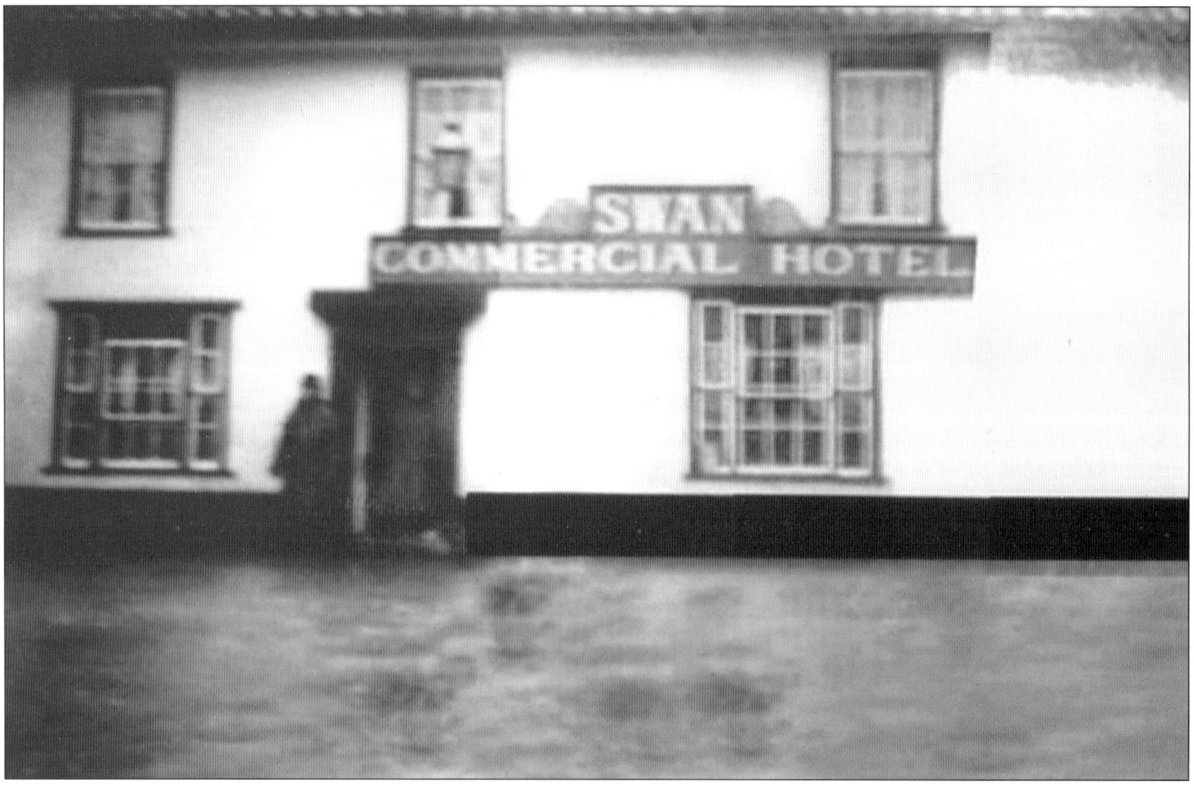

Floods at the Swan Commercial Hotel.

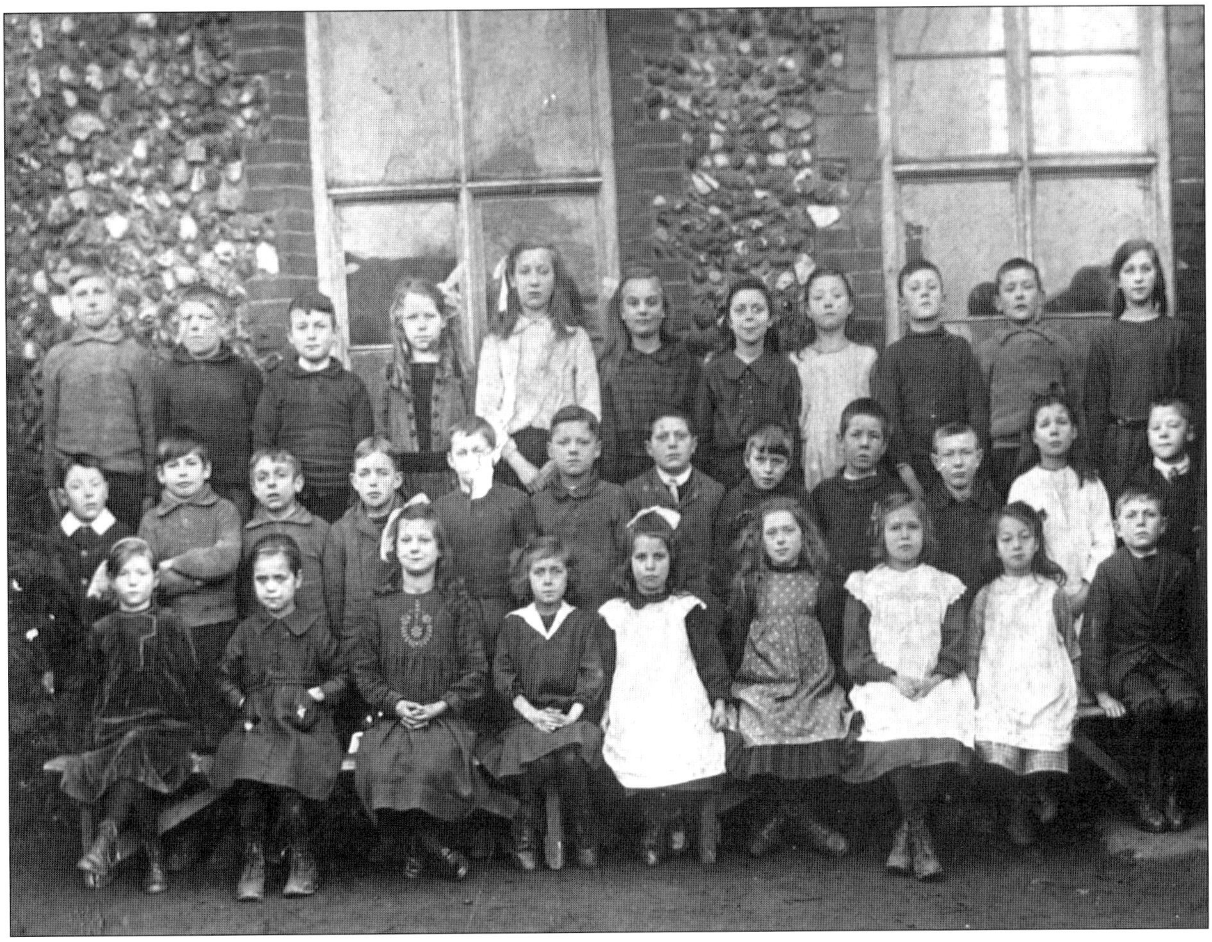

Hempnall schoolchildren.

pieces of crockery. In retrospect, people began to suspect espionage.[27]

The young volunteers were not home by Christmas and before long the first casualties were reported. Leonard Townsend, a lance-corporal in the 1st Norfolks, was killed in 1915 at the Battle of Neuve Chapelle. He had only been married a short time.[28] Private Charles Spink of the 1st Norfolks was wounded in France the same year. He had served in the South African war, but had volunteered again.[29] Mr W. Page died in 1916 and was fortunate to have been reunited with his son, who had been invalided home from France, just a week before his death.[30] William Ladbrooke was believed to be a prisoner of war in Germany in 1918 and Harry Townsend was killed in action in the same year.[31]

Village life changed drastically. Not only were so many young men missing, with news of deaths and injuries arriving all too often, but there was the threat of Zeppelin raids and food and coal shortages. The school was out of coal in January 1915 due to the military authorities controlling the railways, primarily for moving troops. Wagons for transporting coal were also in short supply. In the winter of 1916 the school was without coal despite repeated ordering. The weather being very cold, it was impossible to keep it open. With the absence of so many young men, the dances were discontinued and the Village Institute loaned the school the piano, as it was seldom used and quite neglected.[32]

Percy Ellis was a schoolboy when the war started and remembered seeing a Zeppelin come over the village. On one occasion he was taken to the Norfolk and Norwich Hospital suffering from suspected appendicitis. After a dose of castor oil he was sent home. Taken through a back door, he saw rows of tents packed with wounded soldiers.

In October 1914 a meeting was held at the school to discuss the question of Belgian refugees and to make contributions to the war fund.[33] By 1915 the reality of war was sinking in and men were not so keen to enlist. The schoolmaster, Mr William Morgan Roberts, was asked to canvass in Hempnall and Fritton under the Parliamentary Recruiting Campaign and was granted permission to be absent from school for short periods.

Slates were constantly falling off the school roof and Mr Roberts requested some protection to prevent them falling into the playground. The composition floors of the classroom were so worn that the concrete underneath was exposed and dangerous and the playground needed to be surfaced with macadam, but none of these requests was granted due to shortage of money.

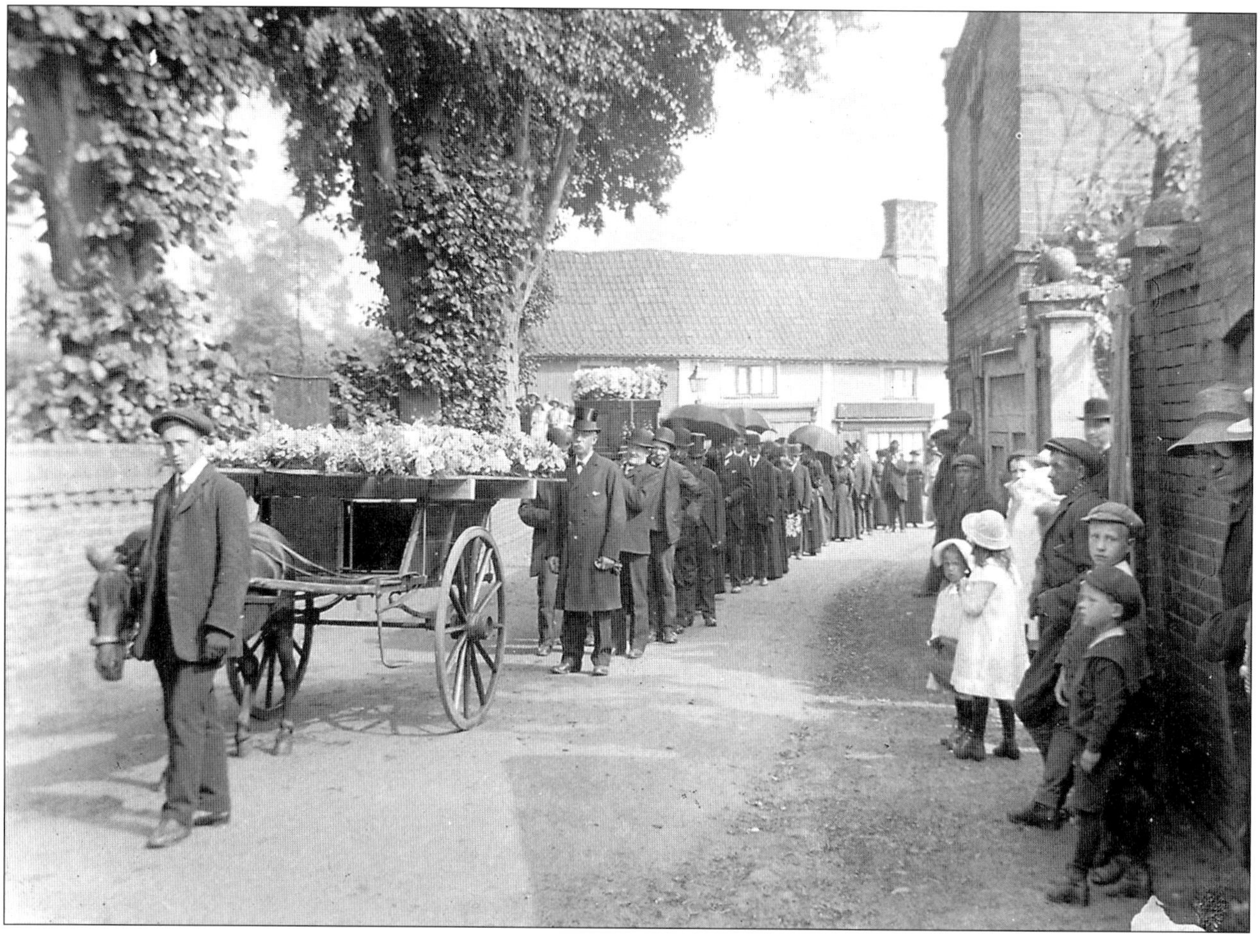

The funeral procession of Samuel Read in 1914.

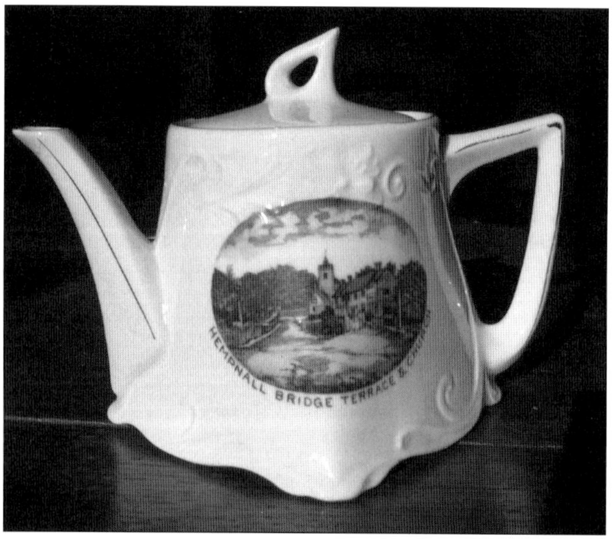

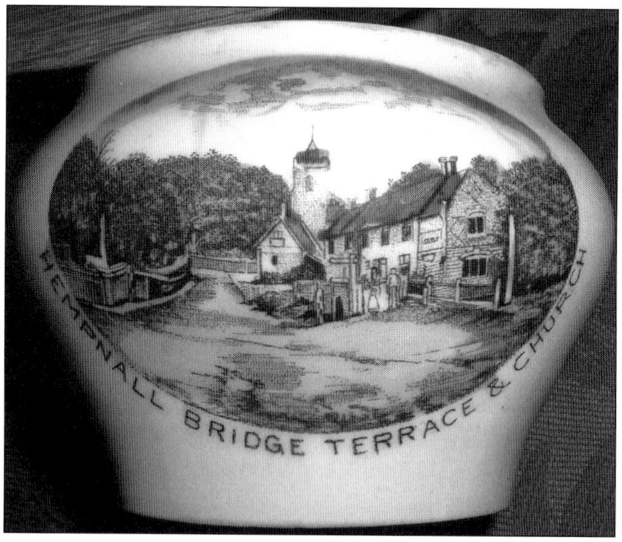

Above, left and right: *Hempnall crockery, c.1913.*

Depwade Council met in 1916 to hear a report on a cottage in Hempnall occupied by Harry Smith. It had one room on the ground floor, with a defective brick floor below the level of the garden. Upstairs the main bedroom was open to the staircase, with no fireplace and just one window. A second bedroom overhung a derelict cottage. The roof was dangerously defective and the outside privy was unsanitary and close to the well. The cottage was declared unfit for human habitation and ordered to be demolished if the recommended repairs were not carried out.[34]

In 1917 women organised an afternoon's entertainment at the Nelson Hall. Mrs Bertrum Barwell's pupils played musical pieces and then *Cinderella* was performed. This was followed by tea in the vicarage garden and £20 was raised for the Red Cross Society.[35]

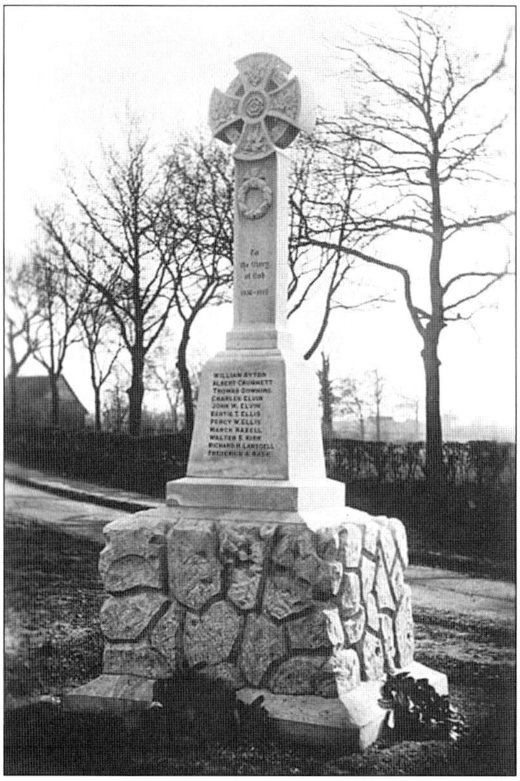

The war memorial on the site of Wesley's Tree.

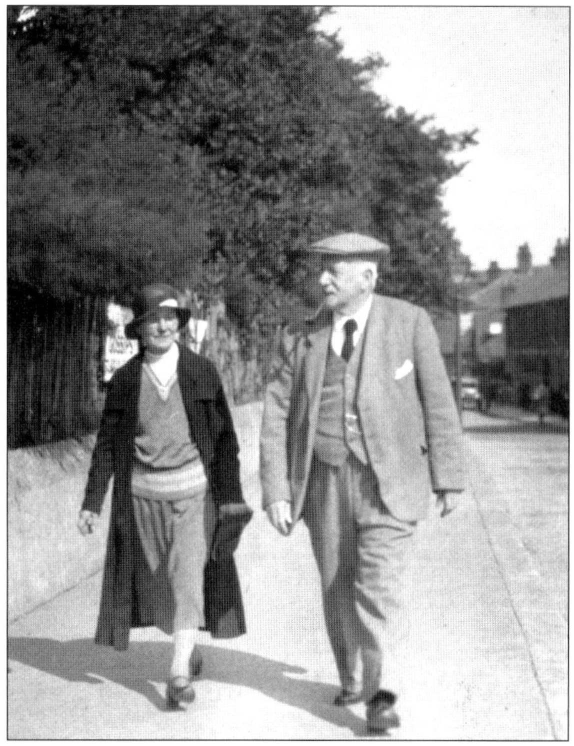

Schoolmaster Mr Roberts and his wife.

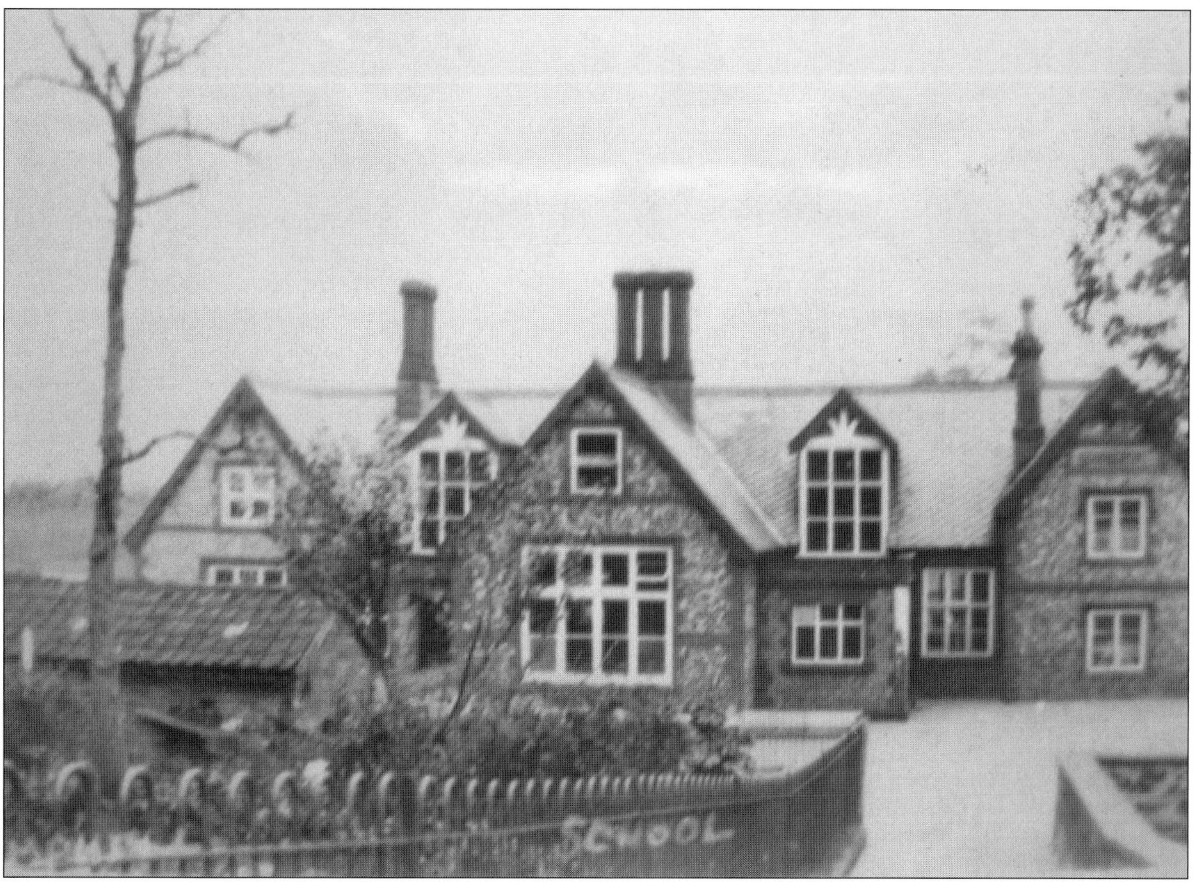

Hempnall School.

A committee was formed to start a Girl Guide group and it was agreed that they could use the school provided they paid for fuel.[36]

The war ended in November 1918. In Norwich all work was suspended as joyous crowds gathered in the market place, and in no time the streets were ablaze with bunting and flags and bells rang out after four years of silence.

A committee was appointed in April 1919 to report on the matter of a memorial for Hempnall men. The first proposal was to build a war memorial in the centre of the plain near the bridge; but when discussions began to focus on the Green at the other end of the Street, the local woodman took the matter into his own hands, felled the great oak there known as Wesley's Tree, and turned it into coffins before minds were changed.[37] It was 26 July 1919 before all the soldiers had returned and then a celebration was planned at the school. The 22 Hempnall men who gave their lives in the First World War are named on the war memorial:[38]

Ayton, William	*Nash, Charles*
Crummett, Albert	*Nash, Fred*
Downing, Thomas	*Pointer, Clarence*
Ellis, Bertie Thomas	*Sheldrake, Arthur*
Ellis, Percy William	*Spink, Charles*
Elvin, Charles	*Sporle, Robert Samuel*
Elvin, John William	*Townsend, Harry*
Elvin, Leonard	*Townsend, Herbert*
Hazell, March	*Townsend, Leonard*
Kirk, William	*Varley, Sidney*
Lansdell, Richard	*Ward, Walter*

A few days before Christmas in 1919, upwards of 500 people gathered to pay their respects to those who had given their lives. The memorial, in the shape of a Celtic cross placed on a huge block of stone, was carved by Mr Harry Parfitt of Long Stratton. There was a short service accompanied by the Hempnall Brass Band and then the Hon. W.H. Cozens-Hardy, MP for the southern division of Norfolk, addressed the assembled crowd, praising the courage of the men, most of whom were volunteers. As the dying strains of the final hymn 'For all the Saints' faded away, bandmaster W. Revell played the Last Post.

References

1 *NM* Saturday, 1 January 1910; *NM* Saturday, 5 February 1910; *NM* Saturday 3 December 1910; *NM* Saturday 2 May 1914
2 *NM* Saturday, 5 September 1913
3 *NC* Saturday, 14 October 1911
4 *NC* Saturday, 24 September 1910
5 *NM* Saturday, 18 April 1913
6 *EDP* Friday, 10 July 1914
7 *NM* Saturday, 9 April 1910
8 *NC* Saturday, 14 May 1910
9 *NC* Saturday, 6 August 1910
10 *NC* Saturday, 17 September 1910
11 *NC* Saturday 25 February 1911
12 *NM* Saturday 4 March 1911
13 *EDP* Tuesday, 2 July 1912
14 *NM* Saturday, 24 August 1912
15 *NM* Saturday, 27 January 1912
16 *NC* Saturday 27 January 1912
17 *NC* Saturday 4 June 1910
18 NRO DC2/4/2 Highway Committee minute Book 3

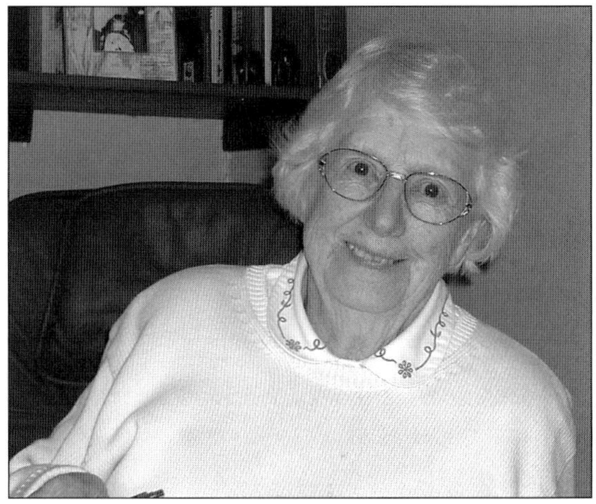

Betty Chapman 1924-2005

19 *EDP* Friday, 30 August 1912
20 Recorded by Betty Chapman from her father's memories
21 NRO C/ED 68/334 Hempnall School Board
22 *NM* Saturday, 12 September 1913
23 *NC* Saturday 13 June 1913. The Revd C.H. Wilford died at Stow Bardolph in 1919
24 NRO BR 37/3/1222 Indenture 2 May 1914
25 *NM* Saturday, 17 June 1914
26 *EDP* Friday, 10 July 1914
27 G.G. Stammers *My Village* p.58
28 *NM* Saturday, 24 April 1915
29 *NM* Saturday, 19 June 1915
30 *NM* Saturday, 29 July 1916
31 *NC* Friday, 11 October 1918
32 NRO C/ED 68/334 30 January 1915, 2 March 1915, 1 February 1915 Hempnall School Board
33 NRO C/ED 68/334 3 October 1914 Hempnall School Board
34 *NM* Saturday, 30 December 1916
35 *NM* Saturday, 2 June 1917
36 NRO C/ED 68/334 27 May 1918 Hempnall School Board
37 NRO DC 2/4/3 Depwade Rural District Council Highways Minute Book
38 *EDP* Wednesday, 24 Dec 1919

CHAPTER 16

The Pace of Change 1920–29

Life was not easy for some of the servicemen who returned to Hempnall. Disabled men were particularly disadvantaged. In 1925 the school needed a new lady caretaker and it was usual for the husband to help with the heavy work. Mrs Walpole was turned down for the post because her husband had lost his right arm in the war. However, James Cawthorne, who had lost a leg, successfully ran a boot and shoe repair business in a hut to the east of the Swan Inn. Others returned to their previous occupations or branched out into new ventures. The Lansdell brothers, who were blacksmiths, moved to premises opposite the school. Albert (Bony) Legood opened a hairdresser's shop in Mill Street and sold monkey-nuts and beer. Alexander Quantrell became a watch and clock repairer, wireless engineer and agent. His brother Reginald became an advertising agent and fountain pen repairer. Walter Ladbrooke took over the butcher's shop near the King's Head and young William Ellis opened a new butcher's shop near the war memorial in 1924. Coby Hickling continued with his general shop and pork butchers at the south end of the Chequers. He had a slaughter-house next to the garage there and the blood drained into the stream behind. The Dunthorne brothers bought James Knights' bakery next to the King's Head and completed repairs in 1929.

War widows faced housing difficulties. A cottage condemned in 1916 had not been demolished, and in 1920 the Sanitary Inspector from Depwade Rural District Council, passing through Hempnall, noticed a woman cleaning the windows. On inquiring how she came to be there, she replied that, as she was homeless, she had approached Mr Bussey and he had suggested she use the derelict cottage. She was trespassing, as the owner of the cottage, who was not Mr Bussey, had no idea she was there. The closing order was lifted and the Mr Jonathan Read, the owner, was asked to put the place in a reasonable state of repair within 56 days.[1]

A shortage of men resulted in women taking over jobs traditionally done by men. Annie Curtis, as well

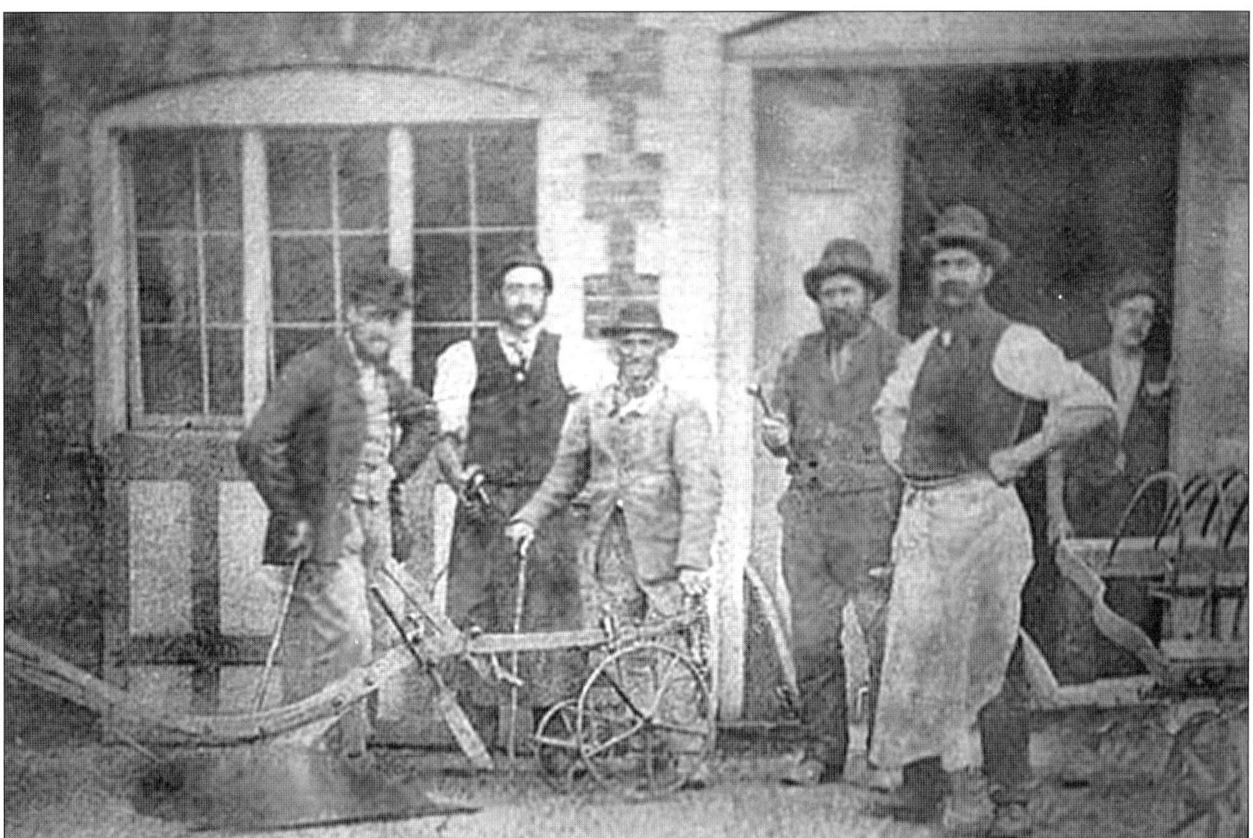

Outside the blacksmith's forge opposite the school. Left to right: *Lewis Lansdell, Henry D'Oyly, Fred Lansdell, Lawson Lansdell, Walter Lansdell, Joe Elvin.*

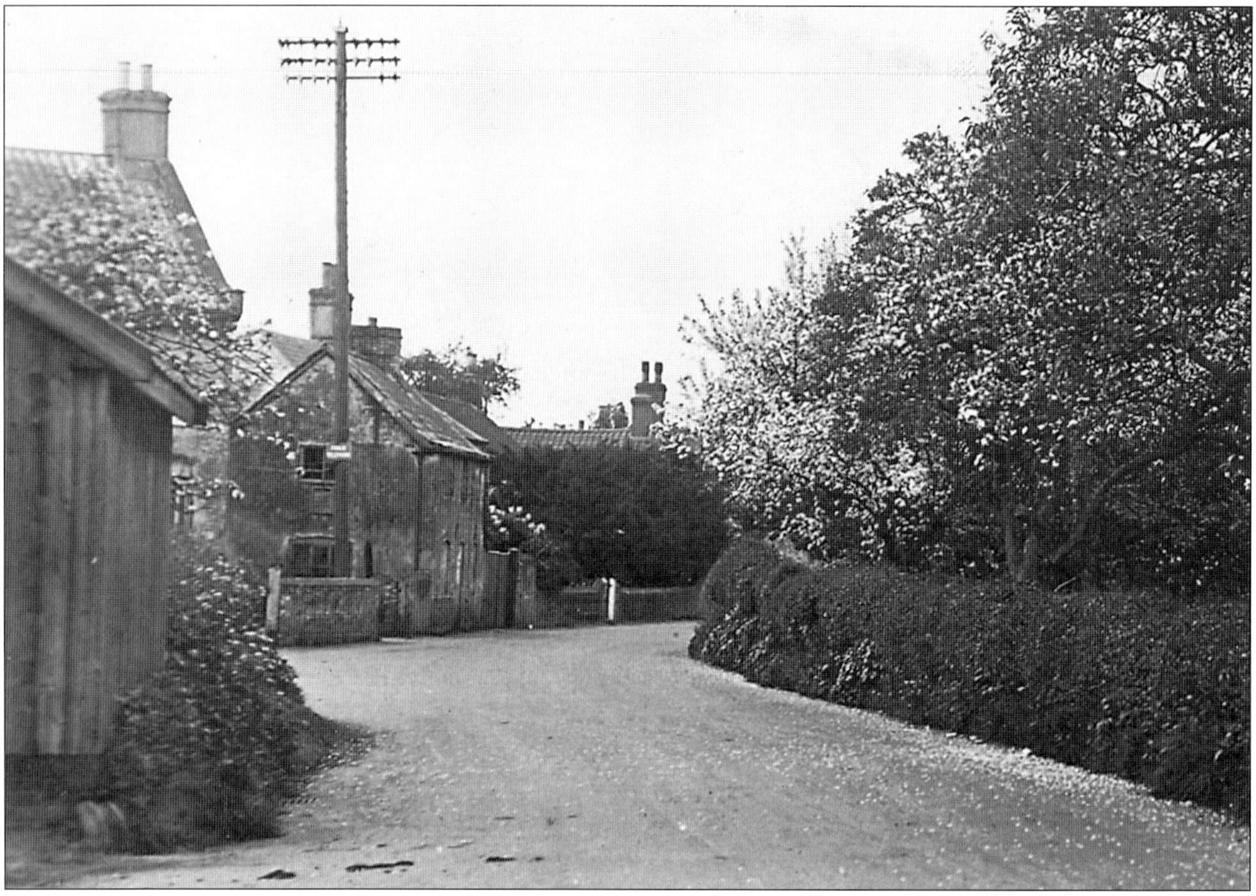

Albert Legood's hairdresser's shop was next to the telegraph pole on Mill Road.

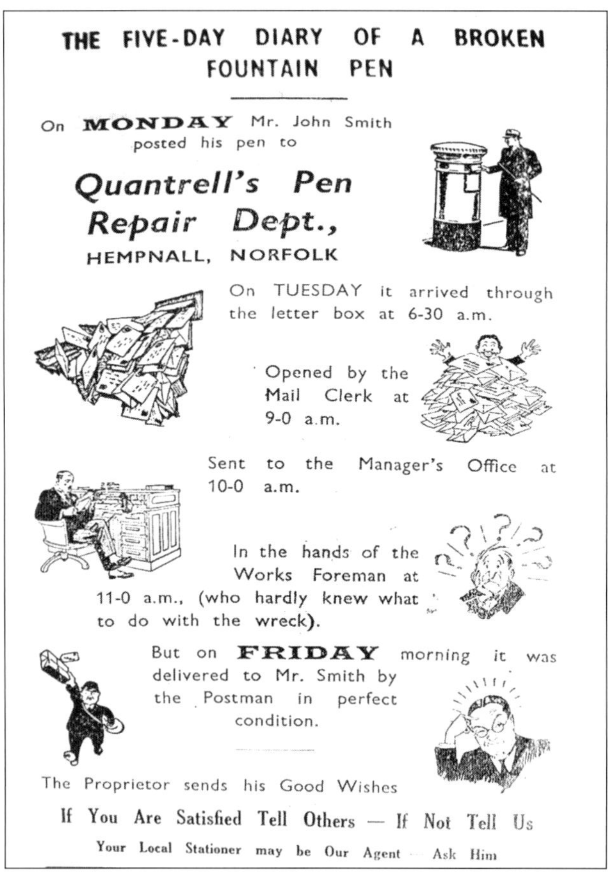

Reginald Quantrell's pen repair advertisement.

as being a nurse, became landlady of the King's Head, and Mrs Francis ran the Nelson Inn.

A strange reminder of the war came in 1921, when James (Slinger) Fryer was digging a pit. He was somewhat alarmed when a column of smoke began issuing from the mud, and exploded into flames. Sergeant Thompson pronounced it to be an incendiary bomb that had dropped from a Zeppelin.[2]

The cricket team reformed and triumphed against Tharston in the 'Soames Bowl' competition in 1920, but were thoroughly defeated by the Pulham Cricket Club in 1927 in the South Norfolk League on a Bank Holiday in torrential rain.[3] Tea was usually provided at the Nelson Hall after matches, followed by a concert in the evening to raise money for the club.[4] In 1925 a fancy-dress dance was held at the Institute to raise money for the cricket club prizes.[5] One of their members, Billy Green, ran a transport business in Mill Road and was a motor car enthusiast. He owned a rare Hispano Suiza car and apparently transported the entire team in, or on it, to away matches.[6]

Dances, parties, whist drives, billiards, draughts, card games and reading were all available at the Institute. Women were invited to become members after 1920, although billiards was only for men.[7] With the additional activities at the Institute, there were no evenings free there for the Foresters. Having been 'turned out' by the Institute's new committee, they approached the school governors for the use of their

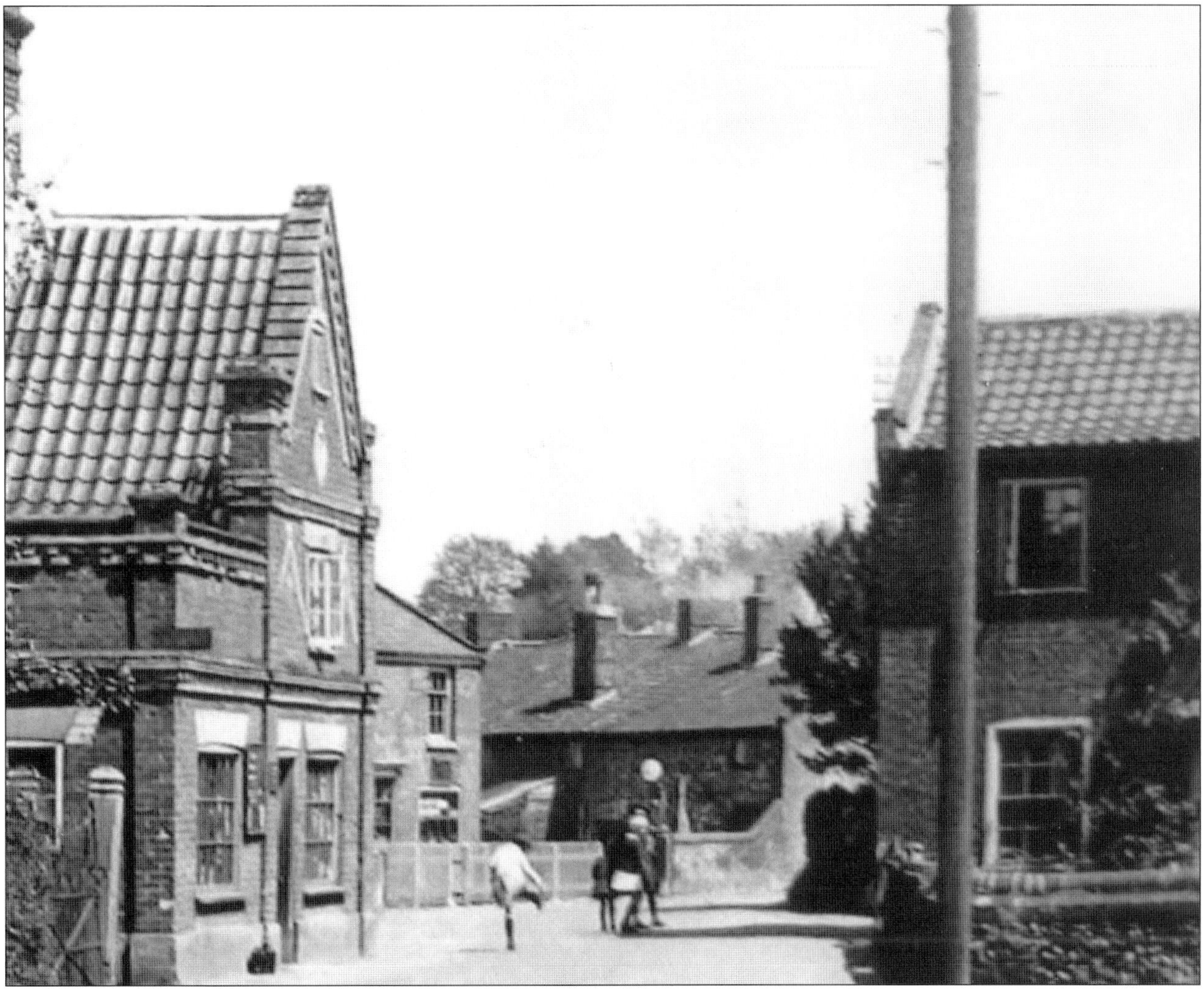

The pork butcher's, part of the Chequers (on the left) *and Rose Cottage* (on the right).

premises, and an agreement was reached stipulating that they made good any damage, cleaned and ventilated the room, allowed no spitting or smoking and locked up no later than midnight.

The football club provided entertainment in more than one way. In the second division of the South Norfolk League they drew against Stoke Holy Cross but lost to Poringland.[8] In the Norfolk County Primary Cup they were well beaten by Harleston, but a dance at the Nelson Hall that evening probably helped to raise their spirits.[9] In 1928 they entered the South Norfolk League, the County Primary Cup and the South Norfolk Charity Shield. They lost to Brockdish in January, beat Flordon and lost to Diss Reserves in March in the South Norfolk League. The club held regular dances at the Nelson Hall, with music supplied either by a group called 'the Magnet' or by the Pulham Jazz Band.[10] On Old Year's Eve in 1928, as, doubtless, in other years, the dancers stopped to listen for the striking of the church clock at midnight before singing the traditional 'Auld Lang Syne'.[11]

August Bank Holiday Mondays were celebrated by a sports day in the pit. In 1922 events included flat races, hurdles, a three-legged race, a slow bicycle race for ladies, a sack race and a tug-of-war between representatives of the Street and the Greens. Another popular activity was the pig hunt. The pig, thoroughly greased, was set loose and the first lady to catch and hold the beast down for a set number of minutes, kept it.[12] The 1924 event was a great success. Hoop-la and coconut shies, donkey and bare-back

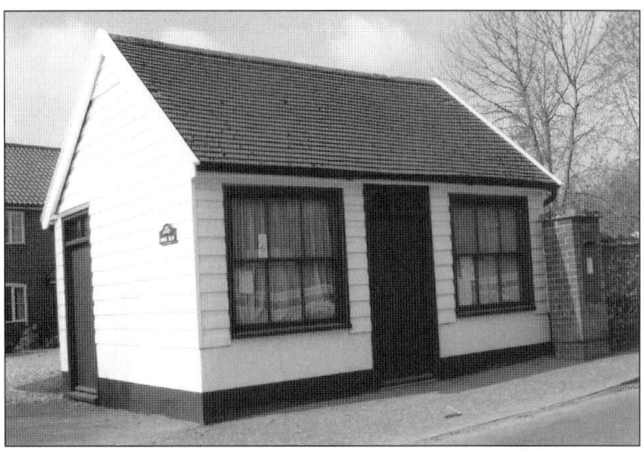

Ellis' butcher's shop, later a Post Office.

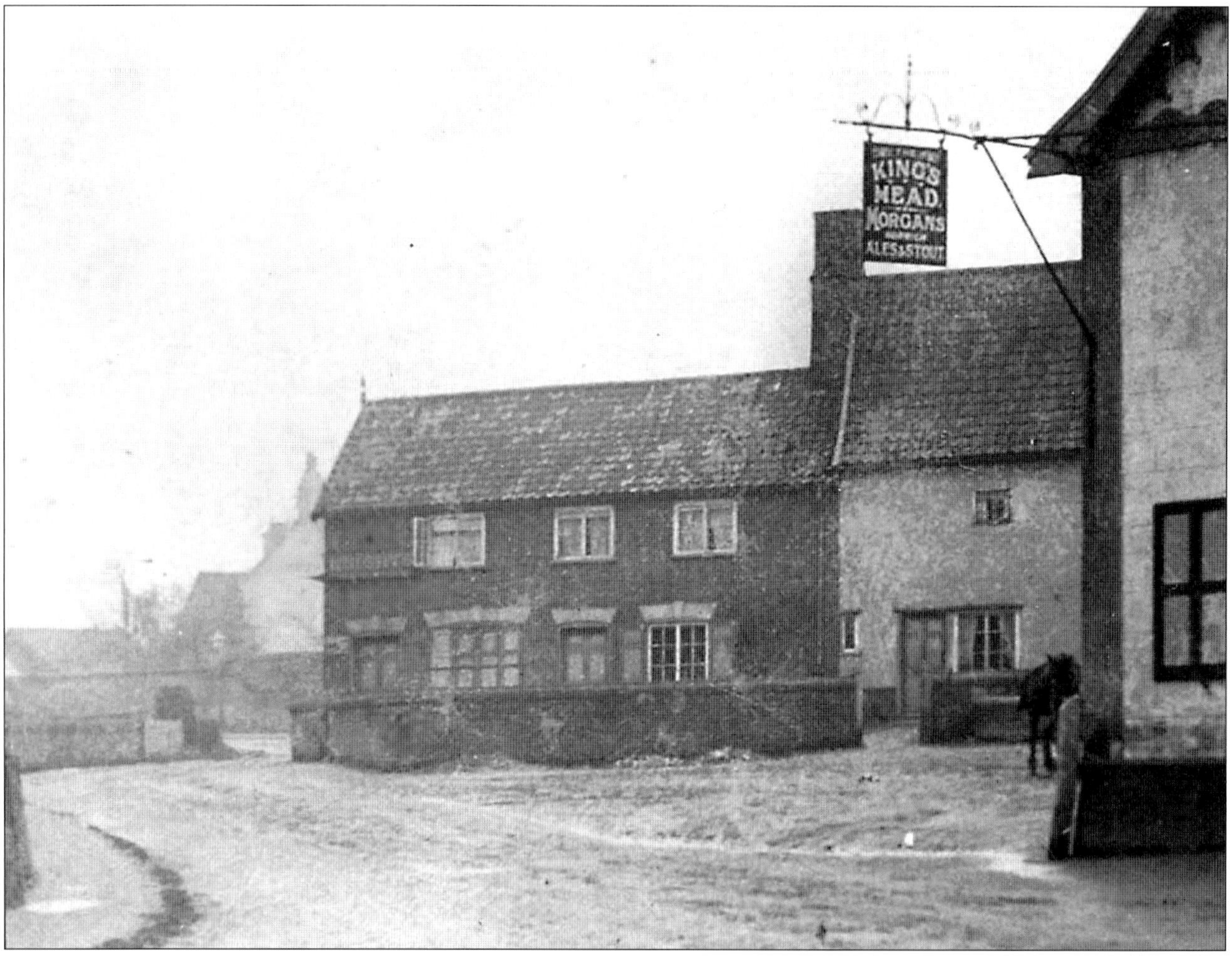

On the left *is the bakery belonging first to James Knights and then to the Dunthorne brothers.*

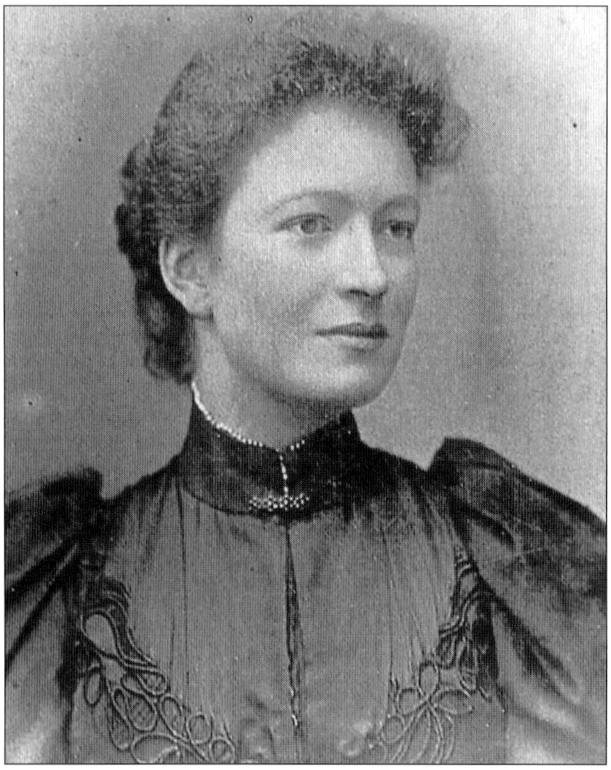

Nurse Annie Curtis.

races enticed 1,434 people to attend. Over 2,000 people were there in 1929, when new events included wheelbarrow and potato races, bicycle musical chairs and high jump.[13]

A tennis club was launched in 1926 and Mrs Goffin offered a piece of meadowland for the court. A tournament was arranged later in the year, part of a fund-raising day for the Wesleyan Chapel. A garden fête was held on Ladbrooke's meadow and a concert in the evening included action songs and drills by a number of girls and members of the Boy Scout troop.[14]

In the '20s, friendly societies joined forces on Hospital Sundays. Decked in regalia and carrying banners, they marched to the British Legion band. Before the war there were two services during the day, but now one was considered sufficient, taken jointly by the vicar and the Methodist minister.

Church and chapel were still central to the lives of many people, and the church choir continued to attract members. A party of over 60 members and friends was conveyed by motors to Yarmouth in 1927 by courtesy of the vicar.[15] Two musical evenings were reported in the newspapers, an organ recital and a performance of Handel's *Messiah*, both held at the Parish Church. The Methodists, eager to attract

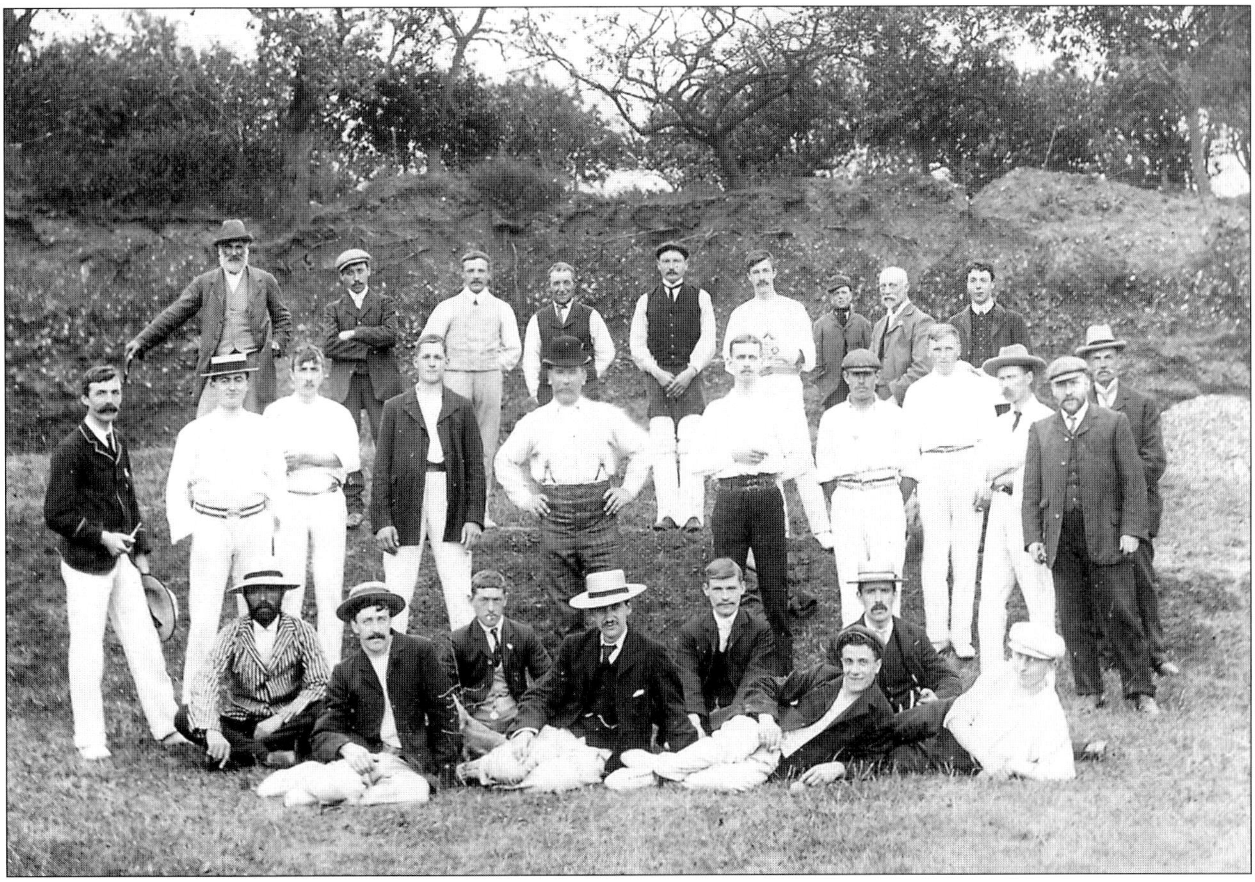

Cricketers in the Pit.

young people, organised a series of fortnightly lectures accompanied by lantern slides.[16]

Inevitably, village life included a brush with the law. When Mary Goffin accused her neighbour, Mary Elvin, of stealing an axe, Goffin threatened to 'do her in'. She was encouraged by her son, who was heard to shout, 'Get her down, mother!' Mrs Elvin had to fly for her life over the hedge.[17] David Lansdell, 16 years old, summoned for discharging fireworks on the highway, was let off with a caution.[18] In 1927 Albert Tyrrell, Fred Barton and Arthur Hipperson had leant their bicycles against a shop when a motor car careered round the corner and crashed into Barton's bike, knocking Tyyell over. The driver failed to stop and continued up the road, weaving from side to side, narrowly missing the bridge. A bus driver spotted the car in a hedge and called the local bobby, who found Harry Laskey, the landlord of the Horse Shoes, somewhat inebriated.[19]

A report on rural slums by Depwade District Council in 1925 deplored the number of insanitary, dilapidated houses in Hempnall and four other villages.[20] It was recommended that four new houses be built in Hempnall. In 1926 the council was still haggling over the price of land. Five owners were willing to sell sites for building and £80 an acre was being considered. It was January 1927 before the contract was signed and work could begin on the council housing.[21]

School records show a different aspect of village life. Every winter, as might be expected, the children suffered from sores, colds and influenza. In the autumn many were absent with diarrhoea from eating too much fruit. There were epidemics of infectious diseases – whooping cough, rubella, measles and chicken pox – which caused the school to close during severe outbreaks. The year 1925 was particularly difficult. It snowed practically every day in February, the summer was very hot and in September ten new children swelled the infant class to 40, making teaching and learning very uncomfortable. October was wet, and 32 children were absent with mumps in one week, together with the infant teacher, Miss Nora Gilden. The infection was still rife in November. In January 1926 the headmaster reported heavy snow and the weather being more severe than for several years. That year scarlet fever, the most dangerous of all the infectious diseases, struck the area and the Beckett and Hipperson families were away for a month.[22]

In 1926 Dr Cecil Gibson opened a surgery opposite the church on four mornings a week, between 10.00 and 10.30. The waiting-room was part of Arnold's office, once the entrance hall of the house. The room was very small, with no window, and contained a wooden bench and a chair. There was no appointment system and patients often had to queue outside. If you were not ill when you arrived, you

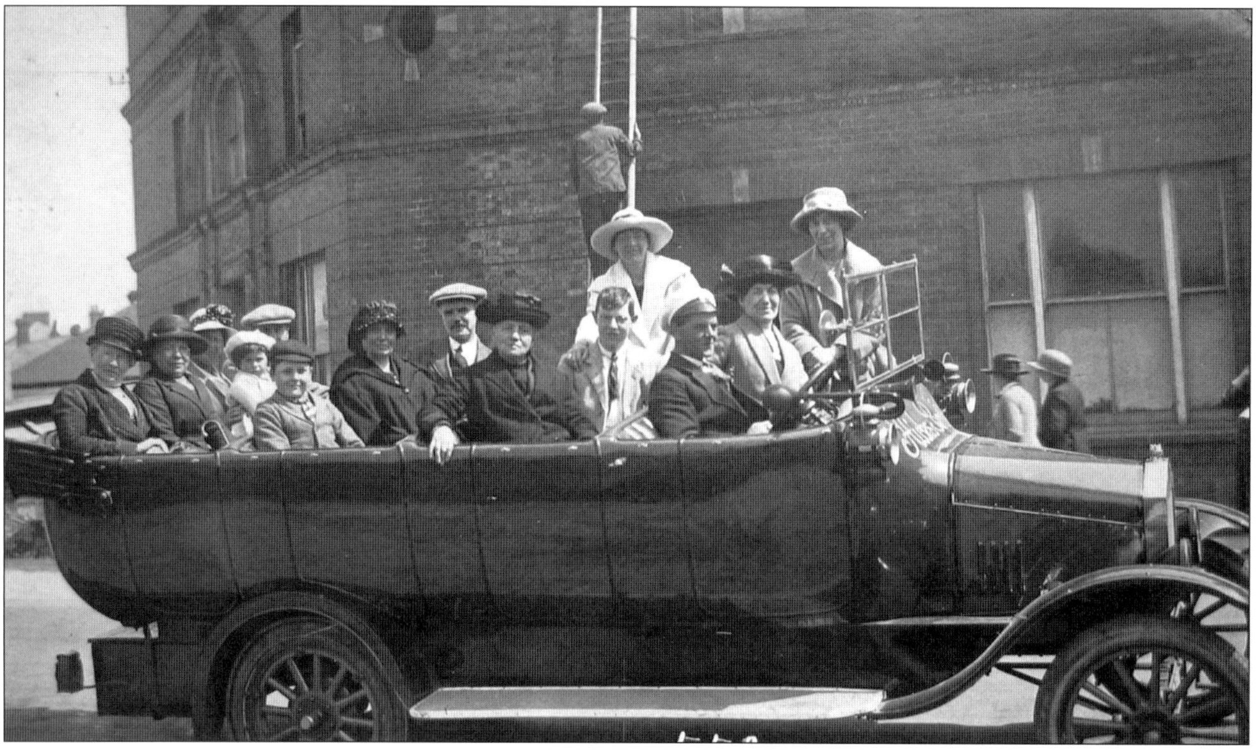

Billy Green driving on a Methodist outing. The passengers include Mrs E. Stammers, Edith Stammers, Allie Stammers and Jack Stammers.

were by the time you left. Miss Cissie Edge was the resident midwife.

Harry Helsdon, one of Hempnall's well-remembered characters, was born in 1908 in a clay lump cottage at Silver Green. It had a dirt floor with a ladder to the rooms above and was infested with rats. He turned this experience to good use. When Harry left school, he spent his time catching rats and skinning rabbits, charging twopence for a rat's tail and sixpence a rabbit. At 16 he landed a job with Charles (Chenny) Tye, earning 1s.6d. a week.

Mr William M. Roberts, the schoolmaster, retired in 1927 and was presented with an armchair.[23] His successor, Mr Eric C. Blaiden, who took up the position in May, almost immediately had to shut the infant class because of an outbreak of measles. The class did not reconvene until after the Whitsun break, exactly a month later. At this time, there were 120 children on the roll. Blaiden appears to have been an innovator, starting a school bank, encouraging a new stamp scheme for savings and reopening the boot club. A cookery class was started at the Lord Nelson for the senior girls. By Christmas the attendance had dropped, with many children suffering from whooping cough, chicken pox and colds. The new master was a disciplinarian and one parent was unhappy with the new regime. She sent a letter of complaint, maintaining that her son had received 'seven clumps in his back', been given 'wireless clouts' and had pens and rulers thrown at him. She did, however, acknowledge that she had had 'a lot of trouble bringing him up'.[24]

In 1927 four Hempnall ladies completed training with the British Red Cross Society, and the following year a concert at the Nelson Hall raised £11.10s. towards the proposed Hempnall District Nursing Association. A full house enjoyed the concluding play, *A Very Lame Dog*.[25]

The parish had lacked a vicarage house since 1744. In the nineteenth century the Manor House next to the church had been rented to the vicars by the lord of the manor after 1813, but owing to several long-lived vicars' widows, Hempnall House, Villa Farm and Fairstead House (now Krons Manor) had been used as vicarages. The Revd Talbot Gardiner bought the Manor House in 1914, selling it in 1926 to the Church Commissioners for a vicarage. It was sold in 1975 and replaced by the present 'Rectory'.[26] In 1927 parishioners of all denominations united to buy a piece of land for £50 to extend the graveyard.[27]

A scheme to supply electricity to the village was proposed in 1927. However, work had still not begun in 1929, when budget problems were reported and technical schemes were being revised.[28] The life of William Forder might have been saved had electricity been installed. He had been unwell and had left a lamp burning by his bedside. Knocking it over during the night, he was burned to death.[29]

Motor cars were superseding horses as the preferred method of travelling. The Revd Francis Howard was proudly photographed by his new vehicle, possibly a Ford Touring Car, advertised at that time in the press for £128. He was also photographed with the Hempnall football team in

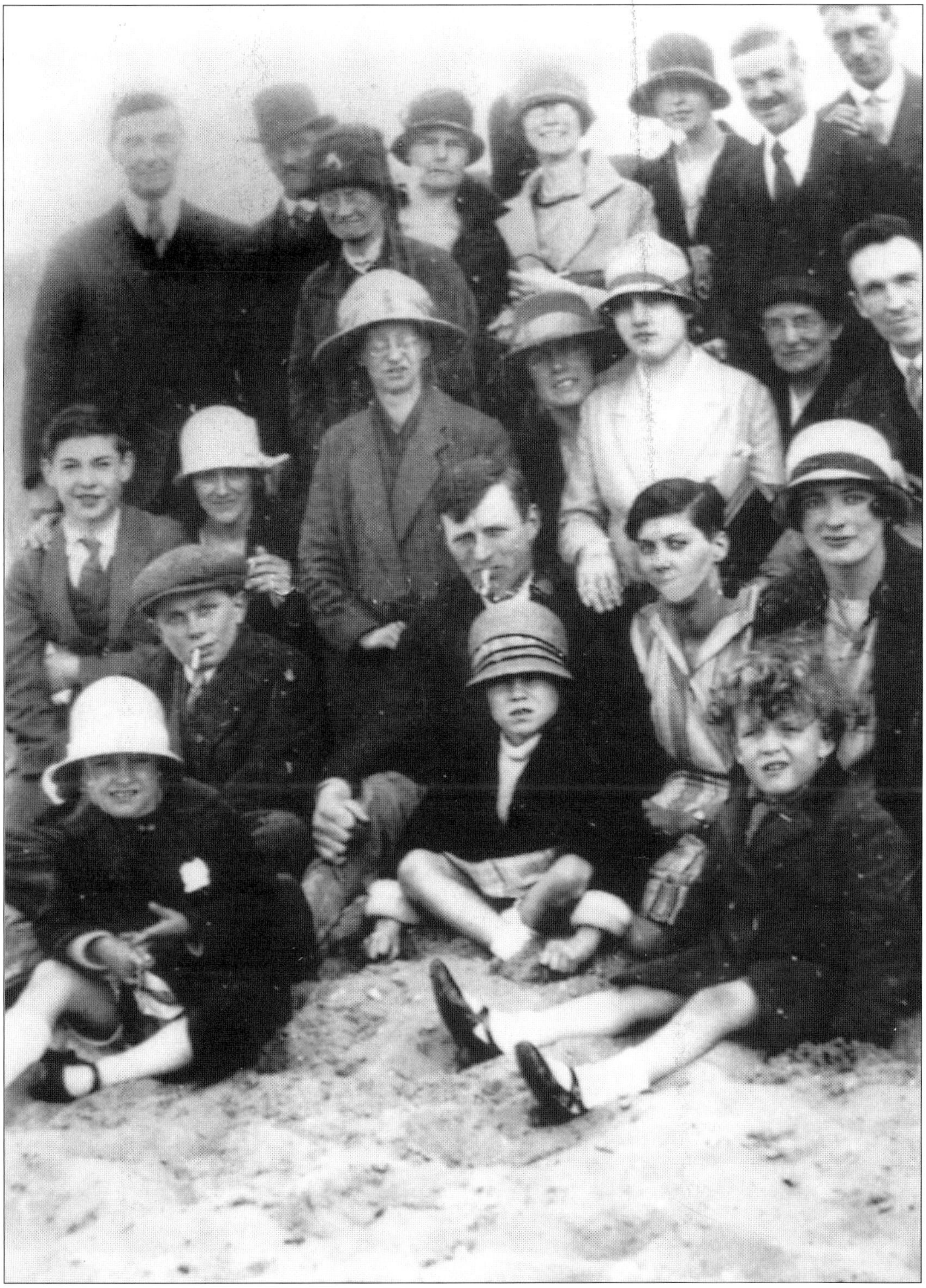

A church choir outing in the late 1920s. The photograph includes Revd F.A. Howard (back row, left, wearing a tie), Mr J. Brighton, Mrs Fulcher, Violet Burton, Rosie Barton, Alec Quantrell, D. Revell, Miss Mary A. Felton, Mrs Cawthorne, Mrs B. Elvin, Bob Spalding and daughter, Mrs Fiddy, M. Brighton, Ethie Thompson, James Cawthorne, Ernie Downing, Chummy Curtis, Dot Curtis and Mrs Curtis.

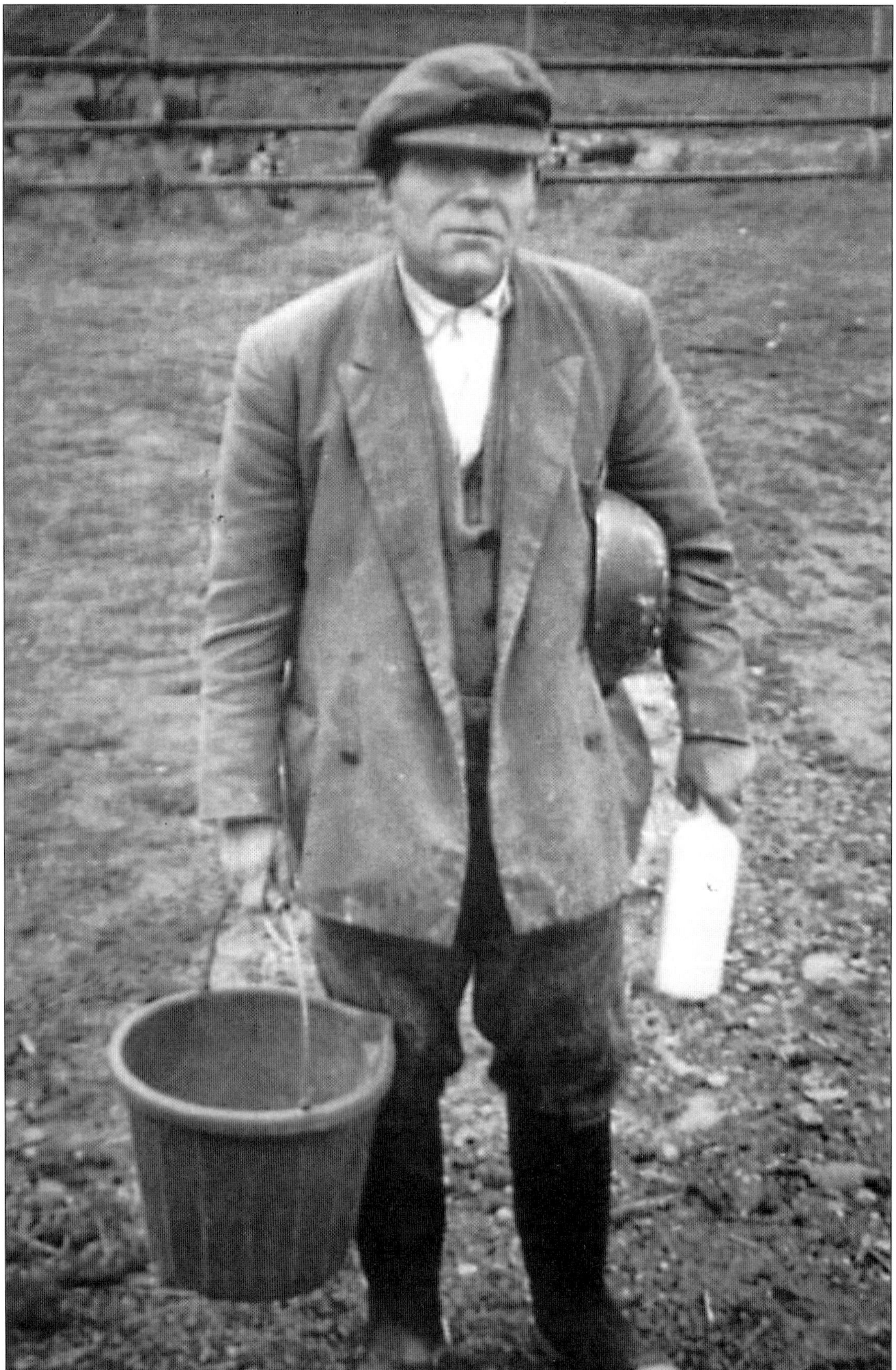

Harry Helsdon, rat catcher.

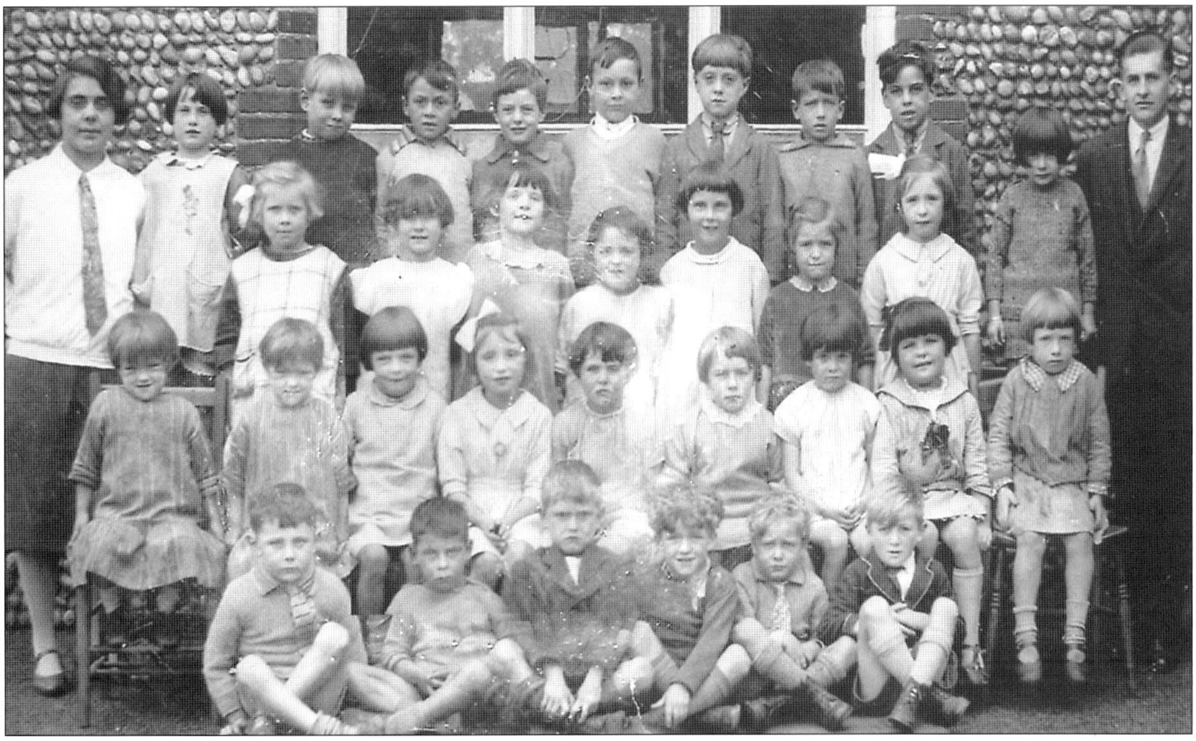

Hempnall School in the 1920s. Left to right, back row: *Miss Gilden, Ada Moore, Wesley Green, Bob Roberts, John Quantrell, Leal Davidson, Peter Townsend, Alan Beckett, Lily Gooderham;* third row: *Ruth Levett, Linda Moore, Vera Goffin, ? Leamon, Daisy Isbell, Joan Taylor, Margaret Penn, Betty Madgett, Mr Blaiden;* second row: *Joyce and Joan Goffin, Benjamin Cunningham, Minnie Penn, Barbara Mcnelly, Molly Revell, Emily McNelly, Annie Matthews, Eileen Pigney;* front row includes: *N. Baker, John Elvin, Jimmy Cawthorne, Bertie Moore, Gerald Tweedale.*

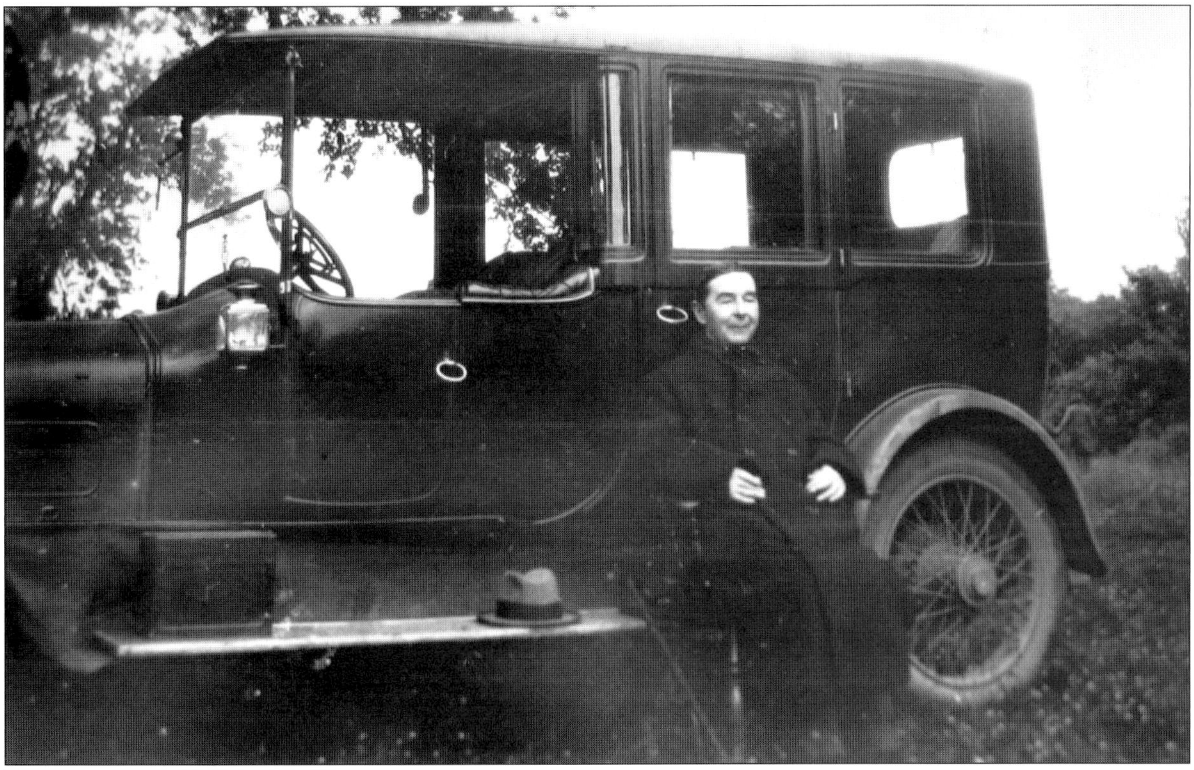

Revd Francis Alfred Howard.

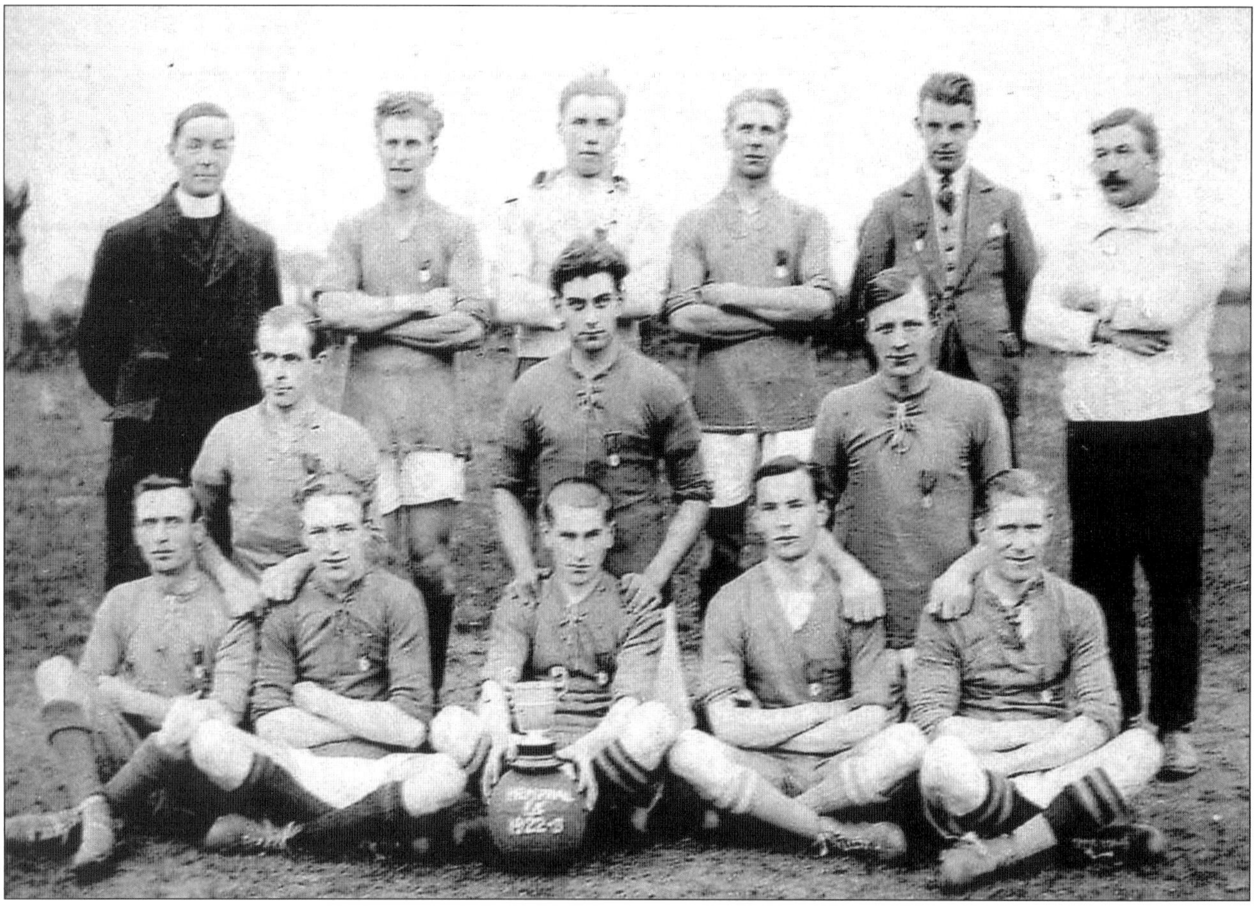

Hempnall Football Team, 1922–23: Left to right back row: *Revd F. Howard, Norman Ellis, Dan Mallett, Percy Ellis, ?, Bill Jacobs;* middle row: *Norman Pechey, Cecil Baxter, Chummy Curtis;* front row: *?, Cyril Jacobs, Reggie Watson, ?, ?.*

1923, the year he became president of the Hempnall Sports Committee.

Unfortunately, cars splashing through the ford at the town watering had seriously damaged the bridge. The Parish Council informed the County Council in September 1924, but the following year nothing had been done and there were fears that the town foot bridge had become a danger to the public. The County Council must eventually have agreed to build a proper road bridge, for a meeting was held at the school in November 1925 to decide if the old town bridge should be left or pulled down. The vote was overwhelmingly in favour of demolition.[30]

Roads too, were suffering from the effects of the motor car, and maintenance was becoming expensive. In 1927 the County Council proposed to take over the responsibility for the road between Hempnall and Fundenhall and were intending to build a concrete bridge to replace the Red Bridge. The estimated cost for the road was £16,953 and £790 for the bridge. Work was well under way in December, when one of the roadmen, Mr G. Pitney, noticed a runaway horse pulling a trap carrying several children and was injured whilst stopping it.[31] There was a white Christmas in 1927, and the January of 1928 was so cold that skating was enjoyed in the pit. By the end of the month the frost had thawed, the snow melted and torrential rain brought floods. The County Surveyor reported that 3,000 yards of the new road had completely collapsed and was obliged to order additional foundation materials – 400 tons of lump slag and 800 cubic yards of flint – at a cost of £725.[32]

The war had accelerated the pace of change in such matters as women's emancipation and the loosening of the class system. Inflation was high, but housing had improved. Social activities had been revived and people were probably looking forward to an improved quality of life with the coming of electricity. The war memorial was a visual reminder of the great loss of their young men, but it was believed that they had not died in vain; for the First World War was the war to end all wars.

References

[1] *NC* Friday, 10 December 1920
[2] *NC* Friday, 29 July 1921
[3] *NM* Saturday, 8 May 1920' *NM* Saturday, 20 July 1920
[4] *NM* Saturday, 20 July 1927. 'The usual concert'
[5] *NM* Saturday, 21 March 1925
[6] *EDP* 18 November 1987. Memories of Billy Green
[7] Minutes of the Institute

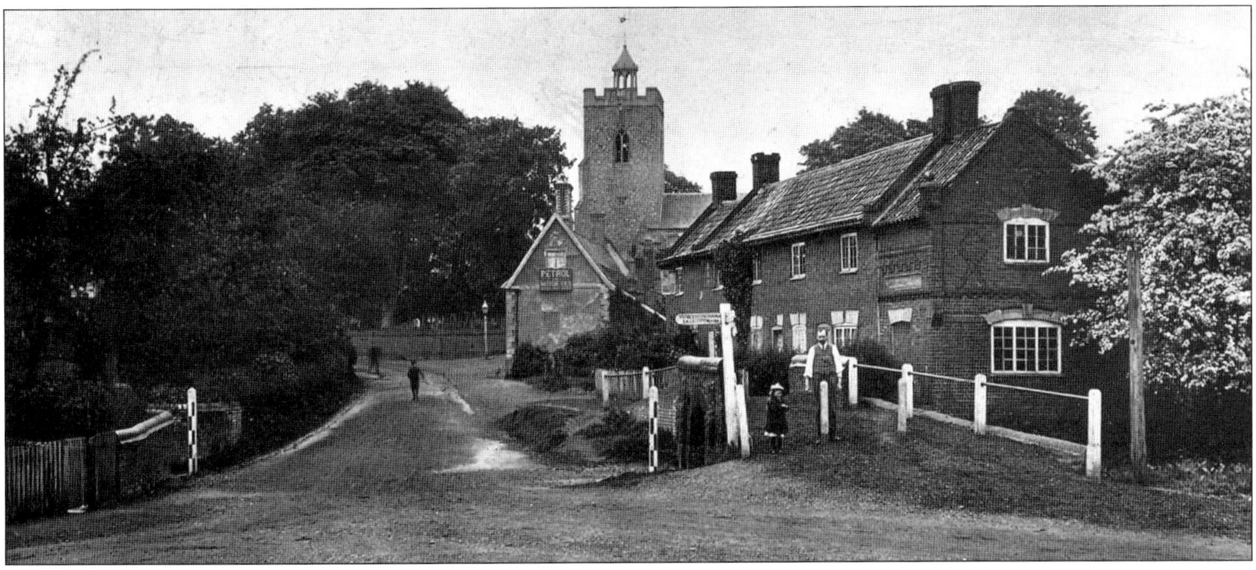

The footbridge before 1927 (above) *and the new bridge after 1927* (below).

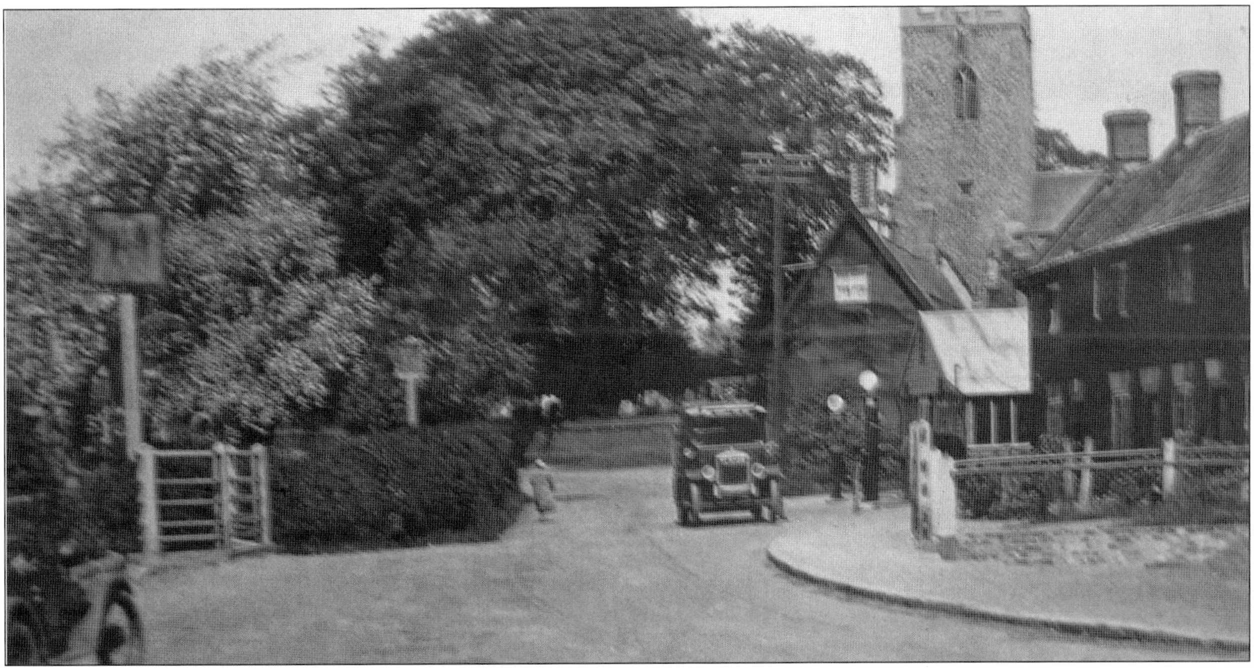

[8] *NM* Saturday, 10 December 1927; *NM* Saturday, 17 December 1927
[9] *NM* Saturday, 22 October 1927
[10] *NM* Saturday, 22 October 1927; *NM* Saturday, 24 March 1928; *NM* Saturday, 14 April 1928
[11] *NM* Saturday, 7 January 1928
[12] *NM* Saturday, 12 August 1922
[13] *NM* Saturday, 10 August 1929
[14] *NM* Saturday, 20 March 1926; Saturday, 26 June 1926
[15] *NM* Saturday 3 September 1927; *NM* Saturday, 17 December 1927; *NM* Saturday, 3 September 1927
[16] *NM* Saturday, 19 February 1927; *NM* Saturday, 5 November 1927
[17] *NM* Saturday, 19 September 1925
[18] *NM* Saturday, 31 October 1925
[19] *NM* Saturday, 10 December 1927
[20] *NM* Saturday, 12 September 1925
[21] *NM* Saturday, 29 January 1927
[22] School log-book owned by the school
[23] *NM* Saturday 3 April 1927
[24] NRO C/ED 68/334 31 October 192. Minutes of Hempnall School Board
[25] *NM* Saturday, 14 January 1928
[26] NRO DN/ADR 26/3/1222. Records of the Church Commissioners
[27] *NM* Saturday, 8 October 1927
[28] *NM* Saturday, 7 May 1927; *NM* Saturday, 10 August 1929
[29] *NM* Saturday, 11 August 1928
[30] *NM* Saturday, 13 September 1924; Saturday, 18 April 1925; Saturday, 21 November 1925
[31] NRO DC 2/4/3. Depwade Rural District Council Highways Minutes
[32] NRO DC 2/4/3. Depwade Rural District Council

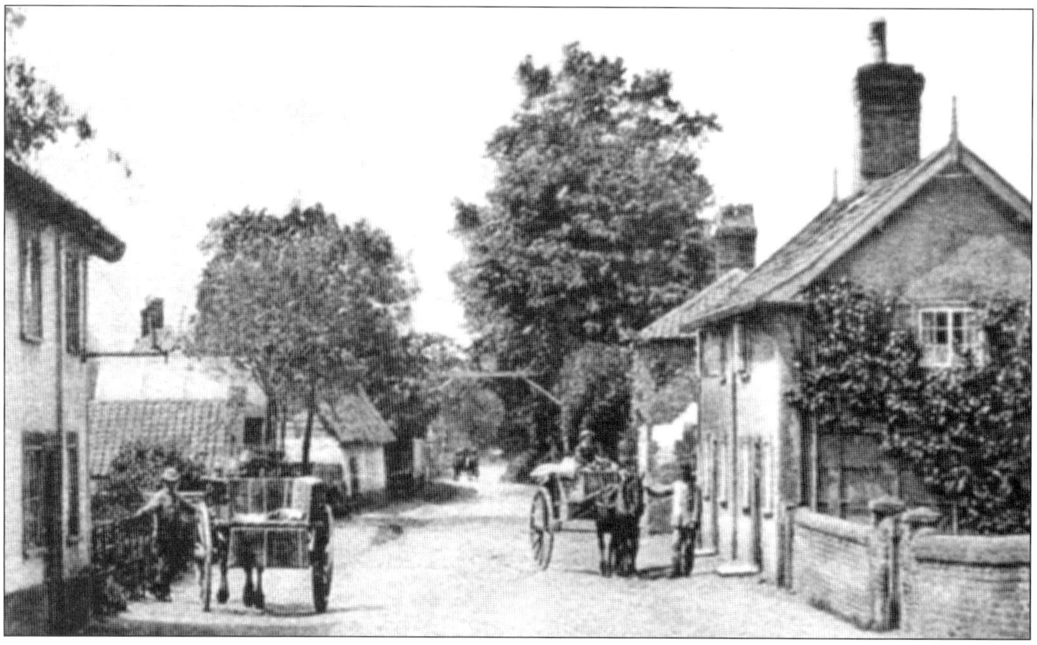

The view along the Street towards the Swan sign.

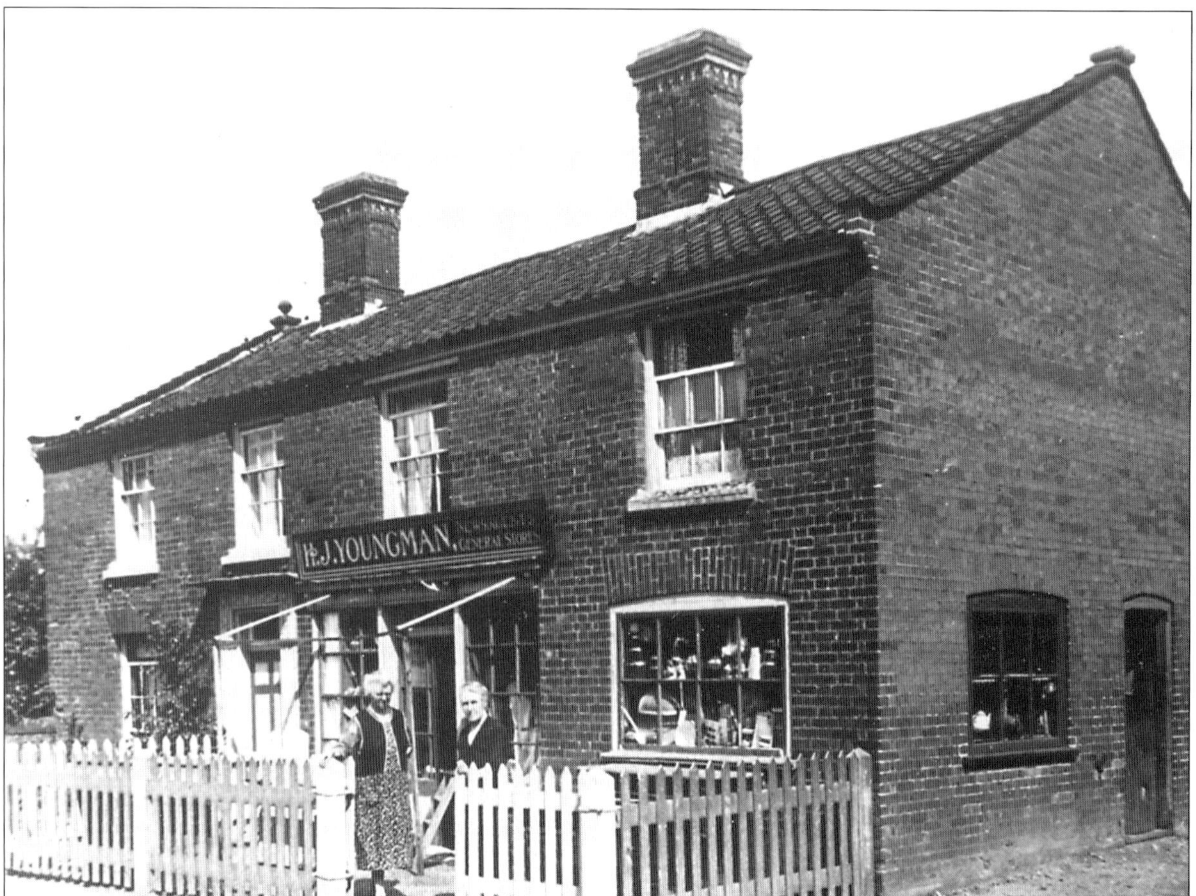

Youngman's shop, next to the Chequers.

✥ CHAPTER 17 ✥

Innovations 1930–39

The Swan Inn, the only public house in the village with a gantry across the road, welcomed Sergeant Major A.E. Saunders in 1930 as the enthusiastic new landlord.[1] He ran billiard tournaments and organised competitions to raise money for the village Nursing Association. Unfortunately, it closed the following year. Accommodation included a large tap room, a parlour, a club room, a newly built lock-up carriage house that doubled as a covered skittle alley, a workshop, a stable and a hay house.[2] Billy Green later bought it, installed petrol pumps and continued his transport business there. He was driving a black Crossley limousine on a dark December evening in 1933 when a lorry, laden with stones and poorly lit by flickering oil lamps at the rear, pulled out in front of him. A pedestrian, coincidentally also named William Green, who lived at Saxlingham, was also involved in the accident. A Red Cross ambulance took the casualties to the Norfolk and Norwich Hospital. The pedestrian died shortly afterwards and William Green from Hempnall died in the early hours of the following day. He was 45 years old.[3]

With the increase in motor car ownership, the village supported three suppliers of petroleum in 1934, each storing 500 gallons. Mr G. Hinchcliffe opened a cycle shop next to the former Swan and took over the petrol pumps, and Mr W.C. Cunningham erected a new garage with petrol pumps in 1937.[4] Other firms sought to enlarge their premises. Arnold's engineering works erected a machine shop in 1935. In 1938, where Kilbourn's garage stands in 2008, Fred Hickling built a new bakery containing a coal-fired oven large enough to hold 250 2lb tins. This was next to the shop that later belonged to Youngman. In 1936 licences for six slaughterhouses were granted to W.N. Ellis, W.J. Ladbrooke, W.J. Legood, H.W. Gooch, J. Leggett and Bertie Mobbs, who had a shop on the Greens.[5]

Stammers' shop regularly stayed open until ten in the evening. Although employees worked long hours there were compensations, such as the annual staff outing, when a coach was provided for a seaside trip. An extension to the shop was added in 1931 and a new drainage system was installed. A partition between the grocery and drapery department ensured that ladies could speak privately to save embarrassment. A machine for topping and tailing currants was operated like a large mangle with a flywheel. In the autumn the sticky mixture attracted the wasps and it had to be kicked and banged to keep them at bay. The raisin stoner was smaller. The stones were wrapped in greaseproof paper and weighed with the fruit, so customers had to pay for them as well. At the end of the grocery counter was the 'tea room', where tea was blended. A large copper tub was filled with Indian and Chinese tea

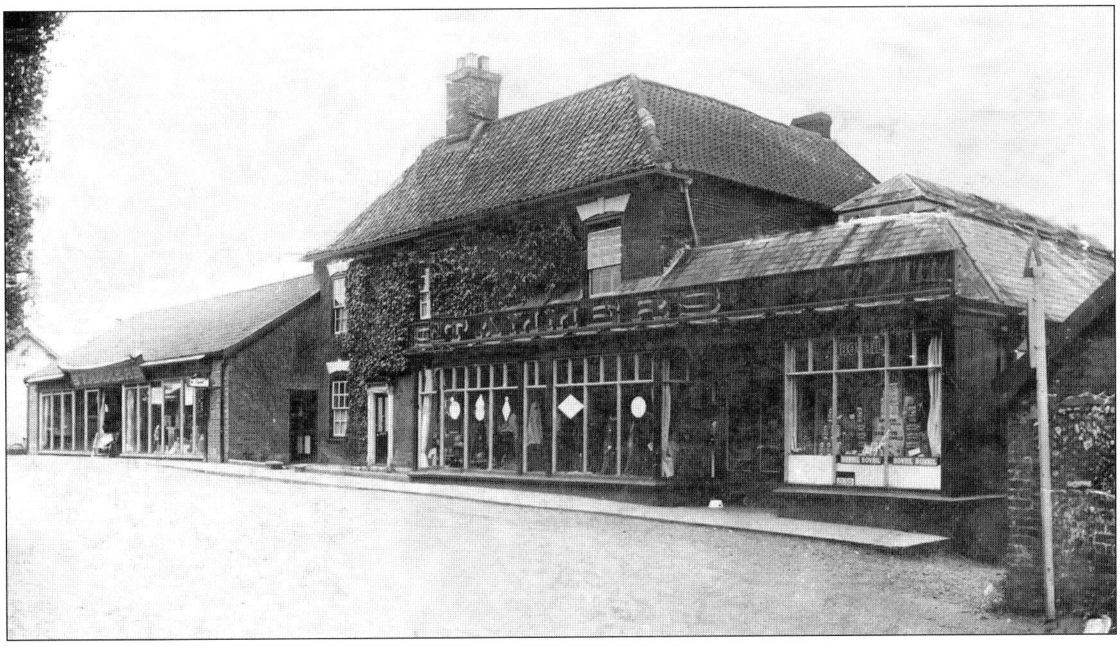

Stammers' shop in the 1930s.

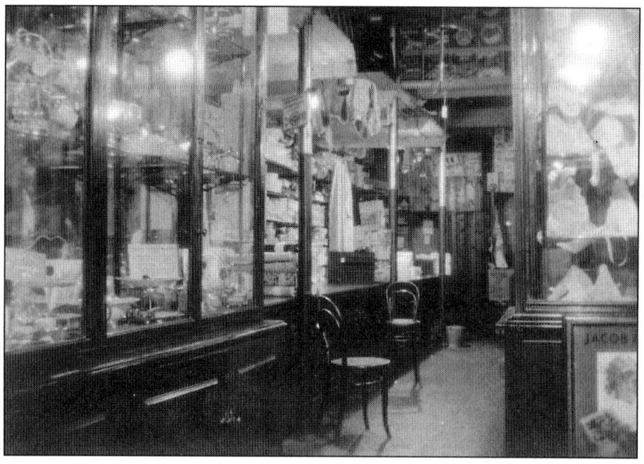

Interior of Stammers' shop, drapery department.

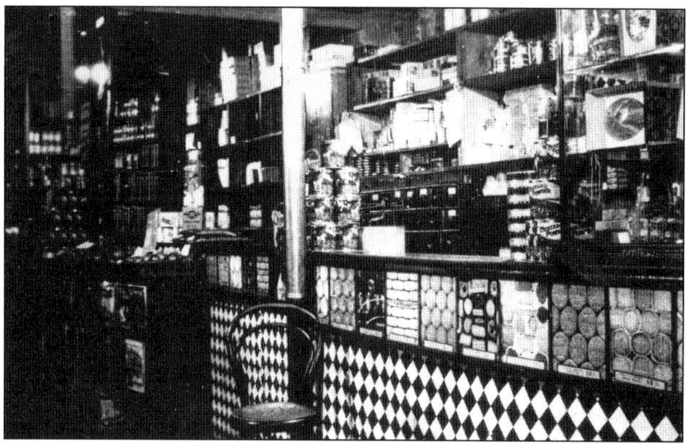

Stammers' shop, grocery department.

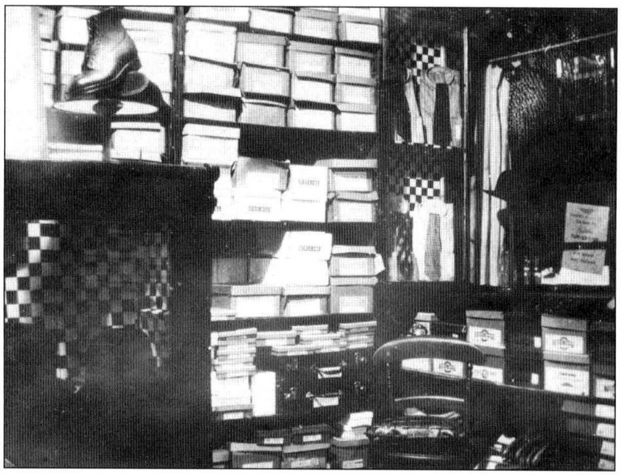

Stammers' shop, boot and shoe department.

and stirred with a copper shovel. Suet was shredded in a mincer, the handle of which had to be kept turning all day over several shifts. At the end of the day the product was poured into large earthenware pots about three feet high. A large wooden spoon was used to transfer the sticky mixture into grease-proof paper and thus it found its way to the customer. Suet was much in demand for making puddings for laborours' lunches.

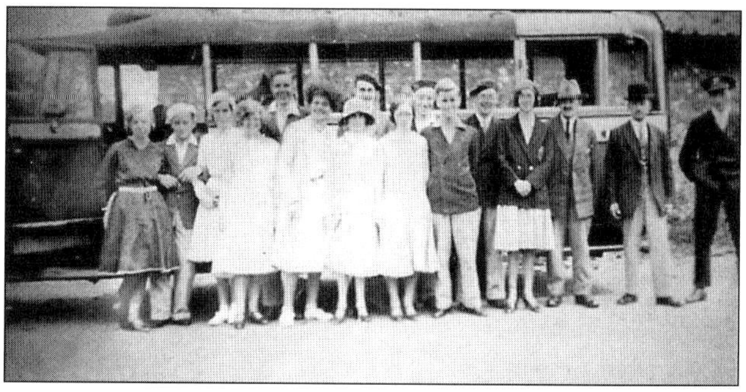

Stammers' shop assistants' outing, c.1930. Among those pictured are Doris Norman, Ray Madgett, Dolly Bush, Mabel Page, Perry Hearn, Ruth Bullen, Bob Spalding, Minnie Goose, George Forder, Ponto ?.

There were annual sales, for which some people queued all night. In 1939 a printed advertisement listed bargains such as curtain fabric at 1s. a yard, men's outsize winter-weight pyjamas at 3s.11d., Suffolk table mangles at £1.15s.6d. and men's black shoes at 6s.11d. a pair. Tinned vegetables and fruit ranged between 3d. and 6d. a tin (1s. is 10d in today's money). Stammers' special blend tea was served free on the first day of the sale. Oil lamps lit the premises and it took a man most of the morning to fill them and trim the wicks. Eventually, Pilgrims of Banham installed a gas generator. A large coke stove on a concrete slab provided the heating. A slow starter, by the end of the day it became red hot and had to be surrounded by sheets of corrugated iron to prevent the staff from overheating. My father remembers going to Norwich to buy sugar from behind a row of shops before the City Hall was built. He bought 25 sacks, each weighing about 2cwt. They were sent by train to Flordon Station and collected the following day. The empty sacks were much in demand, as they were used by farm workers as aprons when performing dirty jobs such as cutting out sugar beet. Women used them as backing for piece rugs.

The Stammers boys took up apprenticeships in Norwich and bought motorcycles. Russell, my father, bought a Rudge for 17s. It had been used on a grass race track and was minus brakes. On one occasion he was concussed after crashing into a tree, and another time, turning a corner at speed and unable to stop, ran into a herd of cows. The farmer commented dryly, after one of his cows leapt a hedge, 'You want to look where yor a-goin, you'll put ha off ha milk.' Apparently the boys used to race to Lakenham Bridge, breaking a few speed limits. It was for the likes of them that 30 mile an hour signs appeared in the village in 1937.[6]

Electricity, supplied by the Norwich Corporation, became available to the village in 1931, although houses on Field Lane had to wait until 1933, and some parts of the Greens were not connected until the 1950s. Fund-raising for connecting the church was underway in 1932 and a local dancing teacher, Madam Osina, organised an entertainment of songs,

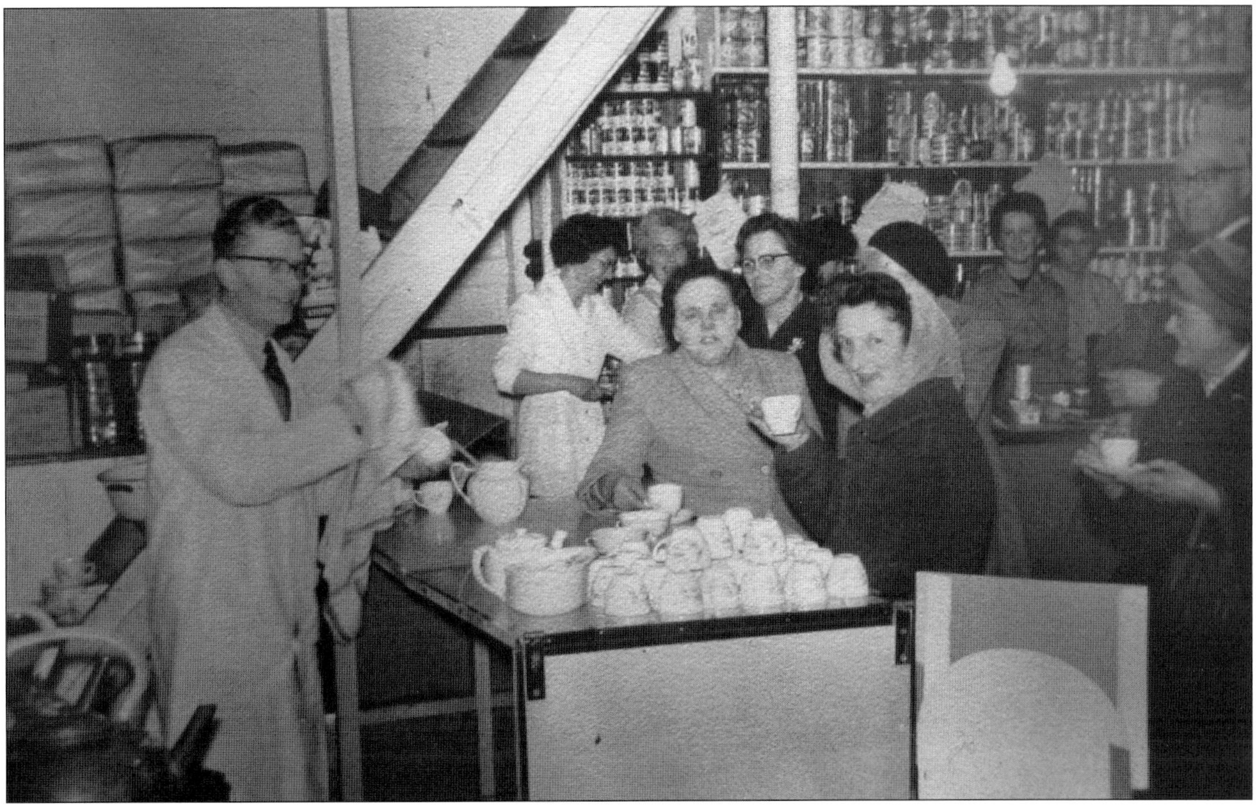

Tea was always served on the first day of the sale.

dances and sketches at the Nelson Hall, raising £9 towards the project.[7] The school governors, however, declined to update the school oil lamps due to the expense. The school was not connected until 1935, when the installation was provided free by the County Council.

My grandfather recollected an old man from Hell's Hole, near the war memorial, who sold vegetables from a coffin. He also remembered Liza Boulter, who made gloves, pushing a pram to Norwich for her raw materials.[8]

Jimmy Kennedy, an unkempt, bow-legged old man with broken teeth, lived in Mill Road. His gate was an old bedstead end. He returned from a May Fair at Bungay one year, apparently with a new spotted horse, but a few days later, after a heavy shower, all the spots came off. He once drove his pony and trap through the main doors of the shop and when my grandfather complained, replied, 'Don't you want my custom?' He would get into fights with the Irish gypsies who came to break ponies in the pit. He would throw bricks at them from his cottage and the Hicklings had to put up shutters in their shop opposite, which adjoined the Chequers. Jimmy died after falling into his fire.

James Fryer, commonly called 'Slinger', ended his days in a terraced house next to the Town Bridge. His dog regularly pinched bacon from the shop before being chased up the road. James used to come in for black 'twist' tobacco to chew, as did Gobbler Becket and Braidy Hazell and others who lived in a

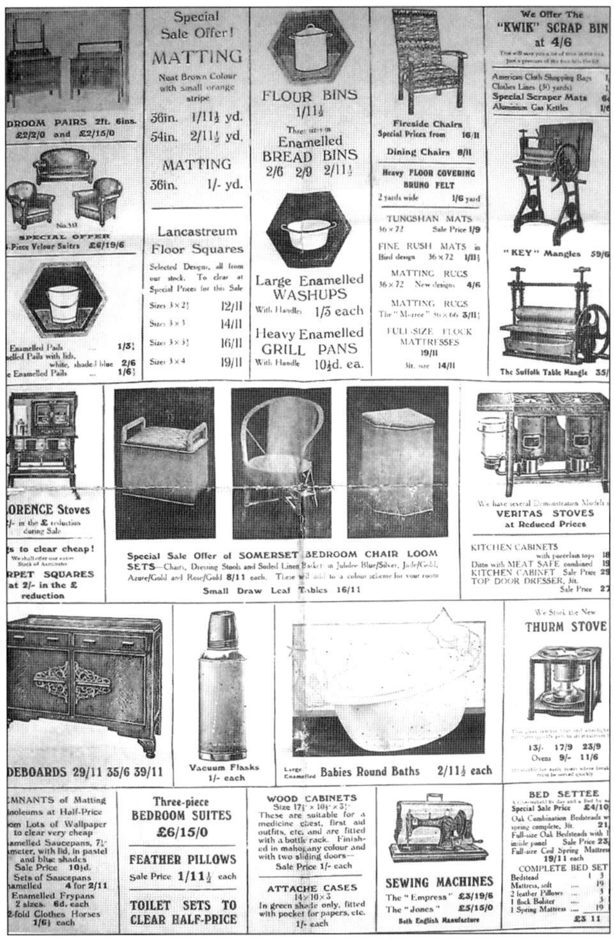

Stammers' advertisements.

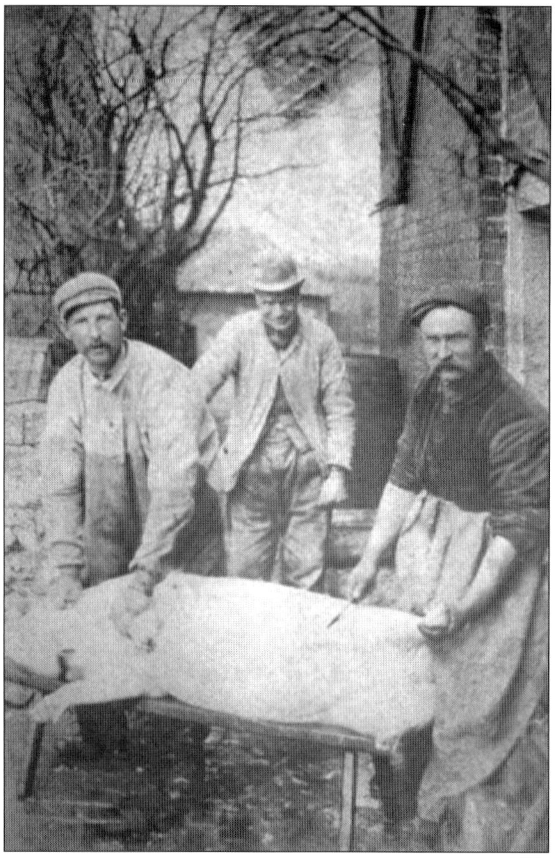

?, Mr Gillingwater and John Crummett. Field Lane tower mill is in the background.

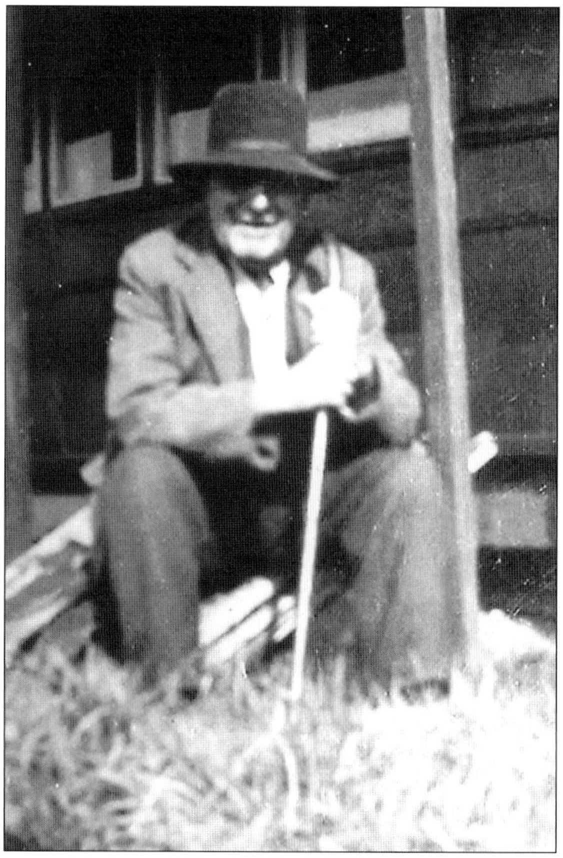

Braidy Hazell, who lived in an old railway carriage on Fairstead Lane.

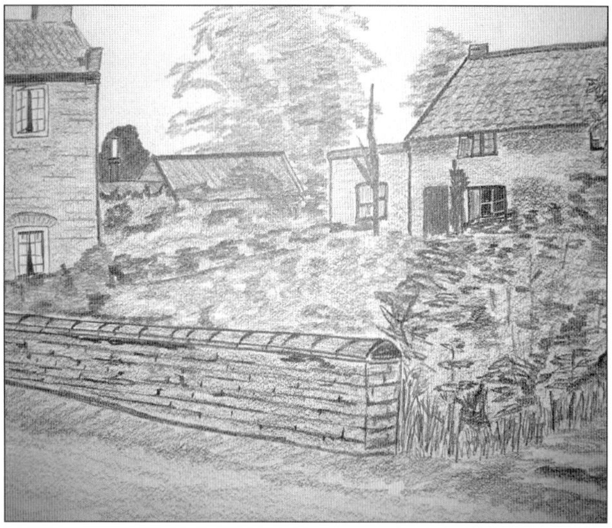

Jimmy Kennedy's house (on the right), *from a sketch by Betty Chapman.*

row of old railway carriages along Fairstead Lane. Slinger, who was a coal merchant, also disposed of night soil for Arnold's works and may have dumped it in his own garden. Betty Chapman remembers seeing him, his horse and his neighbour, Rosie Elvin, looking over his front door, which was of the stable door variety. He had no access to his back yard except through the front door, through which his horse walked to its stable at the back. Mrs Elvin took in washing, and a fierce argument between her and Slinger resulted in a fork full of horse muck over her clean linen. She took him to court at Long Stratton. Apparently, they hired the same car to attend the hearing, he borrowed a long butterfly suit and tall hat, and afterwards they called in at a local for a drink like old friends.[9] In his latter days Slinger was left with one fang-like tooth. The local blacksmith, known as 'Curly' Taylor, offered to extract it at his forge. Three whiskeys were lined up by way of anaesthetic; a crowd gathered, distracting Slinger and allowing Curly to get the alcohol down him. When the deed was done, Curly presented Slinger with a bill for 7s.6d. Slinger frequently fell out with George Baker, his other neighbour, and there were fights. On one occasion Baker was pinned to the ground with a pitchfork about his neck, with Slinger threatening to drown him in his own blood. A travelling fair which visited the village annually set up on the Nelson Plain, opposite Slinger's patch, and there were a few memorable altercations when he had drunk a few pints of 'labourers' beer'.

Other people are remembered for the contributions they made to the village. Mrs Constance Mabel Crawshay, a formidable lady, by 1929 had taken over the running of the cider works. Her husband, Captain Frederick W. Crawshay, took to a bath chair

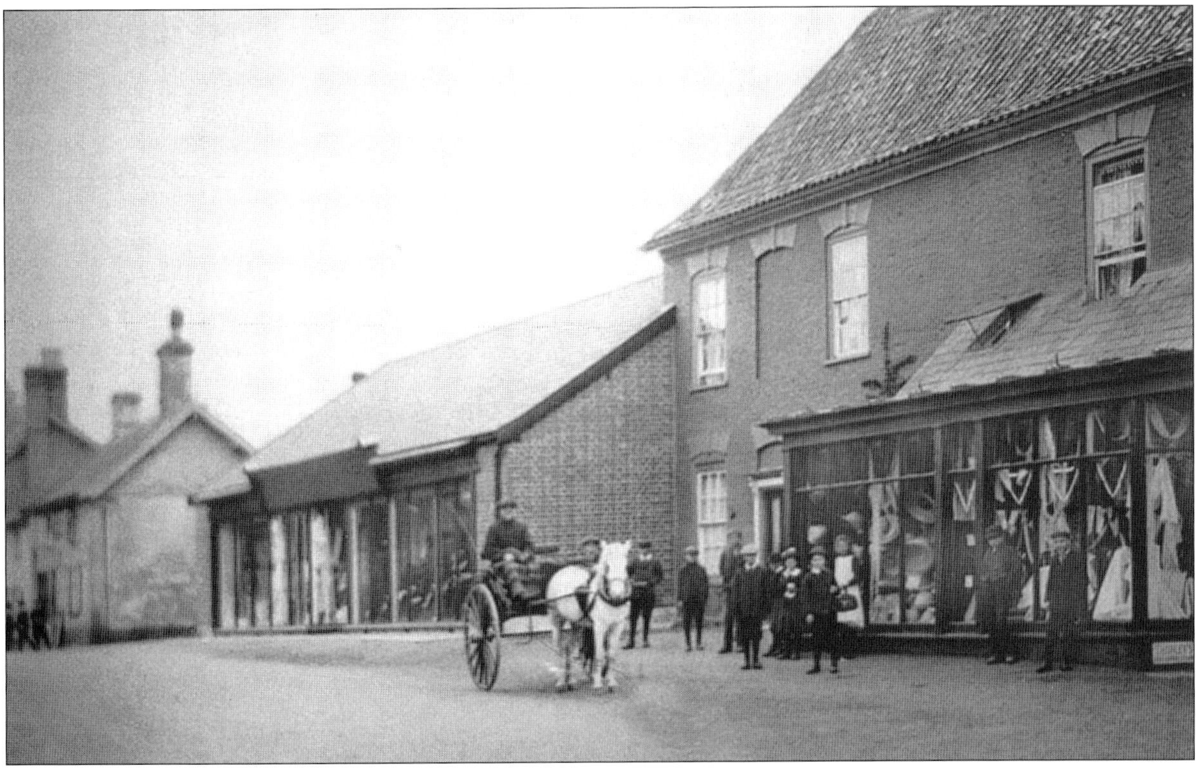

Jimmy Kennedy driving his horse and trap past Stammers' shop.

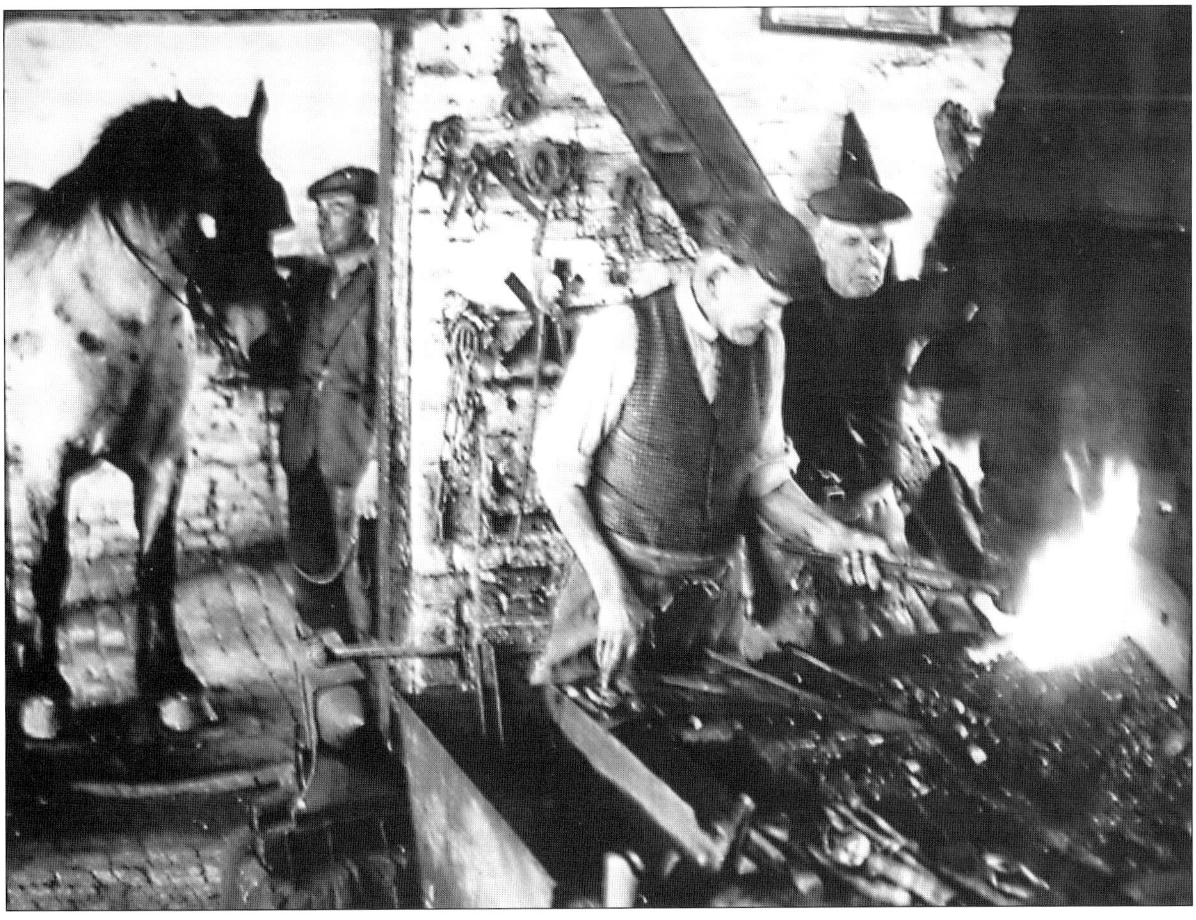

Curly Taylor at the forge. (EASTERN DAILY PRESS)

and timed his visits to the shops to coincide with the end of the school day so that he could pay a child a penny to push him home. She, on the other hand, bought a motor car and was fined £1 in 1933 for driving in Norwich without efficient brakes.[10] Mrs Crawshay became the first president of the Hempnall Women's Institute, begun in January 1934 with a membership of 52.[11] Their monthly meetings, held on Wednesday afternoons, were regularly recorded in the *Norwich Mercury*. There were outings and social evenings and lectures on topics including the history of Norwich Cathedral, invalid cooking and herring fishing. There were demonstrations of rug making and cooking with electricity. Competitions were varied, including the best umbrella made from paper, the best article made from a yard of material and the best nightdress case made from crêpe paper. When Captain Crawshay died in 1937, within six months Mrs Crawshay had announced her resignation from the Women's Institute and had taken herself off to East Africa.

Mr Blaiden, the head teacher, introduced athletic sports in July 1932, the children competing in houses: Fry (blue) Cavell (green), Nelson (yellow) and Walpole (red). Blue house scored the most points on that occasion. He also introduced carpentry for the boys. The children who had school dinners were given Horlicks in 'Belplastic' cups. An 'Ellams Rotary School Duplicator' was bought and a small party of boys visited Hobbies Ltd in East Dereham. However, Mr Blaiden was ambitious and, after completing a refresher course in Norwich, moved to Derbyshire in 1936.

The Revd Arthur Hogarth Oak-Rhind was appointed vicar of Hempnall on 8 November 1932. The following year, a friend of his gave the copy of Rubens' 'Adoration of the Shepherds at Bethlehem' which today hangs behind the communion table, replacing an old piece of tapestry.[12]

Under a slum clearance scheme of 1934, ten village houses were demolished, including a row of terraced houses by the Town Bridge, on the site of Kilbourn's garage. There were two outside toilets to serve these four cottages, and one old man used to regularly take up residence with his pipe and cause a queue. Jimmy Kennedy's house was declared 'a disgrace to the village' in 1937.[13] Four council houses were built in Field Lane in 1936 and a new police house was erected by the war memorial in 1937.[14] A house was destroyed by fire on the Greens in 1935, started when a spark from a fire set a cat alight. The animal ran upstairs and leapt through an open window, setting fire to the curtains which then ignited the thatch.[15] The minor roads in the village had but rough water-bound flint surfaces. In 1937 Fairstead lane was in a terrible condition, full of potholes, and it was a year before the surface was patched. The Hempnall to Puham road was widened to 16ft in 1938. Two gangs of workmen with a steam-roller took seven months to complete the work.[16]

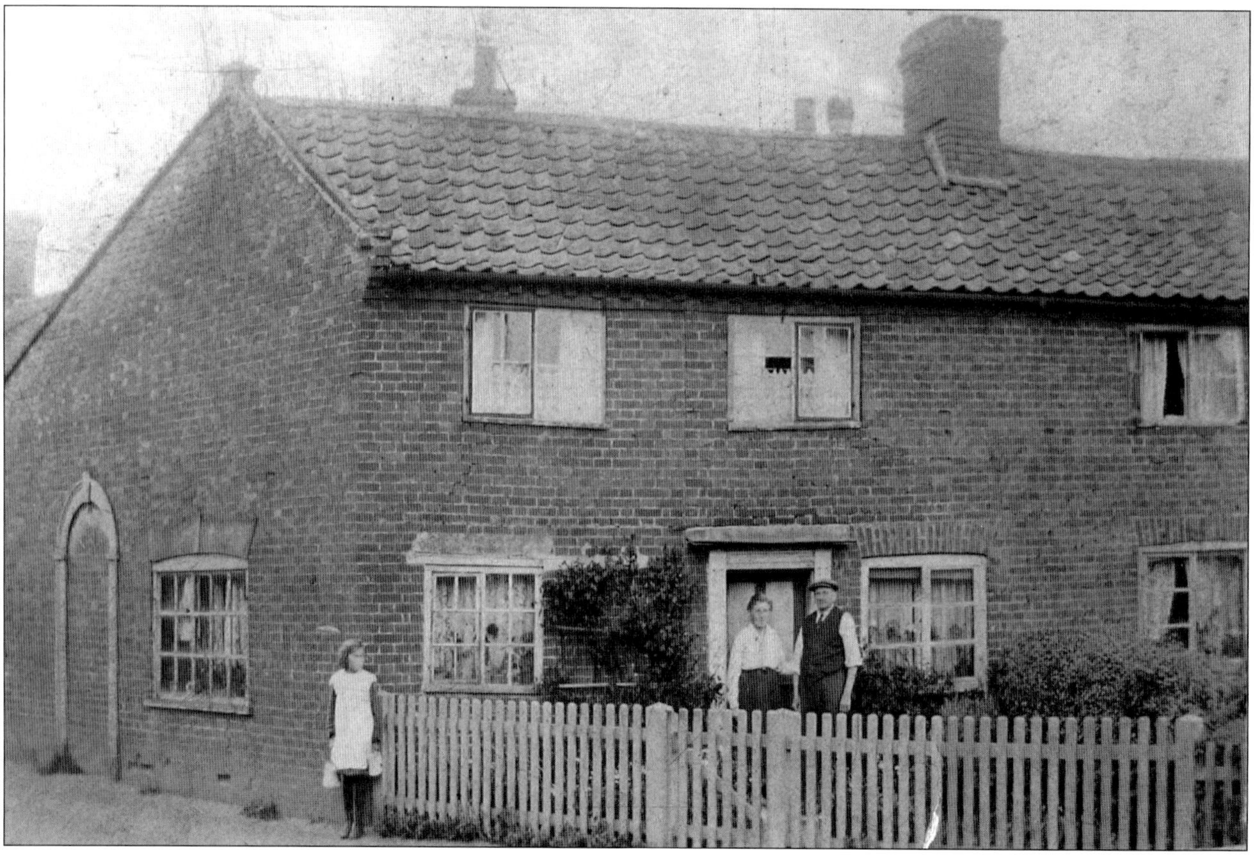

Ruth Buck and James and Alice Leggett outside the cottages on the bridge, now the site of Kilbourn's Garage.

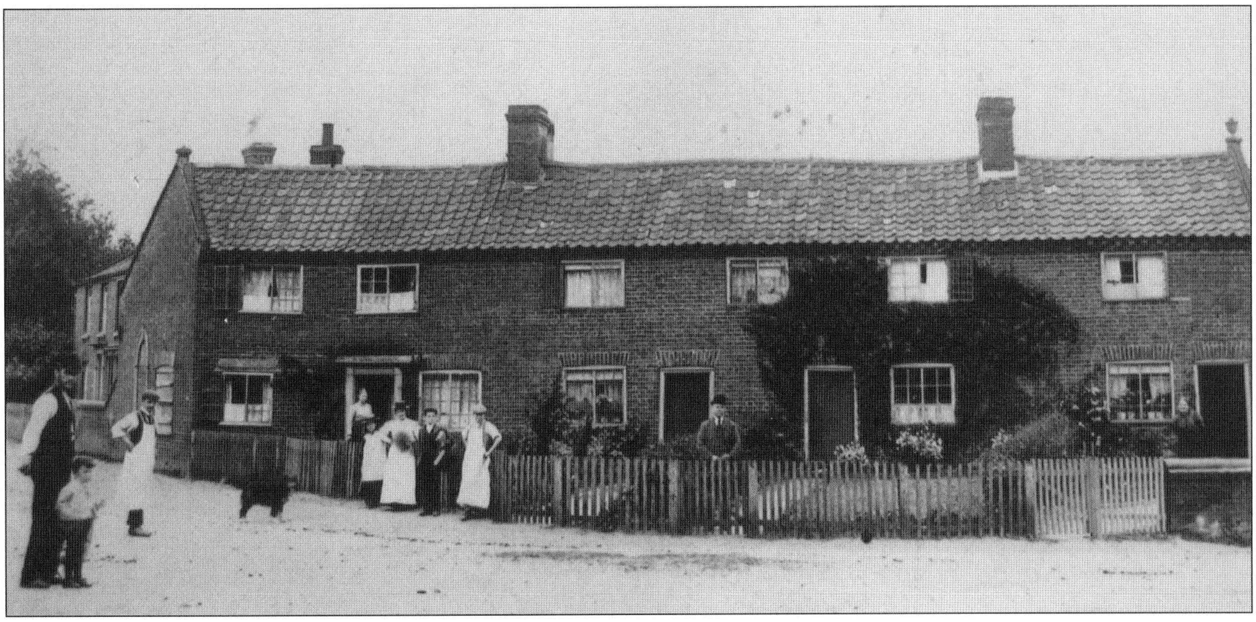

These cottages near the Town Bridge, demolished in 1934, were occupied by the Leggett, Lansdell, Masters and Elvin families.

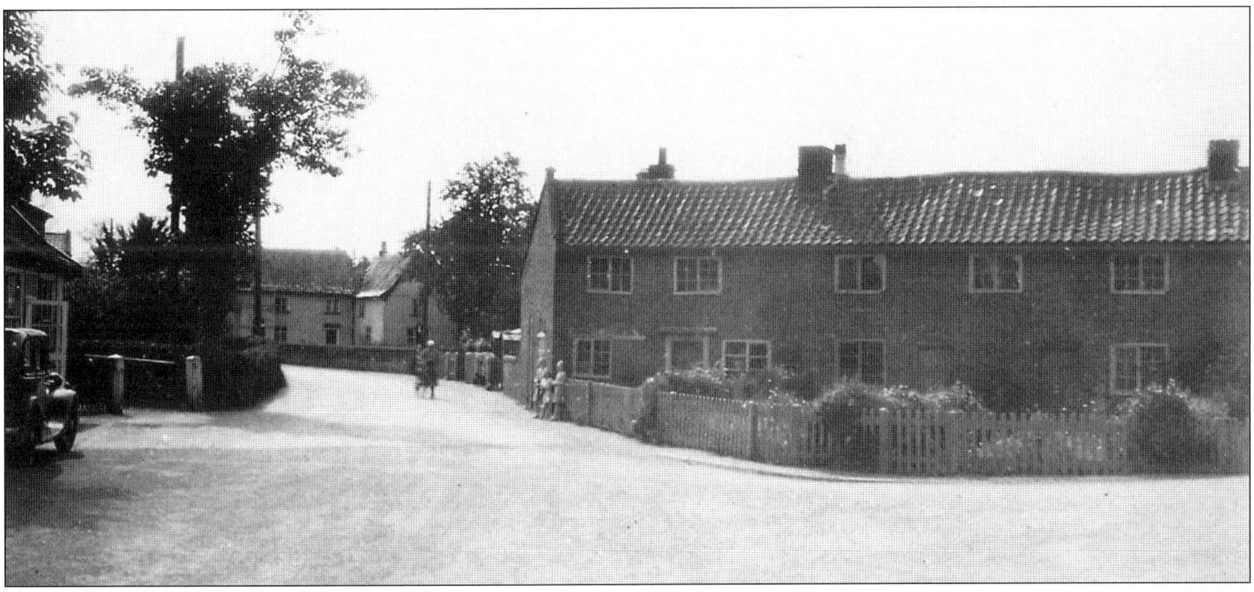

Another view of the cottages near the Town Bridge with the Chequers in the distance.

Stanley Day was one of the youngest men to drive a steam wagon. Arriving in Hempnall in 1931 on his motor bike, he took up residence at the Queen's Head, where he lodged with Topsy and Pip Hollis.

Preparations for celebrating the coronation of King George VI began in March 1937. It was agreed that Mr Metcalf, the headmaster, would organise sports followed by tea for the children, a fancy dress parade and teas for the adults. Mrs Weatherington, landlady of the Lord Nelson, offered the Nelson Hall for a waxworks display followed by a social in the evening. Nearly £42, collected house to house, was spent on 15 stone of beef and three of tinned ham, four gallons of milk, four stone of sugar, five pounds of tea, six pounds of butter, six gallons of pickles, two gallons of piccalilli, 25 four pound loaves, 28 pounds of biscuits, 28 pounds of cheese, 200 pastries, 14 pounds of slab cake and 20 sponge cakes. They were expecting 200 adults and 100 children. The food was supplied by local traders. Mr Dunthorne, the baker, roasted the beef. The bakery run by the Dunthorne family closed in about 1946 after Ray trained as a teacher. It was pulled down in 1949 and a bungalow was built on the site.[17]

The day began with a united service in the Parish Church, but, owing to rain, sports arranged for the afternoon had to be postponed, so there were games in the Village Hall. Slinger Fryer painted his horse red, white and blue, for the occasion. Mrs Crawshay and Mrs Oak-Rhind judged the fancy dress.

Children under 14 were given new sixpences as souvenirs. There was money left over, so it was decided that deserving cases in the village should each be given a hundredweight of coal.[18]

The threat from Germany became more real in 1938. Mrs Sargent from Morningthorpe gave a lecture to Hempnall Women's Institute in February on anti-gas precautions. Men and women were encouraged to train as air-raid wardens – nine were required for the village and five for the Greens. In September the school was closed for half a day to allow the children to be fitted with gas masks. The following month gas masks were ready for delivery to the rest of the population. Householders were advised to create a gas-proof 'refuge' room and to prepare for blacking out windows at night.[19]

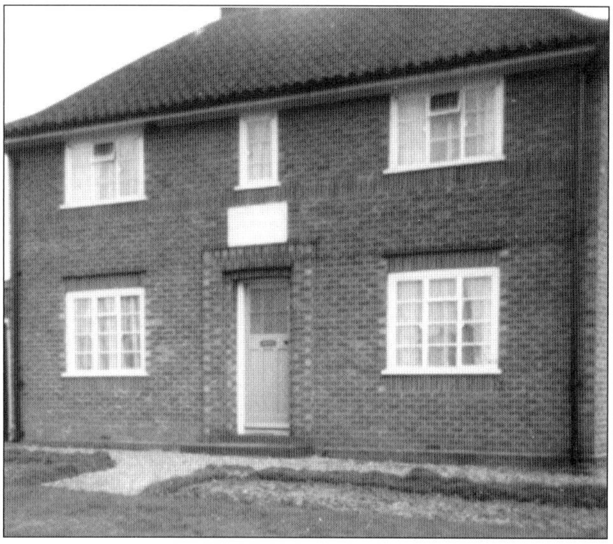

The police house near the war memorial, built in 1937. Now Broaden House.

Meanwhile, efforts were made to maintain the social life of the village. In January 1939 a party of 35 enjoyed *Dick Whittington* at the Theatre Royal in Norwich.[20] The newly-formed Lads' Club held a social evening at the Nelson Hall. Boxing gloves hung around the walls and punchbags and medicine balls were given prominent positions on the platform. Crackers and oranges were supplied and, after dinner, dancing continued into the evening to the music of the Hot Shots dance band.[21] The Women's Institute celebrated its fifth birthday with a party, with members of the Keep Fit movement giving a demonstration.

The evacuation scheme presented a problem for Depwade Rural District Council. Places for about 8,000 children and adults were needed, with the consequent problems of an inadequate water supply and extra refuse for disposal. Parish representatives were asked to remind householders of their responsibly to bury their own waste.[22]

In September 1939, 40 evacuated schoolchildren and two teachers from Edmonton School, arrived in Hempnall. Margaret Baldwin, aged six, described her first impressions when she and her brother William, arrived on the evening of 1 September after a long day's travelling. They were to lodge with my aunts, Edith and Alice Stammers, at Rostrever, now Rosewood. They were well looked after and wanted for nothing, but discipline was strict. William was

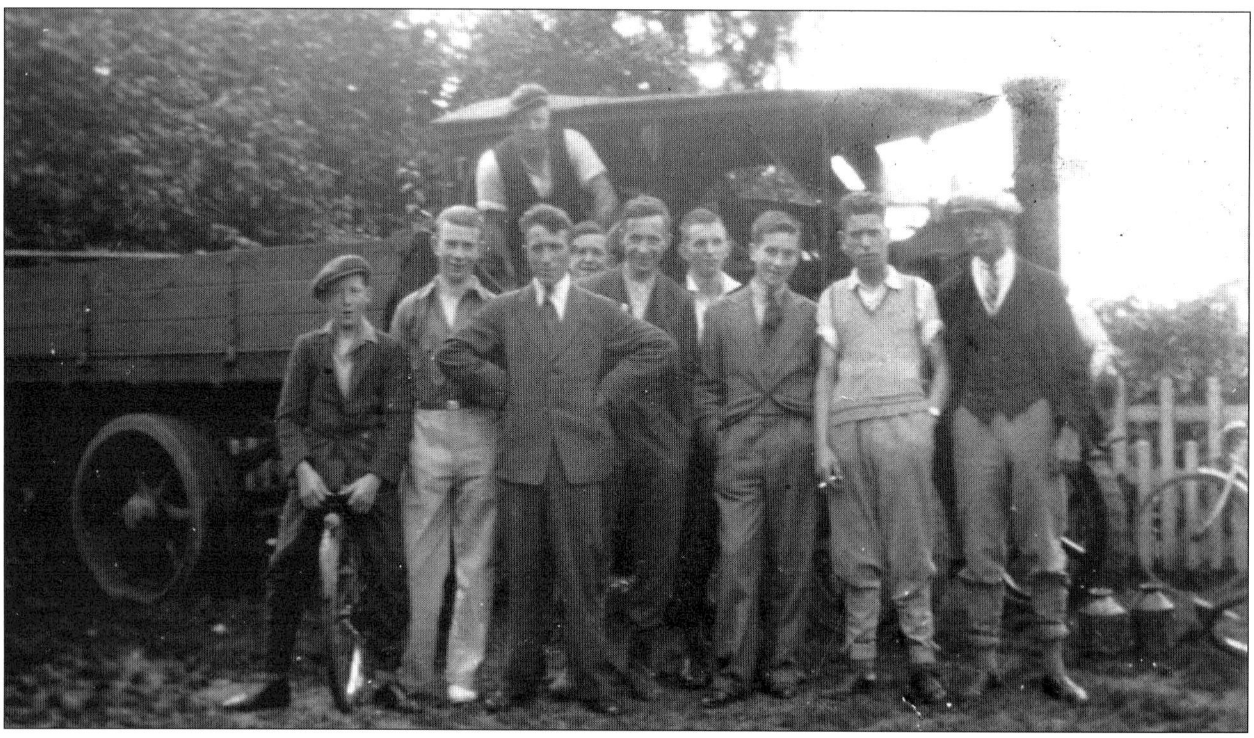

Stanley Day (at the back) *poses with fellow road workers.* Left to right: *Will Beckett, Freddie Baker, Philip Beckett, Claude Beckett, Ray Dunthorne, John Arnold, Tom Hipperson, George Pigney, George Moore.*

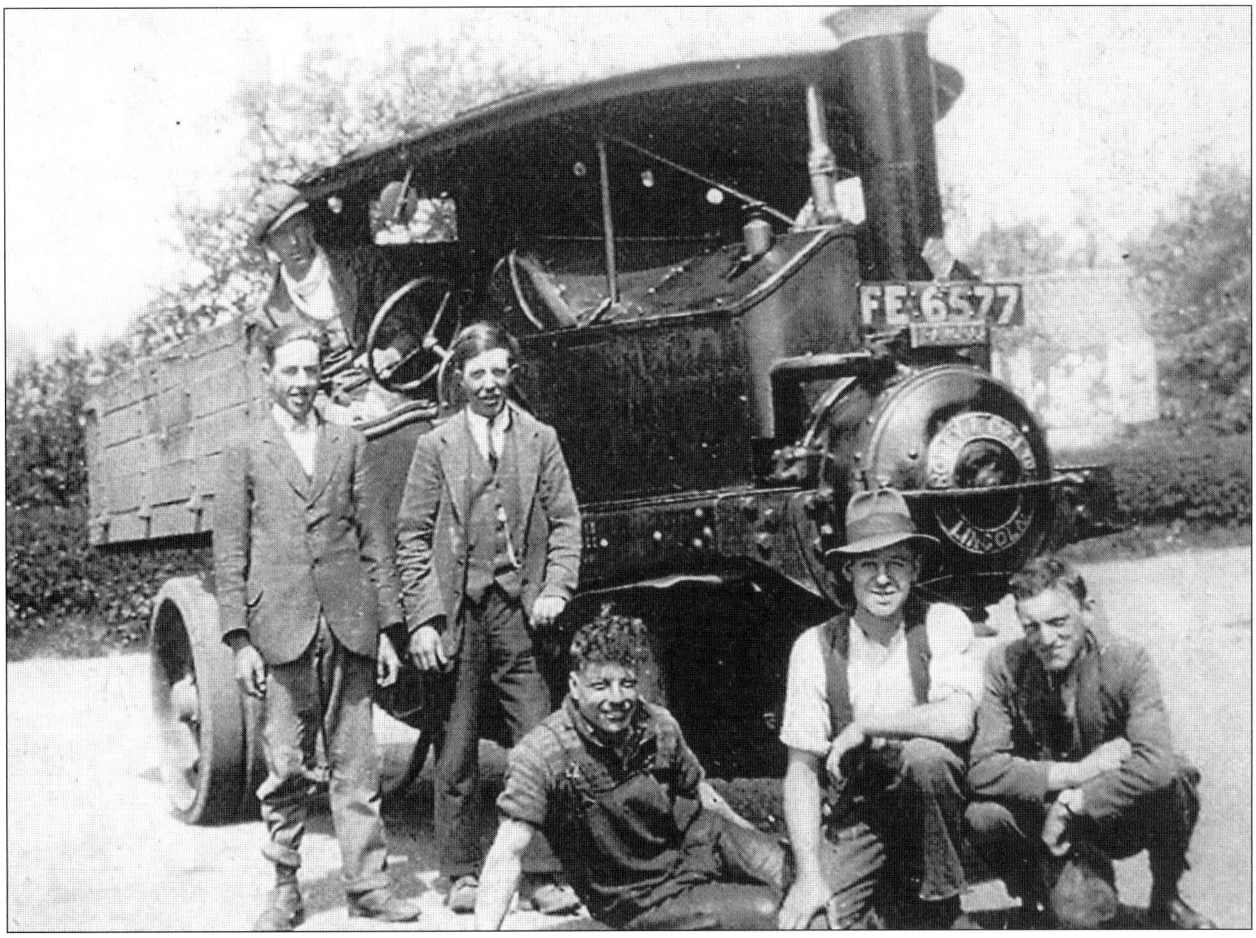

Stanley Day and fellow workers outside the Queen's Head.

often in trouble and wanted to go home for fish and chips and play out after dark. They were soon involved in activities at the Methodist chapel, where they joined the Junior Guild and Sunday school. Margaret remembered the snow and the frozen pond under the tree in the pit that year. Another part of the village she remembered was the abattoir next to the butcher's in Mill Road, and the sounds of squealing pigs and the blood running across the street into the river.

An allowance of 10s.6d. for the first child and 8s.6d. for the next and subsequent children was made to the family with whom they were billeted. In addition, an emergency ration of a tin of corned beef, two cans of evaporated milk, two packets of biscuits and a quarter pound bar of chocolate were provided to help avoid a rush to the local shops, which would cause general shortages. To encourage the London children to settle into country ways, Mrs Burton-Fanning gave some land for a garden.

On 3 September all children assembled at the school and were taken to church for a service. At 11.15 that morning, war was declared. A week later the first air-raid warning was heard and children were taken to safety in the pit.[23] School began on 11 September and was reorganised into four main classes and an infant class. A few days later the school doctor examined the children.

Identity cards and ration books were issued to the population and shops were told to close by 6p.m. The Women's Institute held sewing sessions for the Red Cross Society and organised whist drives to raise money for cigarettes and chocolates for Hempnall men serving in the forces.

Parents came to visit their children in a coach hired at Edmonton. One Sunday morning the Baldwins came out of chapel to see their parents having a glass of beer while they waited. 'We had been there long enough to know the teachings of the Methodists,' wrote Margaret. William was horrified and told them so. This upset their parents so much that they decided to take them home

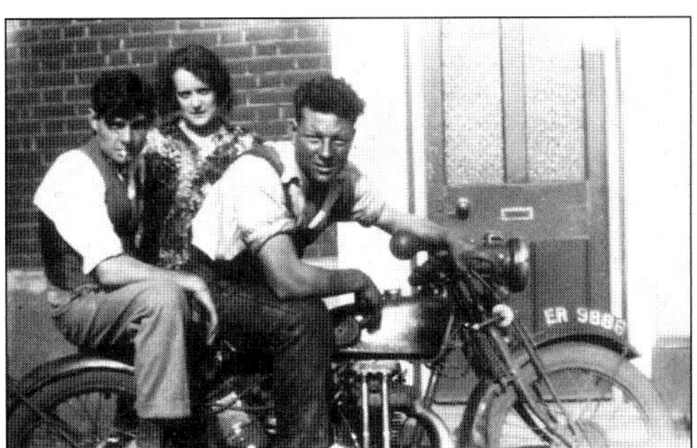

Left: *Stanley Day* (right) *with Topsy Hollis and Pip Hollis.*

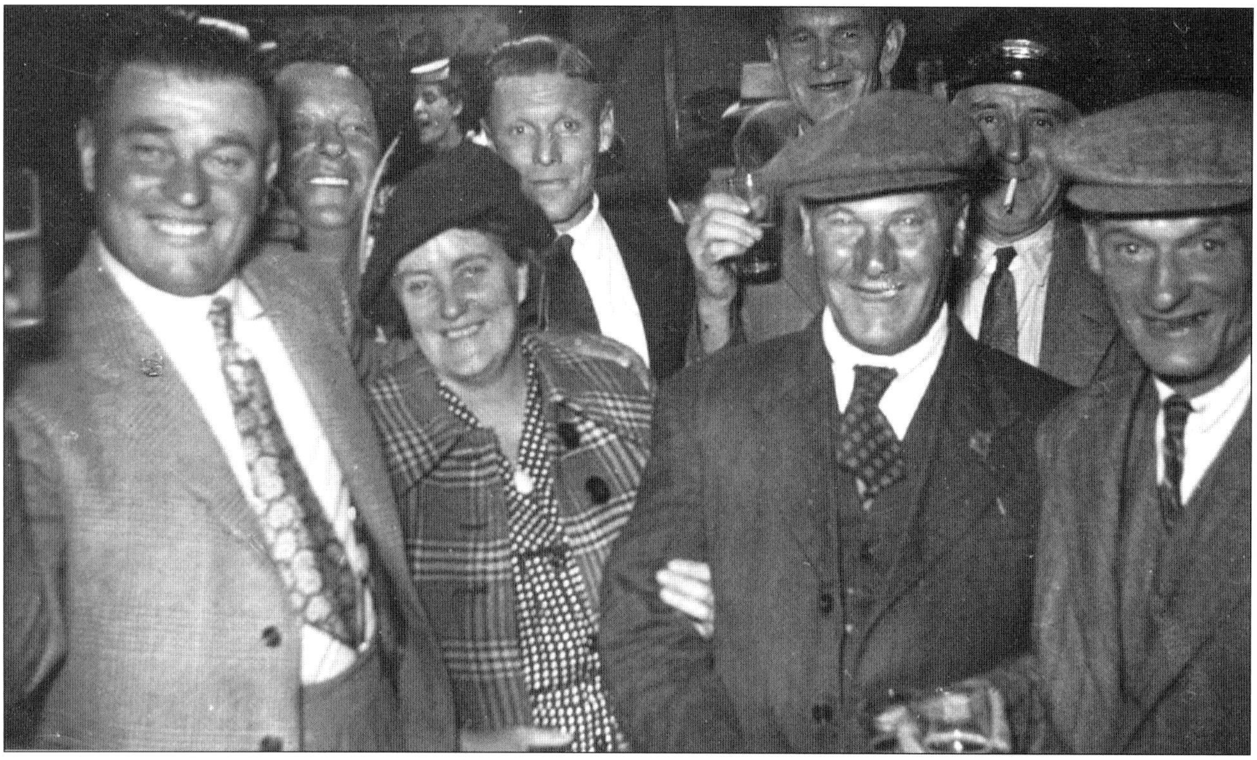

In the Queen's Head are, at the back: *Stanley Day, Bertie Reeder, Walter Ladbrooke, the bus driver;* front: *?, Topsy Hollis, George (Fat) Moore, Jack Townsend.*

then and there. My aunts were very upset, but the children kept in touch and they met again as adults.[24] In fact, 1,000 children returned to Edmonton after just a month, and by January 82 per cent of them had gone home.

References

[1] *EDP* Wednesday, 7 October 1931
[2] NRO BR 32/1 Geldeston Brewers The Swan Lot 36
[3] *EDP* Monday, 1 January 1934; *EDP* 18 November 1987; memories from Billy's son, Wesley, recorded in 1987
[4] NRO DC 2/3/13 Depwade Rural District Minute Book 1930–35. Licences granted to W.C. Cunningham G. Hinchcliffe and Stammers Hempnall (Ltd)
[5] NRO DC 2/3/13 Licences
[6] Parish Council Minute Book, 19 April 1937
[7] *NM* Saturday, 20 February 1932
[8] G.G. Stammers (1969) *My Village* (Norwich) p.50
[9] Remembered by Bobby Tweeddale
[10] *NM* Saturday, 15 July 1933
[11] *EDP* Saturday, 6 January 1934
[12] Depwade Deanery Magazine, July 1933, given by Mary Harris of Westcliff-on-Sea
[13] Parish Council Records, 29 September 1937
[14] NRO DC 2/3/14 Depwade Rural District Council Surveyor's Department
[15] Parish Council Minute Book 1937–52
[16] Parish Council Minute Book 1937–52
[17] Parish Council Minute Book 1937–52
[18] *EDP* Friday, 5 July 1935
[19] NRO DC2/4/4 Depwade Highway Committee Minutes 1930–63
[20] *NM* Saturday, 7 January 1939
[21] *NM* Saturday, 7 January 1939
[22] *NM* Saturday, 25 March 1939
[23] School log-book
[24] Memories of Margaret Baldwin

✦ CHAPTER 18 ✦

A Second Home
1940–49

The threat of gas and bomb attacks was endemic. With fire a major worry, a two-man manual pump was acquired for the village in 1940 and stored in Cunningham's Garage. Seven men were commandeered as fire-fighters and supplied with stirrup pumps and buckets. A Local Defence Volunteer Unit (later the Home Guard) was formed and they assembled in a cottage near the Mill.

James Ladbrooke, district commander of the Local Defence Volunteers, stored equipment and ammunition at the Poplars. Everyone was encouraged to help with the war effort. Collections of waste materials – paper, bones, rubber tyres, clean rags and non-essential metals such as railings and old saucepans – were sorted at a collection point on the site of what, in 2008, is the doctor's surgery.[1] Children were encouraged to help and earned badges for their efforts. Most people kept a few hens and grew their own vegetables. Alec Quantrell was the Salvage Officer in 1944.

Many dug air-raid shelters in their gardens. The Beckett family, who lived near the ford on Bungay Road, made a shelter near the beck with planks topped with earth, which proved unsatisfactory when they were flooded out after heavy rain.

Fred Hickling, a Local Defence Volunteer before he joined the Royal Air Force, was on duty one night with two others in a shepherd's hut used as a look-out along the Saxlingham road when the air-raid siren sounded over Norwich. Fred sped on his bike to warn Major Beck at Hill House. Apparently the major shot out of bed, put on a coat over his pyjamas

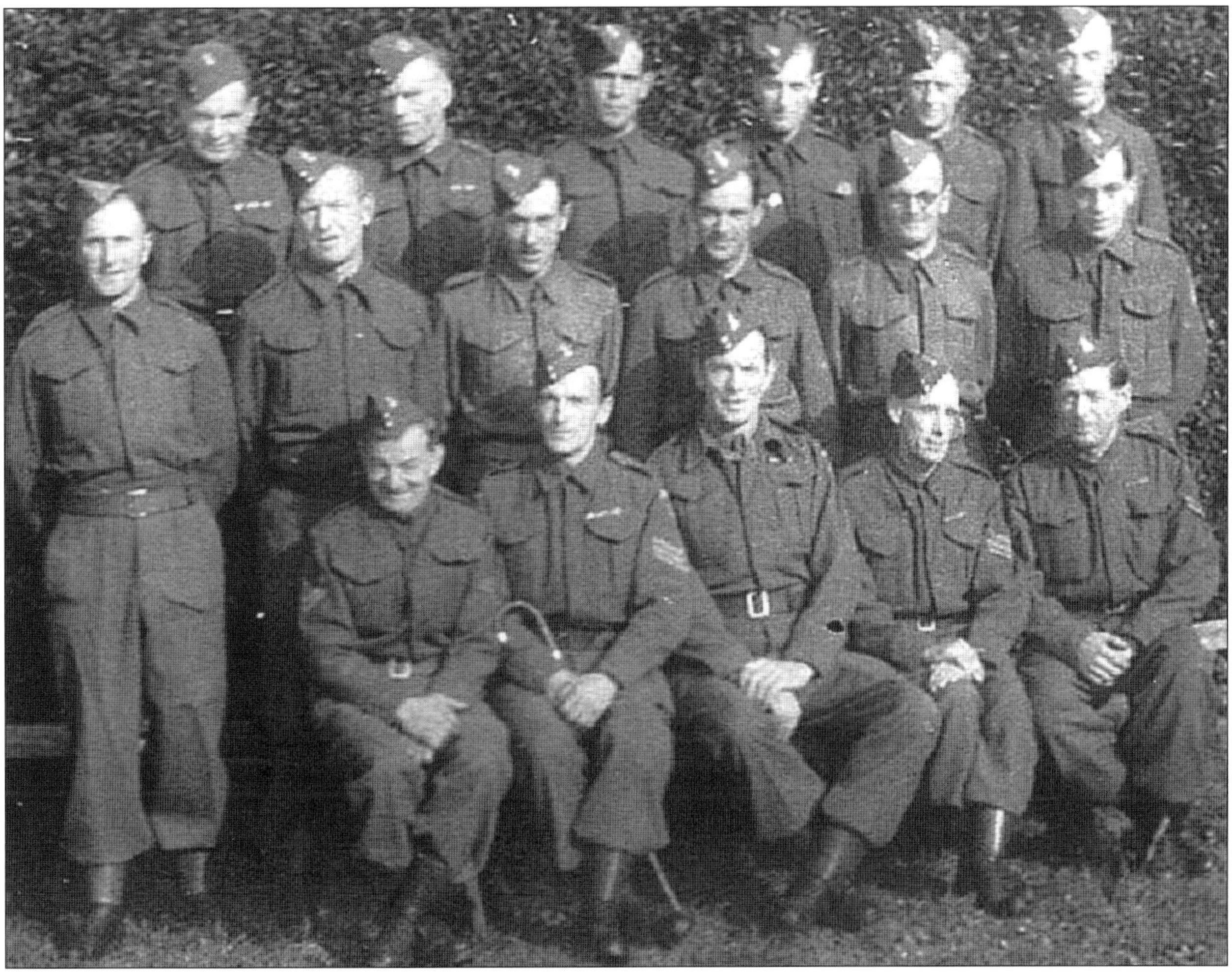

Hempnall Home Guard. Left to right back row: *Mr Stops, Spratt Potter, Will Leathersich, Philip Moore, Jimmy Youngman, Nat Davidson;* middle row: *Norman Ellis, Jimmy Leggett, ?, ? Cunningham, ?, Walter Pigg;* front row: *Ben Hickling, Jimmy Cawthorne, Walter Ladbrooke, Bob Hazell, Jack Waddeldow.*

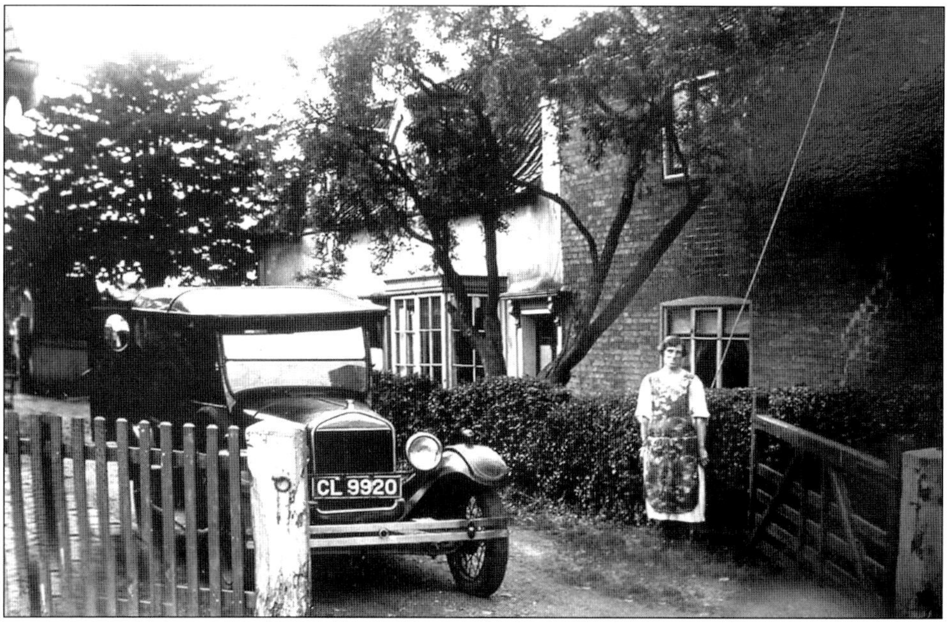

Daisy Page, who worked for the Ladbrookes, outside the Poplars. The old part at the back was copyhold (Custons), earliest known record 1647.

and cycled round the village blowing a whistle. After a while the villagers became used to the warnings and just carried on with their daily lives.

Those serving in the Forces were supported by gifts of chocolate and cigarettes, as well as letters. Those left behind were buoyed by a few social activities, such as the newly formed 'Hempnall Players' and a youth club. The Women's Institute continued to thrive under Mrs Ladbrooke, the new president. A pie scheme, initiated in 1943 at the Institute, operated once a week.[2]

Four new children arrived from Surrey in 1940. In January 1941 there were 18 evacuees and 58 local children on the register. The newcomers had their own teachers and were taught separately. The following year the wall dividing the two playgrounds was taken down, allowing boys, girls and evacuees to mix at playtimes. January 1941 was bitterly cold with heavy snow. A measles epidemic brought attendance down to 17 in total. Jean Poyntz recorded the day when an enemy plane flew very low and machine-gunned the school and children dived under their desks.[3] Gerald Whiting, who remembers the same occasion, heard that the plane was shot down at Lowestoft.

Preparations for a particular family of evacuees involved renovating a cottage on the Greens and donating furniture, kitchen utensils and a pram. The family arrived and before long rumours circulated of coal being stored in the bath and good country food being shunned. That family returned to London. However, most of the new arrivals thrived. They learned how to grow vegetables and an invitation to pick apples invariably caused a stampede. They made local friends and many continued to correspond for years after the war.

My father, uncles and aunt were among those from Hempnall who joined the armed forces. Sergeant John Lansdell was the first RAF casualty. He was shot down in 1940 over Kent after combat with a Messerschmitt, flying a Hurricane with 607 Squadron. He was buried at Hempnall in the Bussey's family plot.

Stanley Day, a steam-wagon driver by trade, had lodged at the Queen's Head until marrying a local girl in 1935. When war broke out, he joined the RAF and drove a 60ft aircraft recovery vehicle, affectionately known as a 'Queen Mary'. He was posted to North Africa in 1943 and then transported petrol and stores around the Middle East, frequently crossing the Suez Canal on a 'Bailey Bridge' with no safety rails, the canal some 60ft below. His Hempnall friend, Gordon Gray, was captured in 1941. Stanley preserved several letters written from the prisoner-of-war camp. Gordon asked to be remembered to all his friends at the Nelson, missed English beer and poaching pheasants with his catapult. In 1942 he recounted a spell of five months in hospital suffering from a cracked skull (the reason not given). He was well enough to escape in January 1943, but was recaptured after three weeks.

Severe flooding in February 1942 drove the family from the schoolhouse to take refuge in the Village Hall for several weeks. The school was appallingly damp and the Parish Council debated an idea to build a new school on a healthier site on the Bungay Road, but this never came to fruition.[4]

Children from the Greens were the first to notice activity in the far south of the parish on the site of the old deer park. Soil was being moved and buildings and supplies appeared. Three dumper truck drivers who were working on the site took the opportunity

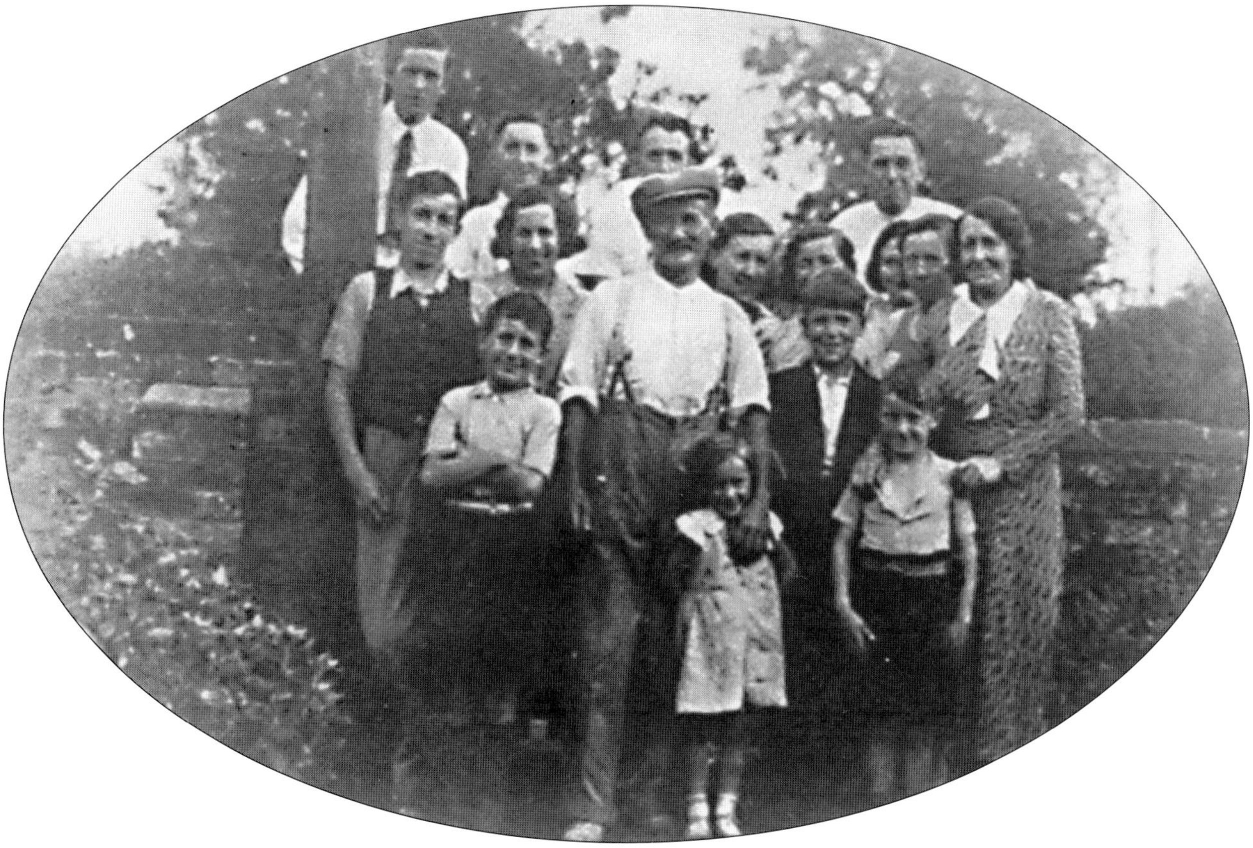

The Beckett family: Left to right, back row: *Lesley, William, Philip, Gilbert;* middle row: *Jo, Beryl, Muriel, Blanch, Eve, Flo, Ruby;* front row: *Basil, Herbert (father), Pamela, Peter, Lionel.*

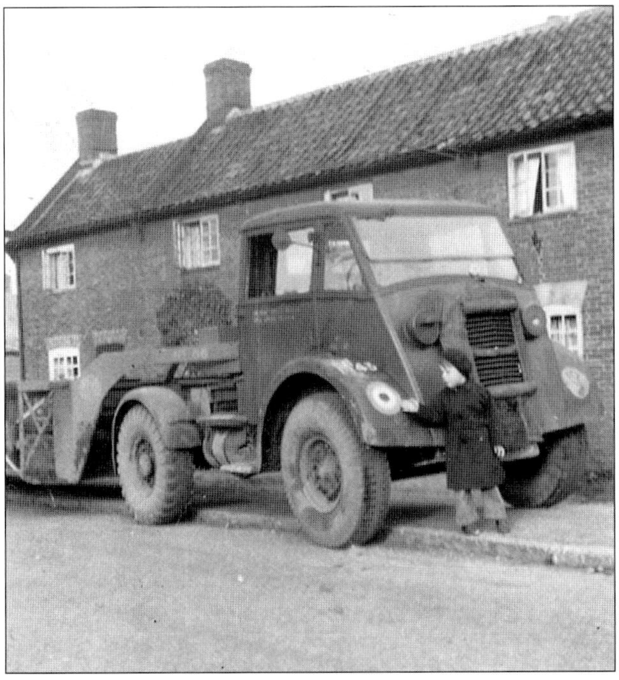

Stanley Day's Queen Mary outside Bridge Terrace.

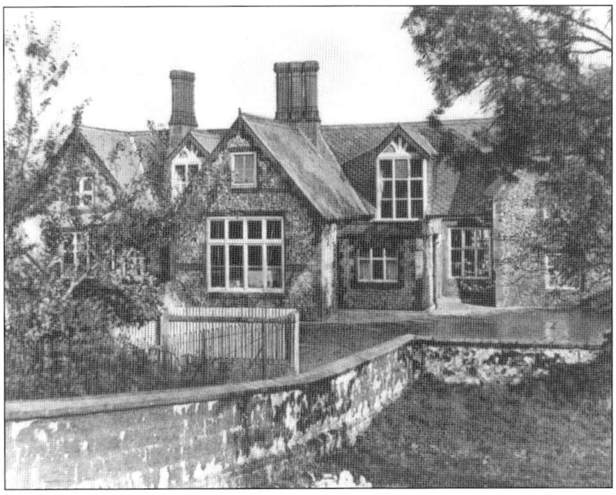

Hempnall School.

to siphon off a few gallons of petrol and steal a new tyre. They were caught because the fuel had been coloured pink. Initially, the airfield was intended for the RAF, but use was transferred to the United States Army Air Force. The first runway was completed in time for the arrival of the 310 Bomber Group with their B25 Mitchell bombers. Though the aerodrome was to be called 'Hardwick', perhaps for security reasons, the entire runway system was in Hempnall parish.

The next few months were spent completing the aerodrome. In all, 13 miles of runway were constructed, with three cavernous hangars, a control tower, fire tender stations, maintenance shops, pump

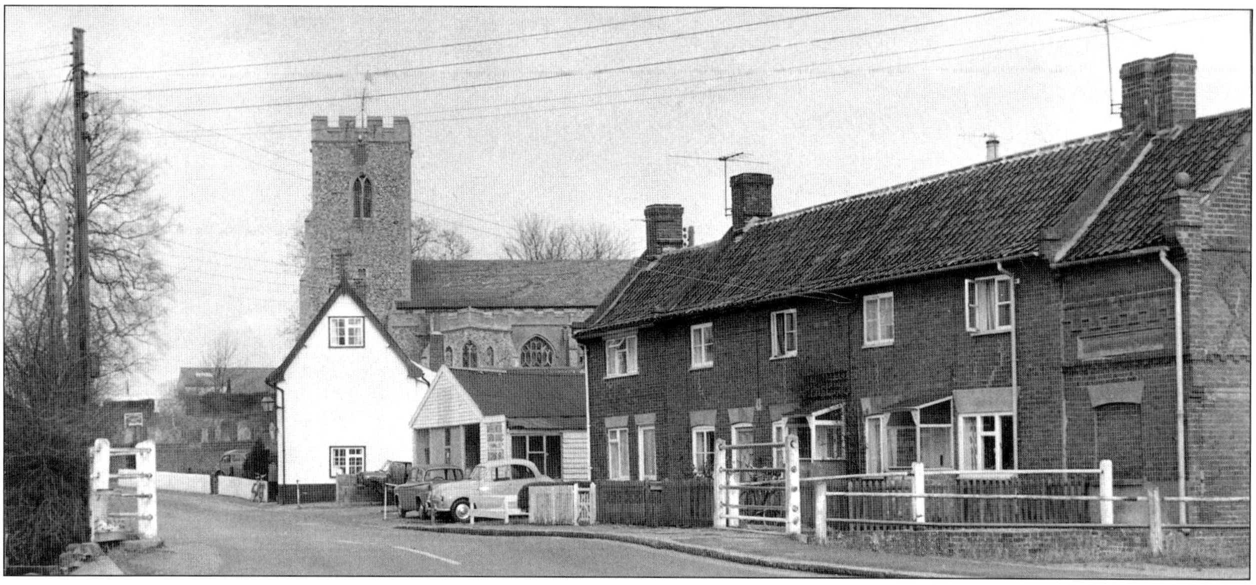

The garage next to the white-gabled Longhouse was used as a social club by the Americans during the Second World War. (EASTERN DAILY PRESS)

houses, Nissen huts, mess halls, a theatre, a chapel, a gymnasium and a sports hall, altogether more than 200 buildings. The 93rd Bomber Group moved in during December 1942, commanded by Ted T. Timberlake. They were nicknamed 'Ted's Flying Circus'. A decoy airfield was constructed on the northern boundary of the parish. Mr Page manned the dummy lights, which were operated from the air base by a connecting cable.

The villagers soon accustomed themselves to the sound of bombers going out on missions, cottage walls shaking to the throb of engines, gunfire, flares dropped by enemy aircraft and the display of searchlights rotating from Musk's farm at Fritton. Over 2,000 men were stationed at Hardwick, 2,900 at the height of the war. It was the equivalent of a small town on the doorstep. Airmen visited the village centre, wobbling on bicycles, and the garage next to the Longhouse was converted into a social club, where they were given the opportunity to play table tennis and enjoy a cup of tea and sandwiches. The Three Horsehoes, the only pub on the Greens, became very popular with the Yanks. Hempnall became their second home.

People on the Greens generously provided afternoon tea and shared their meagre Sunday lunch rations on many occasions. One American serviceman, Mr Murphy, was popular for playing his guitar at Methodist services.

Villagers may have assumed that the Americans had a high level of comfort on the base, but accounts show their staple diet to have been Brussels sprouts, dried beef on toast, tinned spam, powdered eggs, bread and marmalade. Their Nissen huts were poorly heated, winter coal being rationed to a bucket a day.

Perhaps the young Americans about the village helped the locals cope with the absence of their own young men. Dances, very popular with village girls, were held at the Village Hall on Saturday nights.

Letters and the occasional visit on leave were the only contact with village Servicemen. Sadly, not all news was good. Private Reginald Gooch of the 5th Battalion, Royal Norfolk Regiment, died in January 1942 fighting the Japanese. He was 22. He was buried at Kranji War Cemetary. Jack Fraser and Ray Madget, who lived next door to one another in the Street, were both killed. Ray worked at Stammers' shop, before enlisting. He served in the Royal Norfolk Regiment and died in 1943. Jack is believed to have been in the RAF.

During August 1943, when the 93rd Bomber Group was flying missions to North Africa, the return flights were often hazardous. Crash cars, jeeps, fire trucks and ambulances lined up between the hangars, and the atmosphere was tense and quiet for those on the ground. 'Then the roaring thunder of bombers would shatter the peace, planes would be counted as they approached the land strip.'[5] During 1943, 402 men from the base went missing in action or were killed. That Christmas scores of airmen were invited to British homes, where rations were shared. It was the second Christmas in England for most of the men.

At the height of the war, at least one Norwich family with Hempnall connections drove to the village and slept in armchairs, disappearing again at daybreak. Norwich was heavily bombed, and barrage balloons could be seen round the fringe. Village people only went there when absolutely necessary. People looked after the vulnerable and traders did their best. Mr Hickling heated his bread oven on Christmas morning for anyone who had a fowl to cook.

On the evening of 5 November 1943, the Ellis family at Road Green noticed a RAF Mosquito circling the airfield, throwing out distress flares.

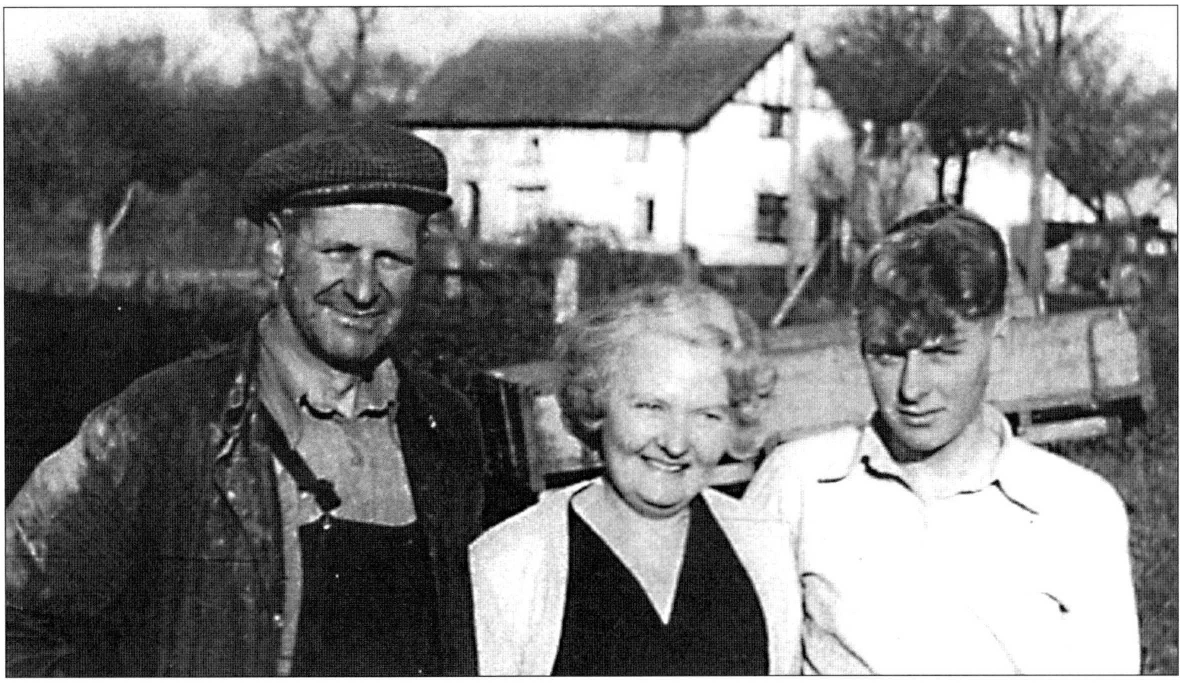

Percy, Florence May and John Ellis outside Moat Farm. Earliest known date 1568. Timber-framed. (Copyhold description: (Gledes with a tenement Spicers).

Suddenly it hit a tree and crashed into a mangold field between the Green and the village. Percy Ellis went to help, but the two young men were dead. The following morning the wreckage was loaded on to a 'Queen Mary' and driven away to Hardwick.

Appalling weather in the early months of 1944 imposed a cessation of missions from Hardwick. The Americans entered a basketball tournament and defeated their rivals, the 44th Bomb Group, at Blackfriars Hall in Norwich. By the end of March, to ease the boredom, they landscaped the base, planted flowers and painted the fences surrounding the Nissen huts white and green. The following month they were back in the skies.

On 22 April 1944, 14 planes were returning from Hamm in Germany when they were chased by Messerschmitt night-fighters, guided by the exhaust flames and landing lights of the B24s. The local radar station fired danger flares from the control tower and searchlights lit the sky. Those Liberators with fuel to spare were flown by the Americans to other airfields. As the German planes swooped down over the airfield with guns blazing, Hardwick's defence gunners took the chance to have their first shot at the enemy. At least one Hempnall family stood outside to watch, oblivious to the danger.[6]

Later that year a crippled Liberator attempted an emergency landing with insufficient power:

> *The pilot dropped his wing tip to avoid the Control Tower, the plane cartwheeled, slamming broadside into the chemical shop... One engine ripped loose and smashed into a supply building. Miraculously only two crewmen were killed.* [7]

Film star James Stewart spent several months on the Hardwick base. He may have been there in 1944, when a Liberator returning from Germany two hours late approached the runway short of fuel. The engine began to splutter and smoke, but the pilot and co-pilot stayed at the controls until the last minute. One airman's parachute dragged him 50 ft on his stomach along the ground until a tree deflated the chute.[8] He walked to a local farmhouse, 'where the folks graciously poured tea'.

On 19 December 1944 an aircraft loaded with 12 500lb bombs crashed at the end of the runway, exploding eight bombs and killing the crew. With another Christmas away from home and yet more of their friends lost to the war, many Americans appreciated the comfort and welcome of English homes. In return, they planned a grand party for 160 local children. Despite the thick fog on Christmas Eve, the children were collected from the surrounding villages and treated to a Walt Disney film and ice-cream. During one summer children were invited to walk to the aerodrome to see a circus.

Neville Day and his friend, Iky Youngs, were standing by the Town Bridge in about 1944, when an American airman parachuted into a meadow, now Roland Drive. While the pilot waited to be collected from Hardwick he gave the boys sweets and chewing-gum. It later transpired that this airman regularly jumped from the aircraft when approaching Hardwick, just for the fun of it.

January 1945 was the coldest for many years. Military and civilians were desperately short of fuel. Plumbing froze and coal reserves for civilians were down to three days. Several Hempnall residents

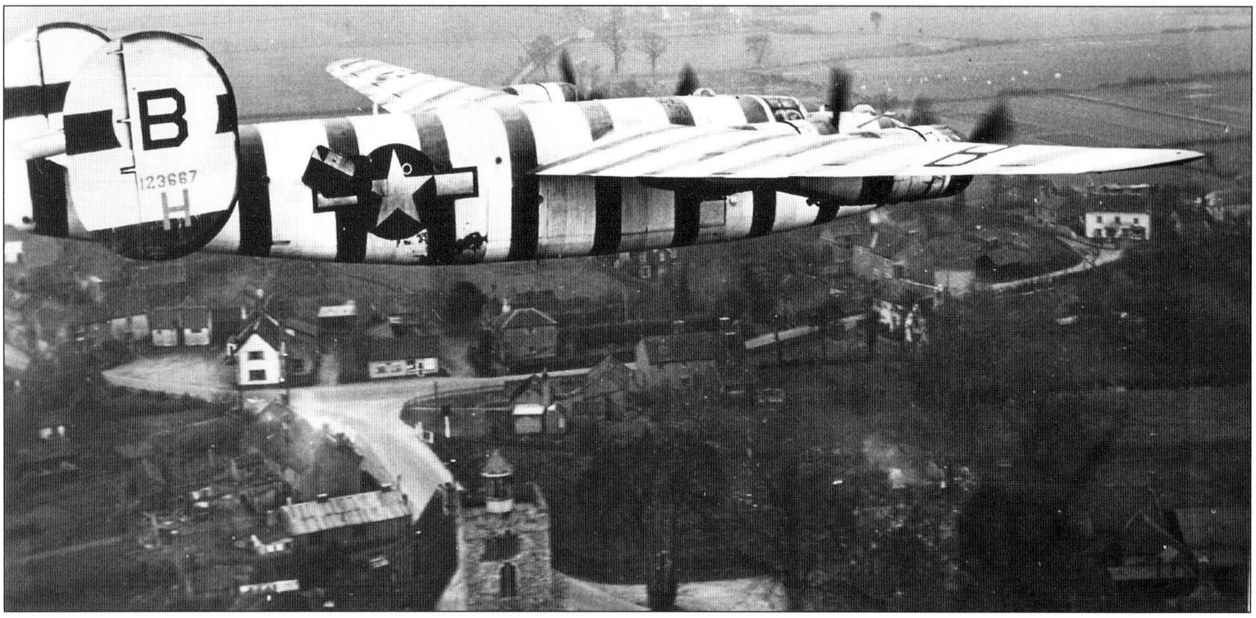

A Liberator flying over Hempnall during the war.

considered the Americans better off and in March were caught in possession of food stolen from the American airbase.[9]

As April approached, secret plans were formulated for the exodus from England. Most of the Americans departed during May and June. As the last group left, the villagers lined the streets and waved goodbye, a solemn and quiet occasion.

Sadly, the day before the war ended, Bob Roberts, a despatch rider from Silver Green returning from Fritton with a message, crashed into a wall near the church and was killed.

Charles Perkins was killed in a plane crash returning from Italy at the end of the war in 1946. Four names were added to the war memorial in October 1947; Perkins's name was added later. Joe Beckett, serving with the 2nd Battalion of the Parachute Regiment, was captured at Arnhem. At the end of the war, when his family heard he was returning, they planned an elaborate homecoming. Some of the girls made themselves red, white and blue dresses ready to meet him. Unfortunately, he arrived late at night and everyone was in bed! However, Joe became a hero in 1949 when he became the Eastern area middleweight boxing champion, beating Ginger Sadd of Norwich, the title holder for a number of years.[10] A committee, chaired by my grandfather, was formed to discuss the best way of welcoming home the Hempnall men and women who had been serving with the Allied Forces. Money was raised through dances organised by the Youth Club, house–to-house collections, an American Concert and Fair, a flag day and a ploughing match. Suggestions for spending the money included a cottage hospital, a playing-field and a bus shelter. It was finally agreed to ask the Forces what they would like. In the end everybody agreed that the money should be equally divided between all members of the Forces, and that next of kin should have the share of those who had died.

A 'Salute Hempnall Week' commenced on New Year's Eve 1945 with a social, including refreshments. A boxing match took place on Tuesday, 1 January, followed by a whist drive on the Wednesday. On Thursday a Christmas fair was organised by the Women's Institute, the Mothers' Union, the Methodist Sisterhood and the Women's Voluntary Service, and in the evening a concert was arranged by Ray Hazell. Carol singing round the village took place the following evening. On Saturday, 5 January, organised by the football club, a children's concert in the afternoon was followed in the evening by dancing to the music of Brighton's Band. Finally, on the Sunday, a concert was held in the Village Hall. After expenses, the total raised was £205.18s.10d, a fitting recognition of the respect and gratitude owed to the members of the Hempnall Forces.

References

1 NRO D2/9/2 Emergency Committee 27 April 1943

2 NRO DC2/3/15 Depwade Minute Book 1940–49, 17 March 1942

3 Diana Ingram, daughter of Jean Poyntz

4 NRO DC2/3/15 Depwade Minute Book 1940–49, 1 March 1943

5 Carroll Stewart (1996) *Ted's Flying Circus. 93rd Bombardment Group (H), United States Army Air Force, World War II* (Lincoln USA) p.100

6 Stewart op. cit., p.310

7 Stewart op. cit., p.356

8 Stewart op. cit., p.422

9 *NM* 24 March 1945

10 *NM* Friday, 7 October 1949

✦ CHAPTER 19 ✦

Postwar 1946–59

When the war ended my parents rented Rostrevor, next to the pit and to Knudsen's poultry farm, from my grandfather. We were not on mains water or sewerage. We had an outdoor 'Elsan' lavatory into which our cat once fell and a friend lost a set of false teeth. My parents dug a huge pit in the garden to dispose of the sewage. We used a hand pump in the kitchen for well water until my father installed an electric pump. My grandparents, at Connaught House next to the shop, had a pump in the kitchen to take water to a tank in the roof, so they had a flush toilet and water in the taps long before us. In the '50s the road was up for weeks as pipes were laid for sewerage. After that we indulged in a twin-tub washing machine instead of the dolly tub in the yard.

I made friends with the Legood children while attending the village school, and we spent happy summer days climbing trees and getting our feet wet in the river. Mrs Baker, who lived opposite at Ivy Cottage, used to dry our shoes and socks for us. She was destined to live to 107, a remarkable woman who was in the Royal Flying Corps in the First World War, before it became the Royal Air Force.

My parents were both involved in the business, Stammers, Universal Providers, later Stammers (Hempnall) Ltd. At that time it operated from two buildings, one for furnishings, the other for grocery and drapery. My father boasted that they could supply anything, from barbed wire to stockings, from salmon to a three-piece suite. Customers were

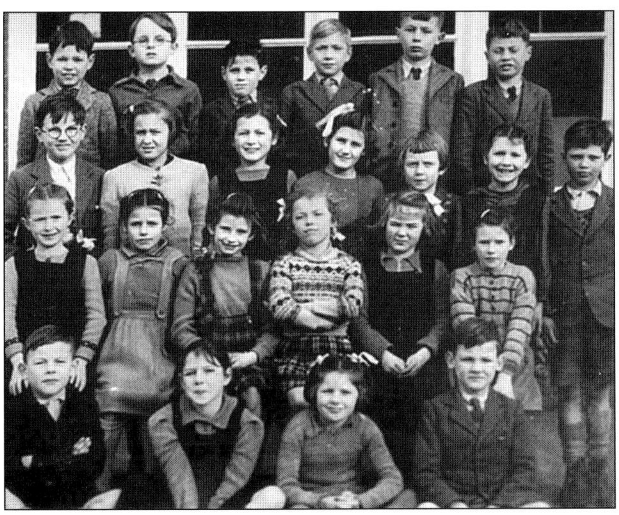

My class at Hempnall School, c.1948. Left to right back row: *St John Perry, Geoffrey Penn, Ivor Downing, Billy Youngman, Billy Legood, George Crummett;* third row: *Philip Buck, Betty Warne, Janet Emms, Brenda Thaker, Violet Haynes, Valerie Taylor, Alan Sutton;* second row: *Margaret Legood, Joan Harwin, Maureen Stammers (author), ? Buck, Joan Roberts, Carol Downing;* front row: *Barry Day, Margaret Gardner, Joy Page, Gerald Brooks.*

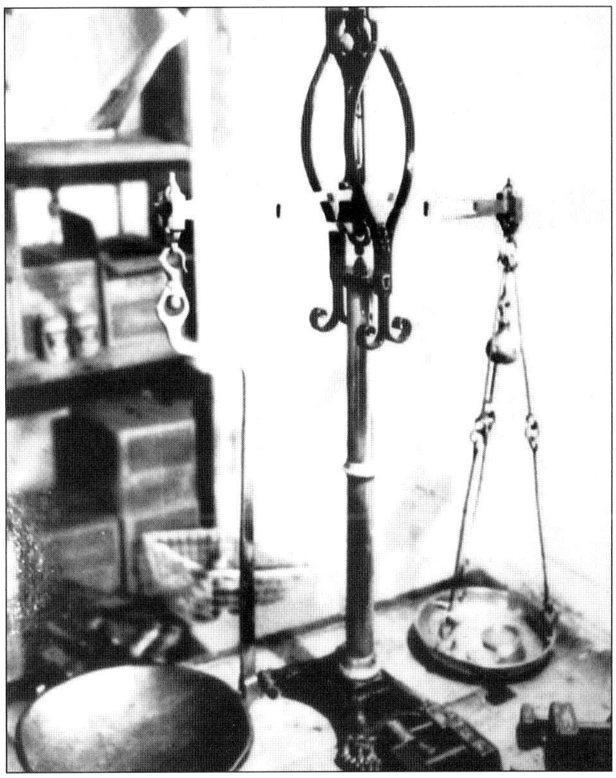

Scales from Stammers' shop.

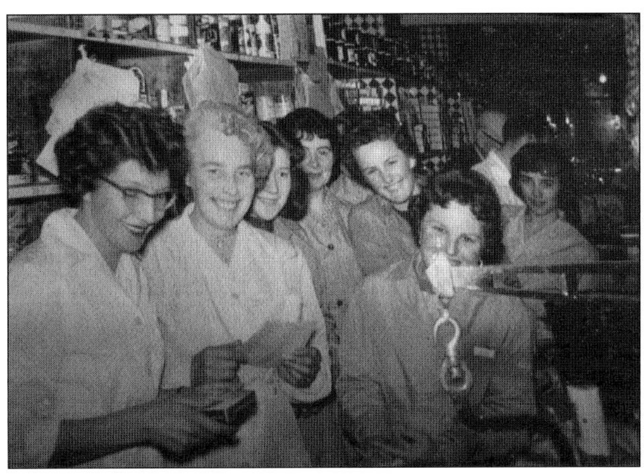

The drapery department. Left to right: *Phyllis Webster, Molly Shepherd, Sheila Punt, Barbara Rackham, Janet Downing, Jenny Harmer;* front: *Ann Downing.*

served individually from counters in the grocery and drapery departments. A delivery lorry was kept in the old tithe barn and a smaller van was parked in the yard. Bacon and cheeses were stored in the cellars below. We sold cutlery with the Stammers name on the blade. Great brass scales weighed loose goods, and broken biscuits could be bought for a fraction of the cost of whole ones. Father had 'schemes' from time to time. He once demolished a staircase in the furnishing department and rebuilt it elsewhere. Behind the scenes there was a large room, always called 'the Ball Room', where whitening balls were once stored. This room contained a cupboard of tiny drawers where nails and screws were kept. Outside was a paraffin tank.

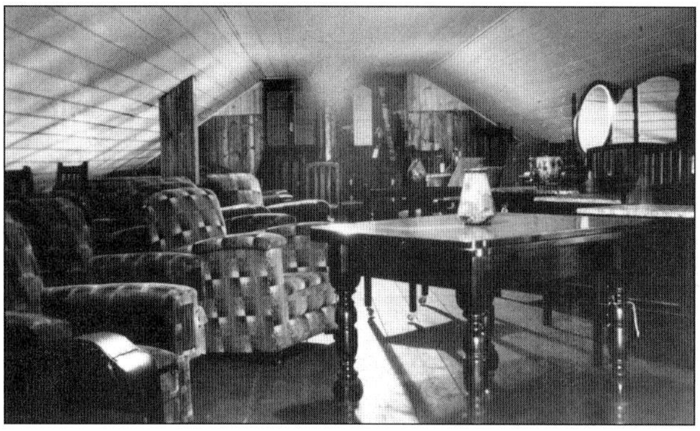

Furnishing department above the hardware department.

Next door to our shop was the blacksmith's owned by Cecil Taylor (Curly). He was kept busy shoeing horses, adding metal rims to cartwheels and making metal shapes to order. Apparently he never had any money and foraged scrap metal from anywhere he could. Robert Lansdell kept a carpenter's shop in the same yard. Forge Cottage, adjoining, had once been three cottages.

We bought our eggs from Isaac Haw, who lived at Lower Croft on Broaden Lane. His garden was a delight to a child, containing a miniature waterway, bridges and gnomes. Tom Dade delivered milk by pony and cart and gardeners would stand by with shovels in case they were lucky enough to find a deposit in the road.

Lockwood's shop, between Stammers' shop and the church, sold sweets. It was once owned by Annie Curtis, nurse and sometime landlady of the King's Head. She died in 1961, aged 87. Later it became a gift and wool shop and then a ladies' hairdresser. March Hazell's shop on Mill Road was impressive for the amount and variety that could be crammed into such a small space, some goods even hanging from the ceiling. Leslie Moulton took over this shop when Mr Hazell retired in 1956, but continued to run his shop on the Greens, which he took over from Mrs Minnie Laskey in 1937.

The Post Office had changed locations several times since the first was opened by March Hazell in

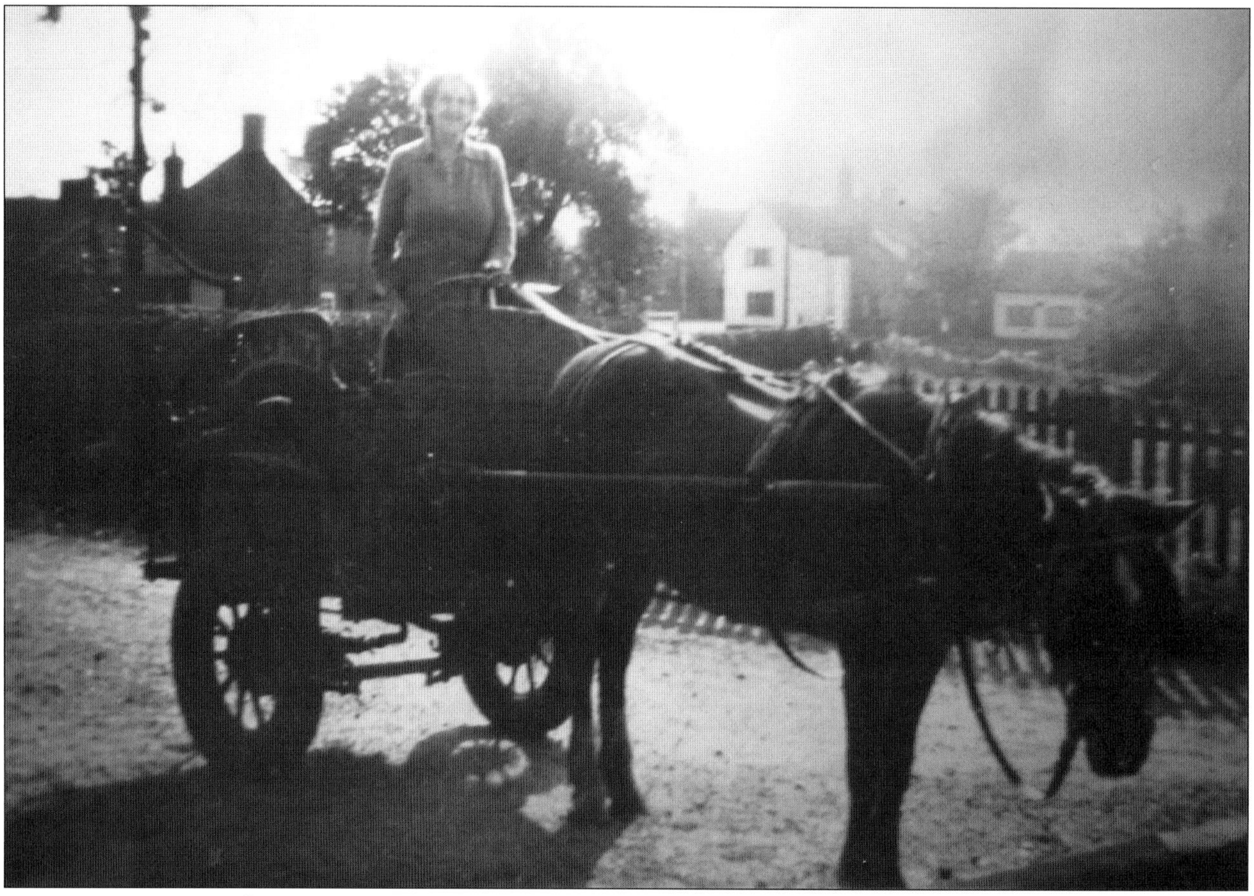

Tom Dade's milk cart, driven by his wife.

the Longhouse. In 1886 Mr Hazell moved it to Mill Road, to a shop formerly owned by Stammers. After a while it operated from Forge Cottage, opposite the school. After that it was run from a small wooden building, formerly Ellis' butcher's shop, and from there it moved to Willow House, where it was managed by Cyril and Ivy Fisher. For a while it moved, with them, to a house, since demolished, opposite the Methodist chapel. Mrs Bringloe sought permission to open a Post Office in part of the Longhouse in 1953 after she and her husband moved from Road Green. It was managed by Betty Wilson for 35 years. Finally, the Post Office became part of the main shop, formerly Stammers, in the Street.

Nurse Maud Hastings moved to Hempnall during the war years and lived at Freemason's Cottage in Mill Road with her daughters. Her house was provided by the Nursing Association. Hempnall gave her a hut to keep the dressings. When she retired in 1952 the village raised enough money to present her with a car.[1] The village was in uproar in 1953 when the Nursing Association planned to install the next Hempnall nurse at a house in Long Stratton. Over 100 attended a protest meeting and signed a petition. After the introduction of the National Health Service, Dr Gibson took on a partner, Dr Morris, who moved into Hill House, opposite Freemason's Cottage. Eventually some stables were converted into a modern surgery and waiting-room. The District Sanitary Inspector was informed of a health problem in 1953 when residents in Field Lane emptied their night soil along Mr Ladbrooke's hedge.[2]

Electricity had not arrived in the Greens, probably because of the expense for house owners. Early in 1954, 47 people objected to the proposed scheme,

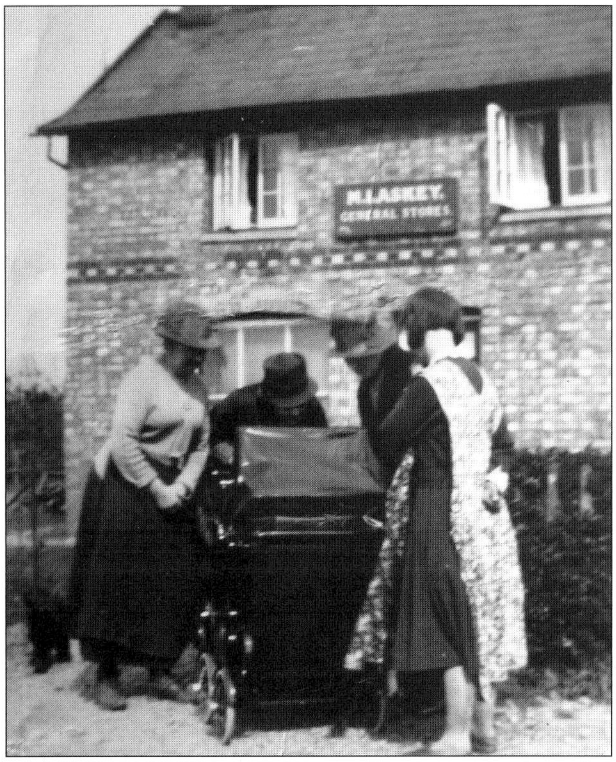

Outside Minnie Laskey's shop on the Greens.

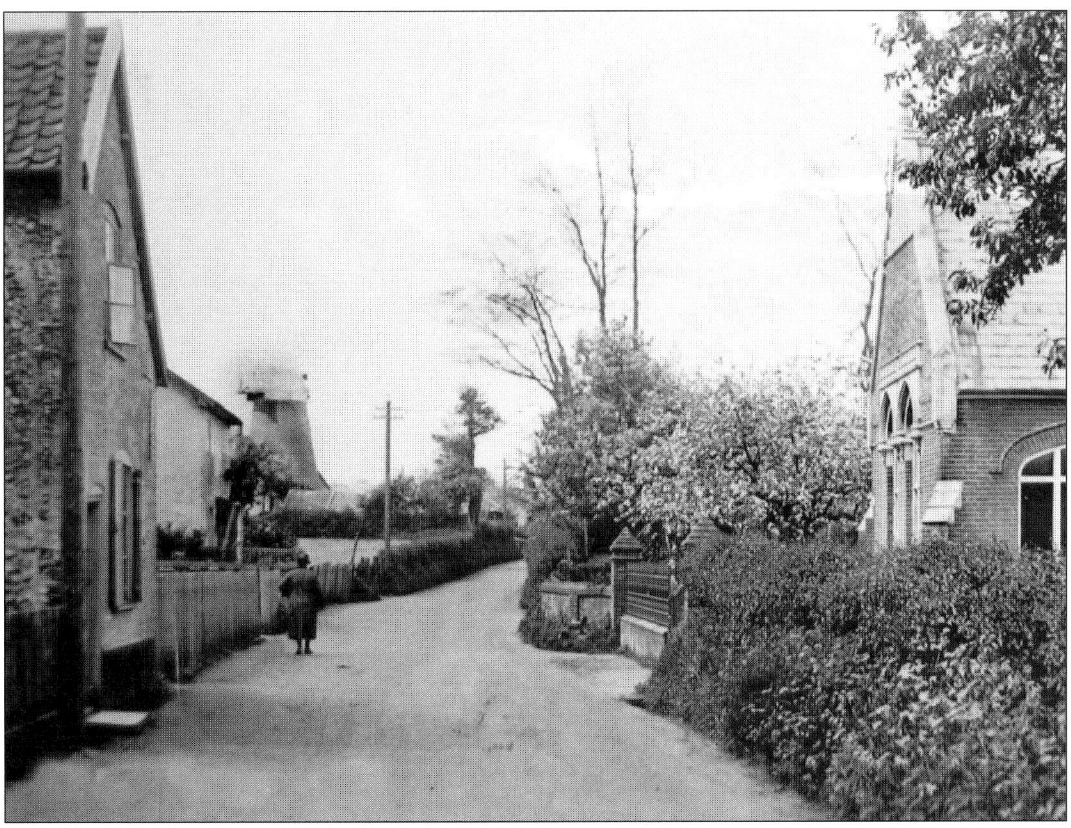

The building on the left was formerly the Post Office in Mill Road, run by Ivy Fisher.

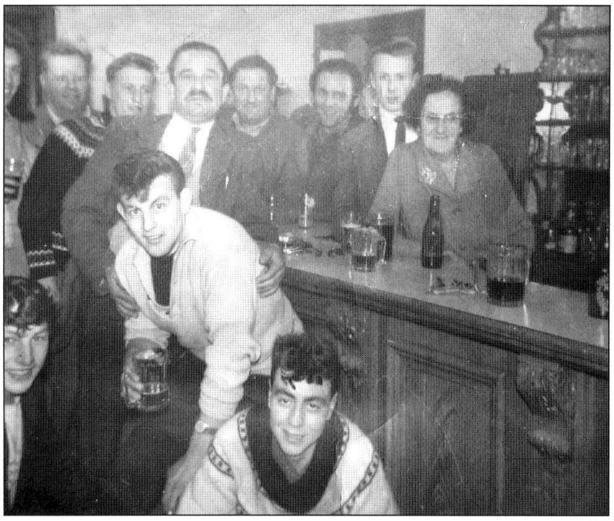

The Darts Club at the Nelson in the 1950s. Left to right back row: Stanley Day, Iky Youngs, Tubby Lynes, Gilly Cracknell, Lydon Bringloe, Mabel Bringloe (landlady). Front: Barry Day, John Vincent.

which had to be abandoned. By the end of the year objectors had been reduced to seven and work eventually went ahead.[3]

The Revd Mr Martin was vicar when I was a child. A Girls' Friendly Society was initiated by Mrs Martin. I remember May Day when a girl from the village was crowned queen and there was dancing round the maypole on the vicarage lawn. In 1950 Monica Cunningham was queen. That year there was a demonstration of keep fit organised by my mother, Kathleen Stammers.

The Nelson Hall was used for many activities in my youth. Every Friday films were shown. The extension of the Lord Nelson near the road was used as a second-hand shop and later became a ladies' hairdressers, the room above a barber's. The pub provided entertainment from pool to darts. In 1950 the Nelson Darts Club had more than 50 members.

Before 1950 football was played in a field adjoining Bungay Road and cricket was played in the pit. In May 1950 Hempnall received a grant for a sports field behind the Village Hall. The Hempnall Playing Field Association planned to raise the remainder through a fête on the following Whit Monday, the traditional date for the old fair. It was always held in the pit next to the school at that time. There were swingboats, bowling for a pig, slow bicycle races and many stalls, but best of all was a high wire to slide down to straw-filled sacks, with no account taken of health and safety, and we loved it. Mr Arthur Arnold, who had a model steam railway in his garden, gave rides.

Mr C.A. Bell, a member of the Norwich Lawn Tennis Association, opened the Hempnall Playing Fields in September 1951. Three other members joined him on the tennis court for an excellent tennis display. At the same time a league cricket match was played between Hempnall and Barford, resulting in a win for the visitors. Early in the evening a ladies versus men cricket match took place. The men had to play left-handed. The match was abandoned owing to poor light, or perhaps because the women were winning! A dance in the evening at the Nelson Hall to the music of the Ace of Spades completed the celebrations.[4]

My parents organised a youth club and spent many happy hours inventing games and activities. Later they joined the Masqueraders, a drama group renamed the Entertainers in 1991. In 1955 they performed *Waters of the Moon*, a comedy in three acts. *When we were Married*, a comedy by J.B. Priestley, was performed in 1958 and *Sailor Beware* in 1959. My father painted the scenery and made the props. The Women's Institute continued to thrive, as did the Mothers' Union, and trips to the coast in Cunningham's coach were a regular occurrence. The vicar's wife, Audrey Cooper, embroidered a banner for Sunday-school parades.

A committee was formed in 1953 to plan for the Coronation of Queen Elizabeth II. Money was to be raised by a house-to-house collection. The cricket and football clubs offered the proceeds from their next two dances and Mr Day offered to organise a darts match. Just over £100 was raised towards the festivities. How different from the 1937 celebrations. Instead of the mountain of beef, pickle and cakes, postwar Hempnall could only afford a 'bag feed' per person, containing a ham roll, an egg sandwich and two cakes, and villagers had to provide their own cup and saucer. Children were given a commemorative mug and old people a tea caddy with tea. The day began with a short service on the playing-field. All events were very successful, although there were a few showers. Mr H.P. Arnold announced items and played music from a loud speaker, and Mr G.G. Stammers presented prizes. A Hempnall baby was born early that morning to Mr and Mrs J. Hardacre and they were given a silver spoon for their child. New council houses were built in 1953 off Field Lane and named Coronation Crescent. These were added to in 1963 and 1972.

Schooling changed in the village. A private school owned by Miss Calver met in the Village Hall until 1947. That year the Secondary School was built at Long Stratton. After the Middle School opened at Stratton, Hempnall School was for young children only. In the 1950s the schoolhouse was incorporated into the school, providing an upstairs office and a boiler room.

Flooding was a regular problem. In 1951 the 'Rons' bridge was repaired by the Tas Drainage Board.[5] A water main burst in January 1957 and water forced its way through the subsoil and gushed into a road. A cavity about six feet by four feet and four feet deep appeared, but fortunately the road did not collapse. The water was eventually turned off

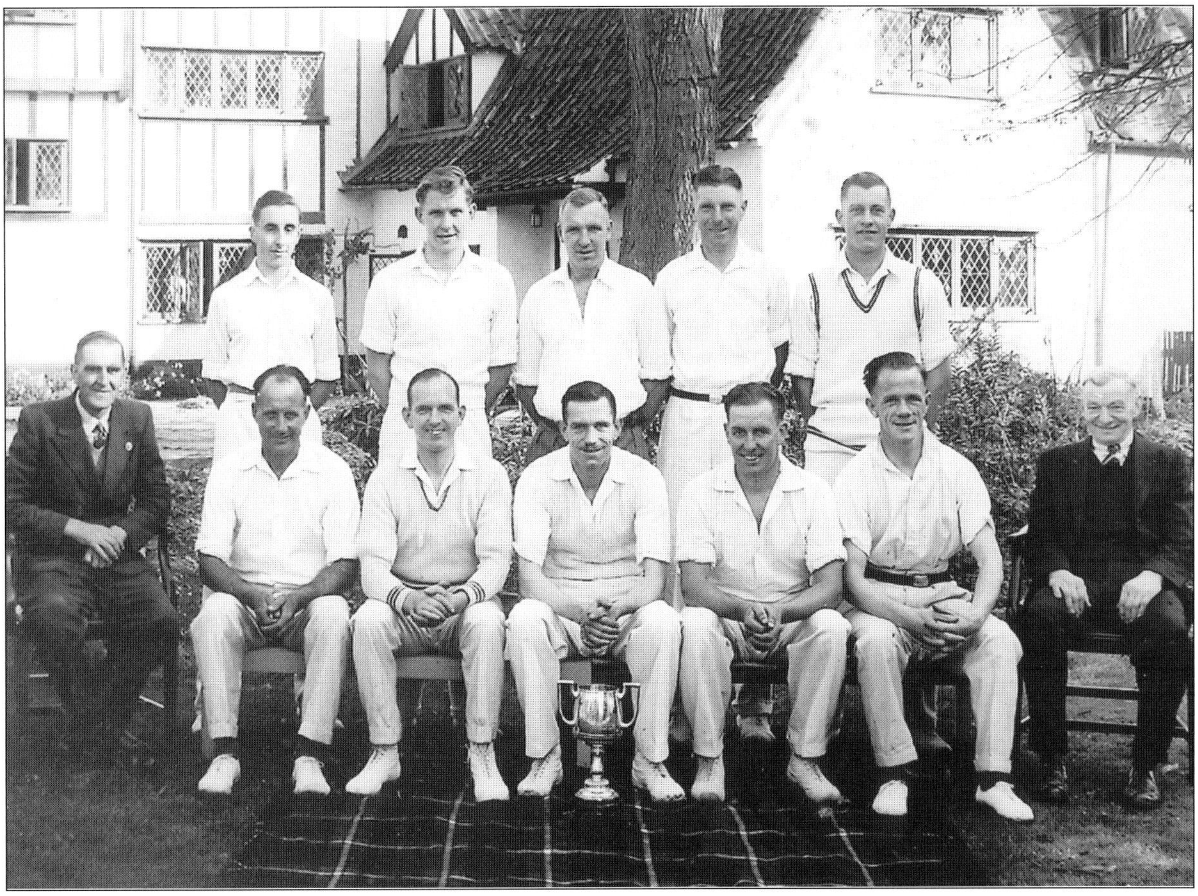

The cricket team outside Krons Manor in the 1940s. Left to right, back row: *Maurice Dunthorne, Lawrence Chapman, Cyril Jacobs, Roy Symonds, Jimmy Helliwell;* front row: *Billy Legood (umpire) Walter Eke, John Arnold, Charlie Downing, Jimmy Buck, Harold Sutton Ben Hickling (scorer).*

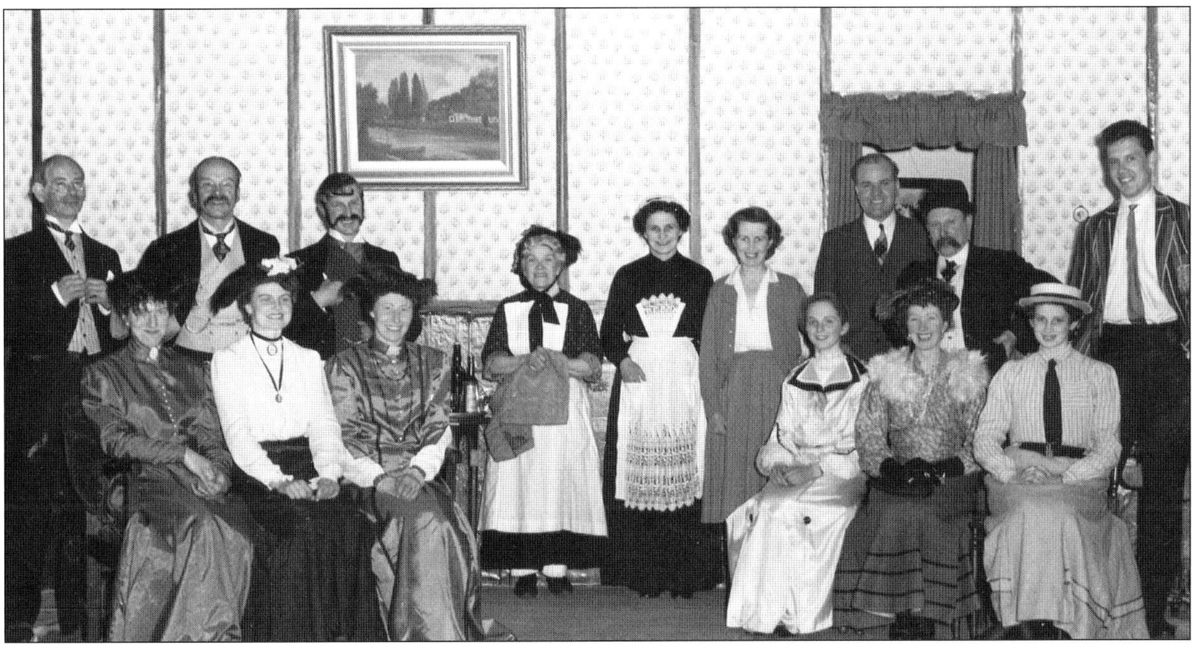

The Masqueraders in When we were Married, *1958.* Left to right, back row: *Russell Stammers, Wilfred Sparks, Bob Webster, Ivy Fisher, Yvonne Hook, Jean Stammers, Bill Hadley (producer), Ray Hazell, Vincent Hadley;* front row: *?, Kathleen Stammers, Muriel Jones, Pat Arnold, ?, Maureen Stammers.*

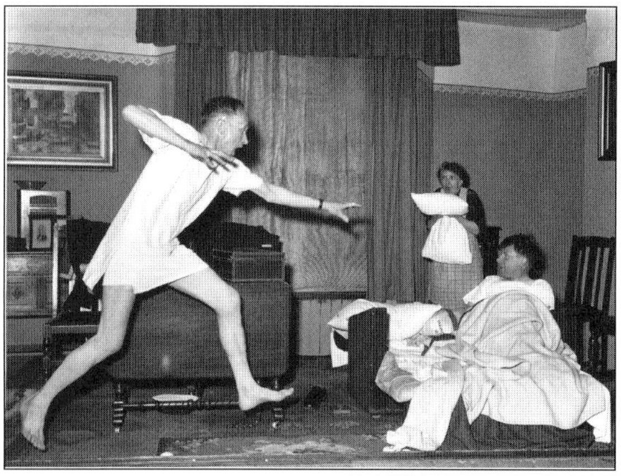

Left to right: *Wilfred Sparks, Ivy Fisher, Ray Hazell in* Sailor Beware, *1959.*

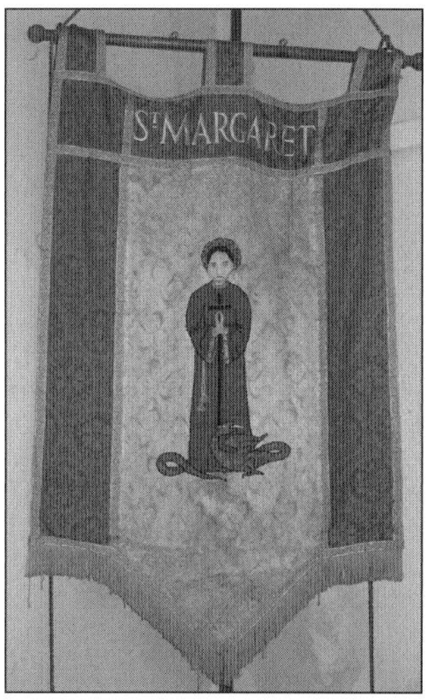

The Sunday-school banner, embroidered by Audrey Cooper.

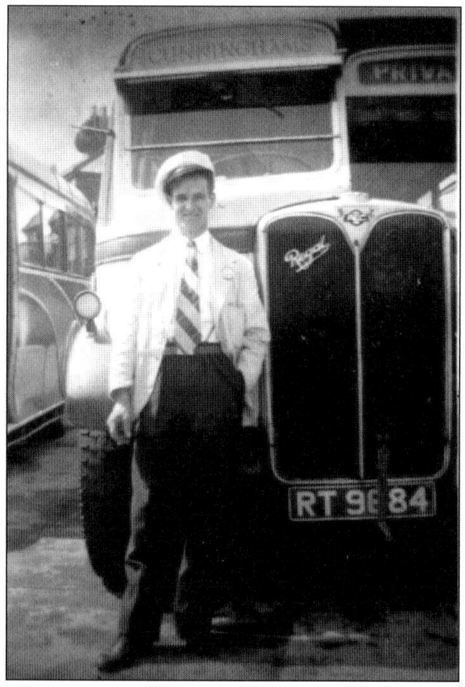

Walter Cunningham.

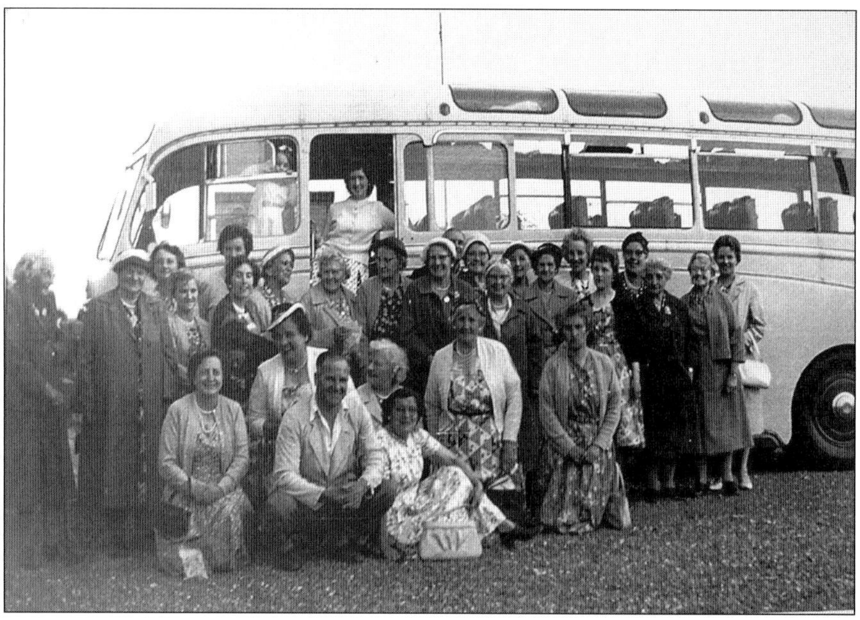

Women's Institute bus outing in Cunningham's coach. Standing in the bus: Pauline Cudden. Left to right back row standing: Mrs Jacob, Mrs Arnold, Betty Arnold,Mrs Brooks,?,Joan Leathersich,?,Mrs Mills,?,?,Mrs Rayson,?,?,?,Mrs Shepherd,Ann Blowers, Mrs Vincent, Mrs Hawkins, Mrs Youngs, ?. Front, kneeling: ?, Mrs Day, Terry Cunningham (driver),Mrs Ellis,?, Mrs Baker,?

and workmen were on the scene from 5.30p.m. until 3a.m.[6] Bungay Road and Silver Green were flooded again later in the year.

On 4 September 1959 a special service was conducted to celebrate the bicentenary of John Wesley's visit to the village. People gathered by the war memorial, on the site of Wesley's Tree. The chairman of the East Anglian district of the Methodist Church, together with the Superintendent Minister of the Alborough Methodist Circuit, conducted the one o'clock service and everyone joyfully sang the hymns of Charles Wesley.[7]

My grandfather retired in 1961 and we moved to Connaught House, a strange building that puzzled me for many years until my elderly aunt Edith told me that in her childhood the now internal stairs were on the outside and led to a hand mill on the roof. My parents developed an interest in caravanning and held an annual Caravan Club rally in the grounds. My father earned a reputation for knocking up structures with six-inch nails. A tree house and a pirate boat materialised. Games were organised and prizes given.

My most treasured memories of the village of my youth feature the outdoor life. On Easter Eve church

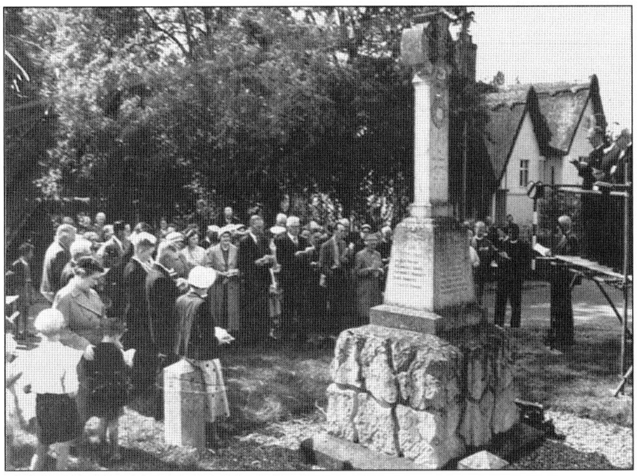

The commemoration of the 200th anniversary of John Wesley's visit to Hempnall, 1959. (EASTERN DAILY PRESS)

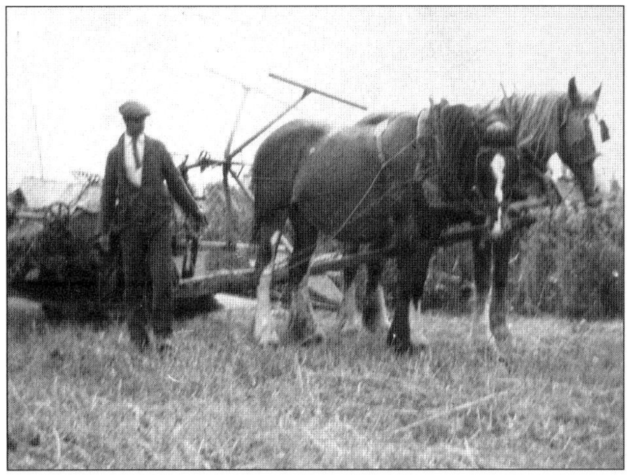

Jimmy Roberts ploughing.

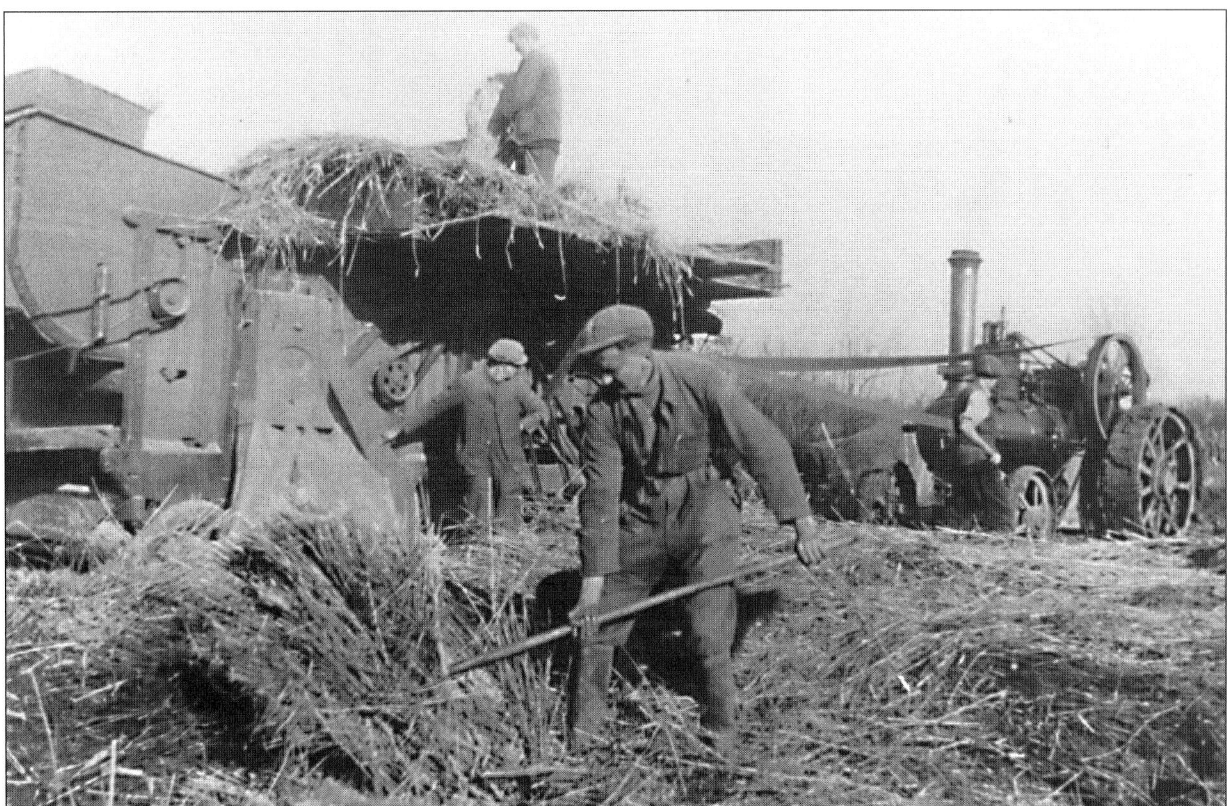

The last threshing on Road Green Farm, 1953. On top of Charlie Moore's threshing engine is Frank Boulter, with Donald Shilling below and Leslie Roberts in the foreground.

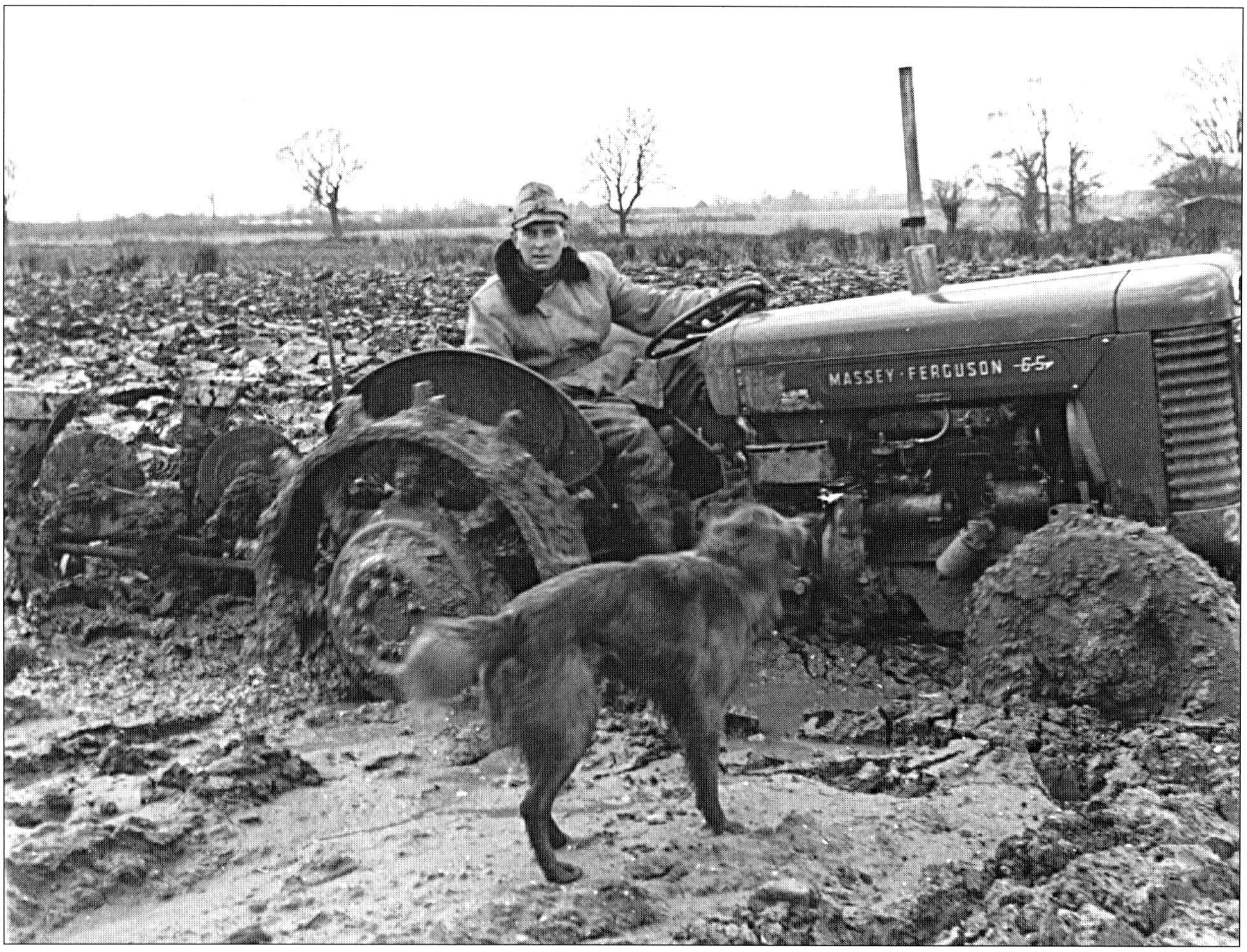

John Ellis ploughing on Moat Farm in 1961 with a Massey Ferguson 65.

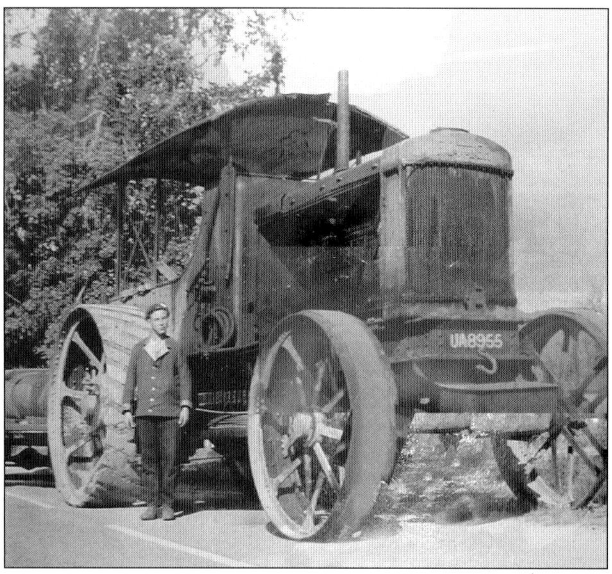

A Fowler tractor in 1959 with 'Sonny' Day.

members would walk along Bussey's Loak to Street Wood, seven acres of ivy-covered undergrowth, with pockets of violets and primroses, small ponds and stately trees. Already reduced from the 96 acres it had been before the First World War, it was nevertheless an enchanting yet formidable place to a child. We collected armfuls of primroses to decorate the church for Easter Sunday. Just a handful of trees mark all that is left of this once proud wood.

Changes to farming methods altered the look of the landscape. Improved methods of weed control enabled the combine harvester to take the place of the old reaper-binders. Haystacks became things of the past and autumn fields were no longer covered with lines of stooks. I witnessed probably the last of a traditional threshing day on a field along Fairstead Lane. It seemed the entire village was there. Threshing commenced around the outside of the field, gradually working towards the middle. Then all the rabbits ran out and were picked off by men with shotguns.

References

[1] Hempnall Parish Council minute-book, 8 April 1952
[2] Hempnall Parish Council minute-book, 2 December 1953
[3] Hempnall Parish Council minute-book, 8 November 1954
[4] NN Friday, 7 September 1951
[5] NRO DC 2/4/4 Highways records
[6] NN Friday, 25 Jan 1957
[7] EEN 5 September 1959

✤ CHAPTER 20 ✤

A Common Thread 1960–2008

My grandfather, Gerald George Stammers, moved to Norwich in 1961, leaving the business in the hands of sons Russell and Colin. After self-service was introduced, the staff turned their hands to assembling orders instead of serving behind the counter. Jack Stammers, a cousin, with Robert Clarke, Fred Levett, Norman Pechey and Fred Wilson, delivered the orders to many scattered villages, covering a radius of about ten miles. The aim was to deliver, no matter what the weather, even though many customers lived at isolated farms and cottages. One winter's day, Jack and his colleagues were obliged to leave the van at the top of a lane, so they packed the groceries in sacks and waded to the customer's cottage through deep snow across a meadow. Jack went into semi-retirement in 1970, the same year that delivery services finally stopped. Furniture ceased to be stocked from that time, owing to rising costs.[1]

In 1981 the Stammers brothers retired, ending a family business that had lasted over 140 years. They sold to Geoffrey and Carolyn Moulton, who had hitherto run a general shop in the village and another on the Greens. In 1987 the Moultons sold the business to Larry and Elizabeth Rippengale, who converted the hardware and furnishing department into a house, changed the original shop to grocery only and opened a delicatessen. In September 2007 the shop

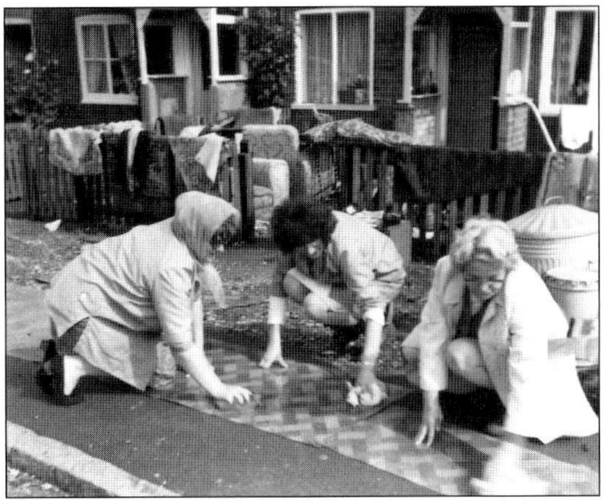

Cleaning up after the 1968 floods at Bridge Terrace

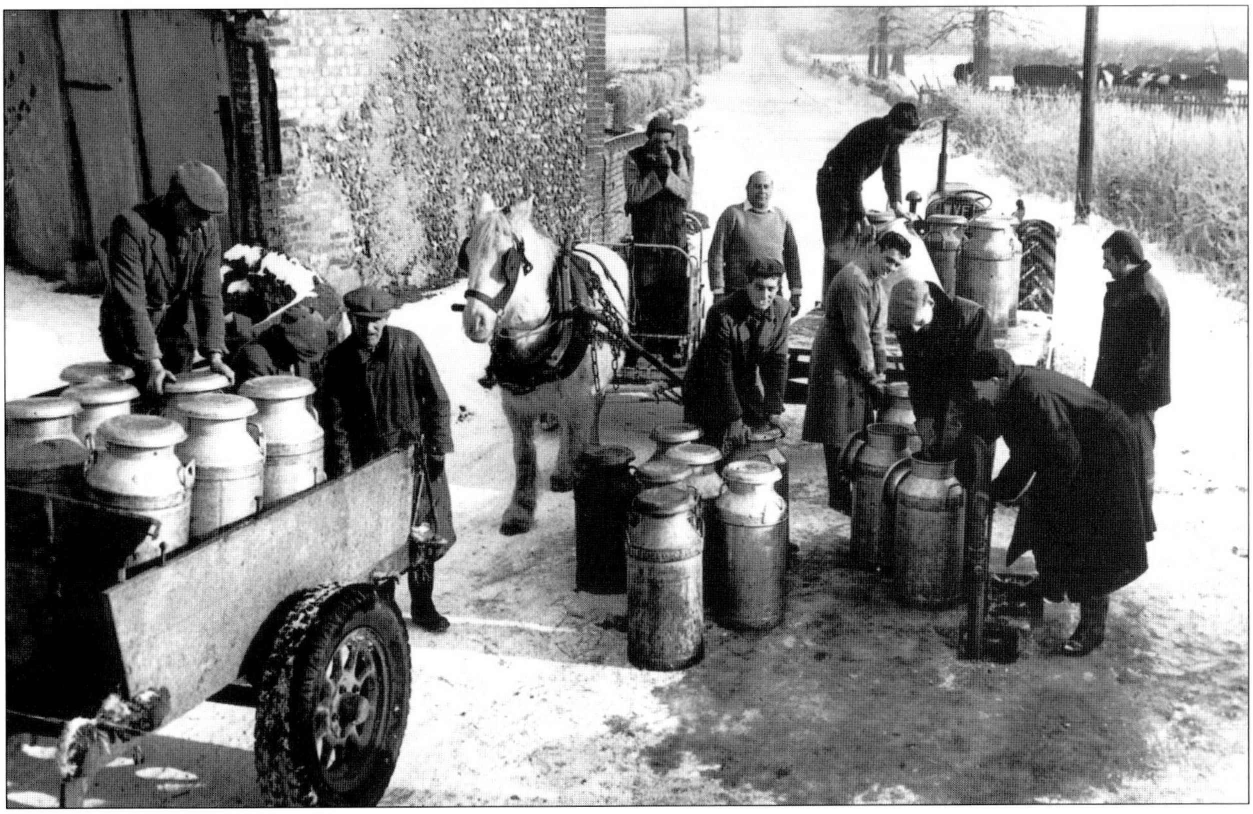

Collecting water from standpipes at Silver Green in 1963. Left to right: Colin MacRae, Mr Crummet, Vic Goddard, Mr Blowers, Deborah the horse, Terry Tyrell, Mr Blowers(brothers),two council workers, Mr Tye (EASTERN DAILY PRESS)

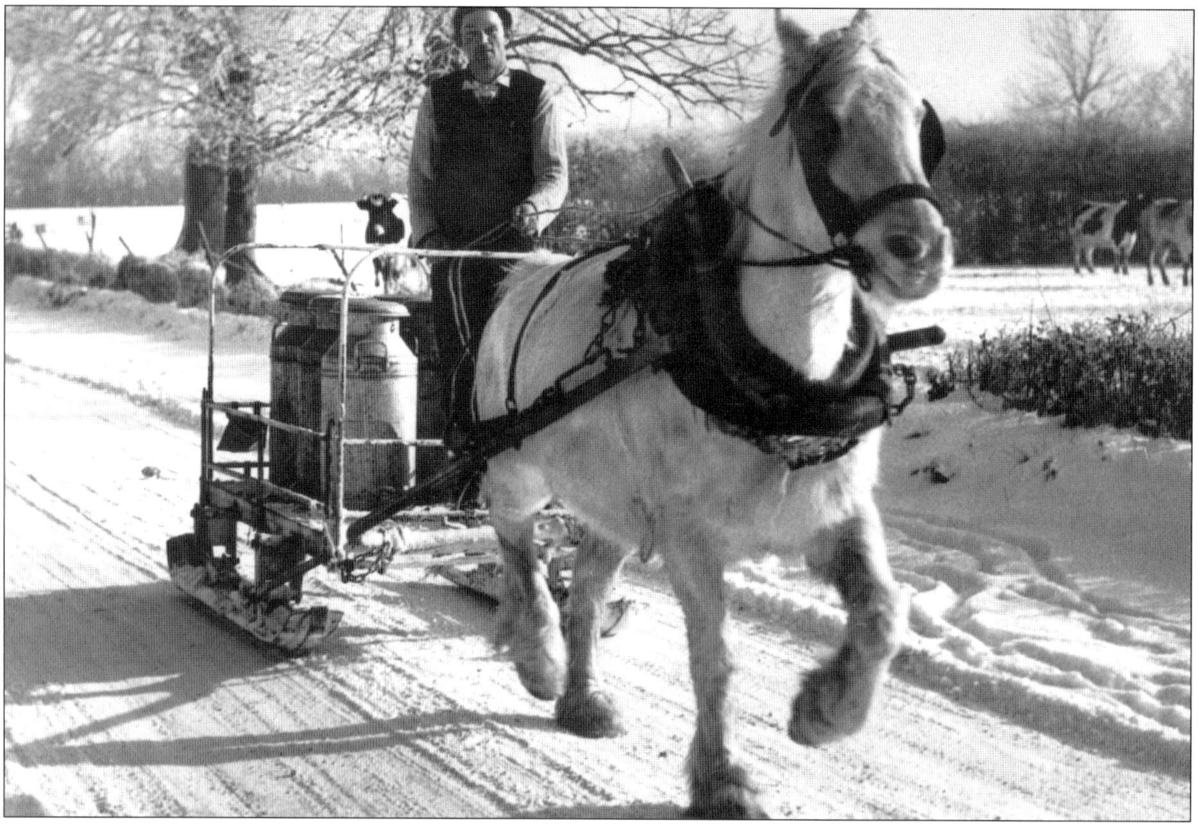

Vic Goddard coping with the snow in 1963. (EASTERN DAILY PRESS)

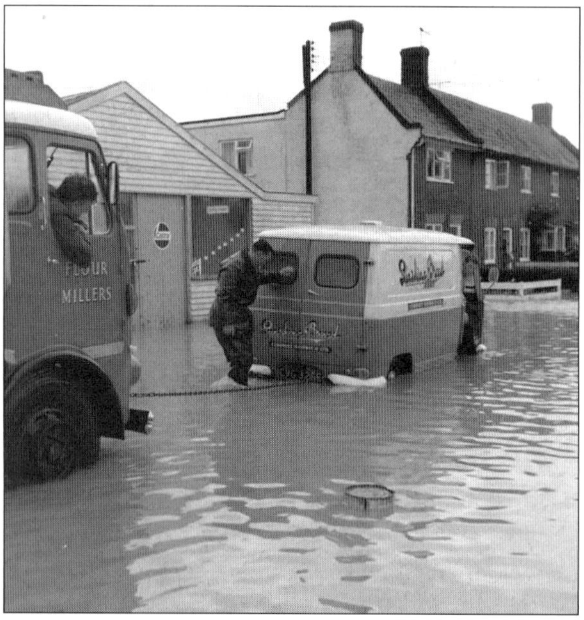

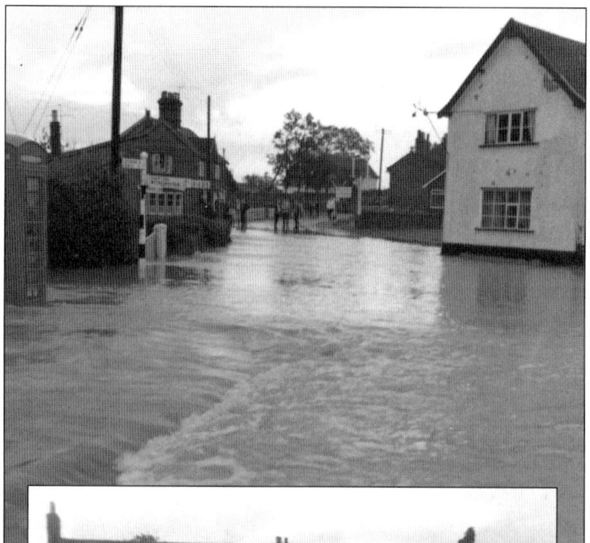

Floods near the Town Bridge (above left) *and by the King's Head* (above right), *1968.*

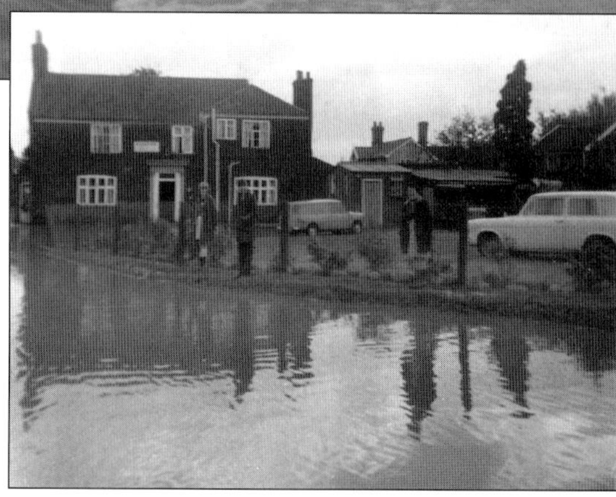

Right: *Floods by the Queen's Head, 1968.*

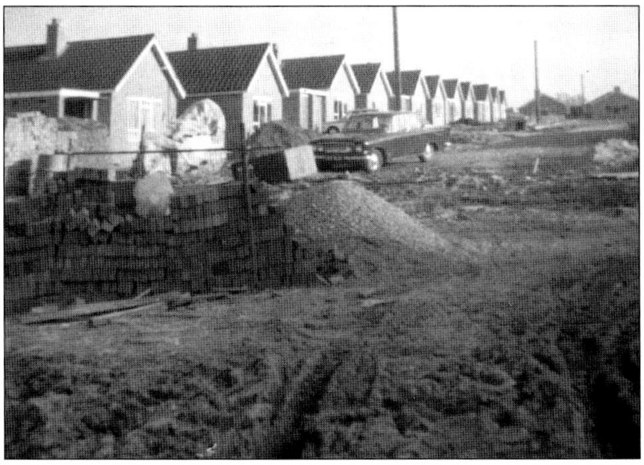

Rowland Drive under construction in the 1960s.

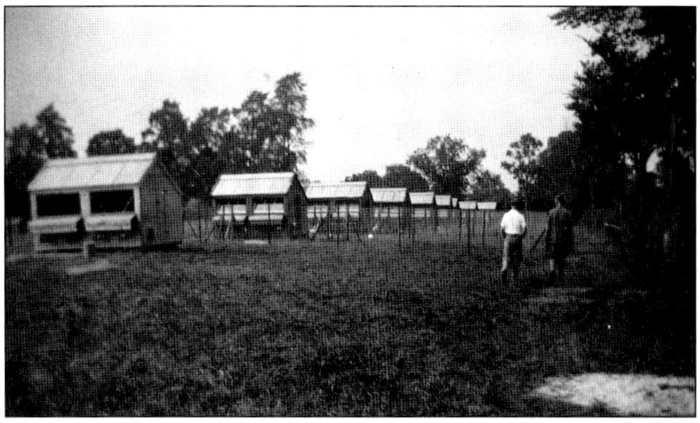

Mr Erik Knusden's poultry farm, now the Old Market Way estate.

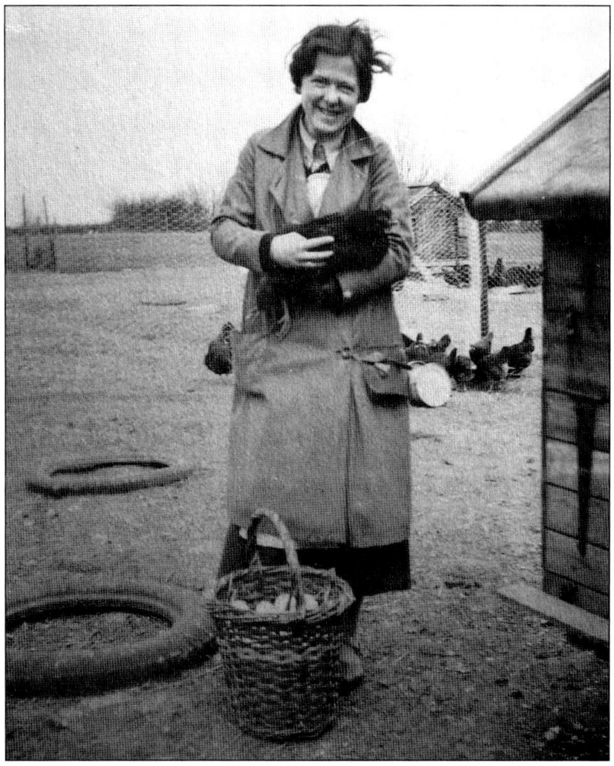

Mrs Karen Knudsen.

was transferred to McColl, an independent neighbourhood retailer.

Arnold's engineering works, like Stammers', provided jobs for many in the village. In the '60s they employed more than 20 men and exported to America, Russia, Australia, India, Turkey and Pakistan. The firm stayed with the Arnold family until 1968, when it was sold and its name was changed to Tarbox Arnold Ltd. By 1988 it was called Norvic Hempnall Precision Products and closed a year later. Richard Delf sold his garage next to the Longhouse and moved to the Arnold's site.

Over the years the traditional entertainment provided by the village public houses became less fashionable. The King's Head, former haunt of local farmers, closed in October 1962, and the Lord Nelson shut its doors in 1997.[2] The Queen's Head ceased trading in 2008. The Horseshoes at Silver Green was almost closed in 1958 by Morgan's Brewery. Fortunately, Terry Tyrrell bought it and renamed it the Three Horseshoes. The spirit of old Hempnall is reflected in the stories of this isolated pub. In those days there was no proper bar and there were spittoons on the floor. Part if it had been old cottages. Hempnall had a resident policeman who, suspecting after-hours drinking, determined to catch the locals. One dark, wet night, as he was spying from the phone box across the road, the landlord slipped out unnoticed and wound a rope round the phone box a few times before tying it off to an oak tree. At another time the same bobby made a dramatic entrance, announcing, 'Got the lot on yew this time!' Explaining that it was a private party, the company walked out and left him on his own. The next morning there was a note on the door telling the landlord to collect the keys from Long Stratton Police Station.

The village continued to suffer the effects of freak weather. Heavy snow fell in 1963 and standpipes were necessary. Vic Goddard of Lower Farm used a horse-drawn sled for delivery and also to collect his children from school. In 1968 heavy rain caused part of the school building to be flooded, as well as the garden, the back courtyard and the entire sports field. The road was under water near the Town Bridge and along Mill Road. A freak whirlwind ripped a third of the slate roof off the Methodist chapel and smashed a window in May 1989.[3] In 1992 lightning struck the home of Emily and Ray Dunthorne while they were on holiday. Fire ripped through the roof, which collapsed. Mrs Dunthorne had taught at Hempnall School for 38 years.[4]

The population increased as new houses were built in Coronation Crescent in 1963 and 1972. Street Farm house was demolished in the 1960s and Roland Drive was constructed. Mr Erik Knudsen sold his chicken farm in the 1960s and construction began on the Old Market Way estate in 1970. Roads were named after Mr Knudsen, landowners and vicars.

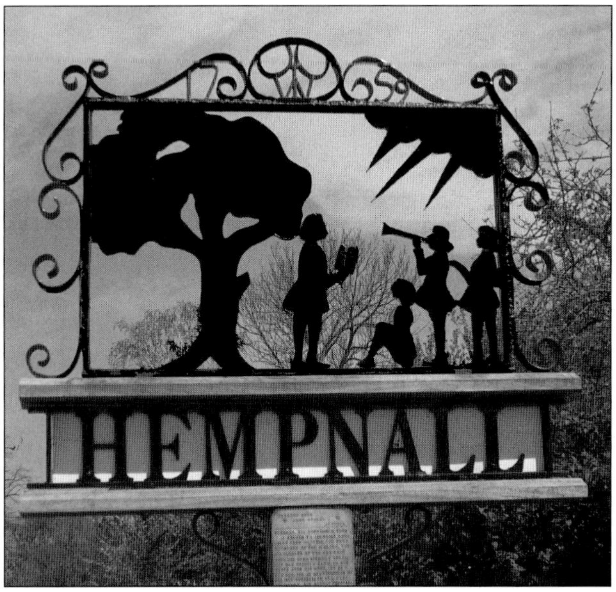

Hempnall village sign, commemorating the visit of John Wesley 1759.

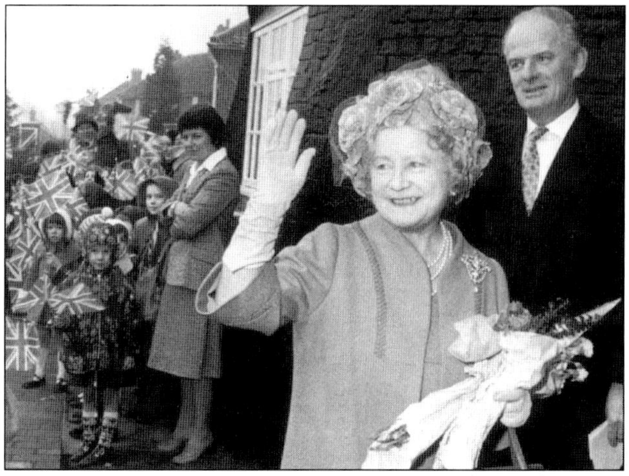

Her Majesty the Queen Mother at the Mill Centre in 1979. (EASTERN DAILY PRESS)

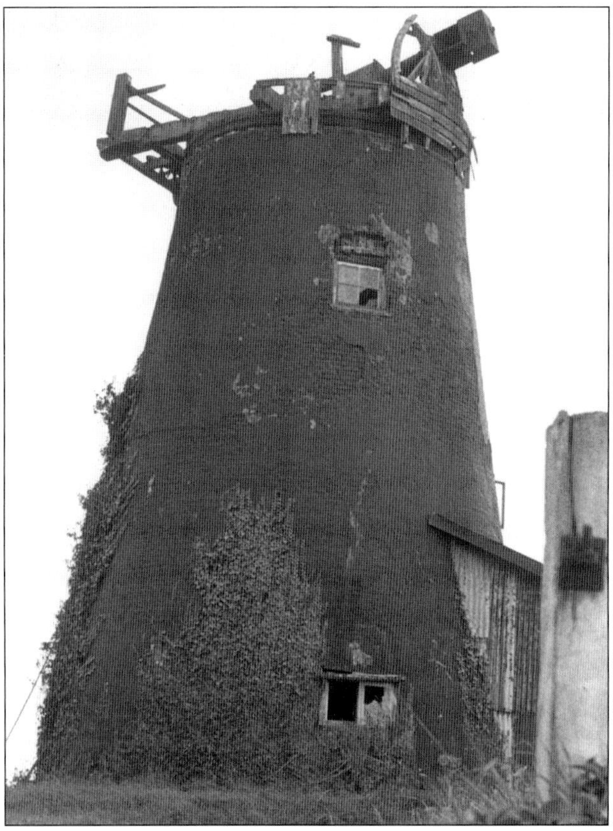

The derelict mill on Mill Road, 1978. (EASTERN DAILY PRESS)

In 1977 a tug-of war team was formed and named the Hempnall Lions. Two years later some of the world's strongest men met at Hempnall for a tug-of-war festival. Apart from having a lot of fun, they raised money for the bus shelter built near the bridge. The tradition of working together for the common good, often with a great deal of enjoyment and imagination, has long been a tradition in the village. For example, in 1988 a group pushed a bed ten miles from Norwich to the Lord Nelson to raise £1,400 for the Great Ormond Street Hospital. A dozen children took turns to ride on the bed and 21 adults helped with the pushing.[5] In 1993 Peter Downing, who lost the use of his legs in a road accident as a teenager, gained a reputation as a sportsman and planned a marathon in his racing wheelchair to raise money for the blind. A group nicknamed 'Dad's Army' laid a concrete base on the village playing-field, enabling the Parish Council to take advantage of the English Basketball Association's offer to provide free goal-posts.[6] In 1993 regulars from the Lord Nelson dragged an ambulance 11 miles in a heatwave to raise more than £100 for the Eccles Ward at the Norfolk and Norwich Hospital; the 25 men dressed in drag and the women in St Trinian's uniforms and cat and bunny costumes.

A village sign, given by the local Women's Institute to mark the Queen's silver jubilee in 1977, was designed by Heather Seager and made by Stan Girling of Mulbarton. My grandfather was invited to unveil the sign, depicting John Wesley, the founder of Methodism, preaching on his visit to the village in 1759. The seat and stonework were built by Mr Philip Beckett using flints and bricks from the village's old mill, and the oak post on which it was mounted was given by Malcolm Dye.[7]

The derelict mill in Mill Road had become a village landmark. Built on land belonging to the Hempnall Town Estates Poor Charity, it was powered by steam and worked by Mr Bristow until 1937. In 1978 an ambitious plan was formulated for its conversion to a day-care centre. The project was financed through the sale of land to the County Council for a proposed school off Field Lane that did not materialise. At that time it was believed that Hempnall was the only village in Norfolk with a centre of this kind and the only example of co-operation between a local charity and a local authority.

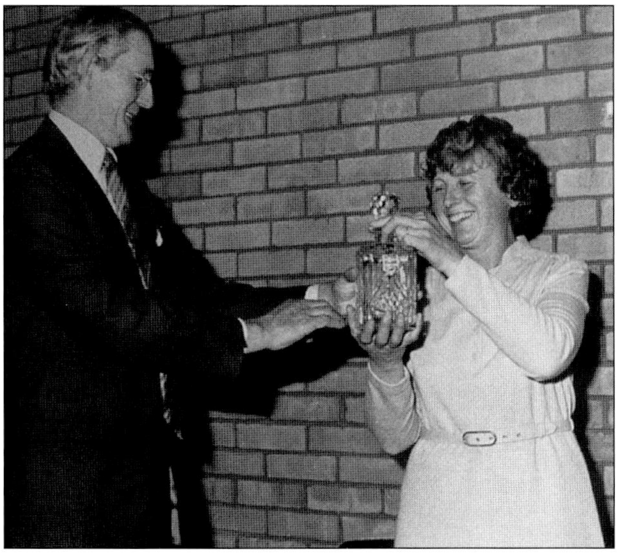

Jimmy Rodgers and Yvonne Davy at the opening of the Village Hall, 1981. (EASTERN DAILY PRESS)

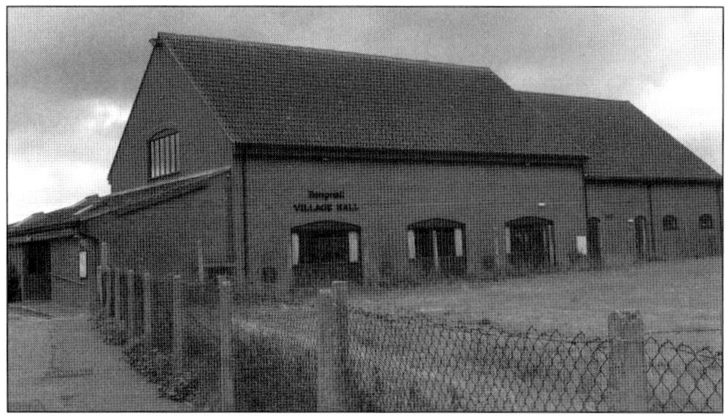

The Village Hall.

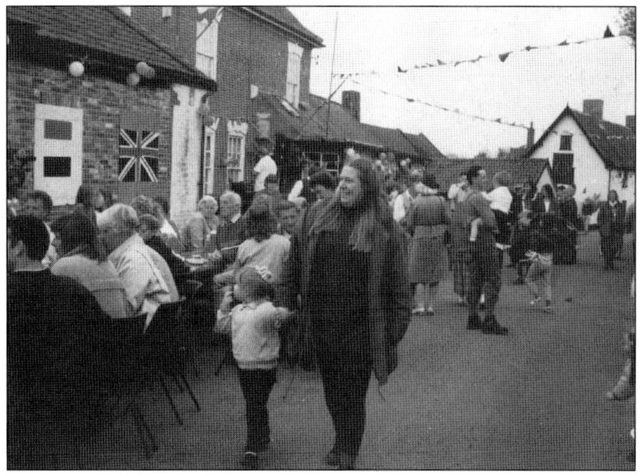

A coachload of Americans returned for the celebration of the fiftieth anniversary of the end of the war.

On Tuesday, 16 January 1979, Hempnall welcomed Her Majesty the Queen Mother. Despite the drizzle and fog, hundreds of villagers were waiting outside the Mill Centre for Day Care to greet her. The building was designed by architects Mr K. King and Mr Michael Sadler and built by Mr Michael Canham of Pulham Market.

After the official opening the Queen Mother joined six villagers for tea. Mr Norman Pechey wore a tie for only the second time in 60 years. The Queen Mother admired the kitchens and the splendid cake made by Mrs Betty Wilson, the postmistress, in the shape of the Centre. As the Queen Mother left, she joked with Mr Pechey that he could now take his tie off. The handicapped were brought to the centre twice a week and it was also used by the elderly men of Hempnall on Wednesday mornings and by the Happy Circle Club for the over-60s.[8] Today it is still used by Social Services for the handicapped. The elderly meet regularly, as do the Women's Institute and an art and craft group. It is a popular venue for meetings.

The idea of building a new Village Hall to replace the old Institute was first put forward in 1976. A committee was formed chaired by Mrs Yvonne Davy. Fund-raising began in earnest in 1978. The Department of Education and Science made a grant of £35,000 and £17,000 was secured from Norfolk County Council. Hempnall's Town Estate Charity supplied another £25,000. The villagers worked together, not only for fund-raising, but also by giving their time and energy to decorate and fit the kitchen. It was finally opened on 11 November 1981 at a cost of £128,000. Today it is used by various clubs for badminton, computer courses, short-mat bowls and football. The playgroup, originally started by Jill Turner at her house, the Chequers, in the '60s, is run from here. Social events take place regularly.

The old Village Hall was sold in 1981 to Martin Battye and became Kirton Designs, making specialist seating for the elderly and disabled. In 1986 they were the winners of a small business efficiency award. It was bought by Kevin Cunningham in September 1999 and converted into a garage.

The new Village Hall scooped top prize in the Best Run Village Hall competition against 44 other entries, just six years after it was opened. The judges were impressed by the outstanding facilities and awarded 366 points out of 400 based on appearance, facilities, management and provision for the community. Caretaker Ernie Downing was reminded of the time his parents ran the old Village Hall. His father was locked in one night but managed to climb out of a window, despite his wooden leg.[9]

On 8 May 1995 the village commemorated the fiftieth anniversary of the end of the war. Thanks were expressed to the members of 93 Bomber Group and several Americans returned for the event, which included a grand parade with bagpipes, a memorial service at the war memorial and a traditional street party.

In November 2001 the new Village Hall welcomed the Princess Royal, president of the Rural Housing Trust, for a seminar on affordable housing schemes. Delegates from more than 40 Parish Councils

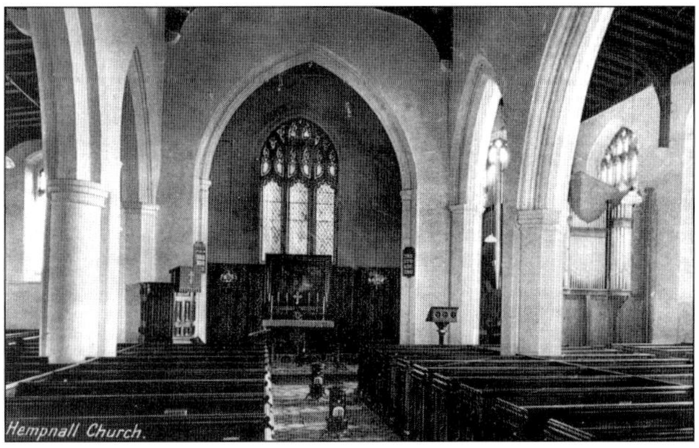

Interior of St Margaret's Church before 1987.

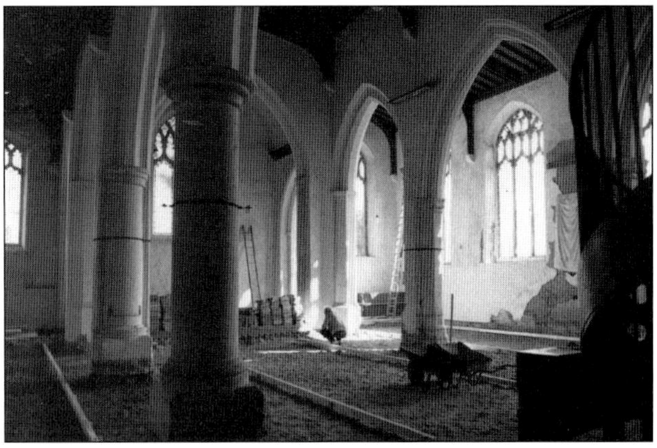

St. Margaret's Church during refurbishment, 1987.

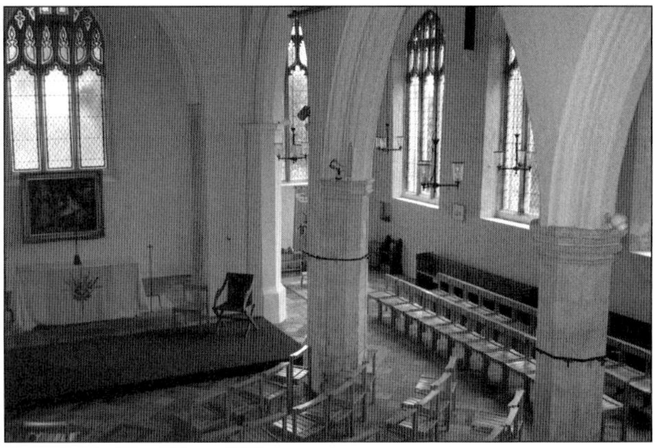

St. Margaret's Church 2007.

attended. The princess signed an official portrait to commemorate her visit.

In 1963 the Hempnall Group of Churches was formed and the Revd. Peter Bradshaw became Rector and team leader.[10]

A major refurbishment of the church took place in 1987. The floor was completely renewed using as many of the original tiles as possible, under-floor heating was installed, old pine pews were replaced by chairs and the walls were repainted. Roy Ladbrooke, the churchwarden, was involved in the project from its early planning. The Feoffees of Hempnall made a grant of £35,000.[11]

The village united in 1990 under the banner of RATS: Residents Against the Tip. Plans had been proposed for a giant rubbish tip on the old airfield. It was estimated that traffic would have increased by over 250 per cent, as 70,000 tonnes of rubbish would have been imported every year. In 1993 the proposal was rejected.[12]

Today the village is split over controversial proposals for a wind farm. Those against call their campaign SHOWT: Stop Hempnall's On-Shore Wind Turbines: many gardens sport posters for or against the scheme, a reminder, perhaps, of what it might have been like during the Civil War, when white roses were grown in gardens to show Royalist support. Such a rose still flowers in the garden of Poacher's Cottage.

My grandfather, who was born in 1890, is the link for me to Hempnall's past. He told me stories about the old men of his childhood. When he was a boy, an old inhabitant told him that the churchyard was so full of bodies that the soil came almost to the bottom of the church windows, so one day a group of men were employed to cart the top layer away. The spoil was dumped on Mill Road and an orchard was grown over the top. He was told that about 40 houses in Hempnall were made of clay lump and after the population declined they were left to rot and simply disappeared into the ground. Grandfather remembered the coming of the bicycle, followed by the car. Through him I feel close to the village of his childhood, for in truth it is not that long ago that most houses were thatched and roads were rough and rutted, with convenient piles of stones left for passing travellers to fill in the odd pothole. He opened my eyes to the possibilities of historical discovery. He saw a rapid change in the countryside and in country life and, fortunately, he recorded a flavour of that in his book, *My Village*.

Village life has always seen changes, but now the danger is that, as the pace of life increases, much more of the past will be forgotten. My hope is that the puzzles and pieces of Hempnall's heritage will give this South Norfolk village a place in history.

References

1 *EDP* Monday, 22 November 1976
2 *EDP* July 1997
3 *EDP* Saturday, 13 May 1989
4 *EDP* Saturday, 20 June 1992
5 *EDP* 8 May 1988
6 *EDP* 17 September 1999
7 *EDP* Monday, 16 October 1977
8 *EDP* Wednesday, 17 January 1979
9 *EDP* Monday, 17 August 1987
10 Jill Turner (2003) Beyond the Parish Pump. (The Hempnall Team Council).
11 *EDP* Friday, 20 February 1987
12 *EDP* Friday, 6 August 1993

List of Surnames

Adcock
Aggas
Aldis
Alexander
Allen
Allington
Andrew
Arnold
Ashe
Asshe
atte Thorne
Atthirne
Ayton
Backler
Bacon
Baley
Baker
Baker
Baldwin
Bancroft
Barber
Barbour
Barham
Barrett
Barton
Bartrum
Barwell
Barwick
Basham
Battye
Baxter
Baynard
Beane
Beck
Beckett
Bell
Bennet
Betts
Bingley
Bird
Blaiden
Bloomfeild
Blundervyle
Boast
Bocheler
Boulter
Boulton
Bowring
Brame
Braybourne
Bressingham
Brighton
Bringloe
Bromvle
Brooke
Broughton
Broun
Brown
Browne
Brundal
Brutton
Buck
Bunn
Burlingham
Burton
Burton-Fanning
Bush
Buskard
Bussey
Butter
Buxton
Buyllen
Bylong
Calver
Cammel
Carentyn
Carr
Carter
Carver
Cator Webb
Chapman
Chettlebrough
Chettleburgh
Clarke
Codman
Cooper
Copping
Coppyng
Cotton
Cowper
Cozens-Hardy
Crabbe
Crawshay
Croune
Crummett
Culley
Culling
Cunningham
Curtis
Dade
Daines
Davidson
Davy
Dawdy
Day
de Brusingham
de Hemenhale
de Rode
Delact
Delf
Devereux
Dowe
Downing
D'Oyly
Dunnet
Dunthorne
Durrant
Dymys
Eager
Eastowe
Eke
Ellis
Ellys
Elsey
Elvin
Fairhead
Fassett
Fellows
Felton
Fidy
Fige
Finch
Fisher
Fitzwalter
Flint
Forder
Forster
Fraser
Freer
Freston
Fryer
Fuller
Funnel
Galyon
Gardiner
Garrard
Gaze
Gedge
Gerard
Gibson
Gillingwater
Girling
Goddard
Goffin
Golafre
Goldsmith
Gooch
Goodard
Gooderham
Goodman
Goose
Gore
Gosling
Gourney
Gowing
Gray
Graye
Green
Grey
Grimston
Grint
Gryms
Gunton
Hadley
Hager
Hall
Halle
Hallmark
Halls
Hammond
Hardacre
Harden
Hardwicke
Hardy
Harrys
Harvey
Hastings
Haw
Hawes
Hazell
Head
Hearn
Hellinge
Helliwell
Hemenhale
Henery
Hickling
Hinchcliffe
Hinderer
Hipperson
Hobart
Hoker
Hollis
Howlett
Huby
Hunt
Hylton
Irby
Jacobs
Jarrold
Jeckyll
Jermy
Jermyn
Johnson
Jones
Kennedy
Kilbourn
King
Knights
Knopping
Knudsen
Knytes
Kyrke
Kyte
Labrook
Ladbrooke
Lansdell
Larke
Laskey
Laurence
Lawn
Leathersich
Leece
Legate
Leggett
Legood
Leicester
Lessy
L'Estrange
Levett
Light
Lloyd
Lockwood
Luckyn
MacRae
Madgett
Mallett
Marten
Martin
Mathews
Mcnelly
Meadows
Meek
Meer
Meers
Melton
Merrison
Metcalf
Miles
Mills
Molle
Moore
Morris
Mortimer
Mott Donne
Moulton
Murphy
Musk
Myngaye
Nash
Neeve
Newman
Nobbs
Norman
Oak-Rhind
Olbarlik
Oldcastle
Osborn
Page
Parfait
Parfitt
Park
Parsons
Passhelwe
Pechey
Peddle
Pedgriest
Penn
Pennywell
Perkins
Peterson
Pigney
Pike
Pitcher
Pitt
Pitts
Pointer
Poll
Pope
Porter
Potter
Poyntz
Pymer
Pynsthorpe
Pytte
Quantrell
Rackham
Radcliff
Randol
Read
Redgrave
Reeder
Revell
Reynolds
Rippengale
Roads
Robard
Robbe
Robberdes
Roberts
Rolfe
Roper
Row
Sadd
Saunders
Scales
Seager
Sendall
Sargent
Severby
Sewell
Sharpe
Sheldrake
Shepherde
Sherdlowe
Sherwyn
Short
Skinner
Skynner
Slipper
Smith
Smythe
Spalding
Spens
Spink
Sporle
Spurgeon
Stammers
Stanton
Stewart
Stone
Stops
Strake
Stranger

Sumford	Thurlow	Turner	Vincent	Watson	Weston
Symonds	Timberlake	Turnour	Waddeldow	Waynyld	Wheatley
Taylor	Todd	Tweeddale	Wale	Wegg	Whitehead
Theviston	Tompson	Tyrell	Ward	Wellington	Wilford
Thirkettle	Took	Van Kemp	Warde	Wells	Wilson
Thompson	Tooke	Varley	Warmoll	Wenn	Wodehouse
Thrower	Townsend	Varney	Warns	Wesley	Woodbine
Thruston Mott	Tristram	Verdon	Watling	West	Youngman

Appendix 1

The Jury at the Leet Court of the Manor of Hemenhale, held 8 June 1387.

NRO MC 1862/MS 35032 Hemenhall Court Roll 1327–98

Walter Asgar	Richard Lece
Robert Baxter	Walter Mone
John Bayborn	John Ponyard
John Bernard	Richard Pynsthorp
William Clobbe	Thomas Schieperde
William atte Cros	John Stacy junior
John Dye	John Stacy senior
William Ede	Hugh Skynner
John Fuller junior	William atte Thorn
Reginald Hail	John Turnour
William Kechen	John Weston
Geoffrey Kybard	

The Jury at the Leet Court of the Manor of Hemenhale, held 24 January 1398

John Stacy	William Alford
Robert Baxter	Thomas Bakere
William Fet	Walter Leece
William Cook	Richard Lece
John Botheler	Robert Ropere
John Lawe	John de Weston
John Bolonye	William atte Thorn
John Sefrey	Giles Taillour
William Ede	John Fuller
John Weston junior	Richard Pynsthorpe
Rogger Atte Cros	John Ward
Richard Winnington	Roger Shaton
Robert Pynsthorpe	Hugh Skynner
Robert Clerk	Thomas Cleron
John Garbald	

Appendix 2

SOME FOURTEENTH-CENTURY ENTRIES FROM COURT ROLLS LISTING RELATIONSHIPS WITHIN FAMILIES.

MC 1862/MS 35032 Hemenhall Court Roll 1327–98

1329 Cecil Alfweht, heir of Robert Alfweht, is admitted to one messuage and two acres. Margery Alfweht, widow, is granted widow's dower. She died in 1347.
1329 Adam Warde and Johanna, his wife, acquire a furlong from Christina le Ward of the tenement Dotis.
1329 Alice de Stauwe and Ralphe atte Green hold land once held by Roger de Stonwe or Stauwe.
1338 Henry Oldbarlik takes on four acres of land from Herman Oldbarlik, paying for the first year 3 quarters and four bushels of wheat and 3 quarters and four bushels of barley.
1340 Cecil Alfweht dies. Sarra Alfweht, his aunt, inherits one messuage and four acres of the tenement Eylward.
1340 Nicholas de Kokefield and wife Sarra, daughter of John Alyward, inherit a messuage and four acres.
1341 John Ailward dies. Sarra, his daughter inherits one messuage and four acres.
1341 Henry Oldbarlik surrenders one messuage and nine acres to his daughter, Isabella, and William Sewell, her husband.
1346 John Walsh dies. John Walsh, son, inherits one messuage and four acres.
1346 Katherine Clubbe dies. William Clubbe inherits one messuage and two acres.
1347 Thomas Blunt dies. Richard, his son, inherits one messuage and one acre three roods of land.
1347 Margery Alfweft dies. Sarra, wife of Richard de Cokefield, inherits one messuage and two acres.
1350 Gwidon Bunns and wife, Sarra, formerly Alfweth, are granted a curtilege with two acres which was Sarra Alfweth's.
1350 Clarica Sigar dies. Thomas Sigar, her son, inherits one messuage with three acres in Boyloundmedowe
1351 Adam Warde dies. Clarissa, his sister, inherits one messuage with 16 acres.
1351 Alicia de Pares dies. Her sister, Clarissa, inherits one messuage and two acres of free land.
1365 Richard de Bressingham dies. John, his son, inherits half a rood in the fee of the lord.
1365 John Whigte and Sara, his wife, are granted two tenements once John Alfweyhe's and Walter Alfweyhe's containing five acres at a rent of 6s. pa

1377 John Coppyng gives two acres of land and one acre of meadow to William, his son.
1377 Cristina and Isabelle Coppyng, sisters, are absent from the manor.
1377 Isabelle de Flordon has married John Elflete de Schotesham without paying merchet
1387 Roger Chaton pays 2s. merchet for the marriage of his daughter, Cristina.
1387 Ralph Gissing and wife Katherine take over part of a wood called Dureys and a part called Spledis.
1387 John Sherwyn, at death's door, grants a messuage to his wife, Matilda.
1387 Bartholomew Kyte and Sibill, his wife, are granted one cottage and four acres called Elnard's tenement.
1387 Robert de Weston, sick unto death, surrenders one cottage called Weston's lying near the vicarage of Hemenhale to John Weston.
1388 William atte Thorn is admitted to one messuage and eight acres from his father, Walter.
1388 Cristina Coppyng and Isabell Coppyng, daughters of John Coppyyng, are living in Norwich. Order for them to be seized. Amerced 3d. each for evading arrest by the bailiff later in the year. In 1390 they were still in Norwich.
1388 Sibil Coppyng bears a child outside marriage. Fined 2s.8d.
1390 John Coppyng dies and his son, Nicholas, inherits a messuage and 16 acres.
1390 Agnes Massy and Joan and Agnes Massy, her daughters, are absent from the manor.
1392 John Galyon is in Beclys, chevage 16d. Anna Galyon is in Bongeye, chevage 8d. In 1393 she had paid 4d. chevage to live in Bungay. In 1396 he paid 16d. and Anna Lavender paid 4d.
1393 William atte Cros dies and Roger ate Cros, his son, inherits his two cottages.
1394 John Seffrey and Margaret, his wife, are granted one messuage and eight acres late Turbett.
1395 Sibil Coppyng marries without permission. Fined 10s.
1396 John Bresyngham dies. Geoffrey Bonewell, chaplain, is next of kin.
1397 Philip Herrs and Joanne, his wife, are admitted to one messuage and four acres – Flordon in Hemenhale.
1398 Richard Pyrnnesthorp dies. Robert, his son, inherits one messuage called Wynters.
1398 Robert Pyrethorp dies and his son, Robert, inherits seven acres called Nichols.
1399 Nicholas Coppyn dies. Thomas is his son, but aged 6. His mother, Agnes, is to take over his messuage called Coppynges until Thomas is of age.

Appendix 3

LAY SUBSIDY
1581 Assessors' Certificates for the Norfolk Hundred of Depwade
(NRS Vol. 18 (NRS 1944) p.103)

Names	Paid	Land or goods
Bullen Henry	£8	lands
Leygoode John	£5	goods
Reynolds William	£5	lands
Estrawe Robert	£4	goods
Haller Robert	£4	goods
Halles John	£4	goods
Roberts Ralph	£4	goods
Sporle John of town	£4	goods
Turner John	£4	lands
Ward Margaret	£4	goods
Weston Thomas	£4	goods
Jermyn Edmund	£3.10s.	lands
Jermy Edward	£3	lands
Bird John	£3	goods
Codnham William	£3	lands
Dowe Henry	£3	goods
Dowe William	£3	goods
Jermyn Ralph	£3	goods

Names	Paid	Land or goods
Richards William	£3	lands
Sendall Jeffrey	£3	lands
Sherwoode George	£3	goods
Skelton John	£3	goods
Sporle William	£3	goods
White Ralph	£3	goods
Chettleborough Richard	£2.10s.	lands
Robberdes Edward	£2.10s.	lands
Jermy Richard	£2	lands
Pytt John	£2	lands
Pyttes Edward	£2	lands
Smyth Roger	£2	lands
Chettleburgh Henry	£1.10s.	lands
Jermyn Ralph	£1.10s.	lands
Sporle John Westgate	£1.10s.	lands
Grey Widow	£1	lands
Gurney John	£1	lands

Appendix 4

1588 MUSTER
NRO AYL 166

Householders
Roger Smith
Robert Caston
Andrew Iker
Jeffrey Sendall
Raphe Robes
John Sherwoode
Edmund Robes
John Turner
Richard Chettleburgh
William Richards
Raphe Jermyn Jun
Ric Jermyn
Thomas Weston
John Randolf
John Halles sen
John Pytt
William Sporle
Adam Loose
Robt Fermon

Cottagers
John Legate
Raphe Jermyn jun
Robt Halles
Ric Weeks
Jeffery Mynges
John Byarde
Henr Chettleburgh
John Meke
Jeffrey Mynges
William Mynges
Thos Warde
John Sporle sen
John Sporle jun
Stephen Rollington
Henr Doroe
Raid Redingmar
Ric Gren
Ric Girlinge
William Dowe
Cord Turner
John Skelton
Nicholas Rechade
William Pytt
John Halles jun
John Ellys
John Chettleburgh

Labourers
Leanard Harper
John Bircham
William Rollman

Gentleman
Charles Jermyn

Artyfycers
Robt Rope
Edmund Robes
Charles Walker
Rob Sporle
Nicholas Spome
Will Harr
James Robes
John Wilkes
Thos Knights
Jeffrey Henry
John Jermes
Rob Clarke
Rob Jermyn
Phillip Jermyn
Henry Harris
Thos Sporle
George Jermyn
Ric Bishop
Ric Birge
Henry Rechards
Will Warde

Appendix 5

POOR ACCOUNTS WITH RATES LIST *NRO NAS 1/1/2/151*

A list of sums of money received and paid to the use of the poor of the parish of Hempnall by Henry Harpley and William Sabourne, churchwardens, and William Bidbanke and Ralph Lynes, outseers made 2 April 1632 for the year now ended

Receipts:	
Received in stock	**46s 11d**
Thomas Turrould	3s.4d.
Richard Coddenham	4s.8d.
John Davye	5s.
Edmund Jermyn	2s.8d.
Ralph Lynes	4s.
William Gootch	3s.
Leanard Turrould	6s.8d.
John Roberts junr	4s.8d.
John Legood	3s.4d.
John Bootye	14d.
Ralph Roberts junr	8d.
Cuthbert Butts clerk	16d.
John Reynoulds	16d.
Thomas Moore	4s.8d.
Ralph Roberts senr	6s.
Henry Maggs	3s.8d.
Jeremy Brame	10d.
Edward Sporle senr	16d.
Edward Sporle junr	4d.
Thomas Porter clerk	6s.
Isaac Skinner	2s.
Roger Roberts	2s.4d.
John Roberts senr	16d.
Robert Turner	5s.
Augustine Chettelborough	3s.
Thomas Gootch	4s.4d.
William Sabourne	20d.
John Middleditch	4s.8d.
Salmon Fox	1s.
William Bidbank	6s.
Mathewe Chettelborough	6s.
Andrewe Dowe	16d.
Peter Curtis	3s.4d.
Richard Chettelborough	6s.
Richard Mendham	1s.
Edmund Johnson	1s.
John Jermyn junr	10d.
John Halles	2s.
William Seawell	2s.6d.
Daniel Halles	3s.4d.
Robert Halles	2s.
Ralph Jermyn	16d.
John Backler	10s.
Robte Chettelborough	8s.
John Chettelborough	16d.
Robte Jermyn	5s.
Thomas Lowe	2s.8d.
of him for Pytts lande	4d.
Mathew Pitcher	7s.
John Jermyn senr	10d.

John Curson	9s.
Francis Halles	8d.
Christopher Jermyn	14d.
Richard Bishop	5s.
Samuel Swatman gen	8s.
Walter Dickerson	4s.
John Weekes	4s.
John Curtis	5s.4d.
John Spillinge	18d.
Christopher Knights	18d.
Henry Weekes	3s.
Nicholas Richards	4s.4d.
Edward Ollyett	3s.8d.
Robert Fayerman	16d.
John Cheney	9s.
Edward Woorre	8d.
For Sallomere	8d.
For farme for 3 neat	9s.
Outdwellers	
Charles Garneys asgines	14d.
Phillip Whithered	4d.
William Goodwin	6d.
John Spendlowe	4d.
Simon Luther cher	2d.8d.
John Purdye gen	2s.8d.
William Shelten	8d.
Roger Legood	8d.
William Coppinge gen	2s.4d.
Roger Fuller	4d.
Robert Howes	10d.
Andrewe Fuller	4d.
William Antells land	8d.
John Randoll	18d.
Thomas Goweinge	18d.
Lawence Potter	2s.4d.
John Freeman	10d.
Thomas Roberts	16d.
Jeffery Goodwin	13d.
George Pytt	5d.
John Theobald gen	4s 8d.
Ralphe Dawson	2s.4d.
Robte Youngs	9d.
Ralphe Smythe	6s.
John Turrould	4d.
John Roberts	2s.
The whole sum is	£15.10s.2d.

Appendix 6

CONSTABLE'S RETURNS *NRO NAS 1/1/2/151*

Distributed to the poore of the parish of Hempnall by the sayd churchwardens and overseers as followeth

To Elizabeth Coleman widdowe 17 April 1631 2d a week for 52 weeks
To Reynould Kirke 17 Apil 1631 12d for 30 weeks
To Henry Kempe 17 April 1631 6d for 45 weeks
To Audrey Kyrke 2d a week for 52 weeks
To Elizabeth Coleman widdowe 13 April 1634 1s a week for 52 weeks
To Rofe Dowe 13 April 1634, 10d. a week for 52 weeks
To Alice Cooke 13 April 1634, 4d. a week for 52 weeks
To Richard Pytt 13 April 1634, 4d. a week for 52 weeks

For keeping of Thomas Blomefeild from 13 April 1634	1s.
For removeing of Alice Cooke and Thomas Blomefeild	10d.
For firewood for Reads wife and Elizabeth Coleman	11s.4d.
For house Farme for Alice Cooke	6s.8d.
Rofe Dowe, Wid Love, Alice Cooke and Ann Johnson for 7… lying cloath for the wid Coleman and Rofe Dowe	5s.3d.
For apparel for Thomas Blomefeild	5s.

Distributed to divers poore people 30 March, 9s. being the same for the towne reate

To Ralph Cobbett	1s.
To the wid Lowe	6d.
To Alice Cooke	1s.
To the wid Herwin	6d.
To Wades wife	8d.
To Abraham Bennett	4d.
To Ann Johnson	6d.
To the widow Dowe	6d.
To Lambert	4d.
To William Taylor	6d.
To wid Hudson	4d.
To wid Knights	4d.
To Thomas Lea	4d.
To William Bythopp	6d.
To the wid Duntt	4d.
To John Bright	4d.
To Thomas Peede	4d.
To Henrie Knights	4d.

Churchwardens
Robt Chettelboroughe
Sam Mayes
Overseers
John Mayhew
Peter Curtis

Appendix 7

VICARS OF HEMPNALL
(Appointed by the Prior of Little Dunmow until the dissolution of the monasteries).
NRO DN/REG 17. Bishop's registers of institutions.
Tanner's Index *DN/REG 30-31*
E.H. Carter The Norwich Subscription Books.

Year	date if known	Name
c.1248		Adam
?		Thomas of Stortford
1303	July 1	Robert de Nuttele
1328	June 4	Thomas Seward de Melford
1331		Thomas de Saxham
1342	May 3	Thomas atte Thorne de Coulyng
1350		Succeeded by John Edmond Cristmesse
1360	January 12	William de Hethill
1368	October 23	Robert Larke de Saundford (Vicar of Hempnall St. Mary)
1397	March 16	John Spencer de Bury
1402	July 1	Richard Parlben
1408		William Machet
1444		Jeffrey Fuller
1480		Nicholas Denton
1503		John Sage (last vicar presented by the prior of Little Dunmow)
by 1552		Robert Talbut
1560	June 18	John Collison
1564		Thomas Fayerman
1591		Richard Cox
1597		George Skynner
1603	April 4	James Lovell
1605	December 16	Thomas Porter
1636		William Barwick
	sequested April 28 1644	
1649	June22	John Potter
1692		John Smith
1697		William Aggas
1724	October22	Joseph Parsons
1774	August 13	Coote Leicester
1793	December 23	John Johnson
1807	September 21	Castres Mott Donne
1819	July 17	Robert Rolfe
1850	November 23	George Thomas Hall (curate of Hempnall from1847)
1885	November 14	Howard Mc Crinck
1886	July 22	Henry William Cooper
1887	July 27	Edward Ewer Ward
1894	May 19	Augustine Brutton
1905	February 11	Charles Edward Hignett Wilford
1913	October 28	John Talbot Gardiner
1921	July 29	Francis Alfred Howard
1932	November 8	Arthur Hogarth Oak-Rhind.
1944	June 8	Sydney Chamberlain Kell
1945	June 30	Frederick Walter Martin
1952	May 18	Carey Cooper

Formation of the Hempnall Group of Churches in 1963

Appendix 8

SOME EIGHTEENTH-CENTURY HEMPNALL CHARACTERS

John Bensley Considerable landowner. May have lived at Willow Farm. He owned a butcher's shop occupied by Richard Watling.

Charles Bunn A farmer owning lands in the west of the parish. He occupied a dwelling-house and 74 acres belonging to Peter Brown.

James Carver A miller. He rented Woodhouse Farm (now Wodehouse) and owned a post mill on Gallow's Hill in Mill Road.

Laomi Cunningham His wife, Mary, absconded from him in 1769. He died 'as it seems of a broken heart from a false wife' and was buried on 26 October 1770. Mary inherited all his property.

Thomas D'Oyly A farmer. He owned Fairstead House, (now Krons Manor). He sold a farm in Topcroft in 1770. His wife died after a long and painful illness in 1777, leaving a will that was never proved, 'she having no assents'. On his death D'Oyly was described as having 'the character of a generous, friendly, and truly honest man'. He was father of the Revd William D'Oyly.

Joseph Parsons The vicar, unlike many clergy of the day, kept in touch with his parishioners and made numerous notes, particularly in the burial register books from 1757 until his death in 1774.
To name a few examples:
Joshua Gryms, an honest industrious man.
William Neeve, an inoffensive quiet man... diligently served the Lord... was just and friendly to many.
Isabelle Carr... of approved conversation in Christ attending the public offices of religion doing good and giving no offence in private. A rare example!
Robert Meadows, taken off suddenly and strangely had grossly offended his aunt. Age 22.

Joseph Parsons, died on Monday, 11 July 1774. The burial register records: 'The Revd Joseph Parsons Master of Arts fifty years the indefatigable pastor of this parish and in all respects the truly exemplary Christian... was buried in a vault under the communion table... aged 77 years one month and sixteen days.'

Thomas Rayner A cooper, an trade traditionally carried out in the village. He owned a house in the street called 'The Stall' (Willow House), once owned by Abraham Bennet, the seventeenth-century murderer.

James Richards A weaver who owned Lundy Green Farm and was constantly plagued by thefts:

10 September 1774 Thomas Stagg, John Philips: theft of cloth from Mr Richards.
12 August 1775 John and Mary Tyler, accused of receiving 72 yards of hempen cloth.
16 March 1776 John Tyler, stealing two pieces of hempen cloth from Mr Richards. (acquitted)
5 October 1776 Stolen in the night, two pieces of hempen cloth, one sold next morning at Barnham, near Thetford. Messrs Richards of Hempnall robbed of 60 yards of hempen cloth cut out of the looms.

Robert Stone A tanner who owned the Hollies. He advertised in 1777 for 30 labourers skilled in Norfolk Husbandry to go to Kilsal in Salop – 'apply at Mr Robert Stone at Hempnall'. A wether lamb was stolen from his lands on 27 December 1778 by John Goose, an old offender.

John Thornley Described as 'gentleman', let his house at Road Green, Hempnall, between 1776 and 1777. It had 'two parlours, one a handsome large room, sashed and wainscotted a few years ago... the other small, hung with wallpaper, a good hall or kitchen... a good cellar with arches for bottles... two small kitchen gardens...coach house.'
Mr Lubbock Thornley, perhaps a son, married Miss Kemp of Tibenham in 1779 – 'an agreeable young lady with a handsome fortune'.

Charles Warmoll Schoolmaster. He owned the Chequers, where he lived, and the Longhouse that was used as a residence for the boarders. In March 1778 a large sow, a hog shot and a small cow were stolen out of his yard. John Ward, an old offender, a deserter from 54th Regiment of Foot, having lately broken out of the City Gaol, was found guilty. He was ordered to serve three years' hard labour on the River Thames.

Appendix 9

HEMPNALL PEOPLE ACCUSED OF CRIMES CONNECTED WITH THE SPINNING AND WEAVING TRADE

Date	Offence	Name of the accused if known
1770	false reeling yarn	Hemnal woman
1776	reeling false and short yarn.	Anne Moore
1782	embezzling 13lbs of wool	Mary Roberts
1784	false reeling yarn	Elizabeth Leech, Martha Tooke, Mary Baker
1785	reeling false and short yarn	Mary Baker, Martha Tooke, Elizabeth Leech
1787	embezzlement of wool	Clare King, Sarah Fuller
1788	false reeling wool	Elizabeth Clarke
1794	possessing wool, the property of different combers	Mary Leech
1800	bleaching grounds robbed, flaxen yarn taken	
1800	false reeling	Wife of William Harris
1801	false reeling	Mary Andrews
1803	false reeling	Richard Ford and Sarah Fuller
1803	stealing linen cloth	William Gardener
1804	false reeling	Sarah Fuller and Mary Grint
1804	possessing wool belonging to different combers	Margaret Fryer
1807	false reeling	Sarah Fuller
1813	embezzling wool	Elizabeth Smith
1818	false reeling	James Penn and Catherine Smith

Appendix 10

ROLL OF HONOUR, FIRST WORLD WAR

William AYTON
13 November 1916, aged 23
7th Battalion, Royal Fusiliers

Albert CRUMMETT
20 July 1917, aged 21
1–6th Battalion, Durham Light Infantry 20

Thomas DOWNING
18 January 1915, aged 26
2–6th Battalion (Cyclist), the Norfolk Regiment.

Bertie Thomas ELLIS ?

Percy William ELLIS
30 December 1917, aged 19
6th Battalion, Duke of Cambridge Own (Middlesex Regiment)

James Charles ELVIN
21 March 1918, aged 46
9th Battalion, Norfolk Regiment.

John William ELVIN
4 September 1918
416th Field Company Royal Engineers

Leonard ELVIN ?

March HAZELL
20 September 1917, aged 23
11th Battalion, Northumberland Fusiliers.

William KIRK ?

Richard Hewitt LANSDELL
31 October 1917, aged 20
1–4 Battalion, East Yorkshire Regiment.

Charles Samuel NASH
15 September 1916, aged 22
9th Battalion, Norfolk Regiment

Frederick Arthur NASH
21 December 1917, aged 19
2–4th Battalion, the Queens (Royal West Surrey Regiment)

Clarence John POINTER
27 March 1918, aged 18
10th Battalion, the Queens (Royal West Surrey Regiment)

Arthur Frederick SHELDRAKE
23 March 1918, aged 26
15th Battalion, the Royal Irish Rifles. The Norfolk Regiment previously

Charles Henry SPINK
3 December 1918, aged 21
7th Battalion, the North Regiment

Robert Samuel SPORLE
6 May 1917, aged 28
13th Battalion, the East Yorkshire Regiment (4th Hull)

Harry George TOWNSEND
27 September 1918, aged 29
1st Battalion, the Norfolk Regiment attached to the 15th French Mortar Battery

Herbert TOWNSEND
4 May 1918, aged 42
101st the Labour Corps

Leonard William TOWNSEND
7 March 1915, aged 29
1st Battalion, the Norfolk Regiment

Sidney George VARLEY
18 September 1916, aged 26
1st Battalion, the Norfolk Regiment

Walter WARD ?

Sources and Bibliography

Manuscript Sources

Barningham Hall in a tin box

Court book A 1650–1713
Court book B 1713–19
Court book C 1719–23
Court book D 1723–41
Minute book E 1727–41
Court book G 1736–63
A number of deeds and sale advertisements with plans and maps
Inclosure Award without map 1818
Tithe Apportionment and map 1842

Shirehall, Norwich

Norfolk Museums and Archaeology Service NWHCM:1958.146, Vol. 2 p.291: F Drawings by A. Rolfe (attrib.) 1845

Own possession

A catalogue of household furniture, china and glass to be sold by auction on Tuesday, 19 October 1858, by Salter & Simpson, formerly belonging to Joseph Cator Webb
Richard Hylton's memoranda (photocopy)

In possession of Hempnall Parish Clerk

Parish Council Minute Books and copy of the Inclosure Award
School: School log-book

Printed original sources

Commission on the Employment of Children, Young Persons and Women in Agriculture, 1867 pp.135, 140, 147, 151, 153. First Report of the Commissioners, with Appendix Part 1 (London, 1868)
Fitzwilliam Museum, Cambridge. EMC No. 1989.0082 (Ref: CR 1989:82. *British Numismatic Journal* 59 (1989) No. 82 coin. NCirc 1990, 198–99. coin
NNR (1822) Norfolk & Norwich 1701 to 1820 inclusive, p.5 (Norwich)
Commission on the Employment of Children, Young Persons and Women in Agriculture, 1867 pp. 135, 140, 147, 151, 153. First Report of the Commissioners, with Appendix Part 1pp.3 -7, 13, 16, 19, 22, 23, 48 (London, 1868)
Depwade Deanery Magazines

Norfolk Record Office (NRO)

AYL 186 Muster 1588
BR 32/1 Geldeston Brewery
BR 37/3/1222 Indenture 2 May 1914
C/aP 3/1 Records of Pulham Market Workhouse
C/Scd 2–17 Land Tax Returns for Depwade
C/Scf 1/421 Railway proposals through Hempnall, 30 November 1835
C/ED 3/101, 3/102, 68/334 Minutes of Hempnall School Board
C/ED 68/334 Hempnall School Board 1915–18
DN/CON/138 faculty papers
Compton Return for the Norwich Diocese 1676 No. 21489
CR 1837 Trust deed to Primitive Methodist Chapel pt 130/1939 pt 145
C/S1/10 1684–93 Quarter Sessions Roll 1
C/Scf1/421 Railway proposal, 30 November 1835
D2/9/2 Emergency Committee, 27 April 1943
DC 2/4/3/13/14/15 Depwade Rural District Council Highways Minute Books
DN/ADR 26/3/1222 Norwich Diocesan Registers
DN DIS Register of meeting. Houses 1751–1810.
DN/FBA/1 A.B Box 389, 11Oct 1744. Faculty bond
DN/FCB/2/2 p. 32 16 March 1755. Faculty Book Protestant Dissenters
DN/REG 21 Book 29 1707/08 pp.273&263. Norwich Diocesan Registers of the Clergy
DN/TER 81/3/1–36. Hempnall Glebe Terriers
DN VIS. Hempnall Visitations
FEL 787 555 X 7 sermon
MC 1862/MS 35032. Hemenhall Court Roll 1327–98
MC 1862/1/1–40, MC 1862/4862X9, MC 1817/9, 843X4, MC 1817/10, 843X5. Copyhold records for the manors of Hempnall, Hempnall Cannons and Hempnall Raffes, 1533–51, 1573–90
MC 1862/5, 863X1 1573–90 Court roll Manor of Hempnall
NAS 1/1/2/154, Dec 4 1633–34. Constables' Returns
NRS 26671 149X2 Indenture
MSS. Rye No. 17 Vol. 2. Church Notes by Thomas Martin
P/BG/55/2. Plans of Hempnall School, 1948
PD 436. Hempnall Church Registers
PD 712/74/5, PD 708/101. Overseers Bastardy Warrants
PD 602/4. Aylsham Baptismal Registers
Norwich Police Charge Book 1836–38
Norfolk Archdeaconry Court wills
Norwich Consistory Court wills

Public Record Office, London (PRO)

ED 2/317. School Board of Hempnall Abstract. Vol. 49 p. 68, 11 Nov 1871
E179/154/697 rot.9 1672–73 Hearth Tax
HO 107/757/11. Census Returns 1841
HO 107/1821/595. Census Returns 1851
MS C135/12 1327. Inquisition Post Mortem
RG 12/1891. Census Returns

Sermons

The Revd. S. Hobson, 'Be Sure Your Sin Will Find You Out: Progress and Consequences of Sin Considered'. (Norwich, 1839). Preached at Hempnall
The Revd Joseph Parsons. Preached at Hempnall and Bedingham, Norfolk, on the 'First Sunday of Reading His Majesty's Gracious Order, for preventing the spreading of the Distemper, which now rages among the Cattle' (London, John Oliver, 1745)
The Revd Joseph Parsons. Preached at the Funeral of Mrs Susan Sporle of Hemenhall, Widow (London, B. Dod, 1746)

British Parliamentary papers

CCR, CChR, CFR, CPR, CFF

Newspapers

EDP, NA, NC, NG, NM, NN

Directories

Craven & Co. (1856) *Commercial Directory of Norfolk* (Nottingham)
Kelly, E.R. (ed.) (1879) *The Post Office Directory of the County of Norfolk* (London)
Peck, Thomas (1802) *The Norwich Directory* (Norwich)

Maps

Xerox copy FX 222/1. Bungay Town Reeve land in Hempnall, 1665
MC 607/1 (MS 33540). Estate of James, Viscount Grimston, 1767
DN/TA 686. Tithe Apportionment with map by Pratt & Son, surveyors, Norwich 1842

Books

Best, G.M. (2003) *John Wesley, A Study of His Life to Commemorate the Tercentenary of His Birth* (Bath)
Bird, Clifford & Yvonne (eds) (1996) *Norfolk and Norwich Clockmakers* (Chichester)
Blomefield, F. (1745) *An Essay Towards a Topographical History of the County of Norfolk* Vol. 2 (Norwich)
Bryant. Norfolk Churches. The Hundred of Diss (Norwich 1915)
Bryant, F.T. Hugh (1906) *Norfolk Churches* 'The Hundred of Depwade', Vol. 17 (Norwich)
Campbell, Lord (1846) *Lives of the Lord Chancellors*, Vol. 5 (London)
Carroll, Stewart (1996) *Ted's Flying Circus. 93rd Bombardment Group (H), United States Army Air Force, World War II* (Lincoln, USA)
Carter E.H., OBE, MA (1937) The Norwich Subscription Books. *A Study of the Subscription Books of the Diocese of Norwich 1637–1800* (London)
Curnock N. (ed.) (1938) *The Journal of the Revd. John Wesley, A.M.*, Vol. 4 (London)
Ede, Janet and Virgo, Norma (eds) (1998) *Religious Worship in Norfolk. The 1851 Census of Accommodation and Attendance at Worship, NRS* Vol. 62 (Cambridge)
Gelling, M. (1987) *Signposts to the Past. Place-names and the History of England* (London)
Gore-Brown, R. (1846) *Chancellor Thurlow. The Life and Times of an XVIIIth Century Lawyer* (London)
Harper-Bill, C. (1996) 'The Medieval Church and the Wider World', *Norwich Cathedral, Church, City and Diocese, 1096–1996* p.290 (London)
Hone, Richard B. (ed.) (1872) *Seventeen Years in Yoruba Country* (London)
Ketton-Cremer, R.W. (1969) *Norfolk in the Civil War. A Portrait of a Society in Conflict* (London)
Pevsner, N. (1962) *The Buildings of England: North-West and South Norfolk* (Middlesex)
Rackham, O. (1986) T*he History of the Countryside* (London)
Smith, A.H. (1956) *English Place-Name Elements* English Place-Name Society Vol. 25 (Cambridge)
Stammers, G.G. (1969) *My Village* (Norwich)
Venn, John & Venn, J.A. (1922) *Alumni Cantabrigienses: a biographical list of all known students, graduates and holders of office at the University of Cambridge from the earliest times to 1900*, Part 1 Vol. 1 (Cambridge)
VCH *History of Norfolk* Vol. 2 p.23 (f.249), ref. 6
Williamson, T. (2003) *Shaping Medieval Landscapes: Settlement, Society, Environment* (Macclesfield)

Articles and Essays

Barton T.F., MA, FSA (transcribed) 'The Registrum of Anthony Harrison Pt 2', *NRS* Vol. 33 p.133
Carter E.H., OBE, MA (1937) *The Norwich Subscription Books. A Study of the Subscription Books of the Diocese of Norwich 1637–1800*, p.167 (London)
Chapman, Elizabeth (1995) *Methodism in Hempnall*
Frankell, M.S. and Seamam, P.J. (trans) (1983) 'Norfolk Hearth Tax Assessment Michaelmas 1664' *Norfolk Genealogy* Vol. 15, pp.9, 10
Hanawalt B., PhD, 'Crime in East Anglia in the 14th century. Norfolk Gaol Delivery Rolls 1307–16', *NRS* Vol. 44
Hopper, N.A., EC *Church Plate* Vol. 15 p.257
Howell, D.E. James (1955) 'Norfolk Sessions Order Book 1650–57' *NRS* Vol. 26, p.38 (244) and p.57 (472)
Hudson, William, 'The Assessment of the Townships of the County of Norfolk for the King's Tenths and Fifteenths as settled in 1334 and 1449', *Depwade Norfolk Archaeology* Vol.12
Hudson, Revd.W. FSA 'The "Norwich Taxation" of 1254, so far as relates to the Diocese of Norwich, collated with the Taxation of Pope Nicholas in 1291', *Norfolk Archaeology* Vol.17, p.108
Jewson, C.B. FSA (1965) 'Return of the Conventicles in Norwich Diocese 1669. Lambeth MS no.639. Lists of conventicles or illegal religious societies in Norwich Depwade Deanery', *Norfolk Archaeology* Vol. 33 (Norwich)
Jewson, C.B. 'Registers of Passengers from Great Yarmouth to Holland and New England, 1637-39' *Norfolk Record Society* Vol. 25
King, The Revd. V. S.W. (1859) 'Examination of an Ancient Cemetery' *Norfolk Archaeology* Vol. V, pp.49–52 (Norwich)
Levy, R. E. (1965) 'The Cartulary of Little Dunmow Priory' (MA dissertation, University of Virginia, USA)
Plunkett, George G. 'Norfolk Church Screens – 1865 Survey' *Norfolk Archaeology*
Peacock, D. (Dec 1996) *Morals, Rituals and Gender Aspects of Social Relations in the Diocese of Norwich 1660–1703* (PhD thesis, York University) 106 NCD DN/DEP 47/51 1665 October
Stone, E.D. 'Norwich Consistory Court Depositions, 1499–1512 and 1518–30' *NRS* Vol. 10 No. 38 fo.60
Stone, Revd E.D., MA (trans.) Williams, P., SSA (ed.) (1944) 'Lay Subsidy of 1581 Assessors Certificates for the Norfolk Hundred of Depwade' *NRS* Vol. 18, p.103 (NRS)
Stone E.D., 'Norwich Consistory Court Depositions, 1499–1512 and 1518–30' *NRS* Vol. 10 No.202 fo.51b, fo.52, fo.52b
'Norfolk Hundred of Depwade' (1944) *NRS* Vol. 18 (NRS)
Walters H.B., FSA (1941) 'Inventories of Norfolk Church Goods' *Norfolk Archaeology* Vol. 27 (Norwich)
Williams, J.F., MA, FSA (ed.) (1946) 'Bishop Redman's Visitations 1597' *NRS* Vol. 18 p.104
Woodward, S. (1831) 'A descriptive outline of Roman Remains in Norfolk' *Society of Antiquaries*

Subscribers

Peter J. Adams, Long Stratton, Norfolk
Joy J. Ainsworth, Hempnall, Norfolk
Audrey Aldrich
Miss J.P. Alexander, Hempnall
Roger J. Allen
Peter J Allison, descendant of family name Elvin (Grandson), Hempnall, Norfolk
Greta Anderson, Barnes, London
Pam Arnold, Hempnall, Norfolk
The Ashford family, Hempnall, Norfolk
Bruce Austin, Hempnall, Norfolk
James A. Ayton, Hempnall, Norfolk
Mr Roger P. Baker
Basil Beckett, Newton Flothan
Mr Will Beckett, Hempnall, Norfolk
David Beckett, Hempnall, Norfolk
Byron D. Beckett, Hempnall, Norfolk
Peter Beckett, Long Stratton
Dennis A. Beckett, Hempnall, Norfolk
Denise J. Bedwell (née Satchell), Tharston (formerly Hempnall)
Anne Benson, Hempnall, Norfolk
Matt, Penny and Thea Bignell
Roy and Cherry Bishop, Meadow Farm, Silver Green
Danny and Margaret Blanchflower
Mrs Ann E. Blowers (née Downing), Hempnall, Norfolk
Lyndon and Barbara Bringloe, Caistor St Edmund
Pauline A. Brookes, Hempnall, Norfolk
Gerald Brooks, Long Stratton, Norfolk
Peggy Brown
Sally Brown
Mr Quinton Brown, Hempnall
Ted Buck, Hempnall
Mr Daniel Burroughs, Hempnall
Mr Gordon D. Cann, Shelton, Norfolk
Drs Mike and Liz Challis, Hempnall House
David Storey and Debbie Chamberlain, Hempnall, Norfolk
Lawrence Chapman, Hempnall
Michael Chappell, Harleston, Norfolk
Mrs J.A. Chellis, Hempnall, Norfolk
Mrs Sheila Clarke (née Leeder), Hempnall
Mr Alan R. Clitheroe, Woodton
Barbara A. Cockerill (née Stammers), Laxfield
J. R. G. Cooper, Attleborough
Nigel and Lynne Cooper, Hempnall, Norfolk
Gwen Cooper, Hempnall
Mr Brian D. Cooper, Hempnall, Norfolk
John Cooper
Mrs Deirdre A. Cubitt, Norwich
David Cubitt, Norwich
Revd Paul Cubitt, Blofield
Dr Robert Cubitt, Grenoble, France
Pauline and Bernard Cudden, Hempnall
Ian and Sylvia Cundy
June Cunningham
Kevin Cunningham
Dagmar June Cunningham, Upper Stoke Holy Cross
Mary Curtis, Hempnall, Norfolk
Mrs Joyce Cushion, Hempnall
Julia R. Davey, Hempnall, Norfolk
Jane Dawson
Kirsten Day
Neville Day, Hempnall
Evelyn Delf, Hempnall
P. J. Earle, Portsmouth
Phoebe Elizabeth Edwards (née Hipperson),
John M. Ellis, Hempnall
Mary and Pat Ellis, Moat Farm, Hempnall
Carol and Paul Evans, Stoke Holy Cross
Les and Jackie Everett, Hempnall
David Ferrey
Julia Field (née Curtis)
Ron Fiske, Morningthorpe
Sylvia and Andy Fox, Hempnall, Norfolk
Carl D. Fox, Hempnall Green
Peter Fryer, Leeds, West Yorks
Richard Fryer, Harden, West Yorks
Mrs Joy Futter (née Keable), formerly of Hempnall, Norfolk
William Futter and Mrs Keable, Hempnall, Norfolk
Pauline J. Ghest, Friskney, Lincolnshire
Ena (née Page) and Malcolm Gibbs, Hempnall
Victor C. Goddard
Wilfrid E. Gooch, Hempnall, Norfolk
Elizabeth and Kenneth Green, Ulverston
Dr and Mrs Steven Griffiths
John and Eileen Hardaker
Robert and Alison Harris, Hempnall
Michala Harrison, Hempnall
C. Hawker, descendant of two Roberts families, Bucks
Kevin C. Hayter, Hempnall, Norfolk
Dinah M. Hazelhurst, Kirkheaton, West Yorkshire
Hempnall Primary School, The Street, Hempnall, Norfolk
Anne High
Daphne Hinsley, Hempnall
Ray and Shirley Hollands, Hempnall, Norfolk
Diana and Michael Honeybone
David and Melanie Hook, Hempnall
Dorothy E. Howard, Beaumont, Alberta, Canada
Charlie Humphreys, Hempnall

Tone Hvidsten, Brevik, Norway
Diane (née Poyntz), Steve, Gina and Katie Ingram, Hempnall
Mr and Mrs Jeffery, Hempnall, Norfolk
Lucy and Carl Jeffery, Hempnall
Mrs Lucy H. Jeffery, Hempnall, Norfolk
Hannah Johnson, Hempnall, Norfolk
Edward Johnson, Hempnall, Norfolk
Rob and Jane Johnson, Hempnall, Norfolk
David and Mary Kaye, Hempnall
Derek and Shelagh Keeler (née Downing), Hempnall
Paul Kilbourn, Hempnall
Queenie Kilbourn, Hempnall
Janet Knox
Sten Knudsen, Cringleford, Norfolk
Joan Ladbrooke
Mr David William Large, Hempnall, Norfolk
Jan and Mike Lee, Hempnall, Norfolk
Brian R. Leeder, Hempnall, Norfolk
Colin Lewis, Hempnall, Norfolk
Peter Lewis, New Ash Green, Kent
William and Linda Lloyd, Hempnall, Norfolk
Sally A. Lymer, Hastings
J.C. MacRae, Hempnall, Norfolk
Ann and Michael Margand, Topcroft
Clifford G. Matthews
Mahala Mehmet (née Sporle)
Ed and Sheila Millar, Hempnall
John and Daphne Milton, Denton
Lesley A. Mitchenal, Hempnall, Norfolk
Robin D. Moore, Saxlingham Nethergate, Norfolk
Lady Mott-Radclyffe, Matlaske
Ian J. Nelson, Hempnall, Norfolk
Mr Peter Noakes, Woodton
Bob and Julie Norman, Hempnall, Norfolk
Lesley Oldfield, Swallow Barn
Colin Oliver, Clare, Suffolk
Neil S. Osborne, Hempnall
Aubrey A. Page
Luke and Catherine Parfitt
Simon Parker, Norwich
Julie Parker, Hempnall
Richard Parker, Bedford
Elsebeth Parry, Debden, Essex
Beryl and Frank Peakall, Hempnall
Daphne Penn, Home Farm
David Penn, Bungay Road, Hempnall, Norfolk
Andrew I. Pointer, Hempnall, Norfolk
Ian Pointer, Hempnall, Norfolk
Daniel Rayson, Hempnall, Norfolk
John Read, Norwich
Allan and Georgina Reeder, Hempnall
Paul S. Reeve, Tasburgh, Norfolk
Christopher Revell, Hempnall
Anita Richmond, Hempnall, Norfolk
Tom Roast, Norwich
Brian R. Roberts, Anglesey, formerly Essex
Audrey E. Roberts, Llandudno, formerly Essex
A.G. Sargent
Peter Satchell, Hempnall, Norfolk
Olivia Mary Saul, Hempnall, Norfolk
Michael John Saul, Hempnall, Norfolk
Rachel Scrafield
Trevor, Patty, Paul and Ian Shurmer, Hempnall, Norfolk
Percy and Irene Smith, Thetford
Margaret Sparham, Hempnall
Michael Sparrow
Michael Stammers, Liverpool
Richard J. Stammers, Bury St Edmunds
J.K Stammers, Norwich
Professor D. K Stammers, Oxford
Mrs K. A. Stevens, Hempnall, Norfolk
Colin J. Stevenson, Hempnall, Norfolk
Joy Stewart (née Page), formerly of Hempnall
Patrick and Christine Stone, Hempnall Green
Beryl I. Sutton
The Rodger Family, Lundy Green, Hempnall
The Walpole Family
Olive Theobald (née Crummett),
Maureen, Brian and Michael Tidder, Hempnall, Norfolk
Rebecca Tozer, Bristol
Mary J. Trudgill, Hempnall, Norfolk
Michael S. Turner, Hempnall, Norfolk
Terence W. Tyrrell, Hempnall, Norfolk
Patricia and the late Donald Webb, Hempnall
Mr Rodric A. Webster, Hempnall, Norfolk
Mrs P.S. Westley, Hempnall, Norfolk
Carolyn Whitham, Long Stratton, Norfolk
Christopher Whitham, Long Stratton, Norfolk
Neville and Betty Wilby, Denton
Paul R. Wildsmith, Hempnall, Norfolk
Mrs E. Williams, Hempnall
Geoffrey Wilson, Thurlton, Norfolk
Jennifer Wilson Tompkins, Long Stratton, Norfolk
Andre and Sue Wingfield, Hempnall
James, Francis and Thomas Wingfield
Charlie W. Woljung, Hempnall, Norfolk
Wood, Fritton Grange, Norfolk
Joy Worman (née Stammers)
Shaun A. Wright, Bungay Road, Hempnall, Norfolk
Rachel Wythe, Moran
Miss Judith A. Yallop, Hempnall, Norfolk
Michael I. Yates, Hempnall, Norfolk
Lorraine, Amy and Sarah Zima, Hempnall